The Reconciliation of the Fundamentals of Islamic Law

VOLUME I

Muhammad b. Hamad Al-Thani Center for Muslim Contribution to Civilization

The Reconciliation of the Fundamentals of Islamic Law

Volume I

Al-Muwāfaqāt fī Uṣūl al-Sharīʿa

Ibrāhīm ibn Mūsā Abū Isḥāq al-Shāṭibī

Translated by Imran Ahsan Khan Nyazee
Reviewed by Professor Raji M. Rammuny

Garnet
PUBLISHING

THE RECONCILIATION OF THE FUNDAMENTALS OF ISLAMIC LAW
VOLUME I

Published by
Garnet Publishing Limited
8 Southern Court
South Street
Reading
RG1 4QS
UK
www.garnetpublishing.co.uk

First Edition

ISBN-13: 978-1-85964-268-9

British Library Cataloguing-in-Publication Data
A catalogue record for this book is available from the British Library

Typeset by Samantha Barden
Jacket design by Garnet Publishing

Printed and bound in Lebanon by International Press:
interpress@int-press.com

First published in
paperback in 2012

Contents

Foreword xi
About this Series xiii
Muhammad bin Hamad Al-Thani Center for Muslim Contribution to Civilization: Founding Board of Trustees xv
Muhammad bin Hamad Al-Thani Center for Muslim Contribution to Civilization: Advisory Committee xvi
Preface by the Editor of the Arabic Text xvii
Preface by the Author xxvii

Introduction by the Author: Preliminary Concepts 1

The first concept: *ʿuṣūl al-fiqh* are definitive 1

The second concept: the evidences relied upon in *ʿuṣūl al-fiqh* are definitive 3

The third concept: evidences and general principles based on induction are definitive 4

Sub-concept: universal principles and *maṣlaḥa mursala* 7

Sub-concept: *ijmāʿ* is a definitive source 8

The fourth concept: the subject-matter of *ʿuṣūl al-fiqh* 8

Sub-concept: disagreements on issues not affecting *fiqh* are also not part of this discipline 9

The fifth concept: an issue not related to conduct need not be taken up in this discipline 10

The sixth concept: two ways of attaining required knowledge 17

The seventh concept: each *sharʿī* discipline is a means of obedience to Allah 19

Sub-concept: only the ignorant deny the merit of knowledge as a whole (the primary and secondary purposes of knowledge) 24

The eighth concept: knowledge preferred by the lawgiver is one that leads to sound conduct 26

Sub-concept: true knowledge is internal (pertains to the spirit) 32

The ninth concept: knowledge is of two types – essential and ancillary 33

The first type 33

The second type 34

Sub-concept: the first type is sometimes merged with the second type 40

The tenth concept: when transmitted and rational sources are combined the transmitted are primary 41
First 41
Second 42
Third 42

The eleventh concept: knowledge acknowledged by the *sharʿīa* pertains to conduct 44

The twelfth concept: the best way of acquiring knowledge is from experts in the discipline 44
The traits and signs of a scholar 46
Sub-concept: methods of acquiring knowledge 47

The thirteenth concept: principles that are a guide for conduct 50
First 52
Second 53

PART I
THE BOOK OF *AḤKĀM* (LEGAL RULES)

1 **The First Category of Rules** 77
The first issue: the *mubāḥ* requires neither commission nor omission of an act 77

The third objection to the claim in the first issue: the claim conflicts with what is established about piety and the relinquishment of its pleasures and temptations 86
The basis of the objection 86
The response to the objection 87
Sub-issue: evidences for not requiring commission of the permissible 88

The second issue: the *mubāḥ* in the wider sense includes all the other categories of the *aḥkām* 92
First: enjoying the good things 92
Second: utilising what is lawful 92
Third: relaxation and enjoyment of nature 93
Fourth: permissible acts whose persistent commission is likely to affect probity (*ʿadāla*) 93
The act recommended by the particular is obligatory under the universal 93
The act disapproved by the particular is prohibited under the universal 94
Wājib and *farḍ* distinguished 94
The rules for different acts vary according to the universal and particular 95

Evidence supporting the distinction between the universal and the particular 97

The third issue: two meanings of *mubāḥ* 98

The fourth issue: *mubāḥ* in which there is no harm 100

The fifth issue: *mubāḥ* is designated as such when the advantage of the subject is taken into account 102

The sixth issue: the five categories of rules are related to acts and omissions on the basis of the purposes of the law (*maqāṣīd al-sharīʿa*) 103

The seventh issue: recommended category (*mandūb*) in the wider sense serves the obligatory (*wājib*) 104

Sub-issue: the *mukrūḥ* serves the prohibited 105

The eighth issue: obligations with a time limit 105

Objection to the above 106

Response to the objection 107

The ninth issue: obligatory rights and the right of God 109

Sub-issue: the first two types are organised on the basis of the demand of a universal or a communal obligation 112

The tenth issue: the category of exemption between the permitted and the prohibited 112

Sub-issue: this category is witnessed on various occasions within the *sharīʿa* 114

Sub-issue: the obstacle to the category of forgiveness should be perceived from various perspectives 116

Sub-issue: rules of the unexpressed category 117

The eleventh issue: the demand for the communal obligation and the universal rules 123

Sub-issue: some details of the communal obligation 125

The twelfth issue: *ibāḥa*, necessity and need 127

The thirteenth issue: balancing the hardships 129

2 **The Second Category of Rules: The Declaratory Rules** **141**

The first type of declaratory rules: causes 141

The first issue: the ability of the subject to perform the act 141

The second issue: legality of causes does not necessarily imply the legal validity of the consequences 142

The third issue: the subject in bringing about the causes does not intend the effects 145

The fourth issue: the determining of causes implies the intention of the lawgiver to bring about the effects 146

The fifth issue: the right of the subject in intending the effects 147

The sixth issue: the two grades of causes 150

The seventh issue: prohibited causes 154

The eighth issue: the occurrence of the cause is equivalent to the occurrence of the effects 159

The ninth issue: effects not in control of the subject 160

The tenth issue: the effects are legally based on causative acts 171

The eleventh issue: prohibited causes are injurious and permitted causes are beneficial 176

The twelfth issue: effects are interests that are to be secured 181

The thirteenth issue: causes based on rationale (wisdom) 185

The fourteenth issue: rules associated with invalid causes 191

The second type of declaratory rules: requisite conditions 193

The first issue: condition is a complementary attribute 193

The second issue: terms related to conditions 193

The third issue: three types of conditions 194

The fourth issue: conditions are like attributes 195

The fifth issue: the cause cannot be implemented without a condition 196

The sixth issue: conditions stipulated with two types of purposes 199

The seventh issue: condition may be given up 200

The eighth issue: three types of rules for which conditions are stipulated 205

The third type of declaratory rules: the obstacles (defences) 206

The first issue: obstacles are of two types 206

The second issue: obstacles are not intended by the Lawgiver 207

The third issue: obstacles may be given up 208

The fourth type of declaratory rules: validity and nullity 210

The first issue: the meaning of validity (two meanings) 210

The second issue: the meaning of nullity (two meanings) 211

The third issue: elaborating the second meaning of nullity 214

The fifth type of declaratory rules: *ʿazīma* and *rukhṣa* (initial rules and exemptions) 216

The first issue: *ʿazīma* is a rule imposed initially 216

The second issue: *rukhṣa* implies *ibāḥa* 220

The third issue: *rukhṣa* is an additional element 224

The fourth issue: *ibāḥa* associated with *rukhṣa* 227

The fifth issue: valid *rukhṣa* of two types 228

In the name of God, the Beneficent, the Merciful

FOREWORD

THE interrelationship and interaction of human cultures and civilizations has made the contributions of each the common heritage of men in all ages and all places. Early Muslim scholars were able to communicate with their Western counterparts through contacts made during the Crusades; at Muslim universities and centres of learning in Muslim Spain (al-Andalus, or Andalusia) and Sicily to which many European students went for education; and at the universities and centres of learning in Europe itself (such as Salerno, Padua, Montpellier, Paris and Oxford), where Islamic works were taught in Latin translations. Among the Muslim scholars well-known in the centres of learning throughout the world were al-Rāzī (Rhazes), Ibn Sīnā (Avicenna), Ibn Rushd (Averroës), al-Khwārizmī and Ibn Khaldūn. Muslim scholars such as these and others produced original works in many fields. Many of them possessed encyclopaedic knowledge and distinguished themselves in many disparate fields of knowledge.

The Center for Muslim Contribution to Civilization was established in order to acquaint non-Muslims with the contributions Islam has made to human civilization as a whole. The Great Books of Islamic Civilization Project attempts to cover the first 800 years of Islam, or what may be called Islam's Classical Period. This project aims at making available in English and other European languages a wide selection of works representative of Islamic civilization in all its diversity. It is made up of translations of original Arabic works that were produced in the formative centuries of Islam, and is meant to serve the needs of a potentially large readership. Not only the specialist and scholar, but also the non-specialist with an interest in Islam and its cultural heritage will be able to benefit from the series. Together, the works should serve as a rich source for the study of the early periods of Islamic thought.

In selecting the books for the series, the Center took into account all major areas of Islamic intellectual pursuit that could be represented. Thus the series includes works not only on better-known subjects such as law, theology, jurisprudence, history and politics, but also on subjects such as literature, medicine, astronomy, optics and geography. The specific criteria used to select individual books were these: that a book should give a faithful and comprehensive account of its field; and that it should be an authoritative source. Readers thus have at their disposal virtually a whole library of informative and enlightening works.

Each book in the series has been translated by a qualified scholar and reviewed by another expert. While the style of one translation will naturally differ from another – as do the styles of the authors – the translators have endeavoured, to the extent it is possible, to make the works accessible to the common reader. As a rule, the use of footnotes has been kept to a minimum, though a more extensive use of them was necessitated in some cases.

This series is presented in the hope that it will contribute to a greater understanding in the West of the cultural and intellectual heritage of Islam and will therefore provide an important means towards greater understanding of today's world.

May God Help Us!

Muhammad bin Hamad al-Thani
Chairman of the Founding Board of Trustees

About this Series

This series of Arabic works, made available in English translation, represents an outstanding selection of important Islamic studies in a variety of fields of knowledge. The works selected for inclusion in this series meet specific criteria. They are recognized by Muslim scholars as being early and important in their fields as works whose importance is broadly recognized by international scholars, and as having had a genuinely significant impact on the development of human culture.

Readers will therefore see that this series includes a variety of works in the purely Islamic sciences, such as Qurʾān, *ḥadīth*, theology, prophetic traditions (*sunna*), and jurisprudence (*fiqh*). Also represented will be books by Muslim scientists on medicine, astronomy, geography, physics, chemistry, horticulture and other fields.

The work of translating these texts has been entrusted to a group of professors in the Islamic and Western worlds who are recognized authorities in their fields. It has been deemed appropriate, in order to ensure accuracy and fluency, that two persons, one with Arabic as their mother tongue and another with English as their mother tongue, should participate together in the translation and revision of each text.

This series is distinguished from other similar intercultural projects by its distinctive objectives and methodology. These works will fill a genuine gap in the library of human thought. They will prove extremely useful to all those with an interest in Islamic culture, its interaction with Western thought, and its impact on culture throughout the world. They will, it is hoped, fulfil an important role in enhancing world understanding at a time when there is such evident and urgent need for the development of peaceful coexistence.

This series is published by the Center for Muslim Contribution to Civilization (CMCC), now a member of the Faculty of Islamic Studies of Qatar Foundation, Doha, Qatar. The Center was established in 1983 under the patronage of H.E. Sheikh Muhammad bin Hamad al-Thani, the former Minister of Education of Qatar, who also chaired the Board of Trustees. The Board comprised a group of prominent scholars. These included His Eminence Sheikh al-Azhar, Arab Republic of Egypt, and Dr Yousef al-Qaradhawi, Director of the Sira and Sunna Research Center. At its inception the Center was directed by the late Dr Muhammad Ibrahim Kazim, former Rector of Qatar University, who established its initial objectives.

Until 1997, the Center was directed by the late Dr Kamal Naji, the Foreign Cultural Relations Advisor of the Ministry of Education of Qatar. He was assisted by a Board comprising a number of academicians of Qatar University, in addition to a consultative committee chaired by the late Dr Ezzeddin Ibrahim, former Rector of the University of the United Arab Emirates. A further committee acting on behalf of the Center comprises prominent university professors who act under the chairmanship of Dr Raji Rammuny, Professor of Arabic at the University of Michigan. This committee is charged with making known, in Europe, in America, in Asia and elsewhere the books selected for translation, and in selecting and enlisting properly qualified university professors, orientalists and students of Islamic studies to undertake the work of translation and revision, as well as overseeing the publication process. In 1997, Professor Osman Sid Ahmad Ismaʿīl al-Bīlī took over as General Supervisor of the Centre.

In January 2009, the CMCC joined Qatar Foundation as part of the Faculty of Islamic Studies. In May 2010 Her Highness Sheikha Moza bint Naser Al-Misnad, the Chairperson of Qatar Foundation, named the Center as Muhammad bin Hamad Al-Thani Center for Muslim Contribution to Civilization. Currently Professor Osman Sid Ahmad Ismaʿīl al-Bīlī is the Director of the Center.

MUHAMMAD BIN HAMAD AL-THANI CENTER FOR MUSLIM CONTRIBUTION TO CIVILIZATION

FOUNDING BOARD OF TRUSTEES

H.E. Sheikh Muhammad bin Hamad al-Thani
Chairman

MEMBERS

1. H.E. Sheikh al-Azhar, Cairo, Arab Republic of Egypt.
2. Director-General of the Islamic Educational, Scientific and Cultural Organization (ISESCO).
3. Director-General of the Arab League Educational, Cultural and Scientific Organization (ALECSO).
4. H.E. the Minister of Education, State of Qatar.
5. H.E. the Minister of Education, Kuwait.
6. H.E. the Minister of Education, Oman.
7. H.E. the Secretary-General of the Muslim World Association, Saudi Arabia.
8. H.E. Dr Ezzeddin Ibrahim, Cultural Advisor to H.H. the President of the U.A.E.
9. Professor Yousef al-Qaradhawi, Director, Sira and Sunna Research Centre, University of Qatar.
10. Chairman, Arab Historians' Union.
11. Professor Cesar Adib Majul, Professor at the American Universities.

Following are the names of the late prominent Muslim figures who (may Allāh have mercy upon them) passed away after they had taken vital roles in the preliminary discussions of the Center's goals, work plan and activities. They are:

1. Dr Kamal Naji, former General Supervisor, Center for Muslim Contribution to Civilization, Qatar (7 October 1997).
2. Sheikh Jad al-Haq Ali Jad al-Haq, Sheikh al-Azhar, Cairo, Arab Republic of Egypt.
3. Dr Muhammad Ibrahim Kazim, former Rector, University of Qatar.
4. Sheikh Abdullah bin Ibrahim al-Ansari, former Chairman, Department for the Revival of Islamic Cultural Heritage, State of Qatar.
5. Muhammad al-Fasi, former Honorary Chairman, Islamic University Rabat, Kingdom of Morocco.
6. Dr Abul-Wafa al-Taftazani, former Deputy Rector, University of Cairo, Arab Republic of Egypt.
7. Senator Mamimatal Tamano, former member of the Philippino Congress and Muslim leader in the Philippines.
8. Dr Ezzeddin Ibrahim (March 2010).

MUHAMMAD BIN HAMAD AL-THANI CENTER FOR MUSLIM CONTRIBUTION TO CIVILIZATION

Advisory Committee

1. H.E. Sheikh Muhammad bin Hamad al-Thani, Honorary Chairman of the Advisory Committee
2. Professor Osman Sid Ahmad Ismaʿīl al-Bīlī, Professor of Middle Eastern and Islamic History at QFIS and Director of the Center.
3. Professor Muhammad Khalifa al-Hassan, Director, Al-Qaradawi Center for Islamic Moderation and Renewal.
4. Professor Ibrahim Saleh al-Nuaimi, former Rector, University of Qatar, Chairman of Doha International Center for Interfaith Dialogue.
5. Professor Husam al-Khateeb, Professor of Arabic Language.

Center's Advisor

Professor Raji Mahmoud Rammuny
Director of the Center's Translation Committee in the U.S.A.
Professor of Arabic Studies, Department of Near Eastern Studies,
University of Michigan, U.S.A.

Preface by the Editor of the Arabic Text

بسم الله الرحمن الرحيم

In the name of God, most Beneficent, most Merciful
Praise be to God and prayers and blessings for the Messengers of God

Al-Muwāfaqāt: the book

As the Noble Book (*al-Kitāb*) is the foundation of the *sharīʿa* and the support of the community, while the *Sunna* has recourse to it for its own meaning, elaborating its unelaborated points, expounding the difficult meanings and making plain its precision, it is imperative for one seeking to derive the rules (*aḥkām*) of this *sharīʿa* on his own to turn to the Book, the *Sunna* and to those principles that emerge from them through definitive means, like consensus (*ijmāʿ*) and analogy (*qiyās*).

Insofar as the Book and the *Sunna* are in the language of the Arabs, which has its own modes and usage – by means of which the manifest and apparent is distinguished from the unelaborated, the actual meanings from the figurative, the general from the particular, the governing definitive texts from the ambiguous, the explicit from the implications, and so on – it is necessary for the person seeking the understanding of the *sharīʿa* to have an adequate knowledge of the language of the Arabs with respect to its modes of address and the meanings conveyed by its syntax. A proficiency of such a level is one of the essential elements of *ijtihād* (interpretation). This has been settled by the specialists in *ʿUṣūl al-Fiqh* (the Foundations of Islamic Jurisprudence) and the most prominent among them is *Imām al-Shāfiʿī*, God be pleased with him, who did so in his book *al-Risāla*.

The obligations imposed by this infallible *sharīʿa*, by agreement, are not merely for bringing people under the authority of the *dīn* (religion), but for the affirmation of the purposes of the Lawgiver in securing their interests both of the *dīn* and of this world. Each rule of the *sharīʿa* expresses: the preservation of one of the necessities (*dīn*, life, reasoning faculty, progeny and wealth), which are the foundations of civilisation preserved by each community, without which all interests of this world would be lost along with salvation in the Hereafter; the preservation of supporting needs, like the various forms of transactions that if found not to support the necessities would have placed mankind in great difficulty and hardship; the preservation of the complementary values, that rely on ethical traits and good practices; and the completion of each of the three forms that lead to their realisation. There is no chapter among the various chapters of *fiqh*, dealing with worship, transactions and crimes, that does not attempt to secure these interests or to realise these purposes, the realisation of which is the main objective of all the rules.

It is known that these three grades differ in their level of importance with respect to their affirmation and the proscription of crossing the bounds set by them. This is a vast sea that requires the elaboration of numerous details as well as of the universal principles so that the purposes of the Lawgiver can be established in them (from the perspective of His intention to lay down the *sharīʿa* initially, His intention to lay it down for conveying their comprehension, His intention in laying it down to require the obligations demanded by them, and His intention to bring the subject under its rules).

The realisation of these purposes, the investigation of their details, the exhaustive treatment of their various branches, and their development by means of induction from their sources in the *sharīʿa*, which amounts to the knowing of the secret of legislation, is a knowledge that is essential for one who strives to derive the rules of the *sharīʿa* from their specific evidences. The reason is that it is not sufficient to examine the specific evidences alone without examining the universal principles of the *sharīʿa*, for otherwise the particulars will become unmanageable with some, apparently, conflicting with the others. Without the universals, the investigator will not have the standard of the purposes of the Lawgiver to decide what he should adopt and what he should let go. It is, therefore, obligatory to consider the particulars in the light of the universals. The particulars operate through the universals in each form of existence. It is this that was indicated by al-Ghazālī, transmitting from al-Shāfiʿī, after giving sufficient explanation of what the *mujtahid* has to take into account during his derivation, when he said: "The universal principles have to be taken into account first and to be given preference over the particulars, as in the case of homicide with a blunt weapon, where the principle of deterrence has to be preferred over the concern for the term used in the particular evidence."

From the above explanation, it becomes evident that there are two major elements of the derivation of the *aḥkām* of the *sharīʿa*: the first is proficiency in the language of the Arabs, while the second is the knowledge of the underlying secrets of the *sharīʿa* and of its purposes.

As for the first element, it was an inborn trait for the Companions and their Followers, who were pure Arabs. They were, therefore, in no need of a knowledge of its rules to be proficient in it, just as they acquired the knowledge of the second element through their prolonged companionship with the Messenger of Allah (pbuh) along with the knowledge of the underlying causes of legislation. They saw with clear comprehension the Qurʾān being revealed and the *Sunna* promulgated in phases according to the arising incidents, and they comprehended the interests and grasped the purposes that the Lawgiver was concerned about in legislation. These were also comprehended by those who paid attention to some of their discussions at the time they adopted their opinions, and who consulted the leaders among them for expounding the rules of the *sharīʿa* that they laid down. For those who came after them, and who did not possess these two attributes, it was necessary to acquire knowledge of those rules that prescribed the forms in which the Arabs used their language and others that elaborated the purposes of the Lawgiver underlying the legislation of the rules.

A number of leading scholars devoted themselves to the compilation of these rules and called them *ʿUṣūl al-Lugha* (the rules of language). As the first element is proficiency in the Arabic language, they recorded in this discipline what was needed, among those determined by the leading scholars, for direct derivation so much so that you will notice that this type of rules form the major part of *ʿUṣūl al-Fiqh*. To these they added material that required the conceptual knowledge of the *aḥkām* and a little of what comprises the introductory material of *ʿIlm al-Kalām* (Science of Theology) and its issues. It was natural, in all that they compiled, to include the core part of *ʿUṣūl* regarding the Book, the *Sunna*, their related matters, and thereafter the discussions of *ijmāʿ* (consensus of legal opinion), *qiyās* (analogy) and of *ijtihād* (interpretation).

They neglected, however, the second element, and did not speak about the purposes of the Lawgiver, except by way of brief hints that are found in chapters on analogy with respect to the divisions of the *ʿilla* (underlying cause) as related to the purposes of the Lawgiver and about having recourse to them. These, with respect to the divisions, they said are of three types: necessities, needs, and complementary values. This they did when it deserved more attention and greater detail as well as exhaustive treatment as compared to many other issues that crept into *ʿUṣūl al-Fiqh* from other disciplines.

From the fifth century (A.H.) onwards, the discipline remained confined to the discussions that were prevalent in the first period with books vacillating between precis, commentaries and various new forms for the earlier material. In this manner, the discipline of *ʿUṣūl al-Fiqh* continued to lack a large part of it, which is the part that deals with one of its essential elements. The situation continued till such time that God, the Glorious and Exalted, sent Abū Isḥāq al-Shaṭibī in the eighth century of the Hijra to take care of this deficiency and to erect this great edifice to fill the huge void in this exalted discipline. He divided these purposes into four major purposes and then discussed each type in detail. To these he added the purposes of the subject in his duty to obey the law. He dealt with the discipline through sixty-two issues and forty-nine sections of his book *al-Muwāfaqāt*. Through these he explained how the *sharīʿa* is based on the securing of interests (*maṣāliḥ*), and it is an eternal system meant for all mankind, assuming that the world will continue till eternity. The reason is that it is concerned with the application of prevalent practices and that the changing of rules with a change in practices does not mean the alteration of the obligating communication itself. In fact, on a change in practices, each practice is referred to a principle of law (*aṣl sharʿī*) that gives a ruling on it. Further, this *sharīʿa*, as he said, is distinguished by its generosity and compassion by virtue of which it carries the masses with it, whether infirm or strong, and guides all, whether intelligent or obtuse.

The other issues discussed in the book

In the renewal and reconstruction of this discipline, the Author did not confine himself to the laying down of the foundations and the establishing of the universal principles that include within them the purposes of the *sharīʿa*; rather he determined for the details of this book a much larger scope, and he attained through their enumeration priceless gems that have most reliable relationships with the spirit of the *sharīʿa* and an intrinsic connection with the discipline of *ʿUṣūl al-Fiqh*.

He laid down, as an opening for the book, thirteen rules including five sections that he deemed a foundational introduction for the book and a beacon for understanding the issues that are treated as principles. From here he moved on to the discussion of the five categories of the rules, both the obligation-creating and the declaratory rules. In this discussion he adopted an approach that is different from the usual approach in the books of *ʿUṣūl al-Fiqh*. He devoted particular attention to the discussion of the *mubāḥ* (permissible category), the cause, the condition, and initial principles and their exemptions. It may be pointed out here that a fourth of the book is about the discussion of these topics through which one attains abundant knowledge and understanding of the *dīn* (religion), laying a foundation here for the part dealing with the *adilla* (evidences) through principles that have a significant role to play in legislation. In that part, he discusses these principles that were settled in the part dealing with the categories of rules, in such a way that we find the parts of the whole book relying on its other parts.

He then dealt with the sources of wisdom and the core rules, whose boundaries are set and basis determined in discussion of the Book and the *Sunna*. These pertain to equivocal meanings, the particular meanings, the constraints for the *aḥkām*, the ambiguous meanings, abrogation, the imperative, prohibitions, particulars, generality, lack of detail, and elaboration of the texts. The knowledge of these issues was revealed to him for he followed the guidance in the sources and tried to remove the veils, and this because he took the Qurʾān as his associate, partner and companion for the days and years of his life, aided in this by research into the meanings in the books of the *Sunna* as well as by the examination of the works of the earlier scholars relying on the opinions of the ancestors, and finally by the employment of the powerful vision granted to him by God. You will feel, as you read the book, that you can see him standing atop a tall mountain peak surveying from there the fountain-heads and sources of the *sharīʿa* viewing all the paths winding through them, and these he describes with his senses, building the foundations as he experiences them, and lays down universal principles through the enumeration of evidences from the *sharīʿa*. Thus, he links a verse, tradition, or report with another verse, tradition or report by supporting this with rational proofs and theoretical bases till such time that all doubt is removed and suspicion eliminated. The truth is, thus, discovered through this method till it reaches the level of the *mutawātir maʿnawī* (definitive in meaning). He follows this method in his discussions and his arguments so thoroughly that he says – in truth – that this method is a significant feature of the book.

He elaborates in these issues the status of the Book among the sources of the *sharīʿa*, to the effect that it is the foundation for all the sources as well as the fact that it gives expression to the *aḥkām* in general terms that necessarily need elaboration from the *Sunna*. Likewise, he also elaborates the disciplines that are associated with the Qurʾān and are, or are not, needed for interpreting it. He delineated the apparent and the concealed meanings of the Qurʾān identifying that concealed knowledge that may be validly used for interpretation as well as knowledge that may not be used. He establishes that the verses revealed in Makka cover most of the universal rules, whereas those revealed at Madina are an elaboration and affirmation of such principles, by virtue of which he explains that the revelation of the Madanī verses was necessary after those revealed at Makka. Abrogation, he elaborates, does not affect the universals; rather it operates upon a few particulars due to sound reasons. Thereafter, he lays down the rule for the balanced and mean path for the interpretation of the Qurʾān upon which the derivation of the *aḥkām* can be structured. The status of the *Sunna* in relation to the Qurʾān is then elaborated with the explanation that it does not go beyond the universal principles during legislation. He elaborates all the points in a manner that leaves little room for doubt about these principles.

He concludes the book by a chapter on *ijtihād* (juristic interpretation) and its related issues elaborating therein the types of *ijtihād*, those that are terminated and those that will go on for ever. Out of those that terminate, he elaborates the types that are based upon two elements: the knowledge of Arabic to an extent that the *mujtahid* understands its modes like an Arab, and the understanding of the *maqāṣid al-sharīʿa* (purposes of the *sharīʿa*) to a level of perfection. After this, he explains the types that are dependent upon one of these elements to the exclusion of the other.

He follows this up with the affirmation that the *sharīʿa* reverts to a single principle in all that is a matter of disagreement among the jurists in the comprehension of the purposes of the Lawgiver with respect to the *aḥkām*. It is on this principle that he then constructs most of the general rules of interpretation. Thereafter, he elaborates the scope of *ijtihād* and the reasons for making errors in it and so on.

What has been mentioned is a mere drop on the shores of *al-Muwāfaqāt*. If it is taken as a guidepost for Muslims through its acceptance among the scholars and employment by the specialists, the book can become a defence against those claimants of *ijtihād* who feed on the crumbs of the pure *sharīʿa*. They make tall claims that they are eligible for undertaking *ijtihād* when in reality they are devoid of the basic means and qualifying attributes. All that they have is mere claims and reliance on whim, for they have given up the affairs of the *Dīn* and believe in unbridled anarchy.

You will then see those who deserve to be called illiterate in matters of the *sharīʿa* adopting some of the particulars in a manner that leads to the demolition of the universals, and they follow what appears obvious to them for they do not have the knowledge of the *maqāṣid* that can serve as a criterion for dealing with such particulars. There is another group of people who employ the evidences of the *sharīʿa* to serve their own ends in the incident facing him. They let their whims govern the evidences till such time that the evidences start serving their interests. In doing so they do not have knowledge of the *maqāṣid al-sharīʿa*, nor do they have recourse to them in submission nor acknowledge what was transmitted to them from reliable ancestors about their understanding of the purposes, nor do they have the vision for undertaking *ijtihād* based on such understanding. All this is due to the pursuit of whims that please the self and that lead to the giving up of guidance based upon evidences, the rejection of justice, the absence of humility, added to which is a lack of knowledge of the *maqāṣid al-sharīʿa* as well as the illusion of having reached the status of *ijtihād*. This invokes the hazard of falling into destruction; may Allah protect us from it.

Reverting to the topic, we would say that the Author of *al-Muwāfaqāt* did not refer even to a single issue out of the issues that are discussed in the books on *ʿUṣūl*, except by way of indication on certain occasions by means of which he seeks to establish a principle or a corollary. Despite this, he is not going beyond the discussions of *ʿUṣūl* for you will find him saying in many of his discussions that if this discussion is appended to what is established in *ʿUṣūl* the purpose will be attained.

The conclusion is that all that is mentioned in the books of *ʿUṣūl*, as well as what is stated in *al-Muwāfaqāt*, is deemed a means towards the derivation of the *aḥkām* from the evidences of the *sharīʿa*. However, the numerous disciplines that are found in *ʿUṣūl*, with the lengthy supporting arguments for their issues, limit its benefit as a means towards an end. An objection is often raised against those who are occupied with it that such knowledge has no use except for one who has reached the status of *ijtihād*. The response that is always given is: Its benefit for one who is not a *mujtahid* is that he comes to know how the *aḥkām* are derived. The response, however, is difficult to concede, because with such knowledge it is only some of the particulars of the means to *ijtihād*, those that are varied and spread out, are uncovered, while others that pertain to the essential element of the *maqāsid* are missing. This can be compared to the case of one who attempts to teach another the art of weaving by giving him instruction in a few varying particulars. The limited benefit of this is not hidden from anyone.

As for the discipline that al-Shāṭibī has mentioned in the four volumes of his book, it is also a part of the means towards interpretation through which we know how the *mujtahids* undertook derivation of the rules, yet it provides a deep understanding of the *Dīn*, a knowledge of the system of the *sharīʿa*, as well as a way of reliance upon the foundations of legislation. Even if we do not reach the level of *ijtihād* through it, or acquire the ability of deriving the rules, we do attain through it a knowledge of the *maqāṣid al-sharīʿa* and the secrets underlying the *aḥkām*. It provides satisfying guidance and illuminates the four corners of the believer's heart driving away doubt and hesitation and gathering together in clear comprehension what was missing. The service provided by this Imām, God be pleased with him, is only for the sake of Allah.

Why has the book not enjoyed wider circulation

It remains to be said that if the status of the book is as mentioned and its excellence as a reference work for *sharīʿa* as described, then why has it remained out of our vision for all these years and has not been granted its rightful share of popularity. Leaving aside its publicity among the eastern scholars, it may be said that if the other books were not more beneficial than it, how could they have become well known?

The response is that this objection is in itself defective, because superiority and inferiority are not dependent upon popularity. Books, in our view, are like men. How many learned men have remained hidden, while useless persons have become famous? What is witnessed is sufficient for negating this view. Take a look at *Jamʿ al-Jawāmiʿ* by *al-Suyūṭī*, with its commentary by al-Maḥallī, which has been for a long time the only book that has been studied at al-Azhar as well as other centres of learning in Egypt despite the existence of *al-Iḥkām* by *al-Āmidī*, *al-Muntahā* and *al-Mukhtaṣar* by Ibn al-Ḥājib as well as *al-Taḥrīr*, *al-Minhāj* and *Musallam al-Thubūt* along with a host of other books dealing with the same discipline that was dealt with by *Jamʿ al-Jawāmiʿ*. Most of these books have been ignored and none of them has surpassed the other with respect to circulation, except for this later period of ours. No two persons will differ about the fact that *Jamʿ al-Jawāmiʿ* is the least beneficial of these books, but has received the greatest attention.

The obscurity of this book can be referred to two reasons. The first is the issues that it deals with, while the second is the method of instruction and writing. As for the first, the discussions in the book are novel and unique and no one prior to the Author has approached them in this way as we have indicated. They emerged in the eighth century of the Hijra when the other methods of the discipline of *ʿUṣūl* had acquired developed forms and those occupied with it had begun to compile it. They occupied themselves with this method through discussions, commentaries, teaching, and learning, thinking this was all that the discipline of *ʿUṣūl* was about. The reason, as we have stated, was that it was for them a means towards *ijtihād* at which they were not adept; therefore, they did not find anything wrong with this method. Even those who had heard of this book did not make the effort to absorb it, to ponder over its discussions in order to derive benefit from them, to link this knowledge with what they already knew, to incorporate it in what they compiled and to direct the students towards it, encouraging them and helping them to understand it.

The second reason is that though Abū Isḥāq's pen moves smoothly and writes lucid Arabic, as has been witnessed in many discussions that are original contributions of his mind and pen, for in these you see an overflowing mind and powerful pen and may read a whole page and find no flaw in the composition and the syntax, yet there are in it occasions where there is a need for legal reasoning based on the sources of the *sharīʿa*, reliance on rational proofs and recourse to settled issues in other disciplines. This may lead the reader to move his comprehension of a word to the next and from there to the following, as if he is walking on the teeth of a comb, because underlying each word is a meaning that he is conveying and a purpose that he is trying to attain. He writes after fully grasping the *Sunna*, the work of the commentators, the discussions of *ʿIlm al-Kalām*, and the special ways of the Sūfis. It was not possible for him to include all this detail in his book. It is from this perspective that one finds it difficult to understand the book, and there is a need for the simplification of its meanings, the elaboration of many of its concepts, and support for the bearing of its burdens. Despite all this, the book is supported in one of its parts by the other parts, and you will find the elaboration of its beginning at the end and that of the end in the beginning.

The reason for my turning to the book and my method of editing

It was often that we heard the advice of the late Shaykh Muḥammad Abduh to his students to understand the meanings of this book, and I have been eager since then to act upon this advice. The difficulty faced by me, and by others, was to have access to a copy of the book. After persistent efforts, we were able to borrow a copy of the book in the script of the Maghrib from a student. The mysteries of the script, the difficulty of the discussions and the demand of the owner for the return of the copy were causes that became obstacles that blocked the way. We, therefore, followed the advice of the poet:

> When you are not able to attain something, give it up and cross over to what you are able to attain.

When God granted me a copy of the book published in Egypt, along with the time to examine it, I began to read it till I reached the end, gladly undertaking the lengthy travel through its ravines and gorges, and searching through its treasures and troves. The knowledge I gained from it increased my faith in the *Sunna* and I praised my nightly journeys and their outcome in the morning. A desire arose in me of re-examining the book with full comprehension by testing what it settles with the measures of the examiner, with recourse to the sources from which he draws his knowledge, verifying the concepts that arise from it, expounding the concise pointers, and elaborating its difficult statements through concise expressions, by extending the hidden concepts and by enveloping the offshoots on which understanding rests, always pointing towards the root at which he aims.

It was not my aim to increase the number of these comments, nor to add to their copiousness by transmitting related texts from other books. I wrote what was required and restricted the desirable to what was sufficient, unless necessity demanded elaboration in those rare cases when understanding ceases. I freed my mind from the constraints imposed by the Author and from being coloured by the assumptions made by him or even from submission to the conclusions required by his objectives. It is for this reason that I have, without hesitation, criticised him on certain occasions and refused to accept those of his elaborations that did not come up to the standard. He himself has declared this method to be appropriate for one who examines what he says, one who seeks the truth from what he has laid down and stated, demanding from him to adopt the method of those who make a choice and not those who reject and doubt. Just as he has recommended verification prior to the seeking of complexities so that a beneficial thing may not be cast aside without consideration. Yes, in the search for knowledge asking who has said this and from where is it coming will not help. Had this been so, many truths would have been wasted through mistakes and forgetfulness. This is the distinction of our religion, Islam, to accept what is sound even from the antagonist, unless it has been prohibited by the Messenger of Allah (pbuh).

Documentation of the traditions in the book

In the Author's search through the sources of the *sharīʿa*, he has recorded close to one thousand traditions from the Prophet (pbuh) in this book. On most occasions he has not traced the chain to the narrator, rather he has mentioned out of the tradition what was necessary for the purposes of evidence for the occasion, often stating the last part of it in another location as is required by the text. At other times he merely gives an indication of the tradition without mentioning anything from it. He desires from such methods the attainment of his goals without prolonging the text beyond limits. The need of the reader is also obvious for he requires the complete tradition along with its status with respect to its strength and weakness, so that the purpose in quoting the tradition becomes evident, help is provided in evaluating the underlying reasoning, and the resulting satisfaction or the lack of it is attained with respect to the context. This strengthened my resolve to undertake this task, which involved hardship and tiring research through the widely spread volumes of traditions with their numerous sources and their multiplicity of references. Consequently, we had to have recourse to thirty-three books of traditions. This burden was borne, on our behalf, by Shaykh Muḥammad Amīn ʿAbd al-Razzāq, who continuously spent long months referring to these sources for deriving the records of a tradition, its various versions, numerous chains, varying texts, so as to arrive at the tradition that was quoted by the Author, and on most occasions the version that he had recorded, and this for ease of access and of identifying its version and status. May Allah grant him the best of rewards for serving this discipline.

Errors and mistakes remaining in previous editions

Two senior and qualified scholars were supervising the editing of the book at the time of its publication taking all possible care to verify it from the original, but corruption of the text and mistakes were to be found in the manuscript that was available to the publisher. In addition to this, the editors were given a very short time for their work. This is sufficient excuse for the two respected scholars in relation to the large number of errors remaining in the book, and the dropping of complete sentences from the book or of words without which the meaning remained incomplete, and the purpose of the Author not served. This became the cause of exercising greater care and thought in this context till Allah made the task easy and the book acquired its pure form with respect to its syntax and words for those who desired it.

I do not claim, even though readers have showered praise, that I did the utmost in the service of the book. Even if it is viewed with good intentions, I would say that it is the first step. If someone musters enough courage to undertake the work then a huge task is laid out for him, and the giving of advice is mandatory for one who has good intentions, because all acts depend on intentions and each person is rewarded according to his intentions.

ʿAbd Allāh Darrāz

Preface by the Author

In the name of God, the Beneficent, the Merciful,
and (with) prayers and blessings on Muḥammad and his family.

All praise is for Allah, who rescued us from the darkness of ignorance through the illumination of knowledge, and through it He granted us the discernment to avoid falling into erroneous deception. He laid down for us in the *sharīʿa* of Muḥammad a lofty standard and a manifest guide. This was the best of His abundant blessings that He showered on us and the best of His venerable gifts that He bestowed on us.

We were, before the shining forth of this light, acting haphazardly with our reason pursuing our interests in an unbalanced way. This was due to reason's weakness in bearing the burden of these interests as well as its involvement with the pressing demands of desire arising within the self, which oscillates equally between these two ends. Thus, we kept placing poison on our ailments in place of medicine, seeking recovery in vain, like a person clutching at water.

We continued to float between these two ends in a sea of doubt and greed, groping in our ignorance for a guiding evidence in a jet-black night, desiring results from sterile comparisons, seeking the symptoms of health in an ailing body, and walking prostrate in the belief that we were on the right path.

All this continued till such time that pure compulsion appeared in divine decrees themselves. Coerced hands were raised towards the One and Only Subduer and the expectations of those in need were redirected towards Him. When the tongues of circumstances expressed true affirmation and the rule of compulsion was established in the objects of deeds, we recognised the Beneficent Lord and His tremendous kindness, and He showed great kindness to us out of His all embracing favour, for we could not have found a solution without His help nor would we have been guided on our own to the right way. He deemed the excuse of our inability acceptable, creating a hope of forgiveness for our mistakes prior to the sending of Messengers. Allah, the Glorious, has said, "Nor would We visit with Our Wrath until We had sent a messenger (to give warning)."[1]

He then sent Prophets, peace be upon them, to different nations, each speaking to them in their own tongue, whether Arab or non-Arab, so as to elaborate for them the path of truth for nations in order that they may hold themselves back from the paths to hell.

He made our group, the last yet the foremost, exclusive through the last brick of the hierarchy of the Prophets and the concluding musk perfuming the message (*misk al-khitām*), Muḥammad ibn ʿAbd Allah. He was an overflowing blessing, a widespread mercy, a far-reaching unlettered wisdom, and a pure Hāshimite flower. He sent him to us as a witness, a giver of good news, a warner inviting to God with His permission, and a brilliant lamp. He revealed to him His clear Book in Arabic, a Book that distinguished between doubt and conviction, and which is not affected by falsehood either from the front or from behind. He (the Messenger) elaborated its text in unequivocal terms and expounded its complete message adequately. He (God) enhanced it with the perfume of praise for the Prophet and described him through a unique aroma for He deemed praise for all his morals and traits an attribute of the Qurʾān. This way the Prophet (pbuh) became the elaboration of the Qurʾān through his words, deeds, and abstentions. The day appeared bright for those with eyes, and guidance was distinguished from guile in the light of the sun without cloud and haze.

We praise Allah, the Glorious, for such praise is in itself a beneficial blessing. We thank Him, and thanking Him is the first of the gains. We bear witness that there is no god but God alone, who has no partners in this Kingdom and He is the Manifest truth. He is the Creator of all that is created. He it is who grants sustenance to the obedient as well as the disobedient in a manner that requires justice and fairness, abundance and gratitude, and which continues through a decree of guarantee. Allah, the Exalted, has said, "I have only created Jinns and men, that they may serve Me. No Sustenance do I require of them, nor do I require that they should feed Me. For Allah is He Who gives (all) Sustenance, Lord of Power, Steadfast (for ever)."[2] And He said, "Enjoin prayer on thy people, and be constant therein. We ask thee not to provide Sustenance: we provide it for thee. But the (fruit of) the Hereafter is for Righteousness."[3]

All this was guaranteed so that they may be free for discharging the trust that was offered to them. When they undertook to bear the trust in return for compensation, they undertook it as an obligation. Would God! if only they had been apprehensive and refused to accept it, and if only they had thought of the grave consequences at the beginning. Yet, they did not care about the consequences as did the skies, the earth and the mountains. It is for this reason that man has been deemed rash and ignorant, but it was God's will that was operative. This is indicated by the clear statement, "We did indeed offer the Trust to the Heavens and the Earth and the Mountains; but they refused to undertake it, being afraid thereof: but man undertook it; he was indeed unjust and foolish."[4] Praise be to Him who runs all affairs with wisdom and measure, in accordance with His will, decisions and standards so that proof against His subjects be established in what they do. He cannot be questioned in what He does, but they will be questioned.

We stand witness that Muḥammad is His servant and His Messenger, is dear to Him and is His friend, the true and the trustworthy, who was sent as a mercy for the world, with the True Religion, and a law that is compassionate towards the subjects. It (the law) speaks with a tongue that is easy to understand, stating that compassion is its trait and generosity its objective, caring for the masses both the weak and strong, guiding all whether intelligent or injudicious, inviting them all with a common call whether low or high, being kind to the subjects whether obedient or disobedient, driving them all from the nose ring whether willing or resisting, and deeming all equal through the rule of justice whether noble or lowly. It grants to one who follows it a high status in this world and the next, while placing the qualities of prophethood between his two sides even though he is not a prophet, granting one who is attributed with it a place of honour so that he becomes a friend of God, and one whom God befriends is the wealthiest of persons even though poor, and he who is removed from Him is the poorest even though he is rich.

The Prophet (pbuh) always invited through it and to it. He spread what he had to give among the humans and the *jinn*. He defended it through proofs derived from within it, and he protected its various aspects through its definitive evidences achieving the aim through his elaboration. He stated through his being and through his speech, "I am a naked (open) warner."

Peace and blessings be upon him and upon his Family and Companions. They understood the goals of the *sharīʿa* and attained them. They established the principles of the *sharīʿa* and linked them to their foundations. They let their minds roam freely in its signs (verses) and acted in all earnestness to seek out its fundamentals and objectives. They concerned themselves thereafter with the elimination of desires and gave priority to the soundness of knowledge. When they occupied themselves with works of welfare they surpassed all others and when they undertook good deeds no one was able to catch up with them. This continued till such time that the sun of distinguishing right from wrong arose on the horizon of their vision illuminating in their hearts the light of conviction. This led to the gushing of springs from their tongues. They were the true heirs of Islam, faith and fairness, and why would they not be so for they were the first to knock at the gates. They became the elect of the elect, the stars through whose light others sought guidance. May God be pleased with them and with those who followed them in the true sense of followers becoming models for guides, their successors in all fairness till the Day of Judgement.

THEREAFTER: O seeker of the realities of higher forms of knowledge – asking for brilliant results of ideas, thirsty for the decked out sources of understanding, hovering around the outer apparent boundary desiring to grasp what is recorded inside it of concealed meanings available through the demolition of these outer sketches – the time has come for you to turn to one whose desires conform to yours, who is gripped by the same anxiety that has taken hold of you. As you have participated with him in this passion, then, turn to the place of his secret revelation so that he may communicate to you his complaints, enabling you to travel with him on the path that he has travelled, to set out like him in the darkness whose light is mixed up with dark patches. When it is time for the dawn, you will give praise, God willing, at the destination of your travel.

He has gone to great lengths in search of this purpose, bearing on the way to it things good and bad, meeting on this course persons with stern and gentle temperaments, and encountering in his various journeys obstacles and facilities. If you like you can find him weary due to hardships of the journey, or exhausted due to the difficulties he faced, or wounded due to the obstacles he had to overcome. Know then that no life can be extremely wholesome or death entirely joyful.

The whole point is that the traveller on this path may not come across someone who can guide him. When the mind becomes tired due to the absence of the light that can serve as a criterion and the heart becomes ill due to a variety of clashes on the way, he will travel on a wrong course associating his name with the wrong people. This happened to him (the Author) till such time that the Beneficent Lord, the Kind and Merciful, who guides whom He likes to the straight path, granted him light, sending to him the spirit of bodies, and the reality behind forms started appearing with their true characteristics and names. Under their protection the truth became evident, the sun of discrimination came shining forth from under the clouds, the weak soul was strengthened and the cowardly heart became brave (gained courage), the truth arrived with all its forces and falsehood was on the run.

He (the Author) gathered together the sound and good (*ḥasan*) traditions with their unique benefits and ideas that appeal to the mind and whose secrets reason can barely unravel and the tongue hardly express, and he gathered them in a manner that separated the well known from the isolated traditions. He tried to verify the levels of the layman and the specialist, the masses and the elect, securing the rights of the follower (*muqallid*) and the independent jurist (*mujtahid*), of the trainee and the trainer, of the student and the teacher, all in accordance with their status with respect to their intelligence (knowledge) and ignorance, their laziness and effort, and their mistakes and accomplishments. He attempted to assign to each thing the level meant for it, to see them in their special position whether small or big, to interpret these things following the middle course which is the attribute of justice and balance, to take two opposites maintaining a straight level for the raised and the lowered, so that everything be free of the two inclinations towards bigotry and laxity, and the two extremes of confrontation and deceit (instigation). All praise is for Allah as is His due on account of His majesty, and all thanks is for Him on account of the excellence of His blessings and the abundance of His magnanimity.

When the concealed secrets began to be revealed and the Gracious God granted success with respect to them and provided guidance, I started collecting their unique meanings, sorting out linguistic irregularities in details and syntax, seeking support from precedents in the sources of the rules and their origins that were manifest and not ambiguous, relying on general induction and not depending on specific individual cases elaborating their transmitted principles along with the related rational propositions. I did this to the extent of my ability and strength, while elaborating the purposes of the Book (Qurʾān) and the *Sunna*. Thereafter, I sought guidance from Allah, the Exalted, for organising these precious gems and for gathering these benefits into meanings that have recourse to their principles helping in their comprehension and attachment, and I merged them with the interpretation of principles of *fiqh* and organised them on a shining and radiant string. The resulting book, thus, came to be divided into five parts.

First: The fundamental concepts of the discipline needed as an introduction to the main objective.

Second: The *aḥkām* (rules) and what is related to them with respect to their concept and legal effect, whether these pertain to the declaratory communication or to the obligation creating communication.

Third: The legal purposes of the *sharīʿa* and the *aḥkām* (rules) related to them.

Fourth: The comprehensive treatment of the *adilla* (evidences) and the elaboration of the concepts related to them in general and specific terms and the discussion of their sources with respect to the manner in which they govern the acts of the subjects.

Fifth: The rules of *ijtihād* and *taqlīd* and the persons associated with each one of them as well as the related conflict, preference, questions and responses.

In each of these five parts there are issues and preliminary discussions as well as detailed aspects through which the required objective is verified and through which they are made more comprehensible.

As the secrets of obligation related to this pure *sharīʿa* are recorded in this, I called it *ʿUnwān al-Taʿrīf bi-Asrār al-Taklīf* (The Sign of Knowledge About the Secrets of Obligation). Thereafter, I moved on from this title to another due to a strange incident that requires amazement from each intelligent mind. In short, I met one day a person whose company I consider a source of benefit for me and whose sessions of discourse I deem a station to be journeyed to and a residence for all delegations (seeking learning). I had already started organising the book and writing it and had given up all other activities for the sake of its arrangement and compilation. He said to me, "Last night I saw you in my sleep (dream) and in your hand was a book that you had written. I asked you about it and you informed me that it was the *Kitāb al-Muwāfaqāt*." He continued, "I asked you about the meaning of this unique title and you informed me that in it you had reconciled the two schools of Ibn al-Qāsim (Mālikī) and Abū

Ḥanīfa." I said to him, "You have shot the arrow directly at the target in this good dream, and you have received a share of prophetic good news. I have begun writing with this objective with a determination to lay down such a foundation for these are principles acknowledged by the jurists and foundations on which earlier ancestors have erected the legal structure." The learned teacher was amazed at the coincidence, just as I was surprised at this reward and companionship of this association.

This book, my sincere bosom friend and faithful companion, will be your support in your travel on the road and a commentary for methods of congruence and reconciliation. It cannot, however, be a source of reliance for all your investigation and verification and your point of recourse to all that concerns you with respect to concepts and confirmation, for it deals with one discipline among the various fields of knowledge and an outline like other outlines as well as the place of conflict of reason and contradiction in understanding. Yet, it will bring you close to your destination, will teach you how to progress within the disciplines of the *sharīʿa* and which way to go. It will stand by you on the way on the back of your mount and will send proposals to the brides of wisdom and then pay the dower on your behalf.

Advance then with determined steps for you have, by the power of God, reached your destination. Receive what is before you of this knowledge for you will, God willing, be successful in what you have attained. Beware of cowardly steps and of lingering on some beautiful path, nor be adamant on mere insistence on your view, without elaboration. Stay away from the lowly ground of *taqlīd* (following another's view without seeking supporting evidence) and make progress by rising up to a higher vision. Hold fast to the guidance you receive for this will enable you to defend your stance, and from this you can seek help, especially when you are faced with feeble questions and minor doubts. Clothe yourself with the fear of God as a distinctive trait and take the attribute of justice as your blanket. Adopt the search for truth as your creed and make acknowledging it for those to whom it is due your ideology. Let not your heart be ruled by selfish obstacles and let not the essence of your intention be deluded by the misfortune of reluctance. Take the position of those who can exercise a choice and not the stance of those who are confused, unless the required meanings become muddled and the meaning sought is not available to the seeker. You are not required to stand aloof if the opponents continue to pester you. The one who is involved with ambiguities is the one who is defeated, while he who is not so involved is well grounded and protected. Blame and censure is for one who storms the prohibited ground for that will cast him into the fire. Do not access the water-hole of bias and do not shy away from conceding a point when the issue is evident for such abstention is the attribute of stubborn persons. It is unwholesome for those who pasture on this land (of knowledge) and an obstacle for the right path.

If something other than this book leads you to deny what is in it, with the novelty and originality in it becoming obscure for you and the opinionated person saying, "It is something the likes of which have not been heard before nor has anything been written within the fundamental or peripheral disciplines of the *sharīʿa* that would resemble its texture or take its form. So beware of the wickedness of its tone and every innovation that it has presented," then, do not pay heed to these confusions without verification and do not aim for assumed benefits without reflection. It is, by Allah, a matter that has been established by verses and reports, its knots have been tied by the elect ancestors, its signposts have been erected by learned scholars, and its foundations have been laid by keen-eyed overseers. Further, when the path becomes clear denial is not required and acceptance of what is gathered by it and consideration of what it presents becomes necessary through acknowledgement. The exceptions are the usual mistakes and errors made by humans and the defects from which the soundness of their ideas suffer. The lucky person is one whose mistakes can be counted, while the scholar is one whose errors are few.

In the light of this, it is incumbent upon a careful (pondering, reflecting) reader to supplement any deficiency that he finds in it. He should form a good opinion about one who gave up his nights and days, who substituted weariness for ease and wakefulness for sleep till such time that he was able to sacrifice for it the sum total of his life and gifted his entire precious time to it. He has now placed the keys of all that he has in front of him. His strength was the strength of trust and he discharged it through what he has stated. Verily, acts are determined through intentions and for each person are what he has resolved to do. One who has resolved to migrate towards Allah and His Messenger will migrate towards them, while he who has resolved to migrate towards this world and what it stands for, or towards a woman he marries, will migrate towards them.

May Allah make us act upon what we have learned, help us in comprehending what we have understood, grant us beneficial knowledge that may make us attain His pleasure, and grant us pure deeds that may be an asset for us on the day we meet Him. He has power over all things and is the most competent to respond. I now begin with the statement of the desired objective and take up the task of making good the promise. Allah is the Helper and there is no power and no strength save in God, the Most High and the Supreme.

NOTES

1 Qurʾān 17:15.
2 Qurʾān 51:56–58.
3 Qurʾān 2:132.
4 Qurʾān 33:72.

Introduction by the Author: Preliminary Concepts

In the name of God, the Beneficent, Most Merciful, and (with) prayers and blessings on Muḥammad and his family.

An introduction to preliminary concepts is needed prior to the examination of the issues in this book. There are over ten concepts.

The first concept: ʿ*uṣūl al-fiqh* are definitive

ʿ*Uṣūl al-fiqh*[1] in the religion (of Islam) are definitive; they are not probable. The evidence for this (statement) is that:

1) these principles are based upon the universal principles (*kulliyāt*) of the *sharīʿa*; and
2) whatever has this form is definitive.

The explanation of the first is evident through induction that leads to definitive truths.[2] The elaboration of the second is undertaken from different perspectives:

The first explanation[3] is that they are either based on rational proofs,[4] which are definitive, or they are based upon general induction[5] from the evidences of the *sharīʿa*, which leads to definitive conclusions as well. There is no third possibility,[6] except for a combination of the two possibilities, and a combination of definitive statements yields a definitive conclusion. These in essence are the ʿ*uṣūl al-fiqh*.

The second explanation[7] is that if they were probable (*ẓannī*), they would not be based on rational proofs, because probable meanings are not acceptable for rational proofs and they cannot be accepted for the universal principles (*kulliyāt*) of the *sharīʿa*. Probable meanings are only to be found in specific rules (individual instances).[8] If uncertain meanings could be associated with the universal principles of the *sharīʿa*, they would be associated with the foundations of the *sharīʿa* itself. As the *sharīʿa* is the primary truth,[9] such association is not permitted in practice[10] – I mean by universal principles (*kulliyāt*)[11] here the necessary principles (*ḍarūriyāt*), supporting principles (*ḥājiyāt*) and the complementary principles (*taḥsīnāt*).

Further, if uncertainty could be associated with the foundations of the *sharīʿa*, it would be possible to associate doubt with it, when there is no doubt in it. So also it would have been possible to alter it and change it. All this, however, goes against the guarantee given by the Glorious and the Majestic for its protection.

The third (explanation) is that if it were permitted to deem a probable meaning as one of the principles of *fiqh*, it would be permitted to deem it as a universal principle of the *dīn* (religion), but this is not the case by agreement, so also here. The reason is that the relation of *ʿuṣūl al-fiqh* with the foundations of the *sharīʿa* is the same as their relationship with the universal principles of the *sharīʿa*. Even though they have different grades within themselves, they are equal in the sense that they are universal principles acceptable to each nation,[12] and they have been included within the meaning of the (guarantee of) protection as necessary principles.

Some jurists maintained that there is no way of affirming the foundations of the *sharīʿa* by probable meanings, because this is the law and we do not render obedience to probable meanings except in particular (individual) cases. It is for this reason that al-Qāḍī Ibn al-Tīb did not include in the meaning of *ʿuṣūl* the details of the underlying causes (*ʿilal*), like the assertion about the conversion (*aks*) of the *ʿilla* (underlying cause), the conflict between the underlying causes, the preference of one cause over another, as well as the details about the rules for reports like the number of narrators and *mursal* reports. All these are not definitive. Ibn al-Juwaynī, on the other hand, for including such issues within the meaning of *ʿuṣūl*, advanced the argument that details that have been erected upon definitive foundations are included by implication[13] in matters indicated by definitive evidences.

Al-Māzarī said: "In my view, even though these rules are probable, there is no justification for excluding them from the meaning of *ʿuṣūl* as is required under the method adopted by al-Qāḍī, who deems *ʿuṣūl* as part of certain knowledge. The reason is that these probable propositions are fundamental general rules that have been formulated not for their own underlying truths,[14] but for checking innumerable matters against them through a relationship that resembles that between general and particular meanings."[15] He aptly points out that Abū al-Maʿālī also does not count them as part of *ʿuṣūl*, but he does it for the meaning that the *ʿuṣūl* according to him are the *adilla* evidences and the *adilla* lead to certain knowledge. He does not find al-Qāḍī (ibn al-Tīb's) method of excluding them from the ambit of *ʿuṣūl*, on the basis of the assumption that we related from him, to be very convincing. This then is what he said.

The response[16] is that a principle in all its formulations must be definitive, because if it is probable it gives rise to the possibility of substitution and such a principle cannot be deemed the practice and through induction a universal principle in religion. There is no difference in this between the formulated principles (*qawānīn kulliya*) and those fundamental principles that have been stated expressly (in the texts).[17] The guaranteed protection in the words of the Exalted, "We have, without doubt, sent down the message; and we will assuredly guard it (from corruption)",[18] means the fundamental expressly stated principles.[19] This is the meaning of the words "This day have I perfected your religion for you"[20] as well. The meaning does not apply to individual cases,[21] for had this been the case no individual instance of the *sharīʿa* could be substituted by another due to the protection. This, however, is not the case and we are certain about such substitution (in individual cases), which is supported by substitution in fact. This is due to the different strengths of probable meanings and the presence of different probable meanings in texts related to particular cases, and even the occurrence of errors in them, for we do find errors in individual traditions (*akhbār al-āḥād*) and even in the (interpreted) meaning of the verses. This indicates that the protection of *dhikr* pertains to principles that are of a general import,[22] and this also makes it necessary that each principle be definitive. This is the response to the statement of Abū al-Maʿālī.

As for the view of al-Qāḍī, the operation of these evidences (texts), whether they are definitive or probable, rests on these principles, which are called *ʿuṣūl al-fiqh*, because reasoning from these texts (evidences) cannot be undertaken unless they are measured against these principles (of interpretation) and are examined through them. This makes it necessary that these principles (of interpretation) be similar in strength to such evidences or even stronger than them. The reason is that you have allowed these principles to govern the meaning of these texts (evidences), so that the evidences that do not meet the standards set by these principles are to be rejected. How then is it possible to deem probable the rules that govern standards for other evidences?[23]

Further, there is no conviction in the assertion that these principles are not intended for themselves so that a lenient view be taken about their being definitive. They govern other evidences and this makes it necessary that there be complete conviction about their status, and they be deemed rules for (measuring) things. Further, if it were true that these are probable rules, all that has been stated above from the beginning, would become necessary. That, however, would not be correct. If all that were conceded, the technical requirement that probable meanings are not to be deemed principles would have to change.

This is sufficient for the absolute expulsion of probable meanings from the domain of principles. Anything operating within these principles[24] that is not definitive is based upon a definitive principle as a consequential sub-rule, and not as the main principle.

The second concept: the evidences relied upon in *ʿuṣūl al-fiqh* are definitive

The principles used in this discipline as well as the evidences relied upon in it are nothing but definitive.[25] The reason is that had they been probable, they would not have yielded definitive meanings of concepts specific to the discipline. This is evident. These principles are either (1) rational – like those that revert to the rational categories of necessary, possible and impossible – or (2) are based on practice, and they move along the same lines as the rational, since among the practical are those that are necessary, possible and impossible, or (3) they are transmitted and the most prominent among these are those that are obtained from reports that are *mutawātir* (continuous) in meaning, or they have been obtained through induction by enumeration undertaken through the sources of the *sharīʿa*.

The *aḥkām* (conclusions of premises) operative in this discipline[26] do not go beyond three: necessary, possible and impossible. To these is related existence (occurrence) and non-existence (non-occurrence).

As for something being a convincing proof (*ḥujja*), it is also dependent on its occurrence for such proof and non-occurrence for such proof. Its existence as valid or invalid is dependent[27] on the three earlier categories. As for their existence as obligatory, recommended, permissible, disapproved or prohibited, these categories have nothing to do with the issues of *ʿuṣūl al-fiqh* insofar as these are *ʿuṣūl* (principles of interpretation). Thus, those who have included them in this discipline have mixed up one discipline with another.[28]

The third concept: evidences and general principles based on induction are definitive[29]

Rational evidences, when they are used in this discipline, are used in combination with transmitted evidences,[30] in identifying their meanings, or in verifying their bases and what resembles these. They are not used independently for legal reasoning, because their employment is for legal matters, and reason (alone) is not the legislator. All this has been settled in *ʿilm al-kalām*.

If this is so, the primary reliance is on the legal evidences (of the *sharīʿa*), and the existence of definitive meanings, according to the well known practice, is non-existent or is at least rare, and by this I mean in the case of evidences that are not continuous (are *āḥād*). Thus, if they are individual reports (*akhbār al-āḥād*) the absence of definitive meanings is obvious. If, on the other hand, these are continuous (*mutawātir*), the derivation of definitive meanings is dependent on (the operation of) premises of which all or most are probable. Something that is dependent on probable meanings is bound to yield a probable result. The reason is that the derivative meanings of these evidences would be dependent on transmitted linguistic and grammatical concepts, the absence of equivocation, the absence of allegorical meanings, the transmission of law and practice, the variance in pronouns, the restriction of general meanings, the removal of ambiguity, the absence of abrogating evidences, the earlier and later evidences by date, and rational conversions. The attainment of definitive meanings with the existence of such factors is difficult. The person who has adopted a safe position will claim that these are all probable in themselves, but yield certain knowledge when they are supported by empirical or transmitted evidence. All this, however, is rare and difficult.[31]

The evidences that are under consideration here, however, are based on induction by enumeration through the entire corpus of probable evidences that converge on a single meaning to yield a definitive meaning. There is a power in collectivity that is not to be found in separation. It is for the same reason that *mutawātir* (continuous) meanings are deemed definitive. This type falls in the same category. If from the induction of all the evidences on an issue a combined meaning emerges that gives certain knowledge, it becomes the desired evidence, and it is similar to what is called *mutawātir* in meaning.[32] In fact it becomes like knowledge we have of the courage of ʿAlī, God be pleased with him, or the existence of Ḥātim (al-Ṭāʾī), a knowledge that is available from numerous incidents reported about them.

It is in this way that the obligation of the five basic pillars was established, like prayer, *zakāt* and others, that is, the obligation is definitive; for otherwise if someone were to argue about the obligation of prayer merely on the basis of the words of the Exalted, "Observe prayer" or another similar text, there would be some discussion about the associated reasoning.[33] It has, however, been propped up by means of evidences and rules external to this so as to grant the obligation of prayer a status of "necessity" in religion about which no one has any doubt, except one who has doubts about the basis of religion itself.

It is due to the obligation arising from such concepts[34] that jurists have relied upon the implication of consensus (*ijmāʿ*), because it is definitive and in turn does away with such controversies. If you were to ponder over the evidences justifying *ijmāʿ* as a binding proof (*ḥujja*), or the individual narration (*khabar wāḥid*) or analogy (*qiyās*) as a binding proof, you would find such justification running on the same lines.[35] The reason is that these evidences are derived from individual cases that defy enumeration, are not confined to a single area[36] and yet convey a single meaning that is the object of the reasoning. When the evidences available to the researcher become numerous, all supporting one another, they collectively convey a meaning that is definitive. This is the case with the sources of the evidences in this book,[37] and these are the sources of the universal principles.

Some of the earlier *ʿuṣūlīs* had, perhaps,[38] given up the recording of such meanings or indicating them, for which reason the later writers on the subject forgot this method. Consequently, reasoning from individual verses or individual traditions became difficult.[39] As they did not consider them to be part of a whole, they pondered over them in their isolated form one text at a time along with the (resultant) objections. This led to the weakening of legal reasoning, which should have been based on the universal principles that convey definitive meanings. When the (individual) texts are understood this way,[40] they do not present any ambiguity. If the general evidences of the *sharīʿa* are understood in the manner adopted by the person raising the objections, a definitive meaning will never be available for the *sharʿī* rule, unless the aid of rational analysis is sought,[41] and reason tries to seek the underlying wisdom behind the *sharīʿa*. It is, therefore, necessary that such a methodology be adopted for the evidences used in *ʿuṣūl*.

The entire Muslim nation (*umma*),[42] in fact all nations, agreed that the *sharīʿa* was laid down for the preservation of the five necessities, which are *ʿaql* (intellect), *dīn* (religion), *nafs* (life), *nasl* (progeny) and *māl* (wealth). The knowledge of these that is available to the *umma* is available by necessity. These necessities have not been established for us through a particular evidence nor are they supported by a particular principle that stands out as the point of recourse. Their compatibility with the *sharīʿa* has become known through a body of evidences that do not pertain to a single category. If they had been based on something particular, it would have been determined as a matter of practice, and those who agree upon them would have had recourse to it, but this is not the case. The reason is that each one of the evidences taken separately are probable, and just as in the case of the *mutawātir* in meaning a particular *khabar wāḥid* cannot be said to convey certain knowledge as compared to the rest of the reports, so also it cannot be identified here, because each one of them taken separately conveys a probable meaning. This is the reality even though the strength of the probable meaning may differ in accordance with the differences among transmitters (of the reports), the particular form of the indicated meanings, the differences among those examining the reports with respect to the power or weakness of comprehension, and the level of the investigation undertaken and so on.

When we examine[43] (the obligation of) prayer, we find the command "observe prayer" related to it in various forms. We find praise for those who observe it, the assignment of blame to those who neglect it, and even the compelling of subjects for its observance and establishing while standing or seated or lying on their sides, like waging of war against those who neglect it or lend support in its neglect as well as all the other evidences supporting such meaning. Likewise, in the case of life where homicide is proscribed, and murder has been subjected to the liability of retaliation in order to prevent it, and its declaration as a major sin that comes close to polytheism, just as observance of prayer has been associated with faith itself. The obligation to meet the needs of one under duress is established. *Zakāt* and charity and looking after one who cannot take care of himself is established. The rulers, judges and kings are under an obligation to establish all this, while the army has been organised to fight those who intend to waste life. Finally, it has been made obligatory on one who fears for his life to satisfy his hunger with anything that is lawful or unlawful out of carrion, blood, and swine flesh. Add to this all that strengthens our knowledge to a certainty about the obligation of prayer and the prohibition of homicide.

This is the case with all the evidences for the pillars of the *sharīʿa*, and this is how the universals are distinguished from individual cases, because the individual cases rely on individual evidences and particular sources. Thus, they remain probable as a consequence of their reliance on probable meanings as against the universal principles that have been derived through induction from evidences without the limitation (of individual texts) and not from specific evidences.

Sub-concept: universal principles and maṣlaḥa mursala

From this preliminary concept another rule is derived: Each principle of the *sharīʿa* that is not supported by a particular text, but is compatible with the fundamental principles of the *sharīʿa*, and its meaning has been derived from its evidences, is valid and can be employed for further extension (of the law) and can be used for subsequent recourse, because this principle has become definitive due to the body of evidences that supports it. The reason is that the evidences do not make it binding that each indicate the rule in a definitive manner when taken individually without the merger of other evidences with it, as has preceded, for this would be difficult.

Under this category is included the *istidlāl mursal*[44] on which Mālik and al-Shāfiʿī have relied. In this method even though no single text supported the individual case, it is supported by a general principle. When a general principle conveys a definitive meaning it enjoys the same strength as an express principle and it is to be built upon in accordance with the strength and weakness of the determined principle, as it may not be preferred in certain cases as compared to the remaining identified principles that conflict with it through the methodology of preference (*tarjīḥ*).

The same is the case with the principle of *istiḥsān*, in accordance with Mālik's view, and this principle is to be used for further extension because its meaning is referred back[45] to the preference of *istidlāl mursal* over analogy (*qiyās*),[46] as has been recorded on the proper occasion.

It is said:[47] that reasoning from a broad general principle to affirm a specific case is not correct, because the wider principle is general and this case is specific and particular, and the general has no relevance to the particular. Although the *sharʿ* (law) has approved the general interest, in what way is it indicated that it has considered this particular and disputed interest?

The response would be that the general principle, if it is structured on the basis of induction, is comprehensive and is like the general class whose rule applies to all its members. As for its being general, it will be explained under its own discussion,[48] God willing, but with respect to its being similar to a class governing its members, the reason is that its required attributes apply to all its members, and it is from here that it has been derived. The reason is that it has been derived from evidences containing commands and proscriptions that are applicable to all the subjects. Thus, it is general in its relationship and is applicable universally with respect to the commands and proscriptions to all.

It is not to be said that it becomes binding in the light of this to take into account each interest, whether it conforms with the intention of the Lawgiver or is opposed to it, because saying this by way of argument is not valid. We say: It is necessary to take into account compatibility with the intention of the Lawgiver, because interests have been deemed interests insofar as they have been determined as such by the Lawgiver. Accordingly, this is discussed at its proper occasion[49] in this book.

Sub-concept: ijmāʿ *is a definitive source*

Not having recourse to the previous principle and the one before it led some of the experts on *ʿuṣūl* to conclude that *ijmāʿ* (consensus of legal opinion) is not a definitive evidence, but is probable. The reason being that the individual evidences considered separately do not have a definitive implication. This way these experts differed from those who went before them and those who came after them. The impact on others of this was that they ceased to reason from textual sources for ordinary matters and gave up the use of *ijmāʿ* for arriving at consensus.[50] Likewise, there are issues other than *ijmāʿ* that have been objected to as probable when they are actually definitive in accordance with this form of reasoning. This, God willing, should be evident.

The fourth concept: the subject-matter of *ʿuṣūl al-fiqh*

The inclusion in *ʿuṣūl al-fiqh* of any issue described in the discipline of *ʿuṣūl al-fiqh* that does not form the basis of any case of the law, of legal procedures, or does not aid in these matters,[51] is superfluous. This is evident from the fact that the title of this subject has been associated with *fiqh* only for an obvious benefit and for ensuring *ijtihād* through it. If a rule does not realise this objective, it is not a principle of interpretation. This, however, does not necessarily imply that everything on which a rule of *fiqh* has been constructed is part of *ʿuṣūl al-fiqh* in general, as this would lead to the inclusion of all the remaining disciplines within *ʿuṣūl al-fiqh* like: grammar, language, derived literal forms, grammatical forms and meaning, *bayān*, *ʿadad*, *masāḥa*, *ḥadīth* and other disciplines that are used for affirming *fiqh*[52] and underlie matters among the issues of *fiqh*. This, however, is not the case and not everything that may be needed for *fiqh* can be counted among its *ʿuṣūl* (principles). What is necessary is that any principle that has been added to *ʿuṣūl al-fiqh*, though no rule of *fiqh* is based on it, is not a principle of this discipline.

On the basis of such reasoning a large number of issues that have been included by later jurists are excluded from this discipline. These are like the issue of *ibtidāʾ al-wadʿ* (initial application),[53] the issue of permissibility[54] whether or not it gives rise to an obligation, the issue of the silent command, the issue whether or not the Prophet (pbuh) is himself bound by the law, and the issue that there is no obligation without an act.

Likewise, it does not become binding[55] that something that is not part of it be included in it and detailed analysis be undertaken in it even when some rules of *fiqh* are constructed upon such principles. These are like the detailed discussions of grammar, like those about the meaning of *ḥurūf* (prepositions), the classification of nouns, verbs and prepositions, the discussions about the actual and metaphorical application of words, of equivocal words and synonyms as well as derivatives and so on.

There is, however, an issue about the rules of Arabic that runs like an artery through *ʿuṣūl al-fiqh*. The issue is that the Qurʾān is in Arabic and the *Sunna* is in Arabic. This does not concern the issue whether the Qurʾān includes non-Arabic words, because it is a matter that concerns grammar and language, but it does concern the issue that the Qurʾān in its syntax, meanings and modes of address is in Arabic.

When this point is established it implies that the methods of interpretation and reasoning from them has to be in accordance with Arab usage insofar as the determination of its meanings and the different and specific modes of address are concerned. There are many people who interpret the legal evidences in the Qurʾān in accordance with how their own reason sees them, and not in accordance with its form. In such an approach, there is a grave error and it goes against the purposes of the Lawgiver. This issue is elaborated in the *Book of Maqāṣid*.[56] Praise be to Allah.

Sub-concept: disagreements on issues not affecting fiqh *are also not part of this discipline*

Providing supporting arguments to strengthen or demolish the different positions taken by the schools is devoid of benefit when disagreement about an issue in *ʿuṣūl al-fiqh* on which *fiqh* is structured, does not lead to a consequential disagreement in the rules of *fiqh*. This is like the disagreement of the Muʿtazila about the *wājib mukhayyar* (obligation offering a choice)[57] or the *muḥarram mukhayyar*,[58] as in these issues each school upholds the same practice. They disagreed about a basic tenet on the basis of a discussion in *ʿilm al-kalām*, and this is repeated in *ʿuṣūl al-fiqh*. The issue is: Whether obligation and prohibition as well as other categories are related to the essence of things[59] or only to the communication of the Lawgiver. There is also the issue of the legal obligation for the unbelievers[60] as discussed by al-Fakhr al-Rāzī, which is evident. These issues have no impact on practice. There are other issues that they have discussed and that have no practical consequence in *fiqh*.

It should not be said that those things in which the disagreement pertains to faith will be assigned the rule of obligation or prohibition as regards faith, and if the dispute also pertains to protection of life or wealth, or the issue of *ʿadāla*, or something else, then it will be assigned the relevant rule in the *furūʿ*. We would say: This is the case with all the issues of *ʿilm al-kalām*; then should all these be deemed a part of *ʿuṣūl al-fiqh*? This, however, is not the case, and the purpose is obvious in what has preceded.

The fifth concept: an issue not related to conduct need not be taken up in this discipline

An inquiry into an issue that is not the basis of practice is an inquiry into something whose soundness is not supported by a legal evidence. I mean by practice here an act of the *qalb* (heart) or of the limbs insofar as it is legally required.[61]

The evidence for this is induction through the *sharīʿa*. We saw that the Lawgiver turns away from that which does not benefit the subject in some practical way.[62] The Noble Qurʾān says, "They ask thee concerning the new moons. Say: They are but Signs to mark fixed periods of time in (the affairs of) men, and for pilgrimage."[63] The response came in a form that concerns practice, and avoids what the enquirer intended through the question about the moon: why does it appear in the early stage fine like a thread and then grows till it becomes the full moon returning to its earlier state? He then said, "It is no virtue if ye enter your houses from the back: it is virtue if ye fear Allah. Enter houses through the proper doors: and fear Allah: that ye may prosper",[64] based on the interpretation of those who interpret it to mean that the entire verse has been revealed for this purpose. The entire response indicated that this question, for purposes of performance, simply refers to approaching the houses from the back,[65] and piety (*birr*) is fear of God (*taqwā*) and not a knowledge of those things that do not yield any benefit in meeting obligations nor are they related to them. After their question about the hour – "They ask thee about the Hour, When will be its appointed time?"[66] – the Exalted said, "Wherein art thou (concerned) with the declaration thereof?"[67] that is, this question pertains to an issue that is not relevant, and all that needs to be known is that it is bound to occur. It is for this reason that the Prophet (pbuh), when he was asked about the hour, said to the questioner, "How have you prepared for it?"[68] He avoided the direct question and turned to something related to it and in which there was some benefit. He did not respond to what he asked. The Exalted said, "Ye who believe ask not questions about things which, if made plain to you, may cause you trouble."[69] It was revealed about a man who had asked: Who is my father? It is related[70] that the Prophet (pbuh) stood up to address (the people) and there was anger on his face. He said, "Do not ask me about things other than those I have warned you of." A man stood up and said, "O Messenger of God, who is my father?" He replied, "Abū Ḥudhāfa." It was then that the verse was revealed. There are other reports in the same two categories. Ibn ʿAbbās said in response to the question of Banū Isrā'īl about the attributes of the cow, "If they had slaughtered any cow, He would have rewarded them, but they went to extremes and God was strict with them."[71] This elaborates that there is no benefit to be derived from such questions.

This meaning is also to be found in the previous verse[72] according to those who maintain that the verse was revealed[73] in the case of the person who asked,[74] "Is this *ḥajj* of ours for this year or for all times?" The Prophet (pbuh) said, "For ever." Had he said, "Yes", it would have become obligatory (on an annual basis).[75] In some narrations he said, "Let me be as long as I do not engage you in a discussion. Those before you were destroyed because of excessive enquiries from the prophets." Their questions were superfluous[76] with no practical benefit, because had they kept silent they would not have ceased to act; the questions then were devoid of practical benefit. It was due to this that the Prophet (pbuh) proscribed "idle gossip and excessive questions",[77] because this becomes the source of useless queries. Jibrīl asked him about the hour of judgement and he said, "The one asked does not know more than the questioner."[78] He thus informed him that he had no knowledge of it. This explained that no legal obligation arose from the question,[79] but as it was necessary to avoid certain acts[80] on the appearance of its signs and to have recourse to God at the time, he did explain those details. The Prophet (pbuh) then ended the statement by explaining to ʿUmar that Jibrīl had come to teach them their religion.

It is, therefore, established that in religion there is no obligation to know the answer to the question about the final "hour", that is, knowledge about the time of its occurrence. Note, then, this meaning in the tradition and the benefit to be derived from the question he was asked. He said, "The most blameworthy of persons is one who asks about a thing that was not forbidden, but becomes forbidden due to his question."[81] This is exactly what we are dealing with here, because if it was not required to be forbidden, what was the point in asking the question. ʿUmar ibn al-Khattāb recited, "And fruits and fodder (*abban*)",[82] and said, "This is the fruit, but what is *abban*."[83] He then said, "We have been forbidden from seeking burdens." The Qur'ān says, "They ask thee concerning the spirit (of inspiration). Say: The spirit (cometh) by command of my Lord: of knowledge it is only a little that is communicated to you, (O men)."[84] According to the apparent meaning this implies that they were not answered and it is a matter whose knowledge is not obligatory. It is related that the Companions once became impatient and said, "O Messenger of God, narrate something to us." Allah then revealed, "Allah has revealed (from time to time) the most beautiful Message in the form of a Book, consistent with itself, (yet) repeating (its teaching in various aspects): the skins of those who fear their Lord tremble thereat; then their skins and their hearts do soften to the celebration of Allah's praises. Such is the guidance of Allah: He guides therewith whom He pleases, but such as Allah leaves to stray, can have none to guide."[85] It is like a rebuttal of what they had asked and implies that it is not required that one ask about things that do not demand obedience. Their impatience increased and they asked for a narration better than the Qurʾān and in response *sūrat Yūsuf* was revealed. See the complete tradition in *Faḍāʾil al-Qurʾān* by Abū ʿUbayd. Ponder over the report about ʿUmar ibn al-Khaṭṭāb and Ḍabīgh[86] who used to question people about things in the Qurʾān from which no *ḥukm taklīfī* emerged, and whom ʿUmar scolded. Ibn al-Kawwāʾ is reported to have asked ʿAlī ibn Abī Ṭālib, God be pleased with him, about "By the (winds) that scatter broadcast; and those that lift and bear away heavy weights",[87] so ʿAlī said to him, "Ask about *fiqh* and do not ask for the sake of questioning." He then responded to him. Ibn al-Kawwāʾ then said to him, "What are these black spots in the moon." ʿAlī said, "A blind person asking the blind", but he then responded to him. He then continued to ask questions, but the report is lengthy. Mālik ibn Anas[88] used to look down upon discussions that did not pertain to conduct. It is reported that he disapproved things like those that have preceded.

The elaboration of there being little benefit in these things is provided from several perspectives.

Among these is the fact that this attention is diverted from matters that are relevant to obligation towards those that are not relevant, because no benefit is derived from them either for this world or for the next. As for the Hereafter, he will be asked about what he was required to do and what he was forbidden from doing. As for this world, the knowledge that he has acquired of these matters does not enhance or decrease his ability to earn his livelihood. As for the momentary enjoyment that he derives, it cannot be deemed compensation for the hardship he encounters in search of his livelihood or for the weariness through searching for it. If it is assumed that there is some utility available through it in this world, then its existence is conditional upon this being affirmed by an evidence from the *sharīʿa*. How many are the enjoyments and benefits that man considers as blessings, but in the reckoning of the *aḥkām* of the *sharīʿa* it is the opposite, like *zinā*, drinking of wine, all types of disobedience, and immoral acts that serve an immediate purpose. Thus, wasting time on things that return no benefit in either of the two worlds, along with suspension of what does return a benefit, is an act that is not required.

Among these is the fact that the *sharīʿa* has elaborated things that improve the condition of the servant in this world and the next in a most complete and exhaustive manner. What does not fall within this category is thought to go against it. This is witnessed in everyday experience. Most of those who occupy themselves with fields of knowledge from which no resultant obligation arises, ultimately lead themselves on to trials and deviation from the right path and this gives rise to disagreement and disputation among them which in turn lead to the severance of relations, enmity and bias, so much so that they split up into sects.[89] When this happens they move out from obedience to the *Sunna*. There is no cause for such a split other than this, because they did not confine themselves to a relevant field of knowledge and moved to those that are not relevant. This is a source of trials for the seeker of knowledge as well as the instructor. The reluctance of the Lawgiver to answer the question, even after acknowledgement of the question, is the most evident proof of the fact that the pursuit of such knowledge is a trial and a waste of time with no gain.

Among these is the fact that attempting to examine each thing and seeking knowledge about it is the occupation of philosophers to whom the Muslims owe nothing. The reason is their occupation with things that go against the *Sunna*. Thus, following them in matters that have this nature is a grave error and amounts to turning away from the right path. The elements of disapproved matters in this are many.

It may be said that knowledge is desirable on the whole, and is to be attained without restriction, and its attainment has been commanded in general and unrestricted forms. These commands include each form of knowledge. Within this is knowledge that is directly related to conduct, as well as knowledge that is not so related. Qualifying one form of knowledge as good to the exclusion of other forms is arbitrary. Further, scholars maintain that seeking knowledge in all its forms is a communal obligation, including magic, the use of talismans, and other forms of knowledge that are far away from conduct. If this is the position of this knowledge, what would be the status of knowledge like mathematics, geometry and the like?

Further, the discipline of *tafsīr* (exegesis) is deemed a part of desired knowledge, but no legal conduct is based on it. Ponder over the story narrated by al-Fakhr al-Rāzī that a scholar passed by a Jew with whom there was a Muslim, whom he was teaching the science of cosmology. He asked the Jew what he was reading out to him. He replied, "I am elaborating for him a verse of the Qurʾān." He asked him in great surprise as to what it was and he replied, "The words of the Exalted, 'Do they not look at the sky above them? How We have made it and adorned it, and there are no flaws in it?' "[90] The Jew said, "I am elaborating for him its structure and management." The scholar approved what he was doing. This is the content of the story and not the actual narration. Then there are the words of the Exalted, "Do they see nothing in the government of the heavens and the earth and all that Allah hath created? (Do they not see) that it may well be that their term is nigh drawing to an end? In what message after this will they then believe?",[91] which include all kinds of knowledge that may be in existence whether rational or transmitted, acquired or gifted, and this is supported by other similar verses.

The philosophers believe that the function of philosophy is to study all that exists without restriction insofar as this will lead to a knowledge of the Creator and all this requires a study of evidences and all creatures. These are matters that indicate the overall approval of seeking all forms of knowledge without restriction.

The response with respect to the first point is that the general command (for seeking knowledge) is restricted, and its absolute form qualified by all the evidences that have preceded. This is evident due to two things. First, that the pious ancestors from among the Companions and their Followers did not indulge in these matters that were not linked to conduct, although they had the best knowledge about what form of knowledge was to be sought. In fact, ʿUmar mentioned this in words like "And fruits and fodder (*abban*)"[92] identifying the obligation that was proscribed. His act of scolding Ḍabīgh is an obvious indication of what we are saying, and no one opposed him in this. They did not occupy themselves with such matters because the Messenger of God (pbuh) himself did no such thing. Had he done so, it would have been transmitted from him, and this indicates the negation of this activity. The second is what is established in the Book of *Maqāṣid* that this *sharīʿa* is *ummiyya* for an *umma* that is *ummiyya*. The Prophet (pbuh) has said, "We are an unlettered nation, we do not rationalise nor do we write the month like this or this",[93] and there are other precedents like this. The issue has been explained in that book. Praise be to Allah.

The response with respect to the second is that we do not accept this in an unqualified sense. The communal obligation is the repelling of each injurious thing and its negation irrespective of the nature of the defect being known, except that it should be known that it is defective and this is known through the *sharʿ* (law). The indisputable argument for this is that Moses (Mūsā) (pbuh) did not possess a knowledge of the magic that was exhibited by the magicians. Yet it was demolished at his hands through something that was more powerful than magic, and that was a miracle. It was for this reason that when they cast a spell over the eyes of the people and put them in a state of amazement through powerful magic, Moses himself was afraid. Had he been aware of its nature, he would not have felt afraid, just like those having knowledge of it were in no fear of it, and these were the magicians. Accordingly, God said to him, "Fear not! for thou hast indeed the upper hand."[94] He then said, "They have faked what they have faked. A magician thrives not (no matter) where he goes."[95] This is its identification[96] after rejection. Had he been aware of its nature, there would have been no need for its identification for him. All that he knew was that they were false in their claim in general. This is the rule for each case falling under this category.

Thus, when the negation and rejection has been achieved, in whatever way this has been achieved, even when this is through the miracle of a friend of God, or it is through a factor external to such knowledge arising out of the discernment of the fear of God (*taqwā*), then this is the desired aim. Consequently, the requirement of attaining such knowledge is not established through the *sharʿ* (law).

The response to the third point is that the discipline of interpretation (*tafsīr*) is desired insofar as the intention behind the (divine) communication is to be understood. When the intention becomes known, what is beyond this is artifice. The matter is elaborated through a case associated with ʿUmar: When he recited

"And fruits and fodder", he stopped at the meaning of *abb*, which is an isolated meaning a lack of whose knowledge does not lessen the meaning arising from the syntax of the verse. The meaning as communicated by God, the Exalted, pertains to food for human beings insofar as He has brought down water from the sky bringing out through it a number of things, some of which directly become food for human beings, like grains, grapes, olives and dates, while others form vegetation for animals becoming food indirectly for humans as a whole. The details of each species remain additional facts that need not be known by man. It was due to this reason – God knows best – that ʿUmar deemed the search for the meaning of *abb* an artifice. Had the syntactical meaning not been clear to him at all, it would not have been an artifice, but a search for its meaning would be required of him due to the words of the Exalted, "(Here is) a Book which We have sent down unto thee, full of blessings, that they may meditate on its Signs, and that men of understanding may receive admonition."[97] For the same reason he enquired from the pulpit about the meaning of *takhawwuf*, which is a word that occurs in the words of the Exalted, "Or that He may not call them to account by a process of slow wastage – for thy Lord is indeed full of kindness and mercy."[98] The response came from a man from the tribe of Hudhayl, who said that the word in their language meant "reducing gradually" and in support he recited the hemistich that meant: "The thickness of its hump is gradually thinned out by the saddle, just as the bow-wood is gradually straightened by the bow-maker." ʿUmar said, "O people, hold fast to the compilations of poetry of your Jāhiliyya (days of ignorance) for they contain the interpretations of your Book."

When questions with respect to the words "By the (winds) sent forth one after another (to man's profit); which then blow violently in tempestuous gusts"[99] started perturbing people in social gatherings, without there being any conduct attached to their meaning, ʿUmar disciplined Ḍabīgh in a manner that is well known. Insofar as the words, "Do they not look at the sky above them? How We have made it and adorned it, and there are no flaws in it?"[100] are interpreted to mean the science of cosmology, such an interpretation is not sound, and it amounts to a meaning that was not known to the Arabs when the Qurʾān was revealed in their language and in terms with which they were acquainted. This meaning will be elaborated in the *Book of Maqāṣid* with the help of God.

The same is the view about each discipline that is attributed to the *sharīʿa*, but which has no practical benefit, and that is something that was unknown to the Arabs. Scholars of science as well as others have indulged in artifice to argue in support of their disciplines through the verses of the Qurʾān as well as through traditions related from the Prophet (pbuh). Likewise, the scholars of numerology have sought support from the words of the Exalted, "They will say: We stayed a day or part of a day: but ask those who keep account",[101] while the scholars of engineering have sought support from "He sends down water from the skies, and the channels flow, each according to its measure: but the torrent bears away the foam that mounts up to the surface. Even so, from that (ore) which they heat in the fire, to make ornaments or utensils therewith, there is a scum likewise. Thus doth Allah (by parables) show forth truth and vanity. For the scum disappears like froth cast out; while that which is for the good of mankind remains on the earth. Thus doth Allah set forth parables."[102] Those dealing with astronomy have quoted the verse "The sun and the moon follow courses (exactly) computed."[103] Logicians have argued that the negation of the "particular negative" argument is understood by way of, "No just estimate of Allah do they make when they say: nothing doth Allah send down to man (by way of revelation): say: who then sent down the book which Moses brought? a light and guidance to man: but ye make it into (separate) sheets for show, while ye conceal much (of its contents): therein were ye taught that which ye knew not neither ye nor your fathers. Say: Allah (sent it down): then leave them to plunge in vain discourse and trifling."[104] Certain forms of the categorical and the hypothetical, they say, are supported by others. Those who are involved with the discipline of *khaṭṭ al-raml* (geomancy) have relied on the words of the Exalted, "Say: Do ye see what it is ye invoke besides Allah? Show me what it is they have created on earth, or have they a share in the heavens? Bring me a Book (Revealed) before this, or any remnant of knowledge (ye may have), if ye are telling the truth!"[105] as well as on the words of the Prophet (pbuh), "There was a Prophet who used to draw lines in the sand."[106] There are other cases besides these that are recorded in books, and all of these imply[107] that these verses are intended for what has preceded.

All this makes known the response to the fourth question, and that is that the words of the Exalted, "Do they see nothing in the government of the heavens and the earth and all that Allah hath created? (do they not see) that it may well be that their term is nigh drawing to an end? in what message after this will they then believe?"[108] do not include in its various interpretations the discipline of philosophy, which was not known to the Arabs[109] and does not suit an unlettered people to whom an unlettered Prophet was sent with a simple and easy religion. Philosophy – on the assumption that it is a required discipline – is difficult in its sources, arduous in its methods, and protracted in yielding results. It is, therefore, not likely that the communication (from God) would require its learning as a prerequisite for understanding the *āyāt* (signs) of Allah and the evidences of His unity, especially for those Arabs who grew up in an unlettered environment. How can this be when philosophy has been condemned by the scholars of the *sharīʿa*, giving arguments for condemnation through what has been stated at the beginning of this issue.

If this is established, then the correct view is that anything that does not form the basis of conduct is not required by the *sharīʿa*. The exception is that knowledge upon which the required conduct depends, like the meaning of words, grammar, the discipline of *tafsīr*, and so on, because there is no difficulty in the assertion that anything on which a required thing depends is also required, either by law or rationally, as has been explained at the suitable occasion. There is, however, another point towards which we must turn, and that is:

The sixth concept: two ways of attaining required knowledge

The knowledge on which depends the identification of required (conduct) may be approached through a method that is approximative and is suitable for the public, and it may be approached through a method that is not suitable for the masses, even though[110] it is deemed a necessity for investigation.

As for the first, it is the required method that has already been indicated. For example, if the meaning of the word *malak* (angel) is required, it will be said that it is one of the creations of God that carries out His orders; if the meaning of *insān* (human being) is required, it will be said that it is a genus of which you are one type; if the meaning of the word *takhawwuf* (fear) is required, it will be said that it is gradual reduction; if the meaning of the word *kawkab* (planet) is required, it will be said that it is something that is witnessed (in the sky) at night; and so on. The meaning of the (divine) communication is understood through this type of approximative knowledge so that obedience becomes possible.

The *bayān* (elaboration) in the *sharīʿa* has come down in this way. The Prophet (pbuh), for example, said, "The word *kibr* (haughtiness) is the denial of truth and looking down upon people."[111] He elaborated the word through such necessary meanings that are apparent to everyone. Likewise, he elaborated the words of the Qurʾān and of *ḥadīth* with synonyms that were easier to understand as compared to the word employed. The Prophet (pbuh) elaborated the meaning of *ḥajj* through his acts and words in a manner that was suitable for the masses, and likewise all other matters. This is the customary practice among the Arabs and the *sharīʿa* is based upon Arabic. Further, the *umma* (Muslim nation) is unlettered, and it is not appropriate that the elaboration be in a manner that is not meant for the unlettered. This has been elaborated (at length), praise be to God, in the *Book of Maqāṣid*. Now, therefore, the concepts employed in the *sharʿ* have approximations expressed in literal synonyms or whatever acts as a substitute elaboration for such approximations.

The second method is not suitable for the masses. As it is not suitable for the masses, it moves out of the ambit of the consideration of the *sharīʿa*, because its methods are difficult to attain and God has not invoked any hardship in religion (*dīn*). For example, if the meaning of the word *malak* is sought, the response will be transferred to a concept deeper than this word to say, "It is an essence that is essentially devoid of matter" or "It is a simple substance possessing perfection and capable of rational speech." If the meaning of *insān* (human) is sought, it will be said, "He is an articulate animal subject to death." It may then be said, what is a *kawkab*? The response would be that it is a body that is "simple, spherical, located in the celestial sphere, with its feature being that it gives out light, rotates on its axis (middle), and is not attached to the sphere". If the meaning of the word *makān* (position) is sought, it will be said, "It is the inner surface of the enveloped mass touching the external surface of the enveloping form." Likewise, all other matters that were unknown to the Arabs, a knowledge of which cannot be attained without spending considerable time in seeking out their meanings. It is evident that the Lawgiver did not intend such concepts nor did He impose a burden for seeking them out.

Further, seeking out the nature of things is like assailing a wall, and even the specialists in the field have acknowledged the difficulty of doing so. Some of them have recorded that it is difficult for them and they were led to say that things cannot be known in reality, because substances have many concealed forms and they are defined through negative definitions. Thus, a specific attribute,[112] if it is found in another essence, is no longer specific. If it is not known, it is not apparent to the senses and is unknown. If this specific attribute is known through something that is not specific to it then it is not part of the definition. Something specific to it is like the specific attribute first mentioned. Thus, it becomes necessary to have recourse to sensory data or what is apparent in other ways, but this is not how essence is defined.

This pertains to the substance. As for accidental attributes, these are defined through their properties, because the specialists in this field have no other way of defining them. Further, what has been stated about substances and other attributes cannot be proved to the effect that there is no other attribute besides them and the disputant can raise a question about this. The person defining may not say: Had there been another attribute, I would have come to know about it. The reason is that there are many attributes that are not apparent. In addition to this, he cannot say: Had there been another specific attribute, I would have discovered another essence besides this one. For we would reply: Reality is discovered when all the properties are discovered; thus, if there is a property that is not discovered a doubt is created about the identification of the substance itself.

This makes it obvious that definitions, according to the conditions stipulated by the specialists, are difficult to formulate. Such definitions cannot be included in the *sharʿī* disciplines that help in its implementation. The meaning that is established is: The essences of this in reality are known only to the Creator, and human endeavours to discover them are no more than a shot in the dark, and it is all a mere conjecture.

As for affirmation that is suitable for the masses, it is necessary that the premises of the evidence adduced be necessary or close to the necessary, as is explained with the help of God, at the end of this book. If that is the case, then it is this fact whose requirement is established in the *sharīʿa* and it is this that has been pointed out by the Qurʾān through examples. The examples are in the words of the Exalted, "Is then He Who creates like one that creates not? Will ye not receive admonition?",[113] His words, "Say, He will give them life Who created them for the first time. For He is well versed in every kind of creation",[114] His words, "It is Allah Who has created you: further, He has provided for your sustenance; then He will cause you to die; and again He will give you life. Are there any of your (false) partners who can do any single one of these things? Glory to Him! and High is He above the partners they attribute (to Him)!",[115] His words, "If there were, in the heavens and the earth, other gods besides Allah, there would have been confusion in both! But glory to Allah, the Lord of the throne: (High is He) above what they attribute to Him!"[116] and His words, "Do ye then see? The (human seed) that ye throw out."[117]

This is the case when an evidence is needed for affirmation, for otherwise establishing the *ḥukm* is sufficient.

The worthy ancestors proceeded in this manner in elaborating the *sharīʿa* for the supporters as well as opponents. Anyone who examines their reasoning for establishing the obligation creating rules (*aḥkām taklīfī*) comes to know that they adopted the easiest of methods and those closest to the understanding of persons desiring opinions without there being any arranged arguments or syntactical organisation.[118] They used to respond spontaneously without bothering about the impact of the composition. As their response was close to the source, it became easy to grasp. Even when the response was similar[119] in rhetorical form to that of those advanced in this field, it was by way of achieving their objective and not for the sake of imitating those who preceded them.

When the mode of address is based upon composite or non-composite syllogisms, and reason has to exert some effort to comprehend the meaning, then, this is not the *sharʿī* mode, and you will not find it in the Qurʾān nor in the *Sunna*, nor even in the speech of the worthy ancestors. It is something that overwhelms the mind and overworks it prior to reaching the goal. It also goes against the methods of instruction. The reason is that legal (*sharʿī*) concepts – in general – require immediate response[120] and what suits them is that which can be understood immediately. If the examination of an evidence is protracted, it will work against these requirements and that is not correct. Further, the methods of comprehension are not all of the same level, nor do they work equally for each requirement, except for what is required by necessity or what is similar to it, for in these there is no known difference. If the evidences (*adilla*) are presented in a form different from this,[121] this requirement will be difficult to meet, and the obligation to know it will become specialised and will not remain general, or it will lead to an obligation that cannot (possibly) be performed, or in which there is an injury, and all these are excluded from the *sharīʿa*. The details of this concept will come up in the *Book of Maqāṣid*.

The seventh concept: each *sharʿī* discipline is a means of obedience to Allah

Each *sharʿī* discipline required by the Lawgiver was required with the objective of serving as a means of submission to Allah, the Exalted, and not for any other purpose. If the consideration of another purpose appears in it, it appears as a secondary goal and not as the primary goal. The evidences for this are several.

The first is what was stated in the discussion of the previous issue, that is, there is nothing in the *sharīʿa* to indicate that a discipline that does not yield a practical benefit[122] can be deemed good. If it has another aim that conforms to the *sharīʿa*, it will be deemed good according to the *sharīʿa*. Had it been good, the predecessors from among the Companions and their Followers would have sought it out,[123] but when this is not found the conclusion about it is drawn accordingly.

The second is that the *sharʿ* (law) has been laid down to require obedience, and that was the purpose in the sending of the Prophets, God's peace and blessings be on them. Allah, the Exalted, said:

> O mankind reverence your guardian Lord, who created you from a single person, created, of like nature, his mate, and from them twain scattered (like seeds) countless men and women; reverence Allah, through whom ye demand your mutual (rights), and (reverence) the wombs (that bore you): for Allah ever watches over you.[124]

> A. L. R. (this is) a book, with verses basic or fundamental (of established meaning), further explained in detail, from one who is wise and well acquainted (with all things): (It teacheth) that ye should worship none but Allah. (Say) verily I am (sent) unto you from him to warn and to bring glad tidings.[125]

> A. L. R. A book which we have revealed unto thee, in order that thou mightest lead mankind out of the depths of darkness into light by the leave of their Lord to the way of (him) the exalted in power, worthy of all praise.[126]

> This is the Book; in it is guidance sure, without doubt, to those who fear Allah.[127]

> Praise be to Allah, who created the heavens and the earth, and made the darkness and the light. Yet those who reject faith hold (others) as equal with their guardian Lord.[128]

That is, they gave obedience to someone else in their worship, and He blamed them for this, saying:

> Obey Allah, and obey the Messenger, and beware (of evil): if ye do turn back, know ye that it is our Messenger's duty to proclaim (the Message) in the clearest manner.[129]

> (He hath made it) straight (and clear) in order that he may warn (the godless) of a terrible punishment from him, and that he may give glad tidings to the Believers who work righteous deeds, that they shall have a goodly reward.[130]

> Not a messenger did We send before thee without this inspiration sent by Us to him: that there is no god but I; therefore worship and serve Me.[131]

> Verily it is We Who have revealed the Book to thee in Truth: so serve Allah, offering Him sincere devotion.[132]

The verses that give a similar meaning are numerous, and all of them indicate that the goal is to render obedience to Allah. They (the Prophets) brought evidences of the unity of God (*tawḥīd*) so that people could turn to the One True God, glory be to Him, who has no partner. It is for this reason that the Exalted said, "Know, therefore, that there is no god but Allah, and ask forgiveness for thy fault, and for the men and women who believe: for Allah knows how ye move about and how ye dwell in your homes",[133] and He said, "If then they (your false gods) answer not your (call), know ye that this revelation is sent down (replete) with the knowledge of Allah, and that there is no god but He. Will ye even then submit (to Islam)?"[134] and He said, "He is the living (One): there is no god but He: call upon Him, giving Him sincere devotion. Praise be to Allah, Lord of the Worlds!"[135]

Similar to these are all those occasions on which the statement about *tawḥīd* (Oneness of God) is made insisting upon the requirement of obedience to God alone or deeming it the fundamental prerequisite. In fact, the evidences of *tawḥīd* are formulated in the Qur'ān in this form whether as a requirement or as an argument. It is evident that obedience to God is the main goal of knowledge, and the verses conveying this meaning are numerous.

The third reason is contained in the evidences that indicate that the soul of all knowledge is action, for otherwise knowledge is devoid of utility and without any benefit. Allah, the Exalted, has said, "And so among men and crawling creatures and cattle, are those of various colours. Those truly fear Allah, among His Servants, who have knowledge: for Allah is Exalted in Might Oft-Forgiving",[136] and He said, "And when they entered in the manner their father had enjoined, it did not profit them in the least against (the plan of) Allah: it was but a necessity of Jacob's soul, which he discharged. For he was, by our instruction, full of knowledge (and experience): but most men know not."[137] Qatāda (commenting upon this verse) said: "That is, in possession of deeds in accordance with what We have taught him." Allah, the Exalted, has said, "Is one who worships devoutly during the hours of the night prostrating himself or standing (in adoration), who takes heed of the Hereafter, and who places his hope in the Mercy of his Lord (like one who does not)? Say: Are those equal, those who know and those who do not know? It is those who are endued with understanding that receive admonition."[138] And, the Exalted said, "Do ye enjoin right conduct on the people, and forget (to practise it) yourselves, and yet ye study the Scripture? Will ye not understand?"[139] It is related from Abū Ja'far Muḥammad ibn 'Alī about the words of the Exalted, "Then they will be thrown headlong into the (Fire), they and those straying in Evil",[140] that these were a people who paid lip service to truth and justice, but went against what they said in implementing it. It is related from Abū Hurayra[141] that he said, "There are grindstones in hell that will crush the evil-doing scholars. This act will be overseen by someone who knew them in this world and he will say, 'Why has this come to pass for you? We used to seek knowledge from you.' They will reply, 'We used to command you to do one thing, but we went in a different direction ourselves.' "[142] Sufyān al-Thawrī said, "Knowledge is acquired to fear God through it. The precedence that knowledge has over other things is that it gives rise to the fear of God." It is related from the Prophet (pbuh) that he said, "The feet of a person will remain planted in their place on the Day of Judgement until he has been asked about five things"[143] – and he mentioned therein – "about his knowledge and what part of it he transformed into action." It is related from Abū al-Dardāʾ, "I am afraid of being asked on the Day of Judgement whether I acquired knowledge or remained ignorant with my reply being 'I acquired knowledge.' None of the verses of the Qurʾān, whether they command action or issue warnings, will remain silent for they will ask me about the obligations arising from them. The verses requiring conduct will ask me, 'Did you act as required?' while those laying down warnings will ask, 'Did you take heed of the warnings?' I, therefore, seek refuge with God from knowledge that has no utility, from a heart that is not devoted, from a self that is never content, and from prayer that is not heard." In the tradition from Abū Hurayra about the three persons who will be the first to be cast into fire on the Day of Judgement, he said, "A person who acquired knowledge and imparted it to others and recited the Qurʾān will be brought forth and informed of the blessings he received and he will acknowledge this. It will be said to him, 'What good deed did you perform in return for these (blessings)?' He will reply, 'I acquired knowledge for Your sake, taught it, and recited the Qurʾān.' It will be said to him, 'You are lying. You did this to be called a *qārī* (reciter), and you were called by this title.' The order will then be passed that he be cast headlong into the fire."[144] The Prophet (pbuh) said, "The person receiving the greatest torment on the Day of Judgement will be the scholar whose knowledge did not benefit him at all."[145] It is related that the Prophet (pbuh) used to seek refuge with God from knowledge that is useless.[146] The wise persons say, "A person from whom Allah has concealed knowledge, He will punish for his ignorance. A greater torment will be given to the person to whom knowledge was offered and he turned away from it, and also to the person whom Allah guided towards knowledge, but he did not act upon it." Muʿādh ibn Jabal is reported to have said, "Know what you wish to know, but know this too that it will not protect you from the wrath of God until you act upon it." This is also reported in a *marfūʿ* tradition from the Prophet (pbuh) with an addition: "The goal of the wise is the preservation of knowledge through their actions and the goal of the ignorant is mere narration." The same tradition is reported from Mālik in a *mawqūf* narration. It is related from ʿAbd al-Raḥmān ibn Ghanm, who said, "Ten Companions of the Messenger of Allah (pbuh) related to me that they used to participate in giving instruction in the Qubā Mosque when (one day) the Messenger of Allah (pbuh) came to us and said, 'Learn what you can as long as you know that it will not save you from Allah's wrath until you act according to your knowledge.' "[147] A man once asked Abū al-Dardāʾ a question and he said to him, "Do you act upon all that you ask?" The man said, "No." He replied, "Then why do you add to God's proof against you?" Al-Ḥasan said, "Judge people according to their deeds and do not go by their statements. Allah will use every statement of a person as evidence against him after verifying whether his deeds confirm his statements or deny them. Thus, when you hear something good from a person give him some time. If his statement conforms with his acts, then it is good and acceptable." Ibn Masʿūd has said, "Everyone has good things to say. If a person's deeds conform with his statements, then this is the one who is successful, but if his deeds go against his statements, then he has ruined himself." Al-Thawrī said, "Traditions are sought after so that with their help the fear of God is attained, for otherwise they would be like all other good statements." Mālik has mentioned that a report reached him from al-Qāsim ibn Muḥammad, who said, "I have seen that people do not like mere statements; what they like are good deeds."

The evidences in support of the above meanings are beyond count, and all these confirm the fact that knowledge is a means among various means. It is not a goal in itself from the perspective of the *sharīʿa*, but one of the means leading to sound conduct. All that has been laid down with respect to the merits of knowledge is established in favour of knowledge insofar as it imposes an obligation for sound conduct.

It is not to be said (as an argument) that the merit of knowledge is established in the *sharīʿa*, that the status of scholars is higher than the status of martyrs, that the scholars are heirs to the Prophets and their status follows that of the Prophets, and that if this is the case, and if the evidence indicating all this is absolute and not qualified, then, how can it be denied that its preference (for itself) is the goal and it is not meant as a means to an end? Besides this, that if it is a means from one aspect, it is desirable for its own self as well, like faith (*īmān*), which is a condition for the validity of worship (*ʿibāda*), but that it is also a means for its acceptance. That even in this case it is desirable for itself.

The reason for not asserting the above is our response: The merit of knowledge is not established in an absolute sense, but only as a means to (sound) conduct. This assertion is made on the basis of the evidence we have adduced recently, for otherwise the evidences will contradict each other, and the verses, traditions, and reports, from the worthy ancestors, will conflict with each other. It is necessary to reconcile all of them. What has been stated recently is an explanation of what has been mentioned with respect to the merits of knowledge and of the scholars. As for faith (*īmān*), it is an act of the heart (*qalb*), a confirmation, and it arises out of knowledge. Some deeds become a means for other deeds, even though they may be desirable in themselves. As for knowledge, it is a means, and the best form of knowledge is the knowledge of God. It does not become a merit for whoever has such knowledge, unless he confirms it according to its requirements, and that is belief in Allah.

If it is said: This amounts to a contradiction, because knowledge of God is not sound as long as His denial is present, the response will be: In fact, knowledge can be acquired even when it is accompanied by a denial. Allah has said about a nation, "And they rejected those Signs in iniquity and arrogance, though their souls were convinced thereof: so see what was the end of those who acted corruptly",[148] and He said, "The People of the Book know this as they know their own sons, but some of them conceal the truth which they themselves know",[149] and "Those to whom we have given the book know this as they know their own sons. Those who have lost their own souls refuse therefore to believe."[150] Knowledge about the arrival of the Prophet (pbuh) was established in their case, but it was elaborated that yet they did not believe. This elaborates for us that faith is something different from knowledge, just as ignorance is different from unbelief. Yes, knowledge in itself is meritorious, sometimes even when it is not accompanied by conduct as a whole, like the knowledge of the rules (*furūᶜ*) of the *sharīᶜa* and the obstacles in the way of obligation, when such cases have not actually occurred in the physical world. Knowledge of such matters is good, and the possessor of such knowledge is worthy of spiritual reward and has attained the goal of scholars; from the perspective of its utility at the time of the occurrence of its object, however, it is not excluded from the ambit of being a means to an end. This is like ritual purification for prayer that has its merit even though the time of prayer has not arrived as yet, or it is the time for prayer, but it is not possible for him to pray due to some legal obstacle. If it is assumed that he has attained ritual purification with the resolve that he will not pray, he will not attain a spiritual reward for ritual purification. Likewise, if he acquires knowledge with the intention of not acting upon it, he will not derive any benefit from his knowledge. We have seen and have heard that a number of Christians and Jews know much about the *dīn* of Islam, and they know much about its principles and detailed rules, but all this is of no benefit to them along with the existence of unbelief, and this by agreement of all Muslim scholars. The conclusion is that a *sharᶜī* discipline is required only from the perspective of what it leads to, and that is (sound) conduct.

Sub-concept: only the ignorant deny the merit of knowledge as a whole (the primary and secondary purposes of knowledge)

No one but the ignorant denies the merit of knowledge as a whole, yet knowledge has a primary purpose and a secondary purpose.

The primary purpose is detailed in what has been discussed already. As for the secondary purpose, it is one that is mentioned by the masses when they say that the possessor of knowledge is respectable, even when it is not essentially like that, or (when they say) that the ignorant is despicable, even when he is in reality respectable. The speech of the person with knowledge is incorporated in poetry and quotations, and his authority prevails over the public, his reverence is binding on all the subjects and he is given a status next to the Prophets. Further, knowledge is beauty, wealth and status that no other status can equal. Those who possess knowledge will live till the end of time, just as all the remaining praised virtues and noble positions will be associated with them in this world. Yet, all this is not the purpose of knowledge in the eyes of the *sharīʿa*, just as it is not the purpose of worship and secluded devotion to Allah, the Exalted, even though the owner of these merits usually attains them (in reality).

In addition to this, there is in the knowledge of things a pleasure that is unmatched by other pleasures, because it is a type of authority over the known thing and its possession. The love of authority (over things) is instinctively liked by the self and the heart is inclined towards it and it is deemed a special prize. All this is proved through experience and simple enumeration. Thus, knowledge is sometimes acquired for the amusement it provides or for the pleasure it gives through its discourses, especially those disciplines in which rationalisation has a role to play, in which investigation is widespread, and in which the deduction of the unknown from the known has practised methods.

However, each secondary purpose out of these secondary purposes is either serving the primary purpose or it is not. If it is servicing the primary purpose, then the intended purpose is sound *ab initio*. Allah has said with respect to praiseworthy matters: "And those who pray, Our Lord! Grant unto us wives and offspring who will be the comfort of our eyes, and give us (the grace) to lead the righteous."[151] It is related from some of the worthy ancestors that they used to say, "O Lord, make us the leaders of the God-fearing." ʿUmar is reported to have said to his son – when he thought that the tree that has been deemed similar to a true believer is the date palm – "Had you said it out loud (before the Prophet (pbuh)), it would have been the dearest thing for me." The Qurʾān quotes Ibrāhīm (Abraham) (pbuh) as saying, "Grant me honourable mention on the tongue of truth among the latest (generations)."[152] Likewise, all those things that may be desired and in which there is a tremendous reward on the Day of Judgement as well as other similar things.

If it does not serve a primary purpose, then the intended purpose is initially incorrect. This is like the attainment of knowledge for ostentation, or for confusing simple people, or for gaining praise from the scholars, or for carrying away the emotions of people, for making worldly gains, and so on. When such a state is displayed in seeking knowledge, the quest for knowledge goes down and the desire to advance increases. The attainment of perfection in what the person began becomes difficult, and he finds it irksome to acknowledge his inadequacy. He finds refuge in the insistence of his own reason and extends his ignorance. He becomes one who issues verdicts on the basis of ignorance when questions are put to him, thus, being misguided and misguiding others. May Allah protect us from this state through His immense bounty.

A tradition says, "Do not seek knowledge to get the acclaim of scholars, nor to argue with the simple minded, nor to make an impression in gatherings. For anyone who does this, the fire is the Fire."[153] He said, "He who attains knowledge through a thing from which the pleasure of God is to be sought, but he uses it for worldly purposes, will not find the fragrance of heaven on the Day of Judgement."[154] In one tradition the Prophet (pbuh) was asked about "concealed desire", and he said, "It is the case of the man who attains knowledge so that people may gather around him (for learning)."[155] The noble Qur'ān says, "Those who conceal Allah's revelations in the Book, and purchase for them a miserable profit – they swallow into themselves naught but Fire; Allah will not address them on the Day of Resurrection, nor purify them: grievous will be their penalty."[156] The evidences bearing similar meanings are many.

The eighth concept: knowledge preferred by the lawgiver is one that leads to sound conduct

Knowledge that can truly be deemed knowledge is one that is acknowledged by the *sharīʿa*. I mean, knowledge whose possessor has been commended by Allah and His Messenger in absolute terms. This is knowledge that leads to action and does not make the possessor susceptible to his whims and fancies in any case, rather it keeps him constrained within its requirements, and makes him follow the course of its rules either voluntarily or by compulsion. The meaning of this statement[157] is that possessors of knowledge with respect to seeking it and attaining it fall into three grades.

The first grade are the seekers of knowledge who have not attained perfection as yet. They are those who are performing *taqlīd* (following opinions of others) in their search. When these persons undertake acts on the basis of this knowledge, they do so according to what is declared to be obligatory and through persuasion based on instigation and intimidation with the burden of obligation decreasing in proportion to the intensity of confirmation (of their knowledge). Their knowledge alone is not sufficient to make them bear the obligation without the aid of external pressure that prompts them to do so, like deterrence, retaliation, *ḥadd* penalty, discretionary punishments (*taʿzīr*) or whatever is similar to these. There is no need here to provide proofs of this as experience of human behaviour provides a proof that is irrefutable.

The second grade of seekers of knowledge are those who rely upon proofs of such knowledge rising above the depths of pure *taqlīd* with perception, to the extent that transmitted knowledge provides this, and which reason confirms in a satisfactory manner and relies upon. Nevertheless, this knowledge is attributed to reason and to the inner self (conviction) in the sense of being an established trait of the human being. It is like something acquired, like preserved knowledge, that is governed by reason and is relied upon through retrieval, becoming like all other stored things. When these persons enter the field of action, another deficiency in addition to the deficiency of mere confirmation, as in the case of the first grade, overcomes them. In fact, there is no correspondence between the two grades. The reason is that the confirming proof denies them the opportunity of open rejection. Among the concealed forms of denial are actions in contravention of the knowledge that is available to them. However, as this knowledge has not as yet become an inherent trait, other established traits like following their whims and fancies are the strongest factors driving them. It therefore becomes necessary to have recourse to an additional external measure; however, in their case it is wider and is not confined merely to *ḥudūd* and discretionary penalties. It extends to other matters like good practices, the requirements of suitable expectations in accordance with the grades they have attained – and the like. For this grade too, the proof is derived from experience, except that it is less apparent than the grade prior to it. Thus, it needs a further examination that is delegated to those who have attained eminence in the *sharīʿa* disciplines and who understand behavioural traits.

The third grade is for those for whom knowledge has become an established trait with the establishing of the intuitive factors through the primary intelligibles, or the secondary intelligibles, without looking at the method of their attainment, because that is not needed here. These persons are not deluded by knowledge or by their whims after the truth has become evident for them. They have recourse to it, even a recourse for their human needs and natural traits.

This is the grade that is intended here. The evidences, in the *sharīʿa*, of the soundness of such knowledge are many. For example, the Exalted has said, "Is one who worships devoutly during the hours of the night prostrating himself or standing (in adoration), who takes heed of the Hereafter, and who places his hope in the Mercy of his Lord (like one who does not)?"[158] He then said, "Say: Are those equal, those who know and those who do not know? It is those who are endued with understanding that receive admonition."[159] He attributed these virtues to those with knowledge for the sake of their knowledge and not for something else. The Exalted said, "Allah has revealed (from time to time) the most beautiful Message in the form of a Book, consistent with itself, (yet) repeating (its teaching in various aspects): the skins of those who fear their Lord tremble thereat; then their skins and their hearts do soften to the celebration of Allah's praises. Such is the guidance of Allah: he guides therewith whom He pleases, but such as Allah leaves to stray, can have none to guide."[160] Those who fear their Lord are the *ʿulamāʾ*, due to the words, "Those truly fear Allah, among His Servants, who have knowledge: for Allah is Exalted in Might Oft-Forgiving."[161] Allah, the Exalted, has said, "And when they listen to the revelation received by the Messenger, thou wilt see their eyes overflowing with tears, for they recognise the truth: they pray: 'Our Lord! we believe; write us down among the witnesses.'"[162] When the magicians who were steeped in this knowledge, which is the meaning of this grade, came to know through their knowledge that what Moses (pbuh) had brought was the truth and not magic or jugglery, they rushed towards belief and faith. They were not prevented from doing so by fear or torment that had been directed at them by Pharaoh. Allah, the Exalted, has said, "And such are the parables We set forth for mankind, but only those understand them who have knowledge."[163] He restricted their comprehension to those with knowledge, which is the intention of the Lawgiver in the stating of parables. He said, "Is then one who doth know that that which hath been revealed unto thee from thy Lord is the truth, like one who is blind? It is those who are endued with understanding that receive admonition."[164] Thereafter, he described those with knowledge through His words, "Those who fulfil the covenant of Allah and fail not in their plighted word",[165] as well as through other attributes.

The substance of the argument is that the *ʿulamāʾ* are those who act. He then said about those with faith – when faith is one of the results of knowledge – "For, believers are those who, when Allah is mentioned, feel a tremor in their hearts, and when they hear His Signs rehearsed, find their faith strengthened, and put (all) their trust in their Lord. Who establish regular prayers and spend (freely) out of the gifts We have given them for sustenance. Such in truth are the Believers: they have grades of dignity with their Lord, and forgiveness, and generous sustenance."[166] Through this He associated the *ʿulamāʾ*, with reference to their acts as required by their knowledge, with the angels, who do not disobey Allah and act according to what they are ordered to do. The Exalted said, "There is no god but He: that is the witness of Allah, his angels, and those endued with knowledge, standing firm on justice. There is no god but He, the Exalted in Power, the Wise."[167] The testimony of God corresponds with His knowledge[168] as contradiction is not possible, while the testimony of the angels is sound and corresponds with what they do, because they are protected against disobedience. The possessors of knowledge are similar to the angels insofar as they are protected through their knowledge. The Companions, God be pleased with them, became sad and restless when an admonishing verse was revealed, so much so that they used to question the Prophet (pbuh) about it, as in the revelation of the verse of *sūrat al-Baqara*, "Whether ye show what is in your minds or conceal it, Allah calls you to account for it",[169] as well as His words, "It is those who believe and confuse not their beliefs with wrong that are (truly) in security, for they are on (right) guidance."[170] Restlessness and fear are the signs of knowledge about what was revealed,[171] and the evidences for this are more than can be enumerated here. All these evidences indicate that knowledge that is acknowledged is one that is a point of recourse for action.

It may be said: All this is not evident for two reasons.

First: The possessor of knowledge, by being firmly established in it, is protected against opposition *ab initio* (by just having such knowledge). If this is not the case, then, those in this grade are at the same level as those of the previous grade. The meaning is that knowledge by itself is not sufficient for acting upon it, nor is it a point of recourse (basis) for action. If such a person is protected through it against opposition, it becomes necessary that the *ʿālim* be obedient as long as he is firmly grounded in knowledge, but the *ʿulamāʾ* with the exception of the Prophet (pbuh) have been found to be guilty of disobedience. This is witnessed, in the first instance, in the words of the Exalted about the unbelievers, "And they denied them, though their souls acknowledged them wrongfully and out of pride."[172] He said, "The People of the Book know this as they know their own sons, but some of them conceal the truth which they themselves know."[173] And He said, "But why do they come to thee for decision, when they have (their own) law before them? therein is the (plain) command of Allah; yet even after that, they would turn away, for they are not (really) people of faith."[174] He further said, "And they knew that the buyers of (magic) would have no share in the happiness of the Hereafter. And vile was the price for which they did sell their souls, if they but knew!"[175] Add to these all other evidences that indicate the same meaning. This establishes disobedience on their part as well as opposition despite their knowledge. If knowledge was able to block all this, they would not be guilty of disobedience.

Second: The second reason lies in what has been stated about wicked scholars, and which is abundant. Among the severest of all such statements is that contained in the words of the Prophet (pbuh), "The severest torment on the Day of Judgement will be given to the scholar whom Allah has prevented from benefiting from his knowledge."[176] In addition, there is the following in the Qurʾān: "Do ye enjoin right conduct on the people, and forget (to practise it) yourselves, and yet ye study the Scripture? Will ye not understand?"[177] And He said, "Those who conceal the clear (signs) We have sent down, and the guidance, after We have made it clear for the People in the Book – on them shall be Allah's curse, and the curse of those entitled to curse",[178] and "Those who conceal Allah's revelations in the Book, and purchase for them a miserable profit – they swallow into themselves naught but Fire; Allah will not address them on the Day of Resurrection, nor purify them: grievous will be their Penalty."[179] Along with these there is the tradition about the three persons whom the fire will touch first on the Day of Judgement. The evidences on this point are many. This point is also evident in the fact that the scholars do not become infallible due to their knowledge nor is it something that prevents them from committing sins. How then can it be said: knowledge prevents disobedience?

The response to the first objection is that being established in knowledge prevents the scholar from acting contrary to it and this on the basis of the preceding evidences as well as on the basis of experienced practice. The reason is that what becomes an established attribute does not part with its owner except in accordance with the usual manner. If he does act contrary to it, then, there are three reasons for his act.

The first is mere stubbornness through which he goes against the requirements of natural instinct. Things beyond stubbornness have greater force. This is indicated by the words of the Exalted, "And they denied them, though their souls acknowledged them, wrongfully and out of pride",[180] and "Quite a number of the People of the Book wish they could turn you (people) back to infidelity after ye have believed, from selfish envy, after the Truth hath become manifest unto them: but forgive and overlook, till Allah accomplishes his purpose: for Allah hath power over all things",[181] as well as other evidences similar to these. The usual basis for this reason is that such an act does not occur except through overpowering whim arising from the love of this world or glory or other things, in a manner that the attribute of whim overwhelms the heart so much so that he does not acknowledge good or reject evil.

The second are lapses arising from oversight from which human beings are not protected. The scholar, as a result of intervening oversight, no longer remains a scholar. This is indicated, for a group, by the words of the Exalted, "Allah accepts the repentance of those who do evil in ignorance and repent soon afterwards; to them will Allah turn in mercy: for Allah is full of knowledge and wisdom."[182] And "If a suggestion from Satan Assail thy (mind), seek refuge with Allah; for He heareth and knoweth (all things). Those who fear Allah, when a thought of evil from Satan assaults them, bring Allah to remembrance, when lo they see (aright)."[183]

This type of reason does not affect the basis of the issue, just as it does not affect the instinctive attributes. Thus, the eye may not see and the ear may not hear due to deep thought or oversight or other factor, thereby removing the benefit of the eye or ear in forming a correct view.[184] Despite all this, it cannot be grasped by the power of hearing or sight. What we are discussing is similar to this.

The third is that he does not belong to this grade of scholars. Knowledge has, therefore, not become an essential attribute for him, or like an attribute, even though he is being counted among such scholars. This has reference to a wrong belief of the scholar about himself or of someone else about him. This is indicated by the words of the Exalted, "But if they hearken not to thee, know that they only follow their own lusts: and who is more astray than one who follows his own lusts: and who is more astray than one who follows his own lusts, devoid of guidance from Allah? for Allah guides not people given to wrong doing."[185] It is also indicated by the tradition, "Allah will not take possession of knowledge snatching it away from people" up to where he said, "People have accepted the ignorant as their leaders, who are asked and give opinions without knowledge, thus going astray and leading others astray."[186] In addition to this, there are the words of the Prophet (pbuh), "My *umma* (nation) will be divided into seventy-three sects of whom the most disruptive for my *umma* will be those who settle issues on the basis of their own opinions."[187] Thus, these people have fallen into opposition under the impression that their ignorance is knowledge, but they are not of those who are firmly established in knowledge, nor from among those for whom knowledge is almost like an attribute. In such a case there is no protection for them in knowledge. The objection applies to these people.

As for those besides these three types, they are included in those who are firmly established in knowledge, in accordance with what is stated by the evidences. There is much in the speech of the worthy ancestors that conveys this meaning. It is related from the Prophet (pbuh) that he said, "Each thing has its rise and its fall, and verily this *dīn* (religion) too has its rise and decline. Its rise lies in what Allah has sent me with so much so that the entire tribe turned into a *faqīh* – or he said in the end – leaving behind one or two disobedient persons, who are suppressed in humiliation when they speak or express themselves – restrained, repressed and curbed."[188] The tradition also says, "A time will come upon my *umma* when there will be a large number of reciters, few *faqīhs*, knowledge will be snatched away, and there will be great commotion"[189] up to the place where it says, "Thereafter a time will come when men from my *umma* will recite the Qurʾān, but it will not go beyond their collar bones, and this will be followed by a time when the hypocrite will enter into a disputation with the polytheist with both giving the same argument." It is reported from ʿAlī, God be pleased with him, that he said, "O bearers of knowledge, act upon it, for the *ʿālim* (scholar) is one who acquires knowledge and then acts so that his knowledge and deeds become compatible. There will soon come a people who will carry knowledge that will not go beyond their collar bones, their concealed acts will be different from their declared acts, and their deeds will conflict with their knowledge. They will sit in circles competing boastfully with one another so much so that one person will become angry at sitting with another and at this he will leave him. These acts of such persons will never rise up (to be reckoned) by Allah." It is related from Ibn Masʿūd that he said, "Become the guardians of knowledge and not merely its transmitters, because knowledge is sometimes protected[190] and not transmitted, while at other times it is transmitted and not guarded." It is related from Abū al-Dardāʾ, "You will not be God-fearing until you attain knowledge and you will not be attributed as one having knowledge until you act upon it." It is related from al-Ḥasan that he said, "A scholar is one whose deeds are compatible with his knowledge. When a person's acts are different from his knowledge it is like the narrator of traditions who hears something and expresses it." Al-Thawrī said, "When scholars gain knowledge they act upon it; when they act upon it they become occupied with it; when they are occupied with it, they disappear; when they disappear, they are sought out; when they are sought they run away." It is related from al-Ḥasan that he said, "It is commendable for a person who excels others in knowledge that he excel them in deeds as well." Another view is reported from him as a comment upon the words of Allah, the Exalted, "Therein were ye taught that which ye knew not, neither ye nor your fathers. Say: Allah (sent it down): then leave them to plunge in vain discourse and trifling."[191] He said, "'Therein were ye taught' means you came to acquire knowledge, but did not act upon it. By Allah, this is not knowledge." Al-Thawrī said, "Knowledge cries out for action. It stays on if there is a response, otherwise it departs." This is the elaboration of the meaning of knowledge that has recourse to action. Al-Shāʿbī said, "We used to seek help for the preservation of traditions through action." A similar view is reported from Wakīʿ ibn al-Jarrāḥ. It is reported from Ibn Masʿūd that he said, "Knowledge does not come from an excess of traditions, for true knowledge is the fear of God." There are many reports that convey the same meaning.

The response to the second question is evident from what has been mentioned. The bad scholars are those who do not act according to their knowledge. They are merely narrators, while *fiqh* is a different matter from what they relate. In the alternative, they are those whose hearts have been completely covered by their own whims. Refuge from all this lies with Allah.

Perseverance in the search for knowledge, developing and understanding of it, and not being content with a little part of it are things that lead to action and having recourse to it, as has been elaborated earlier. This is the meaning in the statement of al-Ḥasan, "We sought knowledge for this world and it took us towards the Last Day." It is reported from Maʿmar that he said, "It used to be said: 'Knowledge continues to be denied to one who seeks it for someone other than Allah, until the knowledge redirects him towards God.'"

It is reported from Ḥabīb ibn Abī Thābit that he said, "We sought out this matter without our intention of acting upon it; the intention to do so arose later." Al-Thawrī said, "We used to seek knowledge for this world, but it drove us towards the Last Day."[192] The same meaning is found in another statement by him, "I used to envy the person around whom people were gathered taking dictation (about knowledge) from him. When I was subjected to the same trial myself, I used to wish that I should come out clean from this trial, without there being anything against me or for me." It is related from Abū al-Walīd al-Ṭiyālasī, who said, "I heard Ibn ʿUyayna, more than sixty years ago, relating a *Sunna*, saying, 'We sought (this discipline of) traditions for other than God so he made us reach the state you are witnessing.'" Al-Ḥasan said, "A group of people desired knowledge (of traditions) without the intention of pleasing Allah and of gaining what He has. They continued seeking it until they desired the pleasure of God and what He has to give." These statements also indicate the validity of what has preceded.

Sub-concept: true knowledge is internal (pertains to the spirit)

A penetrating examination is needed here for affirming this grade and what it really is. The brief response to this is that it is something internal, which is what has been referred to as the fear of God in Ibn Masʿūd's tradition, and that in turn refers to the meaning contained in the verse. He has expressed this in a tradition to the effect that "the first thing that will be taken away from knowledge is the fear of God".[193] Mālik has said, "Knowledge does not come through an abundance in narration; it is a light that Allah causes to descend upon the heart." He has also said, "Wisdom (*ḥikma*) and knowledge are a light through which

Allah guides whom He likes. It does not come through a person knowing a large number of issues, yet it has external signs that are visible (on the person). These are the avoidance of the temporal world and turning towards the permanent abode." This is an expression of acting according to knowledge without any contravention. As for the details of this response, this is not the occasion for them. In the *Book of Ijtihād* an aspect of it has been discussed, so you may have recourse to it if you like. All success lies with Allah.

The ninth concept: knowledge is of two types – essential and ancillary

Knowledge has a part that forms its core and it has a part that is ancillary that does not belong to the core. Knowledge also has a part that belongs neither to the core nor to the ancillary part. This gives three types.

The first type

This is the foundation and the basis of reliance around which search for knowledge revolves and at which the aims of those grounded in knowledge terminate. This is knowledge that is definitive (*qatʿī*) or knowledge that refers back to a definitive principle. The blessed Muḥammadī *sharīʿa* has been revealed in this form. It is, therefore, protected with respect to its principles and its detailed rules (*furūʿ*), as has been stated by Allah, the Exalted, "We have, without doubt, sent down the message; and we will assuredly guard it (from corruption)."[194] The reason is that they refer to the protection of the purposes (*maqāṣid*) through which the affairs of the two worlds are ordered. These are the necessities (*ḍarūriyāt*), the associated needs (*ḥājāt*) and the complementary norms (*taḥsīnāt*), as well as those values that perfect them and complete their various manifestations. These are the fundamental principles of the *sharīʿa* (*ʿuṣūl al-sharīʿa*). A definitive proof has already been established with respect to their acknowledgement as well as for the remaining rules that rely upon them. There is no doubt that these are the essential knowledge having a deep foundation and essential pillars.

Now, even though these are laid down (prescribed) and not rational, matters laid down often go hand in hand with rational propositions in yielding knowledge that is definitive. Knowledge within the *sharīʿa* is like this on the whole, because such knowledge has been derived through general induction that organises its multiple cases. Such knowledge becomes gathered in the mind as general principles that are established in broad terms not yielding to dimunition or alteration, and governing others rather than being governed. These are the very attributes of rational general principles. Further, rational general principles have also been derived from actual existence, which is something that is laid down (given) and not rational. These become similar in form to the legal universal principles of the *sharīʿa* (*kulliyāt sharʿiyya*) when considered from this vantage point, and the distinction stands removed.

Accordingly, this essential knowledge[195] has three distinctive traits by virtue of which it differs from other types of knowledge.

First: generality and continuity – It is for this reason (of generality and continuity) that the rules of the *sharīʿa* are applied to the acts of the subjects in an absolute way even though the individual cases are never ending. Thus, the *sharīʿa* governs all obligatory acts and all acts of commission and omission in their individual and collective forms. This in essence is the meaning of its being general. Even when a specific rule is to be found in its textual or rational sources, it refers back to the generality, as is the case with *ʿarāya*, the imposition of *diya* upon the *ʿāqila*, *qirād*, *musāqāh*,[196] one *ṣāʿ* for deception through a goat's swollen udder[197] and other similar things. All these refer to principles belonging to the categories of *ḥājiyāt* and *taḥsīnāt* or to what is complementary for these, and all these are matters that are general. There is no specific rule that in reality is not general. Examination of these rules within their categories of *fiqh* will make this evident.

Second: it is knowledge established without any diminution – It is for this reason that we do not find abrogation to be operative on them (the principles) once they are established, nor is there any restriction of their generality, nor qualification in their absolute meaning, nor the lifting of one of their rules. No diminution is to be found in them either with respect to the subjects in general, with respect to particular subjects, with respect to time, or circumstance. In fact, what was established as a cause will remain a cause for ever without repeal, what was established as a condition will for ever remain a condition, what was established as a *wājib* will for ever remain a *wājib*, and what was established as a *mandūb* will remain a *mandūb*. Likewise, all other types of rules. There is no diminution in them, nor can these be altered. If the continued existence of duty to Allah (*taklīf*) is presumed without ever ending, the same is to be said about the related rules.

Third: it exists as governing knowledge and not as one that is governed – This is the meaning underlying its utility in regulating conduct in a suitable manner. It is for this reason that the disciplines of the *sharīʿa* are confined to those that have utility for conduct, or those that regulate it. There is nothing that goes beyond this. You will not find anything in conduct that regulates the *sharīʿa*, for this would convert it from being the governing element to an element that is governed. Likewise, everything else that is to be reckoned as a type of discipline.

Consequently, any knowledge that attains these three attributes forms the core of knowledge. The meaning of this, and its proof, have been made evident within this book. All praise is for Allah.

The second type

As for the second type, it is knowledge that is confined to the ancillary and does not form the essential core, nor is it definitive, nor is it linked to a definitive base, rather it is probable, or it does not rely on a *qaṭʿī* base; however, one of the essential traits has been dropped from it, or even more than one trait. It is probable and something that perturbs reason when approached initially and at the first examination without there being a shortcoming in itself, or it does so due to an external concept. When such is its nature, it is proper to reckon it as part of the second type of knowledge.

As for the absence of the first attribute, it is continuity, and this prevents it from being part of core knowledge. The reason is that lack of continuity strengthens the aspect of rejection and weakens the aspect of acknowledgement. The contradiction within it indicates weakness of reliance upon it with respect to the subject of this knowledge, bringing it closer to coincidental matters that are unintended. Thus, it cannot be relied upon and cannot be used for further extension based on it.

The absence of the second meaning is its proof, which is denied by core knowledge and its principles. Thus, it gives out a ruling in a certain case and thereafter it goes against its given ruling on certain occasions or under certain circumstances, its ruling is an error and is void insofar as it applied a ruling to something that is not absolute, or it applied a general ruling to a situation that is particular. The person examining it, therefore, loses faith in its ruling. This is the meaning of moving out from the ambit of core knowledge.

As for the absence of the third attribute, which is that it is governing knowledge, one on which others are based, it acts as a preventing factor as well. The reason is that even if it conforms with reason, it has no immediate utility except the mere pleasing of the self, becoming equal to all that is pleasurable. If it does not conform with reason, then, it is to be rejected outright, like the discussions of the Sophists and those who follow them.

There are examples for the absence of these attributes to which others besides these issues can be linked.

First: a derived rule pertaining to the taʿabbudāt *(matters of ritual obedience) in which the meaning cannot be rationalised* – A derived rule pertaining to the *taʿabbudāt* (matters of ritual obedience) in which the meaning cannot be rationalised in some specific sense, like minor ablution (*wuḍūʾ*) being specific to some particular limbs; or prayer in a certain form with raising of the hands, standing in the erect posture, bowing and prostrating, that is, its being specific to a certain form and not others; or fasting being specific to the day and not the night; the determination of the timings of prayer as specific to determined moments to the exclusion of other times of the night or the day; the making of *ḥajj* (pilgrimage to Makka) as being specific to certain known acts at known places and at a certain mosque; and things similar to these that cannot be rationalised in any way which knowledge does not envelop.[198] Now, some people come up with an underlying rationale (*ḥikma*) that they attribute to such things, believing that this is the purpose of the Lawgiver under these circumstances. All this is based upon conjecture[199] and guesswork that is not continuous for the relevant category, nor is the prescribed conduct based on it. This amounts to taking up isolated cases and attributing underlying causes to them even after the transmitted knowledge is available. Perhaps, some such knowledge is what can be reckoned as part of the third type, as it amounts to an offence against the *sharīʿa* being a claim about which we have no knowledge and for which there is no *dalīl* (evidence).[200]

Second: transmitting traditions and reports through certain required modes that are not at all necessary – The second example is that of transmitting traditions and reports through certain required modes that are not at all necessary; their adoption is not required. This is like the continuous traditions that have been transmitted in a required manner in the earlier times, but without an accompanying intention of transmitting them. The later scholars made them binding with the stipulation of an intention to transmit. The transmission of such a tradition with such intention was deemed sufficient investigation for it. Thus, its proper verification of authenticity (*istikhrāj*) was not needed and this tradition alone was the object of focus. This was the position even though the accompanying intention to transmit it did not affect consequential action, although action was present along with it. The reason is that the absence of such intention within its channels of transmission does not negate acting according to what is required by such traditions, as is the case with the tradition, "Those who show mercy will be shown mercy by the Merciful (al-Raḥmān)."[201] They made it necessary in this case that it be the first tradition that the student has heard from his Shaykh (for intentional transmission). However, if he heard it from him after someone else had heard it from him, it does not prevent benefiting from the implication of the tradition. This condition is not applied in a continuous manner[202] in all the prophetic traditions or even most of them so that it can be said that it is intended as a condition.

Requiring something like this can only be treated as ancillary and not core knowledge.

Third: being fastidious (meticulous) (taʿannuq) *in the authentication of a tradition through a large number of channels* – Being fastidious (meticulous) (*taʿannuq*)[203] in the authentication of a tradition through a large number of channels, not with the intention of requiring its *tawātur* (continuous narration), but for counting it as one that has been received through a large number of *shaykhs*, and through multiple directions, even though it amounts to a *khabar wāḥid* when it reaches the Companions or their Followers or others. Being occupied with this is to be occupied with ancillary knowledge not with core knowledge. Abū ʿUmar ibn ʿAbd al-Barr has recorded from Ḥamza ibn Muḥammad al-Kinānī, who said, "I recorded a single tradition from the Prophet (pbuh) through two hundred channels, or close to two hundred – the narrator was not sure about the exact number." He said, "This pleased me considerably and I was proud of it too. I then saw Yaḥyā ibn Maʿīn in a dream and said to him, 'O Abū Zakariyya, I have recorded a tradition from the Prophet (pbuh) through two hundred channels.'" He said, "He kept quiet for a moment and then said, 'I am afraid this will fall under the category of "The mutual rivalry for piling up (the good things of this world) diverts you (from the more serious things), until ye visit the graves."[204]).' " This is what he said and it appears correct upon reflection. The reason is that recording it through a few channels is sufficient for achieving its purpose. Any excess over this is superfluous.

Fourth: kinds of knowledge acquired through dreams – The fourth example is about kinds of knowledge acquired through dreams that cannot be categorised as some sign of good news or a warning. There are many people who argue for and against academic issues expressly on the basis of dreams and what they conclude from them. Such conclusions, even though they may be sound, have dreams as their basis and this is something that is not acknowledged in the *sharīʿa* for legal reasoning.[205] This is like the dream of al-Kinānī mentioned above. What Yaḥyā ibn Maʿīn has said about it is sound, but we do not rely upon it as evidence,[206] unless we have verified it from our knowledge pertaining to a state of wakefulness. Thus, adducing evidence for it will pertain to a state of wakefulness and not sleep. The dream will be mentioned by way of general interest. This is how we classify what has been recorded from the scholars with respect to evidence on the basis of dreams.

Fifth: the issues on which there is disagreement, and no practical consequence flows from such disagreement – Such issues are counted within ancillary knowledge, like the issues indicated earlier within the discussion of *ʿuṣūl al-fiqh*. Many such issues are found in the remaining disciplines as well. There are many such issues in the Arabic language, like the derivation of the verb from the verbal noun, the issues of *Allahumma* (O God), the issue of *ashyāʾ*, the issue of the basis in the word *ism*. Although the discussion of these issues is based upon continuous principles, there is no beneficial yield from such disagreement. Thus, those issues are excluded from core knowledge.

Sixth: reliance on verses of poetry for affirming technical and practical meanings – This is seen in abundance in books by those who practise *Sufism* for purposes of elaboration of their stations. They extract the meanings of verses and form their morals in accordance with their implications. In fact, this belongs to ancillary knowledge[207] insofar as there is an inclination in dispositions towards refined verses and one is emotionally moved towards the desired objective. It is for this reason that those who deliver sermons have adopted this as a practice and made the verses part of their sermons. When we examine the matter in its own right, then adducing evidence of meaning if it yields a technical (*sharʿī*) meaning it is proper, otherwise not.

Seventh: legal reasoning for establishing meanings on the basis of the acts of those with sound conduct – This is based merely on a good opinion about them and is nothing more than this. It may happen that their acts provide a proof on occasions, as has been stated in the *Book of Ijtihād*. When such evidence is adopted in the absolute sense in the case of those about whom a good opinion exists due to the inclination of people towards them on account of their merits and uprightness, as long as this is free of objections, then it is part of such knowledge.

It is not, however, part of core knowledge due to the absence of continuity in the soundness of their conduct and also due to the possibility of a change in it. It is adopted, if deemed sound, as part of this (ancillary) source.

Eighth: the statements of those having spiritual authority – Reasoning on the basis of their statements[208] is exactly what we are dealing with here. The reason is that their followers exaggerated in the service to their masters so much so that they turned away from all others. They inclined towards this approach to such an extent that they rejected outright everything else besides Allah, and gave full expression to the implications of their statements. Statements such as these are not bearable for the majority and it is these that they objected to. Even when these statements are true, they operate within their own sphere and are not applicable in the absolute sense, because for most people they amount to an injury or an obligation to do the impossible. Perhaps, they deem blameworthy much that is not blameworthy except in certain cases and under certain circumstances. Accepting them in the absolute sense is like committing the invalid, as against accepting them in general terms. Thus, this type of knowledge is not part of the core, rather it is ancillary and complementary.

Ninth: extrapolating the principles of one discipline to another – Extrapolating the principles of one discipline to another so that issues are settled in one on the basis of principles from the other without combining two principles into one true principle. The illustration is that narrated about al-Farrāʾ, the grammarian, when he said, "One who excels in one discipline has all the other disciplines made easy for him." Muḥammad ibn al-Ḥasan (al-Shaybānī), the *qāḍī*, who was present in this session and who was his first cousin, said to him, "You have excelled in your discipline, so take this issue that I present to you and that belongs to a different discipline. What do you think about a person who makes a mistake in his prayer and then offers prostration for the mistake, but he now makes a mistake in these prostrations?" Al-Farrāʾ said, "There is no further liability on him." He asked, "How is that?" He replied, "The reason is that *taṣghīr* in our discipline cannot be shortened further. Likewise, the error in prostrations of error; there are no further prostrations for it, because it amounts to shortening of the *taṣghīr*. The prostrations of error are a compulsion (exception?) in prayer, and compulsion cannot be made compulsory further." The Qāḍī said, "I did not know that women gave birth to the likes of you."

Now you can see the weakness in the combination between *taṣghīr* (diminution) and *sahw* (forgetfulness) in prayers, because no real principle gathers the two so that one issue may be settled by the other. If a common principle had combined the two, however, these would not be reckoned in this ancillary category. The illustration of this is the story of al-Kisāʾī and Abū Yūsuf, the *qāḍī*, in the presence of (Hārūn) al-Rashīd. It is reported that Abū Yūsuf visited al-Rashīd when al-Kisāʾī was having a light conversation with him. Abū Yūsuf said, "This Kūfī has wiped you out and dominated you." He said, "Abū Yūsuf, he has come up with things that I find highly pleasing."

Al-Kisāʾī turned to Abū Yūsuf and said, "May I ask you about an issue?" Abū Yūsuf said, "Grammar or *Fiqh*?" Al-Kisāʾī said, "*fiqh,* in fact." Al-Rashīd laughed at this, till he scratched the ground with his feet. He then said, "You are going to learn *fiqh* from Abū Yūsuf?" He said, "Yes." He then said, "O Abū Yūsuf, what do you think about the case of a person who says to his wife, 'You stand divorced that (*an*) you entered the house', and he uses *an* (that) instead of *in* (if)?" Abū Yūsuf said, "If she enters the house, she stands divorced." He said, "You have made a mistake, O Abū Yūsuf." Al-Rashīd laughed and said, "What then is the correct answer?" He replied, "When he says *an* (that) the act becomes binding and divorce is effective, but if he says *in* (if), it is not binding." It is said that Abū Yūsuf always used to visit al-Kisāʾī after this. This issue is based on a rule of language that forms the basis of decision in both disciplines.

These examples guide the investigator to what lies beyond them so that he knows what is to be taken from the disciplines and what is to be left alone. In many of these disciplines, the initial interest of the investigator usually overwhelms the mind and he may spend his entire life in it, leaving behind nothing that can be taken for the purpose of conduct and belief. All his effort will be lost in the search for knowledge. Allah is the Saviour.

Among the examples in this category is what has been related by some Shaykhs. Abū al-ʿAbbās al-Bannāʾ was asked a question and it was said to him, "Why don't you make *inna* operate upon *hādhān*, in the words of the Exalted, "*Innā hādhān la-sāḥirān* (They said: these two are certainly (expert) magicians[209])"? He said in reply, "When what is said does not affect the thing about which it is said, the operator does not affect what is being acted upon." The questioner said, "Sir, what is the operation of '*inna*' upon the statement of the unbelievers about the prophets?" The person responding said, "O so and so, I brought you a petal that was presenting its full beauty. You wish to erase this beauty with your hands and then demand from it such beauty", or he said something similar. When you reflect in your mind what is in this response, it will be evident what relationship it has with core knowledge.

The third type of knowledge belongs neither to core knowledge nor to ancillary knowledge insofar as it does not rely on a definitive principle or on a probable principle. It is a type that is referred to its principle or to another so as to nullify it, when such a principle is deemed valid within acknowledged disciplines and is one of the principles pertaining to conduct or beliefs, or it is a type that rises up to negate the truth and verify falsehood in general terms. All this is not knowledge at all, because it refers back to its principle by nullifying it, and it is neither established, nor governing, nor continuous. Further, it is not part of ancillary knowledge, because ancillary knowledge is deemed good by reason and it is sought out, for it is not accompanied by a repelling factor nor does it display enmity towards the disciplines. The reason is that ancillary knowledge possesses a basis on the whole upon which further knowledge may progress. This is different from this type, which does not have any such attribute.

If some persons are inclined towards it or deem it good, then, that is due to some temporary ambiguity, and due to confusion between it and the type that goes before it. Perhaps, it was acknowledged by ignorant people on the basis of some principle, people who inclined towards it due to this reason. The reality of such a principle is an illusion and is imaginary; it has no truth in it. To this one may add ulterior motives and whims, like strange knowledge acquired by seeking out the less known, clamouring about knowing what those grounded in knowledge do not know, boasting that beyond these well known concepts are those that are known only to the elect and that they are the elect; and many things similar to these from which the desired object is not available. Those who seek such knowledge face humiliation when they are put to the test, as has been elaborated by al-Ghazālī and Ibn al-ʿArabī as well as others who have dealt with such matters.

An example of this is what the Bāṭiniyya have said about the Book of Allah by moving away from its apparent meanings and saying that what is intended is what lies behind these apparent meanings and that there is no way of knowing this by way of reason and investigation. Such knowledge, they say, is acquired from the Maʿṣūm (infallible) imam by following such an imam without questioning. Their reliance – in all that they say – is upon the discipline of *ḥurūf* (characters) and astronomy (astrology). In the later times, the damage caused is beyond repair. Thus, claims upon the *sharīʿa* through things similar to what the Bāṭiniyya allege multiplied in number and increased to such an extent that besides causing other damage their knowledge became incomprehensible in itself. This type of knowledge includes what is advocated by the Sophists and the Mutaḥakkimūn (those who claim wisdom). All this has no basis upon which further knowledge can be structured. It has no fruit that can be utilised, and it therefore cannot have a relationship with true knowledge.

Sub-concept: the first type is sometimes merged with the second type

Sometimes the first type is counted as part of the second type. This is conceived by the mixing of one discipline with another, like a *faqīh* (jurist) basing a legal issue on a point of grammar. The issue is first settled by a method that is similar to that of the grammarian and not on the basis of an accepted premise, and thereafter the jurist refers the issue to this premise. What he should have done was to say that it has been settled in grammar and he should then have constructed upon it. When he did not do this and started discussing it for validating it, organising it and reasoning according to it, just as a grammarian would do, he did something that was superfluous and was not needed. Likewise, when he is need of a numerical issue. He is supposed to come up with a postulate so as to settle the issue within his discipline. If he starts discussing it in a manner that a specialist in numerical problems would do in his own discipline, it is something superfluous that is counted as ancillary knowledge if it is deemed part of this discipline. The same is the case with the remaining disciplines that come to the aid of other disciplines.

It is also possible that the first type may become part of the third type. This happens when someone boastfully talks about academic issues in a discipline when he is not qualified to do so or he discusses, going against the approved methods of training, complicated issues with one who does not have the capacity to comprehend them and can understand simple problems alone. Such a person is bound to face difficulties. It is with reference to such a person that ʿAlī, God be pleased with him, said, "Talk to people about things that they can understand. Would you like them to attribute falsehood to Allah and His Messenger?" This becomes a trial for some of the listeners, in accordance with what is elaborated in this book.

When the first type can be treated as part of the third type, it is easier for the second to be treated as part of the third type, as it lies closer to it than the first. Thus, it is proper for a scholar undertaking academic instruction to be careful about the preservation of these concepts, otherwise he cannot be deemed a teacher and is in need of an instructor who can teach him.

From this it is concluded that it is difficult for a person examining this book to do so beneficially or seek benefit from it, unless he is well versed in the discipline of *sharīʿa* with respect to its principles and detailed rules, its transmitted and rational evidences, and does not insist upon blind following and does not have bias for a particular school. If he is in this position, there is an apprehension that it might become topsy turvy for him insofar as there is a trial in it, although it is wisdom (*ḥikma*) in itself. God grants success in doing what is right.

The tenth concept: when transmitted and rational sources are combined the transmitted are primary

When support is sought from transmitted evidences and reason, it is on the condition that the transmitted evidences will be given precedence so that they are the ones that are followed. Reason will be relegated and it is subservient to transmission. Reason will not be permitted a free play during investigation, except to the extent that may be determined by transmission. The evidence in support of this is of several types.

First

If it were permitted to reason to go beyond the sources of transmission there would be no use of the boundary determined by transmission, and the presumption is that a boundary has been determined for reason by transmission, therefore, when this boundary is traversed reason is no longer beneficial. This is null and void in the *sharīʿa*.

Second

It is determined in *ʿilm al-kalām* and in *ʿuṣūl al-fiqh* that reason cannot independently determine what is good and bad (*ḥusn* and *qubḥ*). If we assume that it can cross the limits fixed for it by the *sharʿ* (law), it will be able to determine independently what is good and what is bad. This amounts to a discrepancy.

Third

If the foregoing were permissible, it would be possible to annul the *sharīʿa* through reason. This is impossible and void, and the elaboration is: the purpose of the *sharīʿa* is to lay down limits for the subjects with respect to their acts, statements and beliefs, and this is all that it includes. If it were permitted to reason to cross one limit, it would be permitted to cross all limits, because what is established for one thing is also established for what is similar to it. The crossing of a limit means it is nullified, that is, the limit is not sound. If it is permitted to nullify one, it is permitted to nullify the rest. This is not maintained by anyone due to its obvious impossibility.

It may be said that this is not valid due to several reasons.

First – This view is the view of the Ẓāhirīs, because they adopt the apparent meaning of the texts without adding to its meaning or taking away from it. The result is the negation of the role of reason on the whole, and this leads to the negation of *qiyās* (syllogism), which was agreed upon by the ancestors.

Second – Restriction of the meanings of texts has been established for a reason as has been mentioned by specialists in *ʿuṣūl al-fiqh*, for example in "Allah hath power over all things",[210] "He hath power to dispose of all affairs"[211] and "Allah is the Creator of all things".[212] This amounts to a deficiency in the implication of the general meaning; therefore, an addition should also be permitted as it carries the same meaning,[213] and also because stopping prior to the limit amounts to crossing. Thus, both amount to nullifying the limit according to your reasoning. If nullification is permitted with a deficient meaning, it is permitted with an additional meaning. As this deficiency is not treated as nullification of the limit, the other should not be treated as nullification either.

Third – The *ʿuṣūlīs* have a principle that rules against this position. The principle is: If a suitable meaning is clearly the first meaning to be understood when the text is mentioned, it is proper to control this meaning by restricting it or adding to it. They illustrate this through the words of the Prophet (pbuh), "The *qāḍī* is not to render judgement when he is angry." Thus, they proscribed, on the basis of the underlying meaning of being upset, the handing down of a judgement in all cases leading to such a disturbed state. They permitted it when anger does not perturb the *qāḍī*. Thus, you see them doing all this as required by reason in the case of a transmitted text without halting at the original meaning. This goes against what you have deemed to be a principle.

The response is that what is stated here does not affect what has been settled earlier.

First – *Qiyās* (analogy) is not merely a rational process,[214] it is used under the control of the evidences (*adilla*) in accordance with the meaning they give it, whether absolute or qualified. This is elaborated in its proper place in the *Book of Qiyās*. When the law (*sharᶜ*) indicates to us that the linking of a case not expressly mentioned by the texts with what is expressly mentioned is an acknowledged method, that it is one of the methods intended by the Lawgiver and ordained by Him, and the Prophet (pbuh) has indicated that it be acted upon, then, where is the independence of reason to be found in this? In fact, it is something to which the *sharᶜī* evidences are accustomed. It works up to the extent to which they permit it and ceases to function when they want it to cease.

Second – As for the second, it will be discussed in the section on general and particular meanings – God willing – showing that separated evidences are not to be restricted. Even if it is conceded that they are restricted, the meaning of such restriction does not imply that the intended apparent meaning is being altered by the texts. In fact, they elaborate, through *sharᶜī* evidences indicating this, that the apparent meaning is not intended at all in the communication. Reason also operates in the same way. Thus, in the words of the Exalted "He hath power to dispose of all affairs",[215] reason has restricted the meaning to imply that this text does not apply in general terms to include the Supreme Being and His attributes, because this is impossible.[216] In fact, the meaning is that it includes all that is besides this. Reason, in this case, has not gone outside the ambit of transmission in any way. If this is the case, it is not possible to apply analogies of crossing the limits here.

Third – As for the third objection, the linking of all cases of emotional disturbance with anger is a category of analogy, and the linking of a case not expressly mentioned with one that is, amounts to permissible *qiyās*. When we examine the case of restriction through slight anger it does not amount to a ruling of reason; it amounts to understanding the meaning of emotional disturbance and it is known that slight anger does not give rise to emotional disturbance. Thus, rendering judgement is permissible even when it exists, based on the reason that this is not what is intended by the communication.

This is what the *ᶜuṣūlīs* say in settling this meaning: that the unqualified meaning of anger is carried by the word, but the conceptual meaning has restricted it. The matter is resolved more easily than by having recourse to restriction. Thus, the word *ghaḍbān* (angry) is on the pattern of *faᶜlān*, which is used to indicate full involvement of the meaning from which it is derived. Thus, the word *ghaḍbān* is employed for the person who is overwhelmed by anger, like the word *rayyān*, which implies fully watered (saturated), and *ᶜaṭshān* implies one who is very thirsty, and so on. All this means that it does not apply in an unqualified manner to the meaning from which it has been derived. It is as if the Lawgiver has proscribed the handing down of a judgement by one overwhelmed by anger, as though He were saying: the *qāḍī* is not to render judgement when he is very angry or overwhelmed by anger. This is the person who is emotionally disturbed. The meaning of restriction is, therefore, removed and the proscription of slight anger is no longer intended within the implication of the word (and not its meaning). Analogy may be constructed upon emotional disturbance due to anger for all kinds of emotional disturbance. Reason has not crossed the limits here either.

In any case, reason does not govern transmitted texts in all matters similar to these. This brings out the validity of what has preceded.

The eleventh concept: knowledge acknowledged by the *sharīʿa* pertains to conduct

When it is established that knowledge acknowledged by the *sharīʿa* is one upon which acts are based, it becomes all knowledge that is covered by the *sharʿī* evidences. What the evidences require is knowledge about which it is required from the subject that he acquire it in general. This is evident; however, what the *sharʿī* evidences encompass are the sources of *sharʿī* knowledge. This is mentioned in the *Book of the Adilla Sharʿiyya*, as will be coming up, God willing.

The twelfth concept: the best way of acquiring knowledge is from experts in the discipline

Among the most beneficial paths to knowledge that lead to the desired objective is its acquisition from its specialists, the *mutaḥaqqiqīn*,[217] who verify it to perfection and completion. God creates man in a state where he knows nothing. He then instructs him and grants him perception; and guides him to ways of securing his interests in his life in this world. What He teaches him, however, is of two types. One type is necessary and is given to him without knowledge of where it has come from or how. It is instilled in him through the act of creation like feeding at the breast and suckling after emerging from the body into this world. This knowledge pertains to the senses. Further, there is knowledge like his knowledge about his own existence and that two opposites can never come together, which is knowledge that belongs to the rational faculty.

The second type of knowledge is acquired through instruction. He senses this need in the first instance as he did for movements that were necessary, and this is like vocal sounds, speech in the form of words, and knowledge about the names of things. These pertain to the senses. Then there are rational forms of knowledge in the acquisition of which reason has a role and function to perform. This knowledge pertains to the rational faculty.

Out of these, our discussion pertains to knowledge that needs investigation and perception. This form necessarily requires an instructor. Although people differ in their abilities, is it possible to acquire such knowledge without an instructor? The possibility is conceded, but the fact in actual practice is that there must be an instructor. This is agreed upon as a whole, even though there is some disagreement about details, like the disagreement between the majority of the *umma* and the Imāmiyya, who are those who stipulate the existence of an infallible *imam*. The truth lies with the majority, who do not stipulate infallibility on the basis that this is exclusively for the Prophets, peace be upon them. Despite this the Imāmiyya acknowledge that the ignorant person needs an instructor whether his instruction pertains to knowledge or to conduct. The agreement of the people over this in actual fact and its being found in practice are sufficient to show that this is necessary. They sometimes say, "Knowledge existed in the breasts of men, it was then transferred to books, but the keys remained in the hands of men." This statement indicates that the prerequisite for the acquisition of knowledge is the existence of men (teachers), because there is no goal beyond these two stages in their view. The basis for this is found in a sound (*ṣaḥīḥ*) tradition: "God will not snatch away knowledge by snatching it from the people, rather He will take it away by taking away the scholars."[218] In such a case, it is men who are the key without doubt.

Once this is established, knowledge is not to be acquired except through those who are well versed in it. This is self-evident and agreed upon by all reasonable men. The conditions they stipulate for a learned man, whatever the field of knowledge, are that he be aware of its fundamental principles and the foundations on which it is based; that he should be able to spell out its objectives and be able to identify what is binding due to these objectives, and he should be in a position to dispel all doubts that may arise with respect to the discipline. When we look at the conditions they stipulate and then look at the *imams* among the worthy ancestors in the disciplines of the *sharīʿa*, we find them meeting these conditions to perfection.

They do not, however, stipulate freedom from mistakes, because the details of every discipline can be mixed up, one with another, especially when they become numerous. Perhaps, the proliferation of the details can be conceived as being based on differing principles[219] within the same discipline and they become confused or their link with a principle becomes concealed where the scholar is not careful and refers them to some principles when they are in reality linked to other principles; or the variety of doubts can be contradictory leading to confusion where the scholar chooses the preferable interpretation and so on. All this cannot be treated as an objection against the scholar nor does it affect his being treated as an *imam* who is followed. If he falls short of meeting the conditions, his status will be reduced from one of perfection to the extent of the shortcoming. He cannot then attain the status of perfection, unless he makes up the shortcoming.

The traits and signs of a scholar

The scholar who is well versed (*mutaḥaqqiq*) in knowledge has certain traits and signs that conform to what has preceded even though he may contradict them in his investigation.[220] These are three.

First: Acting upon knowledge he has acquired so that his words and deeds become compatible – If these are not compatible, he is not qualified for being a teacher from whom knowledge can be acquired, nor can he be followed with respect to his knowledge. This idea is elaborated in its complete form in the *Book of Jihād*. Praise be to God.

Second: He should be a scholar who has been trained (taught) by shaykhs in the relevant discipline – He should have acquired knowledge from them and should have enjoyed their companionship. Such a person is more qualified to be attributed with the merits that the teachers possess. This was also the case with the worthy ancestors.

The first case of such companionship was that of the Companions (God bless them all) of the Prophet (pbuh) and their learning from his sayings and acts with their full reliance on what came from him whatever the consequences and in whatever form it was communicated. They[221] grasped the essence of what he intended or did not intend, so much so that they came to know, and were convinced, that it was the undeniable truth, a wisdom whose laws could not be broken, and no deficiency could surround the perfection of its boundary. All this came out of an abundance of companionship and the intensity of their persistence. Ponder over the case of ʿUmar ibn al-Khaṭṭab during the truce at al-Hudaybiyya[222] when he said, "O Messenger of Allah, are we not on the right, and these people on falsehood?" He (pbuh) replied, "Of course." He said, "Is it not true that our slain go to heaven, while their slain go to hell?" He replied, "Of course." He said, "Then why should we bear this disgrace for our *dīn* (religion) and return when Allah has not issued a decree between them and us?" The Prophet (pbuh) said, "O Ibn al-Khaṭṭab, I am a Messenger of Allah, and Allah will not neglect me ever." ʿUmar went away, yet he was not patient, and in a state of anger he came up to Abū Bakr and said something similar to him. Abū Bakr (R) replied, "He is the Messenger of Allah, and Allah will never neglect him, ever." The narrator says that it was then that revelation descended upon the Messenger of Allah (pbuh) conveying a message of victory. He sent for ʿUmar and recited it to him. ʿUmar said, "O Messenger of Allah, was it then victory?" The Prophet (pbuh) said, "Of course." ʿUmar was pleased and he retracted from his earlier stance.

This is the benefit of companionship, submission to scholars, and exhibiting patience with them on occasions of ambiguity till such time that the proof comes to light. In such a case, Sahl ibn Ḥunayf said during the Battle of Siffīn, "O people, take your views with suspicion. By Allah, I had an opinion on the Day of Abū Jandal and if I had been able, I would have defied the order of the Messenger of Allah (pbuh)."[223] He said this as they were facing some confusion, but then *sūrat Fatḥ* was revealed after they became depressed due to the intensity of the confusion, and ambiguity of the order. Yet, they submitted and gave up their views till such time that the Qur'ān was revealed. Their confusion and perplexity was removed.

Such incidents became a fundamental principle for those who came after them. The Followers of the Companions adopted the same attitude towards the Companions as they had adopted towards the Prophet (pbuh), and by virtue of that they became learned (*faqīhs*) attaining the peak of perfection in the disciplines of the *sharīʿa*. It is sufficient for the validity of this principle that you will not find a scholar whose teachings have become known among people without his having a model teacher who had become known in his own time. Whenever a deviant sect is found and whenever someone opposes the *Sunna*, he will be found lacking this attribute. It is for this reason that Ibn Ḥazm al-Ẓāhirī was looked down upon, because he did not consider obedience to teachers and following their instruction as necessary. Exactly opposite to this was the approach of the scholars grounded in knowledge, like the four jurist *imams* and those similar to them.

Third: Emulation of those from whom he has acquired knowledge and adoption of their method – This[224] is just like the Companions following the Prophet (pbuh) and the Followers of the Companions following the Companions. It was the same in each generation. Mālik stands out among those similar to him, I mean in exhibiting this attribute with great intensity, for otherwise this attribute was present in all others, but Mālik became famous for acquiring this attribute to the extent of exaggeration. When this attribute is dropped, it gives rise to many types of innovation. The reason is that the giving up of emulation is an evidence of something new that the person guilty of it has come up with, and the basis for this is the pursuit of whims. This idea will be verified in the *Book of Ijtihād* through strength acquired from God.

Sub-concept: methods of acquiring knowledge

When it is established that it is necessary to acquire knowledge from those who are qualified, (we maintain that) there are two ways of acquiring such knowledge.

First method: oral knowledge – The first is oral knowledge (acquired face to face). This is the most beneficial of the methods and the most secure, and this is due to two reasons. The first is the unique bond that Allah, the Exalted, has created between the teacher and the taught. To this, whoever has pursued knowledge will stand witness. There are so many issues that the student reads from books, memorises and reflects upon, yet does not understand. When the teacher speaks to him about the same issues, he comprehends them at once gaining knowledge through attendance. This understanding is sometimes attained in the usual way from the circumstances and the elaboration of complex issues in a manner that the student has not thought of before or it is acquired in an unusual way as a gift from Allah to the student due to his standing at attention in front of the teacher in obvious want and need of what the teacher has to impart to him. This is something that cannot be denied and is pointed out by the tradition, which says, "When the Messenger of Allah (pbuh) died, the Companions denied their own selves too." There is also the tradition of Hanzala al-Usaydī when he complained to the Messenger of Allah (pbuh) that when they are in his presence and company they are in a state that pleases them, but when they move away from his company they are also removed from this state. He replied, "If you maintain the attitude that you have when you are with me, the angels will spread their wings to provide you shade."[225] ʿUmar ibn al-Khaṭṭāb said, "I sought success from my Lord in three things", and these are all the benefits of the company of the learned, because matters are revealed to the student in the presence of the teacher and they are not revealed during absence, and this light stays with him to the extent that he follows his teacher, his method, and to the extent that he emulates him.

This method of acquiring knowledge is, thus, beneficial on all counts. Among the earlier ancestors, very few used to write for they looked down upon this. Even Mālik considered it disapproved.[226] What should we do, it was said to him. He replied, "You should memorise and understand till such time that your hearts light up with knowledge for then you will not be in need of writing." Disapproval of recording knowledge is also narrated from ʿUmar ibn al-Khaṭṭāb. The people have been provided an exemption in the case of forgetfulness or when the knowledge of the *sharīʿa* is about to be effaced.

Second method: studying the works of writers and compilations of the compilers – This is also a beneficial method, but with two conditions.

The first is that the reader understand the aims of the desired discipline and that he have knowledge of the terminology used by the specialists in that field, sufficient to enable him to study the books. This is attained by the first method with face to face instruction by the scholars or by a system that relies on this method. It is this meaning that is found in the statement of the person who said, "Knowledge resided in the hearts of men; it was then translated into books, but the keys to the knowledge remained in the hands of men." Books alone, however, do not benefit the student without an introduction by scholars. This is what is witnessed and practised.

The second condition is that the books of the earlier scholars in the intended discipline be studied, because they were better grounded in the discipline as compared to the later scholars. The basis of this statement is experience and reports. As for experience, this is what is witnessed whatever the discipline. The later scholars have not exhibited the same depth of knowledge in a discipline as has been shown by the earlier scholars. The works of the specialists in a discipline, whether applied or theoretical, is sufficient proof. The acts of the earlier scholars in ordering the affairs of this world and the next are different from those of later scholars, and their knowledge was more sound. The soundness of knowledge in the disciplines of the *sharīʿa* exhibited by the Companions was different from that exhibited by their Followers, and these Followers were unlike those who followed them, and so on till the present times. Anyone who studies their lives, statements and stories, will be amazed at the truth of this meaning.

As for reports, it is stated in a *ḥadīth*, "The best of generations is my generation, and then come those who follow them, and then those who follow them."[227] In this tradition, there is an indication that the status of each following generation with respect to one that went before it will be like this. It is related from the Prophet (pbuh) that he said, "At the beginning of your *dīn* will be prophethood and mercy, followed by domination (*mulk*) and mercy, domination and coercion, and then cruel domination."[228] This is not possible unless good becomes scarce, while evil competes with it gradually gaining ground. What we are discussing is included under this absolute meaning. Ibn Masʿūd is reported to have said, "There is no year that is not followed by one with more evil. I do not say that it rained more in the previous year or that there was more fertility in one year than the other or that the ruler was better in one year compared to the other; rather I mean the disappearance of the best among you and the disappearance of your scholars. Finally, a group will rise up who will settle things according to their personal views thus attempting to demolish Islam and defiling it." The same meaning is found in a sound (*ṣaḥīh*) tradition, "Knowledge will be snatched away by the taking away of the scholars along with their knowledge leaving behind ignorant people who will be asked to settle matters and they will do so on the basis of their personal views, thus, being misguided and misguiding others."[229] The Prophet (pbuh) said, "Islam began in estrangement and it will revert to the estrangement with which it began. Blessed be the estranged people." It was said, "Who are the estranged people?" He replied, "The estranged people of the tribes."[230] In one narration it was said, "Who are the estranged people, O Messenger of Allah?" He replied, "They are those who set matters right when things go wrong with the people."[231] It is related from Abū Idrīs al-Khawlānī, "Islam is bare with the people attached to (covering) it, but they will be torn away thread by thread." Some have related that "the *Sunna* will wither away one at a time like a rope loosened knot by knot". Abū Hurayra recited the words of the Exalted, "When comes the help of Allah, and victory"[232] and then said, "By Him, in whose hands is my life, they will move away from it in huge numbers (*afwājan*) just as they entered it." It is related from ʿAbd Allah that he said, "Do you see how Islam is fading away?" The people replied, "Yes, like the colour of a dress and like the fat of an animal." ʿAbd Allah said, "This is similar." When the words of the Exalted, "This day have I perfected your religion for you, completed my favour upon you, and have chosen for you Islam as your religion"[233] were revealed, ʿUmar began to weep. The Prophet (pbuh) said, "What makes you weep?" He said, "O Messenger of Allah, we were in a state when our *dīn* was on the increase. Now that it is complete, it will not be increased at all, but will go down." The Prophet (pbuh) said, "You have spoken in truth."[234] The reports in this category are many and they indicate the diminution of *dīn* and worldly matters." The greatest of all such diminution is in knowledge, and it is a deficiency without doubt.

Thus, the books of the earlier scholars, their words and lives are the most beneficial for one who wishes to exercise care in acquiring knowledge of whatever form it is, especially the knowledge of *sharīʿa*, which is the strongest tie and the greatest protection. Allah, the Exalted, grants success.

The thirteenth concept: principles that are a guide for conduct

Each principle that is adopted as a guide for conduct is acted upon in accordance with the practice required by it in a manner that does not go against its basic elements or conditions or it is not acted upon in such a manner. When it is acted upon in such a way it is a valid principle; otherwise it is not.

The explanation is that in an academic discipline the presumption is that acts come into existence in conformity with it without default, irrespective of acts being those of the *qalb* (inner resolve), of speech, or whether these are acts pertaining to the limbs. If the acts proceed, in the normal course of things, in accordance with it and without default, then it is a true discipline with reference to such acts; otherwise it is not a discipline that relates to such acts, because of the default exhibited. This is not valid as it amounts to conversion of a field of knowledge into ignorance.

The example, in the field of *sharīʿa*, whose principles we are trying to establish, is that in the discipline of *ʿuṣūl al-dīn* going against a report about Allah the Exalted, and a report about the Messenger of Allah (pbuh), is not allowed, while in *ʿuṣūl al-fiqh* the rule of there being no obligation to do the impossible is established, and with this is associated the negation of obligation in which there is abnormal hardship. Therefore, each *sharʿī* principle in whose application there is an exemption of this nature is not continuous, and cannot be deemed valid in practice. It is, therefore, not a principle that can be relied upon nor is it a rule that provides a legal basis.

This takes place in the comprehension of statements, modes of address[235] and undertaking of acts.

As for the comprehension of statements, the example is found in the words of the Exalted, "And never will Allah grant to the unbelievers a way (to triumph) over the believers."[236] If it is interpreted to mean a report, then, the fact reported is not continuous due to the occurrence of numerous cases when an unbeliever (*kāfir*) does have domination over a believer – where he imprisons him and humiliates him. It is, therefore, not possible that the meaning be applicable to cases other than the one to which it actually applies, and that is the verification of the *ḥukm sharʿī*. It is to be interpreted to mean that they will not able to make them change their faith.[237] Another example is to be found in the words of the

Exalted, "The mothers shall give suck to their offspring for two whole years."[238] If it is interpreted to mean the establishing of a *ḥukm sharʿī* it is continuous and a benefit is derived from it. If, however, it is interpreted to mean that it is a report concerning mothers, there is no additional benefit[239] in it that goes beyond what was known already.

The example of the modes of address is in the words of the Exalted, "On those who believe and do deeds of righteousness there lies no blame for what they ate (in the past), when they guard themselves from evil, and believe, and do deeds of righteousness, (or) again, guard themselves from evil and believe, (or) again, guard themselves from evil and do good. For Allah loveth those who do good."[240] This form of address is general here and implies all kinds of *matʿūm* (food) and that there is no harm in consuming them when this condition is met. Among these is *khamr* (wine). This apparent interpretation, however, renders invalid the mode of address[241] by negating the cause (reason) for which the verse was revealed after the prohibition of *khamr*. The reason is that when Allah, the Exalted, prohibited *khamr*, He said, "On those who believe and do deeds of righteousness there lies no blame for what they ate (in the past), when they guard themselves from evil, and believe, and do deeds of righteousness."[242] This is a negation of the prohibition. Thus, permission and prohibition are gathered together, and this makes it impossible for the subject to comply.

It is here that ʿUmar ibn al-Khaṭṭāb found fault with the person who interpreted the verse saying that it refers to the time before the prohibition of *khamr*. He said to him, "When you fear God, you avoid what Allah has prohibited."[243] The reason is that it is not proper to say to the subject, "avoid this" following it up with an emphatic prohibition that requires strict compliance and then say, "If you do it, there is no blame on you." Further, Allah has informed us that it keeps one away from the remembrance of Allah, from prayer, and gives rise to enmity and hatred among those who have mutual compassion in the path of Allah. After settling the rule of prohibition, it amounts to a negation of it[244] due to the words of the Exalted, "when they guard themselves from evil, and believe, and do deeds of righteousness",[245] if it is consumed after prohibition. It is not possible for the occurrence of the true fear of God, as that will amount to a hardship or the performance of what is impossible.

With respect to the understanding of acts, this principle is the foundation of the issue. It is also the basis for upholding *istiḥsān* (preference of the stronger rule) and *maṣlaḥa mursala* (interest not directly supported). The reason is that when the unrestricted interpretation of a principle leads to hardship or to what is not possible according to the *sharīʿa* or even rationally, then, the principle is not applicable in a valid manner and continuously. It cannot, therefore, be applied in the absolute sense. This is also the principle for those who discuss the difficult meanings in the Qurʾān and the *Sunna*, due to what becomes binding when the sources of such meanings are interpreted in the general or absolute sense leading to the contradiction mentioned earlier, unless such meanings are restricted to serve the requirements of uninterrupted application and continuity, in which case they become valid meanings. Within this discussion is included that of exemptions (*rukhaṣ*), for the principle governs them and distinguishes between situations where exemptions are available and where they are not.

Anyone who does not observe this principle as one of the principles of the *sharīʿa* is not secure against error. In fact, you will often find this principle eliminated from the principles of those who pursue ambiguous meanings, as well as included among the principles of those few sects that deviate from the straight path. Likewise, it is missing from the issues of *ijtihād* that are disputed among the recognised *imams* and earlier jurists.

I will now illustrate this for you through two issues about which a discussion took place with some contemporary scholars.

First

One of the scholars of al-Maghrib wrote to me about a topic that includes a discussion of "what study is obligatory upon a person seeking the Hereafter and how he should act for attaining it". He wrote in the letter: "If occupation with an affair keeps a person away from his prayer even for a moment, he is to vacate his inner self of it by giving up the affair, as is done by the God-fearing, even if it is worth fifty thousand." I considered this issue to be difficult, and I wrote to him saying: "As for the fact that the person is required to free his thoughts of the affair, it is true, but as to vacating his mind of it by giving up the affair altogether, I do not know what type of obligation this is. Had this been obligatory in unqualified terms, it would be obligatory on all the people to give up their real estate, houses, villages, wives, children and other things[246] that are likely to occupy their thoughts during prayer. On the same analogy, giving up wealth can become a cause for occupying his mind during prayer greater than his occupation with wealth. Further, if poverty is the reason for distraction then what is he supposed to do? It is often that we find that the cause of distraction is want, especially when the person has dependants and he cannot find a way to support them. It is one of these things that keeps most people occupied. Thus, is it binding on such a person to give up the thing that distracts him in prayer? This is something that is not understood. The practice in *fiqh* and *ijtihād* with respect to worship is to resist distracting thoughts in particular. It is recommended to give up what has in its nature to distract, like wealth and other things, if such giving up is valid according to the *sharīʿa*, and is something whose absence is not effective in leading to something that is similar to what is given up or something greater than it. Thereafter, the rule for the prayer in which distraction has occurred needs to be examined as to whether the state of the person who performed the prayer requires repetition by way of obligation or recommendation or dropping such repetition, but this is a separate discussion." This is the result of the issue.

When this message reached him, he wrote back saying something that amounted to conceding what had been said. This is correct, because the view about giving up all this in the absolute sense is not sound in fact, because of the different states of people. Thus, it is not correct to rely upon it for purposes of *fiqh* in any case.

Second

The issue is that of piety requiring the giving up of things due to disagreement. Many of the later scholars considered giving up disagreement in obligatory acts to be a requirement and they moved such disputed issues to the category of the *mutashābihāt* (ambiguities).

I have since long pondered over this issue, so much so that I wrote about it to al-Maghrib and Ifrīqiya, but a reply that would satisfy me did not reach me. In fact, if it was like all other existing disagreements, the majority[247] of the issues of *fiqh* being disputed, and if such disagreement is acknowledged, most of the issues of the *sharīʿa* would be treated as *mutashābihāt* (ambiguities) and that would go against[248] the approach of the *sharīʿa*. Further, piety would become a severe hardship as it would not be possible for anyone in most forms of worship, transactions and every other obligatory act to give them up due to disagreement. This is the crux of the issue.

One of them responded saying: "The meaning of a disputed issue being part of ambiguities (*mutashābihāt*) is that it is something disputed with respect to the supporting evidence and views about it are equally strong or similar." Most issues of *fiqh* are not like this, in fact those described to be like this are very few for one who ponders over the consequences of the subject under examination. Accordingly, those that can be classified among the *mutashābih* will be very few. As for piety in its essence, even though it belongs to this category alone, it is intensely difficult, and it cannot be attained except by one to whom Allah has granted an excess of strength for countering prohibited acts. The Prophet (pbuh) has said, "The heaven is concealed behind deception."[249]

I wrote to him saying: "What you have said in your response is not clear, because it applies to the *mujtahid* alone, and the *mujtahid* displays piety when there is a conflict of evidences (*adilla*), not when there is a conflict of views. What you have said, therefore, does not apply to what we are discussing. As for the *muqallid* (follower), the author of this special piety wants him to move out of disputations towards consensus (*ijmāʿ*), even when the person issuing the verdict for him is the best among the disagreeing jurists. The layman under usual circumstances does not know whose evidence is stronger and whose evidence is weaker. He also does not know whether their evidences are equally strong or similar. The reason is that this is known only to the person who is qualified to judge this. The layman does not have this ability. The difficulty arises through reliance on the disagreement that is accepted and this accepted disagreement is found in most of the issues of the *sharīʿa*. The disagreement that is not acknowledged is minor,[250] like disagreement about the *mutʿa* marriage (temporary), *ribā al-nasīʾa* (usury in case of delay alone), unnatural lust with women, and whatever is in the same category.

Further, the equality of evidences[251] or their similarity is something additional to the examination undertaken by the *mujtahid*. It is possible that for someone the evidences may be equal or similar, but they are not so according to others. Thus, the layman cannot have a standard on which he can rely for avoiding or not avoiding disagreement. It is also not possible for him to have recourse to the *mujtahid* for this, because what guides him towards avoidance or non-avoidance is in itself the decision of the *mujtahid*. Following his decision alone in this amounts to performing his *taqlīd* alone (following him alone) without the need for moving away from disagreement, especially when this *mujtahid* claims that the opinion of his opponent is weak and is not to be relied upon. The same is the case if he has recourse to the other *mujtahid*. The layman will continue to be in a state of confusion if he pursues such matters. Anyone who creates a difficulty for this *dīn* will be overwhelmed by it." This is what was confusing for purposes of the question and his (following) response did not clarify the issue:

"When we ponder over the basis of the issue, we find a distinction between this type of special piety and other types of piety that we elaborated. The remaining types of piety are attained easily with respect to occurrence, even though they are strong when it comes to opposition of the inner self. The piety requiring the giving up of disagreement is difficult to attain with respect to occurrence, even though it is not difficult with respect to countering the self. The intention of the questioner became evident through (the factors of) hardship and difficulty of attainment, but it was not what you indicated." This is what he wrote. Here the discussion between us ended.

Anyone who ponders over such a resolution of the issue will realize that what this person has said in response is not always applicable (continuous)[252] and is not sound in actual fact, because of the inclusion of hardship in its occurrence. It is, therefore, not proper to rely upon it nor deem it a principle for further reasoning. There are many examples of this, so hold on to this principle as it is of immense benefit, and many of the issues of piety are settled through it. It is also used for distinguishing between ambiguities as well as for judging what is an ambiguity[253] and what is not. Within this book there are similar issues that we shall resolve, God willing.

NOTES

1 The learned Editor of the book gives the following note: The term *ʿuṣūl* is applied to mean universal principles (*kulliyāt*) that are expressly stated in the Book (Qurʾān) and the *Sunna*, like "no injury is to be inflicted and none is to be borne", "no bearer of burdens can bear another's burden", "there is no hardship for you in religion", "verily, acts are determined through intentions", "he who dies without associating anything with God enters heaven", and so on. These principles are also considered *adilla* (evidences), like the Book, the *Sunna*, consensus (*ijmāʿ*) and the like. These are definitive (*qatʿī*) without dispute. The term *ʿuṣūl* is also applied to mean rules (*qawānīn*) that have been derived from the Book and the *Sunna* and through which the specific evidences (*adilla juzʾiyya*) are weighed and measured during the derivation of the rules of law (*aḥkām*) from the evidences. These rules (*qawānīn*) are the technique (*fann*) of *ʿuṣūl al-fiqh*. Among these are those that are definitive, by agreement, and those about which there is a disagreement as to their being probable or definitive. Thus, al-Qāḍī and those who agreed with him maintain that among these *ʿuṣūlī* issues are some that are probable. The Author while attempting to prove that these issues are definitive relies on the three primary evidences as well as on other evidence that he adduces for responding to al-Māzarī who objected to al-Qāḍī's view. In the end he declares that whatever is probable is removed from the discipline of *ʿuṣūl* and is to be discussed as ancillary to this discipline. The comments of the learned Editor are sound and our initial reaction was to leave the reader to make his own judgement about a very powerful statement made by al-Shāṭibī. Yet, for someone not thoroughly acquainted with the discipline of *ʿuṣūl al-fiqh*, the discussion about *ʿuṣūl al-fiqh* being definitive may become somewhat confusing. The issue is complex and touches the very foundations of the true meaning of the discipline itself. We shall attempt to simplify it as far as is possible.

The first question to be raised is: why does the Author consider *ʿuṣūl al-fiqh* to be definitive? What purpose will be served through such a presumption? The term definitive or *qatʿī*, with respect to the *ʿuṣūl* here, implies that these *uṣūl* convey a single unalterable meaning that is not subject to change. Thus, the statement "the Qurʾān is a source of Islamic law", if it is definitive, and it is, conveys that no one has the right to question this statement or to alter and amend it or even consider it open for discussion. As far as this statement is concerned, no Muslim, whatever his school or affiliation, will disagree; the Qurʾān is a binding source of law. Can we say the same about the *Sunna*, that is, can we state as a definitive principle that "the *Sunna* is a binding source of Islamic law"? According to al-Sarakhsī and many other writers on *ʿuṣūl*, anyone who denies this statement as a whole is to be imputed with *kufr* (unbelief). See al-Sarakhsī, *ʿUṣūl*, vol. 1, 318. Are we to say the same about consensus of legal opinion (*ijmāʿ*)? According to al-Shāṭibī, yes it is a *qatʿī* principle, even though the consequences of disagreeing may not be as serious as those for the *Sunna*. Can we say the same for syllogism (*qiyās*) in the context of Islamic law? The idea would be that the principle that "*qiyās* is a binding source of law" is not open for discussion as it is definitive (*qatʿī*). In fact, al-Shatibī appears to be going much further. To understand exactly what he means we have to explain the meaning of *ʿuṣūl al-fiqh* in somewhat different terms.

The term *aṣl* has many meanings for purposes of Islamic jurisprudence, like root, source, original rule, and so on, but for the jurist, the term *ʿuṣūl*, insofar as it is a discipline, implies "a body of principles" that he uses to interpret the texts. See Ṣadr al-Sharīʿa, *al-Tawḍīḥ*, vol. 1, 41–45. These principles of interpretation are formulated by the Muslim jurists in the form of general propositions that have a major premise, a minor premise and a conclusion. The major premise of these propositions serves as the principle. Such a principle is referred to as a *qāʿida uṣūliyya*. Thus, for example, a proposition may be stated as follows:

> The *aḥkām* of Allah are established through the sources of Islamic law [minor premise]. **The Qurʾān is a source of law** [major premise]. Thus [conclusion], each time a *ḥukm* is found in the Qurʾān it is proved as the *ḥukm* of Allah. See Ibid., vol. 1, 45.

The major premise in the above proposition, which emerges as a principle, is that **the Qurʾān is a source of law**. This is what is usually stated when we are talking about *ʿuṣūl al-fiqh*. The emphasis, however, is always on the last sentence; namely, **each time a *ḥukm* is found in the Qurʾān it is proved as the *ḥukm* of Allah.** This latter statement focuses on the intention of the Lawgiver; it is the result of the effort that the *mujtahid* has made to understand the texts. It tells the *mujtahid* that if he is able to find a *ḥukm* in the texts of the Qurʾān that *ḥukm* stands proved or established as the *ḥukm* or rule laid down by Allah.

The same is the case with the *Sunna* as well as *ijmāʿ*; when it is said that they are sources of law. The emphasis is identical. The same emphasis is applied by the Sunnī schools of law when they are formulating a principle for *qiyās*. Thus, when the jurist maintains that analogy (*qiyās*) is a source of law, the emphasis will always be on the fact that "each time analogy is successfully used to discover the law (from the Qurʾān and the *Sunna*) a *ḥukm* of Allah is discovered or proved". Ibid. This is so as *qiyās* is merely a method of discovering a law laid down in the Qurʾān and the *Sunna*. The law is actually being proved from the two primary sources.

The jurist, in this way, arrives at four fundamental principles of interpretation related to the four sources of the law. These four principles can easily be substituted for the term *adilla* used below for the view of al-Qāḍī. These four principles, however, are not the only principles used in this discipline. Each school formulates principles for the additional sources that it accepts and acts upon them. The emphasis is the same as for the first four sources with respect to the resulting rule being the *ḥukm* of Allah.

A large number of other principles that apply to literal interpretation are also part of *ʿuṣūl*. A few examples of such *ʿuṣūl* are given below.

1) Each time a *ḥukm* is discovered in the Qurʾān it is said to be proved. [Unanimous.]
2) Each time a *ḥukm* is discovered in the *Sunna* it is said to be proved. [Unanimous.]
3) Each time a *ḥukm* is discovered though *ijmāʿ* it is said to be proved. [Unanimous, though al-Shāfiʿī had some reservations.]
4) Each time a *ḥukm* is discovered through *qiyās* it is said to be proved. [Unanimous for the existing Sunnī schools.]
5) Each time a *ḥukm* is discovered through the opinion of a Companion it is said to be proved. [Not unanimous; the Ḥanafīs consider it binding, but the Shāfiʿīs do not.]
6) Each time a command (*amr*) is found in the texts it conveys an obligation, unless another evidence indicates the contrary. [Not unanimous.]
7) Each time a proscription (*nahy*) is found in the texts it conveys a prohibition, unless another evidence indicates the contrary. [Not unanimous.]
8) Each time a *ḥukm* is expressed in general terms it applies to all its categories with a certainty, unless restricted by an equally strong evidence. [Not unanimous.]
9) The *ḥukm* is proved through the persuasive power of the *dalīl* and not through the number of evidences. [Not unanimous.]

These are only a few out of a large body of rules called the *qawānīn uṣūliyya*. They have been stated so that the reader may get an idea of the tools employed by the jurists. There are, for example, a large number of sub-rules for *qiyās* that are mentioned within this concept by al-Shāṭibī.

Are all these principles and sub-principles definitive according to al-Shāṭibī? Let us first focus on *qiyās* and assume that the principle "*qiyās* is a binding source of Islamic law" is definitive. This principle has many sub-principles like "the details of the underlying causes (*ʿilal*), like the assertion about the conversion (*aks*) of the *ʿilla*, the conflict between the underlying causes, the preference of one cause over another". Likewise, there are sub-rules for reports "like the number of narrators and *mursal* reports". The statements in quotation marks have been lifted from the discussion of the first concept, as the reader will notice.

Al-Shāṭibī argues through the statements of other writers. He first quotes a jurist called al-Qāḍī al-Tīb, who says that such sub-rules are not definitive, they are probable, and thus cannot be counted as part of *ʿuṣūl al-fiqh*, because *ʿuṣūl al-fiqh* are *qatʿī* (definitive). He then quotes al-Juwaynī to imply that these sub-rules are definitive too as these are "details that have been erected upon definitive foundations". He means thereby that these too should be treated as *qatʿī*, and the term "definitive foundations" obviously means the broader principle of *qiyās*. He follows this up by al-Māzarī's statement who deems al-Qāḍī's method of considering *ʿuṣūl al-fiqh* as definitive to be unconvincing and says that "even though these rules are probable, there is no justification for excluding them from the meaning of *ʿuṣūl*". This view, however, negates al-Shāṭibī's opening statement that the *ʿuṣūl* are *qatʿī*. Al-Māzarī also points out that Abū al-Maʿālī does not consider them to be part of *ʿuṣūl* either, but that is because he considers *ʿuṣūl* to be the first four principles mentioned above and which are considered the *adilla*.

Al-Shāṭibī responds to these views in different ways, but his response to al-Qāḍī's view is meant to settle the point:

> As for the view of al-Qāḍī, the operation of these evidences (texts), whether they are definitive or probable, rests on these principles, which are called *ʿuṣūl al-fiqh*, because reasoning from these texts (evidences) cannot be undertaken unless they are measured against these principles (of interpretation) and are examined through them. This makes it necessary that these principles (of interpretation) be similar in strength to such evidences or even stronger than them. The reason is that you have allowed these principles to govern the meaning of these texts (evidences), so that the evidences that do not meet the standards set by these principles are to be rejected. How then is it possible to deem probable the rules that govern standards for other evidences?

Here we leave the reader to form his own view.

2 The editor says: When we scrutinise all the issues of the discipline of *ʿuṣūl*, we are certain that these are based on the three universal principles (*kulliyāt*) of the *sharīʿa*. The empirical enumeration (induction) of all the individual cases is possible as these issues are limited in number.

3 According to the editor, the conclusion drawn from this is that the universal principles (*kulliyāt*) of the *sharīʿa* are either based upon rational proofs or on general induction through the sources of the *sharīʿa*, and both result in definitive conclusions. Thus, these universal principles are definitive and consequently the issues of *ʿuṣūl* that are based upon them are also definitive.

4 That is, they rely on the three rules of rational analysis that he (the Author) will be mentioning in detail under the discussion of the second concept.

5 The editor says: It is not established in practice that those who, for example, derived the principle "*al-amr lil-wujūb* (each command necessarily gives rise to an obligation)" took into account each command that was issued by the Lawgiver so that the well-known claim about general induction leading to certainty can be affirmed. What is required here, however, is certainty that amounts to decisive conviction. For this purpose the preponderant enumeration of each type of command is sufficient, and which is found for the three purposes (*maqāṣid*) of the *sharīʿa*: necessities (*ḍarūriyāt*); supporting needs (*ḥājiyāt*); and complementary principles

(*taḥsīnāt*). This type of enumeration is sufficient for being counted as general induction that leads to certainty. The reason is that the cases of commands that the investigator has not come across will not be excluded from cases that he has encountered; thus, this fact will not disturb the soundness of the principle.

6 This will come up under the second concept in addition to the usual. Perhaps, he has widened the concept by arranging them under the rational.

7 Editor: This amounts to proving the required fact by negating its opposite. The reason is that the consequence of accepting it as probable is a conclusion that is not permitted in practice, which is the association of probable meanings with the foundations of the *sharīʿa* or the admitting of doubt in them or the possibility of altering them, for all this is void.

8 Editor: And not in the universal principles of the *sharīʿa* due to his words "if uncertain meanings could be associated ..." This is the heart of the argument.

9 Editor: Keeping in view the fact that this has been derived through general induction, his words "they would be associated with the foundations of the *sharīʿa* itself" are valid. The foundation of the *sharīʿa* is definitive as it is the primary principle from which all other rules and principles have arisen. Insofar as the primary principle is definitive and the generation (of the rules and principles) from it is by way of general induction, the rule for the derivative principle is the same as the rule for the primary principle and vice versa.

10 Editor: The reason is that after establishing an evidence for the principle and its being definitive, it becomes difficult in practice to associate a probable meaning with it in place of a definitive meaning. He did not say "rationally", because there is nothing to prevent the reason of a particular individual from assigning a probable meaning to it, on the basis of an evidence, even after certainty has been attained. It is, therefore, not necessary to assume that this is rationally impossible.

11 Editor: That is, those that are the point of recourse for the issues of *ʿuṣūl*.

12 Editor: This is a figure of speech, because it does not occur in all the issues of *ʿuṣūl al-fiqh*, even in those on which they have agreed. What are acceptable to each nation are some basic principles alone. It would have been better if he had not advanced this type of argument when he was arguing for the definitive nature of *ʿuṣūl* and their primary concepts.

13 Editor: It is evident that such an argument would lead to the claim that the derived rules (cases) are also definitive.

14 That is, they are not to be adopted as such until their proof is given in a definitive manner.

15 Editor: Perhaps, he means that a principle in relation to specific categories is in the nature of the general word (*ʿāmm*) with respect to its incidents. As a probable meaning may be associated with individual evidences with respect to their implied meanings, there is no reason why a general principle cannot be applied to them in the same way as the general word to its particular meanings with which a probable meaning may be associated.

16 Editor: That is, on behalf of al-Qāḍī. Al-Qāḍī, even though he has said that *ʿuṣūl* (*al-fiqh*) are these rules (*qawānīn*), it does not negate the claim that they are definitive, because anything that is probable cannot be counted as part of *ʿuṣūl*. Thus, whether he intends by the term *ʿuṣūl* evidences like the Qurʾān and the *Sunna* as well as others, or he means thereby these principles, they must be definitive. From this we also come to know that his words "these probable propositions are fundamental general rules" are the words of al-Māzarī and not those of al-Qāḍī. It is obvious that the benefit of the dialogue between al-Qāḍī and al-Māzarī is to clarify the point and to refute the confusing statements made by al-Māzarī so as to determine that the *ʿuṣūl al-fiqh* in whatever way these are understood are definitive, whether these are treated as principles or as evidences like the Book and the *Sunna* and the expressly stated fundamental principles of the *sharīʿa*.

17 Editor: This is a mere claim, unless it is deemed a consequence of what has preceded, in which case the *fā* will have to be dropped.

18 Qurʾān 15:9.

19 Editor: This is conceded, but it has been generalised to include those that are derived.
20 Qur'ān 5:3.
21 Editor: The statement that contradicts this will come up later for he states in the "ninth concept": It is for this reason that the *sharīʿa* in its principles and detailed issues stands protected. It is, however, possible to reconcile the two statements by saying that his intention here is to deny protection to the derived cases (*furūʿ*) in themselves, while it is there to grant them protection by adducing adequate evidence for one who is attentive towards him with sound understanding. If some deem them unsound, while others deem them sound, they are protected as a whole.
22 Editor: That is an expressly stated general principle, as he stated earlier. This statement goes against his view that it is necessary that each principle be definitive. If his purpose is to assert the view of Abū al-Maʿālī, and that certainty is found in expressly stated principles without recourse to the derived rules, there is no benefit in such a statement that would revert to his claim that principles in *ʿuṣūl al-fiqh* are definitive. If an analogy is to be constructed for the derived rules (*qawānīn*) upon the expressed principles, as is to be understood from his statement that there is no distinction between the expressed and other principles, then it is an analogy for which a proper underlying cause has not been mentioned.
23 Editor: That is, the definitive evidences that are examined through these principles. It is sometimes said that they are deemed rules (*qawānīn*) for the derivation of the specific cases (rules) whether these are definitive or probable, but they are not rules for the definitive evidences. The specific rules (*furūʿ*) derived through these rules are probable, and there is no problem with this.
24 Editor: This is a retraction from support to a large category although it is acceptable and understandable. Among the issues (rules) of *ʿuṣūl* are those that are definitive and agreed upon by all and among them are those that are subject to examination with many arguments for and against them. See al-Asnawī's commentary on *al-Minhāj fī Taʿrīf al-ʿUṣūl*. With this conclusion he has excluded a large number of principles that are mentioned in *ʿuṣūl* and he has done this en bloc without identifying the categories that are excluded. This makes the number of principles left behind as definitive and those deemed probable an unknown category. The statement diminishes the utility of this concept.
25 Editor: Necessary or implied as has preceded in the first concept. What applies there applies here too.
26 Editor: That is, those that constitute the premises do not exceed three whether these are rational, experiential or transmitted. It is sometimes stated in *ʿuṣūl al-fiqh* that such and such is a proof (*ḥujja*) or is not a proof. This is not part of a premise, rather it is a consequence of these premises. As it is an accidental attribute the proof of whose subject is required and such proof is identified by means of these premises.
27 Editor: Because it is more general in terms of its evidence than merely being obligatory or permissible or impossible, that is, rationally or in experience, not as a specific rational category.
28 Editor: They mentioned these in the category of premises due to a need arising in *ʿuṣūl* for elaborating the concept and for ascertaining their evidence in the affirmative or the negative, as in case of the rule "the imperative necessitates an obligation and the prohibitive a prohibition". He has himself mentioned it and gone into details for its determination. Unless he means thereby that such and such act is obligatory or prohibited, for example, as this belongs to the purely derived cases (*furūʿ*) that have nothing to do with the premises.
29 Editor: This preliminary concept is in the form of an elaboration and defence of what is stated in the previous concept.
30 Editor: That is, the evidences employed in the discipline are not formulated through rational premises alone. One of the premises may be rational, while the rest may be from the *sharīʿa*. They are sometimes employed for identification insofar as the entire evidence is from the *sharīʿa* and helps in the verification of the conclusion through a rational evidence. On

occasions the rational and experiential premises are not employed for proving a universal principle; rather they are used for proving the effective cause (*al-manāṭ*) that is, for the application of the principle to one of its categories. This is done by undertaking an examination as to whether a category falls under the domain of a principle so that it may be governed by it. It will be coming up later that this study refers to a command, to different crafts or to customary practice in trade and agriculture as well as other things, except that it is to be observed in this context that *taḥqīq al-manāṭ* (verification of the cause) is the work of the independent jurist (*faqīh*) and is not the subject of the issues of *ʿuṣūl*. The same is said with respect to *tanqīḥ al-manāṭ* (refinement of the cause) and *takhrīj al-manāṭ* (derivation of the cause), that will be coming up for discussion in the fourth volume, because all of these are tasks for the *faqīh* and not the *ʿuṣūlī*. It may, however, be said that there is nothing to prevent the claim that *taḥqīq al-manāṭ* is also related to the issues of *ʿuṣūl*, but in a manner that is different from the technical meaning assigned to it here.

31 Editor: That is, it does not provide conviction about it with respect to its being general for all the evidences as is required.

32 Editor: It is not *mutawātir* in meaning. The reason is that all this occurs in one form alone like a large number of different incidents that together indicate the courage of ʿAlī, for example, in a manner that is direct. As for these, some of them directly indicate the obligation of prayer, while others do so indirectly though obligation is derived from them, like praise for one who undertakes it, blame for one who misses it, severe warning for one who neglects it, and making it binding for the subject to establish it even if this is done while lying on one side when he is unable to stand, waging war against one who neglects it completely and so on. It is for this reason that he deemed them similar to *mutawātir maʿnawī* and not continuous in meaning itself.

33 Editor: That is, it is probable reasoning based upon probable premises that have been pointed out.

34 Editor: Instead of enumerating all the individual evidences and engaging in the discussion of each evidence, they avoid the method that can cause disturbance and mention consensus that eliminates such disturbance, because otherwise each evidence taken alone is probable and does not communicate a definitive meaning.

35 Editor: This is similar to *mutawātir maʿnawī* (continuous in meaning).

36 Editor: As we have indicated, it is for this reason that it is like the continuous in meaning, but is not exactly that.

37 Editor: He has structured the book on this method and it runs throughout the book.

38 Editor: He is using the word perhaps and is not saying clearly that they did give it up, because al-Ghazālī has indicated this while providing the legal justification for consensus, as will be pointed out. It was excellent that al-Ghazālī by his indication in the context of consensus led al-Shāṭibī to utilise it in an outstanding manner and to expand the meaning into this. In fact, he made it the distinctive feature of his book, as he says in the end.

39 Editor: That is, on the basis of each individual verse without merging it with the remaining verses and traditions so that its examination would be the examination of this whole body of texts that convey continuity.

40 Editor: That is, on the basis of an agreement that becomes like consensus of the individual evidences conveying the required meaning.

41 Editor: That is, through induction and the examination of the evidences organised on the same method, it will give a probable meaning unless reason is given a role in *sharʿī* rules. We say that reason comes to the same conclusion on its own and this makes the meaning definitive due to it, even though the transmitted evidence was probable. Reason according to us, however, cannot perceive this directly, but views it from behind the *sharīʿa*. This inductive method, therefore, becomes a means for giving definitive meanings to the transmitted evidences.

42 Editor: An illustration of an important *ʿuṣūlī* issue that cannot be established through a specific evidence. It is established by something resembling the continuous in meaning through evidences that have not been laid down for the same context or under the same topic.

43 Editor: Two further examples of important issues from the substantive legal matters.

44 Editor: That is, the *maṣāliḥ mursala* (additional interests), and these are those that are not supported by a specific *sharʿī* evidence, either a text or *ijmāʿ*, and either by way of acknowledgement or rejection. The example is that of the collection of the Qurʾān and recording it in writing. There was no individual text for this from the Lawgiver. It is for this reason that Abū Bakr and ʿUmar hesitated in the first instance, until they verified that the interest of the preservation of the *dīn* was one of the purposes of the law. Similar to this are the organisation of the *dīwāns* and the compilation of the *sharʿī* and other sciences. For example, in the compilation of the rules of grammar there was no specific evidence, but it was evidenced by a universal definitive evidence that was compatible with the purposes of the *sharīʿa* and its propositions so that the rule of this issue could be derived from it, reasoning that it was something required by the *sharīʿa*, even though it was dependent upon intermediaries for cataloguing under it.

45 Editor: Based on some interpreted meanings of *istiḥsān* – the other meanings will be coming up in the fourth part – leading to the conclusion that it is to be preferred over the apparent meaning and over analogy. Thus, Mālik prefers its restriction through *maṣlaḥa* (acknowledged interest) and Abū Ḥanīfa through a *khabar wāḥid*. It is for this reason that he attributes it here to Mālik.

46 Editor: That is, adopting an individual interest as against a universal interest. This is illustrated by the *ʿariyya* sale of dates by estimate. It is the sale of moist dates for dry dates and this involves prohibiting *gharar* (uncertainty) on the basis of a general evidence, except that it was permitted to remove hardship for the two parties to the contract of *ʿariyya*. If it were to be prohibited it would prohibit the *ʿariyya* contract *ab initio*, and this would lead to an injury. If the general evidence were to be applied generally to it, it would lead to injury and, therefore, the contract had to be made an exception. Its detailed explanation will be coming up in the tenth issue of the *Book of Ijtihād* in part four. Among these issues is the examination of the private parts for medical reasons and this has been permitted against the general evidence, because the pursuit of the general evidence in such a case leads to an injury and harm that does not conform with the *maqāṣid al-sharīʿa*. Thus, *istiḥsān* examines the implications of the evidences and takes into account their consequences to the maximum. If in certain specific issues, the matter goes against the general interest that is the purpose of the Lawgiver, the general evidence is covered in such a case and an exemption is created in conformity with the *maqāṣid al-sharīʿa*. In the *sharīʿa* such examples are numerous and spread over many areas. Even though there is no specific text for the justification of *istiḥsān* yielding specific evidences it is something that is compatible with the propositions of the *sharīʿa* and its meaning is derivable from the detailed source evidences. Thus, it is a universal *sharʿī* principle on the basis of which the rules are to be derived.

47 Editor: This objection is directed towards both *maṣlaḥa mursala* and *istiḥsān* as each is reasoning on the basis of a universal principle to derive a particular rule. The distinction between them is that the second is the restriction of the evidence through *maṣlaḥa*, while the first is the affirmation of the evidence on the basis of *maṣlaḥa* for an issue for which there is no specific evidence.

48 Editor: In the first part of the third volume.

49 Editor: In the eighth issue at the beginning of the *Kitāb al-Maqāṣid* in the second volume.

50 Editor: That is, the lack of agreement about the *mutawātir maʿnawī* in the tradition, "My *umma* will not agree upon an error", on the basis of which al-Ghazālī has argued for the legal justification of *ijmāʿ*. Their examination of the traditions on the topic is the individual examination of each of these traditions, which has led them to give up reasoning for the legal

justification of *ijmāʿ*. They argue either by reasoning from it on the basis of ordinary matters like witnessed circumstances or by those that are transmitted and usually take it into account. As for reasoning for it on the basis of *ijmāʿ* being definitive it is due to the error of one who opposed it, along with there being a semblance of being a source (refer to Ibn al-Ḥājib). It is through this explanation that we know the meaning of the use of the word employment by him.

51 Editor: That is, directly and not indirectly, as is the case with taking help from derivations of the following disciplines. He intends thereby that the preliminary concepts he has discussed in his book rely on direct assistance and that makes them part of *ʿuṣūl* as against remote concepts, like those he will take up in the discussions to follow.

52 Editor: Affirming *fiqh*, but not for its derivation. It is for this reason that he said "among the issues of *fiqh*" and not "issues of *fiqh*".

53 Editor: Add to this the issue of the word used prior to its employment, neither as an actual application nor a figurative use, and so on.

54 Editor: He talks about the issue of permissibility in five issues that will come up soon. You may examine them on the basis of the rule laid down in this concept in order to know the distinction between permissibility being an obligation creating rule in the first instance and these issues, insofar as he has deemed this to lie outside the scope of *ʿuṣūl*, while he has considered those five issues to lie within *ʿuṣūl*.

55 Editor: He refers earlier to a type of issue that cannot be properly included in *ʿuṣūl al-fiqh*. He has determined that its rule to be every issue on which *fiqh* is not based. He has illustrated this through a number of legal rules as well as rules of language, like the issue of initial application. This is another type and it is one on which *fiqh* is based, but it is not one of the issues of *ʿuṣūl* rather it is a topic of another discipline, and its discussion properly lies in its own specific discipline. These are like the rules of grammar and language. Through this explanation it becomes known that his statement (and subsequent discussion of it) is a nominal sentence linked to another. Perhaps, in the original manuscript it is a verbal sentence that has been changed. It is well known that the discussions of grammar and language are brought into *ʿuṣūl* not because they are its issues but preliminary matters on which its derivation is closely based. Yes, they should not have expanded upon the discussions or have recorded them as if they are issues of this discipline, for they are verified in another discipline. Perhaps, this is what the Author means.

56 Editor: In the first issue of the second part of the Book of *Maqāṣid*.

57 Editor: The majority said that the *wājib* is a single type that is unknown and is verified externally for one of these specified categories with respect to which a choice has been given. The Muʿtazila said that all of them are *wājib*. The imam (al-Ḥaramayn) said in *al-Burhān* said that they acknowledge that one who gives up all does not sin in the same way as one who gives up the *wājibāt*, and one who gives up all is not given the spiritual reward (*thawāb*) meant for the *wājibāt*. Thus, there is no practical benefit of this disagreement, rather it is merely theoretical, on which a difference in practice cannot be based. Accordingly, it is not proper to engage in a discussion of its evidences in the discipline of *ʿuṣūl*.

58 Editor: The earlier jurists said that one unidentified act out of these be prohibited and the meaning is that the subject can give up any of them by way of substitution and he cannot combine them in a single act. The Muʿtazila said that this is not permitted, and in fact all are prohibited; the giving up of one is, therefore, sufficient for purposes of obedience. The evidences and refutations are all mentioned in the case of *wājib mukhayyar*. Accordingly, there is no practical benefit of even this disagreement. This is what the Author intends, and it is obvious.

59 Editor: Perhaps, the correct word would be "acts". This pertains to the rule of good and evil rationally. The Muʿtazila, who uphold it, maintain that the command to undertake an unknown act is not sound, because it is not known whether reason deems a command to undertake an

unknown act as morally sound. The majority of the jurists maintain that obligation and prohibition are to be determined through the address of Allah and reason has no role to play here and, thus, there is no moral goodness or badness in acts, except through the commands and proscriptions of the Lawgiver. Accordingly, there is nothing to prevent the command to undertake one undetermined act out of several things, as in the case of the options in expiation where the subject has a choice to deem one of the things as determined. This is the interpretation that is the basis of the issue of *mukhayyar* in the light of the rule of *taḥsīn* (good).

60 Editor: Please refer to al-Asnawī, who has mentioned a number of practical benefits of the issue with respect to the execution of his manumission and repudiations of divorce. There are about ten disputed cases. Yes, he did restrict his statement according to the statement made by al-Fakhr al-Rāzī. Al-Rāzī maintains that there is no purpose in obligation except the doubling of penalty for them in the Hereafter. Consequently, there is no *fiqhī* practical benefit of the issue in his view. However, after the elaboration of these legal cases and their coming to the knowledge of the Author, he should have eliminated this issue of obligation for the unbelievers from this discussion of his.

61 Editor: The *mubāḥ* (permissible) is not legally required, as will be coming up in his discussion. The rule he applies to it requires that the reasoning underlying the derivation of the *mubāḥ*, and the knowledge that a certain act is *mubāḥ*, is not preferred by the *sharīʿa*; however, this is not evident and granting it substance is somewhat vague.

62 Editor: Does this not belong to the category of acknowledging the creations of Allah that lead to the strengthening of faith and an increase in understanding of the powers of the Creator, glory be to Him, by way of obedience to the verses requiring the subjects to ponder over what is in the earth and the skies? It is for this reason that they said that the obligation arising out of the question in the verses is one of the modes of address of the Wise Lord, that is, He knows best about the condition of the questioner through the meaning conveyed to Him by the Messenger of Allah (pbuh). Accordingly, if the Prophet (pbuh) had given him the answer he required, there would have been a benefit in terms of satisfaction of the heart, except that He thought it best for him in terms of his state to turn his attention to the movement of the moon instead of focusing on the movement that he did not understand, and its understanding was difficult for most of the Arabs, as this would not have suited the office of prophethood. Thus, turning to the state of the questioner, and its examples, through what suits the office of prophethood, had the response conformed to the questions, it might have led to the benefit of satisfaction. Ponder over it.

63 Qurʾān 2:189.

64 Qurʾān 2:189.

65 It is recorded by al-Bukhārī in his *Ṣaḥīḥ*, vol. 3, 621, Tr. No. 1803.

66 Qurʾān 79:42.

67 Qurʾān 79:43.

68 Recorded by al-Bukhārī and Muslim. Al-Bukhārī, *Ṣaḥīḥ*, vol. 10, 557, Tr. No. 6171. Al-Ḥāfiẓ al-ʿIrāqī says while undertaking the documentation of the traditions of *al-Iḥyāʾ* that it is agreed upon by the two Shaykhs and is a tradition of Anas, Abū Mūsā and Ibn Masʿūd and so on.

69 Qurʾān 5:101.

70 Editor: Reported by the two Shaykhs, al-Bukhārī and Muslim.

71 It is recorded by Ibn Abī Ḥātim, *al-Tafsīr*, vol. 1, 215–16.

72 Editor: The verse that says, "Do not ask ..."

73 Editor: This discussion is found in the second issue of the rules for questions and answers in the part on *ijtihād* at the end of the book.

74 Editor: He asked after the revelation of the verse whether Allah has imposed the obligation of *ḥajj* for the people, as will be coming up in volume four by the Author.

75 Editor: This sentence is the result of combing two traditions with two different incidents, as is understood from the Arabic syntax, and as is known from the examination of the chapter on the *ḥajj* of the Prophet (pbuh) in Muslim and in the chapter on the obligation of *ḥajj* a single time. The source for this is that when *ḥajj* was made obligatory, a man said, "Is this for every year, O Messenger of Allah?" The Prophet remained silent till the man had repeated his question three times. He then said, "Let me be as long as I do not engage you in a discussion. Those before you were destroyed because of excessive enquiries from the prophets." The person asking the question here was al-Aqraʿ ibn Ḥābis. As for the second tradition, it is about the *ḥajj* of the Prophet (pbuh). Sarāqa ibn Mālik said, "Is this *ḥajj* of ours for this year or for all times or for ever?" The Prophet (pbuh) said, "In fact it is for ever."

76 Editor: He asked this question after having gained knowledge according to his needs. The reason is that the apparent meaning of the verse is absolute, which is that their *ḥajj* does not become obligatory except once in a lifetime. The verse was sent down in this sense in the meaning that responding to numerous questions is likely to be harmful by increasing an obligation that was not there or through an answer that may be reprehensible for the questioner, even though it was not intended to be so, because the response that creates ease is that *ḥajj* is obligatory once only.

77 Editor: "Allah has deemed idle gossip, the wastage of wealth and excessive questions reprehensible for you." It is related by al-Bukhārī, and this version is from him – as well as by Muslim and Abū Dāwūd – from al-Mughīra, Abū Yaʿlā and Ibn Ḥibbān, in his *Ṣaḥīḥ* as a tradition by Abū Hurayra.

78 Editor: It is part of a lengthy tradition reported by al-Bukhārī, and is recorded *al-Taysīr* from the five Shaykhs, except al-Bukhārī, in a form that is lengthier. All agree upon the segment reproduced here.

79 Editor: For otherwise he would have informed the Prophet (pbuh) of it. If this did not concern him, who was the object of knowledge and divine information, then what can be said of others.

80 Editor: As is pointed out by a tradition of al-Tirmidhī without elaboration, "There will be turmoil close to the Day of Judgement ..." till it reaches the words that nations will sell their religion in return for this world.

81 Editor: Recorded in *al-Taysīr* from the two Shaykhs as well as from Abū Dāwūd.

82 Qurʾān 80:31.

83 Editor: That is, he turned their attention to the fact that there is something unknown so as to build upon it an academic benefit.

84 Qurʾān 17:85.

85 Qurʾān 39:23.

86 Editor: In the ninth issue in *Kitāb al-Ijtihād* his name is stated as Ṣabīgh. He said that he beat him and drove him away as he used to ask many questions about Qurʾānic knowledge that was not directly related to action.

87 Qurʾān 51:1–2.

88 Editor: This is explained clearly in the seventh issue in the third section of *Kitāb al-Ijtihād*.

89 Editor: The illustration is their disagreement about the salvation of the parents of the Prophet (pbuh). As the people disputed this it led to discord.

90 Qurʾān 50:6.

91 Qurʾān 7:185.

92 Qurʾān 80:31.

93 Editor: It is reported by al-Nasāʾī as well as Muslim giving precedence to writing over rationalising.

94 Qurʾān 20:68.

95 Qurʾān 20:69.

96 Editor: That is, this is identification for Moses that this is magic and the one practising it will not thrive. It occurs after denial and the lack of identification by Moses (peace be upon him).

97 Qur'ān 38:29.
98 Qur'ān 16:47.
99 Qur'ān 77:1, 2.
100 Qur'ān 50:6.
101 Qur'ān 23:113.
102 Qur'ān 13:17.
103 Qur'ān 55:5.
104 Qur'ān 6:91.
105 Qur'ān 46:4.
106 Editor: A Prophet used to draw lines in the sand and what conformed with it was deemed so. It is related by Aḥmad, Muslim, Abū Dāwūd and al-Nasā'ī from Mu'āwiya ibn al-Ḥakam. It is said that this Prophet was either Idrīs, Daniel, or Khālid ibn Sanān. Ibn Khaldūn has commented upon this in the *Muqaddima* in a section entitled "Anwā' Madārik al-Ghayb".
107 Editor: That is, all that is recorded in these books is adduced to claim certainty about the fact that the meaning of these verses is as they claim. He means to say that these are artificialities that do not conform with the Arabic language and its usage.
108 Qur'ān 7:185.
109 Editor: When we examine the sound tradition, "Report from me even if it is a single verse, for it is possible that the recipient will understand it better than the transmitter (listener)", along with the knowledge that the Qur'ān is meant for all mankind and that its audience is not the Arabs of the first period exclusively or even the Arabs as a whole including the first period and other periods; rather it includes non-Arabs as well. When we look at it from this aspect it is not necessary that we restrict ourselves to the meaning of the Qur'ān, its secrets and hints as is desired by the Author. How do we reconcile what they invite to and what is established with respect to the fact that it does not exhaust itself after a particular meaning? The best thing to do is to maintain a balance. All meanings that are not supported by the language and that do not fall under the purposes of the legislation may be treated in the way the Author has indicated. As for meanings that the language does not deny and that can be found to conform to the purposes from a particular perspective may, without obstruction, be added to the meanings of the Powerful Book, and among these is what pertains to the examination of the creation of Allah, through pondering and reflection, and which strengthens faith and increases understanding and comprehension.
110 Editor: He will dispute the fact that it really amounts to investigation due to its inability to reach the underlying reality of things. It is for this reason that he says, "even though".
111 Editor: Reported by Muslim and al-Tirmidhī.
112 Editor: If the existence of what he deems a specific attribute is known outside its nature, it is not specific, and if it is known outside it, it is concealed. If we define it with an attribute that it not specific to it, it will not amount to its definition. If, however, we define it with something that is specific to it, the statement will apply to it and it will be like the particular that is the object of the statement, thus being linked. It is, therefore, necessary to have recourse to a specific attribute apparent to the senses and so on. This is rarely achieved, and many of the definitions of entities are not perfect.
113 Qur'ān 16:17.
114 Qur'ān 36:79.
115 Qur'ān 30:40.
116 Qur'ān 21:22.
117 Qur'ān 56:5.
118 Editor: Like syllogisms in logic.
119 Editor: That is, it may have conformed with the organisation of syllogistic reasoning without their having intended to follow the logicians in the organisation of their arguments; rather it was based on their intention to attain their objective. The form, therefore, conformed with

organisation as will be coming up in the case of the tradition, "Each intoxicant is *khamr* and each *khamr* is prohibited." This, however, is rare, as will be expounded in the last issue in the book.

120 Editor: That is, the meaning is required in the time following the address without delay, which depends upon logical reasoning and analytical consistency that in themselves require a lengthy thought process. This is not something that yields satisfaction in view of the numerous legal meanings required daily.

121 Editor: That is, a form other than that required by the necessities and associated attributes.

122 Editor: Like purely theoretical sciences. As for the applied sciences, like engineering, chemistry, medicine, electronics and others, they are not included in his statement and it is not proper that he intends them for these are sciences upon which the preservation of the purposes of the law depends including the necessities, needs, and so on. Further, the securing of interests includes them, and they are a means of worship as well, because worship is the act of the subject in the affairs of this world as well as the Hereafter in a form that secures the interests of the worshippers and in a manner laid down by their Lord and not their own whims, as will be discussed by the Author.

123 Editor: Not valid. How many *sharʿī* disciplines are there that were not pursued by the ancestors due to the lack of need for them. The closest example for us is the discipline of *ʿuṣūl*, which was not initiated during the period of the Companions and their Followers.

124 Qurʾān 4:1.

125 Qurʾān 11:1, 2.

126 Qurʾān 14:1.

127 Qurʾān 2:2.

128 Qurʾān 6:1.

129 Qurʾān 5:92.

130 Qurʾān 18:2.

131 Qurʾān 21:25.

132 Qurʾān 39:2.

133 Qurʾān 47:19.

134 Qurʾān 11:14.

135 Qurʾān 40:65.

136 Qurʾān 25:28.

137 Qurʾān 12:68.

138 Qurʾān 39:9.

139 Qurʾān 2:44.

140 Qurʾān 26:94.

141 Editor: In al-Bukhārī and Muslim, it is related from Abū Wāʾil from Usāma in a different form. Please refer to volume 4 of *al-Taysīr* in Bāb al-Riyāʾ.

142 Editor: It is mentioned in *Kitāb Rāmūz al-Ḥadīth* by Shaykh Aḥmad Ḍiyāʾ al-Dīn from al-Daylamī from Abū Hurayra, except that a different word is used for "grindstones" and the word "evil-doers" is not mentioned with scholars. In al-Bukhārī the meaning of the tradition is recorded.

143 Editor: It is recorded in *al-Taysīr* from al-Tirmidhī with the following words: "The feet of a person will remain planted in their place on the Day of Judgement until he has been asked about four things." In al-Tirmidhī, however, there are two narrations, one of which mentions five, but he has declared it weak. In one, the words are "what he has done with respect to his knowledge" and in the second, "about his knowledge and what he turned of it into action". About the second he says that it is a sound tradition. It is stated in *al-Targhīb wa-al-Tarhīb*, after transmitting the tradition from al-Tirmidhī that it is related by al-Bayhaqī and others and that it is a tradition from Muʿādh ibn Jabal: "The feet of a person will remain planted in their place on the Day of Judgement until he has been asked about four things."

144 Editor: Related by Aḥmad, Muslim and al-Nasāʾī, while it has been recorded completely in *al-Maṣābīḥ* among the sound traditions. It is related in *al-Taysīr* in a different version. It says therein: "O Abū Hurayra, the first three are the first creation of Allah over whom the fire will rage on the Day of Judgement."

145 Editor: It is reported by al-Tabarānī in *al-Aṣghar* and by Ibn ʿAdī in *al-Kāmil* as well as by al-Bayhaqī in *Shaʿb al-Īmān* with the words: The persons receiving the greatest torment. Al-Manāwī says: al-Tirmidhī and others have declared it as weak. Al-ʿIrāqī says in his documentation of the traditions of *al-Iḥyāʾ* that it is reported from Abū Hurayra through a weak chain.

146 Editor: From Zayd ibn al-Arqam, God be pleased with him, that the Messenger of Allah (pbuh) used to say, "O Lord, I seek refuge with you from knowledge that does not benefit, from a heart that is not afraid, from a self that does not desire, and from a call that is not answered." It is recorded in *al-Targhīb wa-al-Tarhīb* from Muslim, al-Tirmidhī and al-Nasāʾī and it is a segment of a lengthy tradition.

147 Editor: There are two versions that are different from this in part. The first is from Ibn ʿAdī and al-Khatīb with a weak chain reporting from Abū al-Dardāʾ, while the second is from Abū al-Ḥasan al-Arkham in *Amāliya* from Anas (ʿAzīzī).

148 Qurʾān 27:14.

149 Qurʾān 2:146.

150 Qurʾān 6:20.

151 Qurʾān 25:74.

152 Qurʾān 26:84.

153 Editor: It is reported by Ibn Māja and Ibn Ḥibbān in his *Ṣaḥīḥ*, while al-Bayhaqī has reported it from Jābir with the words: "Do not compete through it in gatherings." Ibn Māja has also recorded it in a similar version as a tradition of Ḥudhayfa (*Targhīb*).

154 Editor: It is reported in *al-Targhīb wa-al-Tarhīb* with a slight variation in words from Abū Dāwūd, Ibn Māja, Ibn Ḥibbān in his *Ṣaḥīḥ*, as well as al-Ḥākim. He said that it is a sound tradition meeting the conditions laid down by al-Bukhārī and Muslim.

155 Editor: It is related in *al-Jāmiʿ al-Ṣaghīr* from al-Daylamī in *Musnad al-Firdaws* from Abū Hurayra with the words, "Avoid the concealed desire of the scholar who loves people gathering around him for learning." Al-ʿAzīzī has said that it is *ḍaʿīf*, while al-Manāwī quotes Ibn Ḥajar as saying: "In it is Ibrāhīm ibn Muḥammad al-Aslamī, who is *matrūk*."

156 Qurʾān 2:174.

157 Editor: The first three are the first creation of Allah over whom the fire will rage on the Day of Judgement.

158 Qurʾān 39:9.

159 Qurʾān 39:9.

160 Qurʾān 39:23.

161 Qurʾān 35:28.

162 Qurʾān 5:83.

163 Qurʾān 29:43.

164 Qurʾān 13:19.

165 Qurʾān 13:20.

166 Qurʾān 8:2–4.

167 Qurʾān 3:18.

168 Editor: He uses the word testimony in its apparent meaning. The commentators say that it means the adducing of evidence (*adilla*), and the adducing of evidence from the cosmos for this. Thus, testimony is used in the sense of what it indicates: "Soon will We show them Our Signs in the (furthest) regions (of the earth), and in their own souls, until it becomes manifest to them that this is the Truth" (Qurʾān 41:53).

169 Qurʾān 2:184.

170 Qurʾān 6:82.
171 Editor: The reason is that when their knowledge, by compulsion and coercion, led them to its purposes, and they were afraid that they might do something that would not be in accordance with these purposes, because it was beyond human ability, they would then not be safe from the anger of Allah, as is found in the second verse, and their reckoning would be on this basis, as is stated in the first verse. It is for this reason that they were perturbed till something removed this state from them.
172 Qurʾān 27:14.
173 Qurʾān 2:146.
174 Qurʾān 5:43.
175 Qurʾān 2:102.
176 Editor: This tradition has preceded with a very slight difference in words.
177 Qurʾān 2:44.
178 Qurʾān 2:159.
179 Qurʾān 2:174.
180 Qurʾān 27:14.
181 Qurʾān 2:109.
182 Qurʾān 4:17.
183 Qurʾān 7:200–201.
184 Editor: As if he is falling in some ditch that he cannot see, or an animal harms him when he could not hear its movement or voice so as to avoid it. All this is something that comes over him against his nature and so also the negligence of the scholar.
185 Qurʾān 28:50.
186 Editor: Reported by the two Shaykhs (al-Bukhārī and Muslim) as well as al-Tirmidhī.
187 Editor: The Author will say about this in the ninth issue in the Book of *Ijtihād* that it has been mentioned by Ibn ʿAbd al-Barr with an unsatisfactory chain. The version there differs slightly from this version.
188 Editor: It is mentioned in *Kitāb Rāmūz al-Ḥadīth* by Shaykh Aḥmad Ḍiyāʾ al-Dīn, as will be coming up: Each thing has a rise and fall. The rise of this *dīn* is that an entire tribe will have an understanding of the *dīn*, so much so that even one or two ignorant persons will not be found, and the fall of this *dīn* will be when all the people of the tribe will be ignorant and only one or two individuals will be found who have knowledge, and even these two will be despised and humiliated not finding any one to assist them or support them. It is related by Abū Naʿīm from Abū Amāma.
189 Editor: It is recorded by al-Tabarānī in *al-Awsat* and by al-Ḥākim from Abū Hurayra.
190 Editor: Perhaps, the word is *yurʿā* here and also the next.
191 Qurʾān 6:91.
192 Editor: This is the same statement as that of al-Ḥasan above.
193 Editor: It is related in *al-Taysīr* from al-Tirmidhī as a lengthy tradition and it says: The first knowledge to be lifted will be the fear of God.
194 Qurʾān 15:9.
195 Editor: Its principles and substantive issues.
196 Editor: The generality of the proscription about *gharar* (uncertainty), the absence of liability of one person for the act of another, the vitiation of the transactions based upon lack of knowledge about the price or wages for example, include all these issues through their apparent meaning; however, when there are in fact rational causes the rule is associated with the general meanings stated. Their rules have been adopted against the rule conveyed by the apparent meaning. They applied them in the meaning of exemptions and said that these are specific issues. In reality these are also general principles that have arisen from the three basic purposes of the law.
197 Editor: Note its position in the syntax in this context, although they said: It is merely a matter of ritual obedience.

198 Editor: That is, circle around it.

199 Editor: Thus, it belongs to the category from which two characteristics are missing and it is based on the probable.

200 Editor: Like the prohibition of taking up the drawing of pictures. It is said that the underlying cause is the fear that it will lead to their admiration and then worship for the sake of attaining nearness through idol worship. When such a danger does not exist now, there should be nothing to prevent doing this. This amounts to the derivation of the underlying cause through conjecture and the pursuit of whim.

201 Editor: Related by Aḥmad, Abū Dāwūd, al-Tirmidhī, who said it is *ḥasan ṣaḥīḥ*. In one version the word Allah is used in place of al-Raḥmān.

202 Editor: Two characteristics are missing from it as in the preceding example.

203 Editor: This is something from which the benefit is missing on the basis of accompanying practice. The reason is that as long as it refers to the excessive number of narrators in some grades and does not refer to all the grades, so that strength is created in the tradition, there will be no benefit in it nor can it be used for preferring one tradition over another.

204 Qurʾān 102:1, 2.

205 Editor: That is, such reasoning has not been deemed by the *sharīʿa* to be an evidence for legal rules even though it is used for enlightening the believers.

206 Editor: This belongs to the category of the probable that is not continuous and no practice is based upon it.

207 Editor: For it is not definitive nor usually based on the definitive, nor is it continuous in general.

208 Editor: Continuity is missing from them, and adopting their views and statements for continuity and in the absolute sense gives rise to harm or the obligation to do the impossible. Thus, discussion about their statements belongs to ancillary knowledge.

209 Qurʾān 20:63.

210 Qurʾān 2:284.

211 Qurʾān 6:102.

212 Qurʾān 39:62.

213 Editor: Each one of them is a process, and where a deficiency is permissible an excess is possible too. This is how this reasoning is understood in general so that the later evidence may have a new benefit, and that is that they share a desired common specific meaning on the basis of the problem in his statement, "As this deficiency is not treated as nullification of the limit, the other should not be treated as nullification either", unless the *waw* and *li-anna* are an excess in the text. Thereafter, the examination of the issue remains that the basis of the claim is the crossing of the limits of the *sharʿ* and its nullification through reason, whether this is through deficiency or excess. Consequently, the meaning may be that he deems the same reduction that is required by the generality to be a transgression, and objecting through it he says that what you have treated as rule here goes against another rule and that is restriction through reason, as that too is a deficiency. Thereafter, he builds, upon restriction through reason and its being a deficiency that has been limited by the law, the problem of excess according to the method he has determined, just as he saw a problem through excess and reduction in the third problem. He makes an effort to respond to the second problem from the perspective of deficiency and negates it, and then says that it is not proper to construct analogy for transgression from this, and that implies that he has taken the objection of deficiency to be included in his statement, "amounts to a deficiency" – that is, this is a problem and he then treats it as an introduction and says that excess is permissible.

214 Editor: Ponder over this to grasp the basis of the first problem, because that is wider than the denial of analogy and that requires a clear response, that is, reason is subservient to the evidences and serves them, and this is what we claim.

215 Qurʾān 6:102.

216 Editor: Induction through the *sharīʿa* indicates that there is no clash between reason and the core issues, and considering it impossible becomes permissible or obligatory. It is on this basis that reason undertakes its activity of restriction under the supervision of transmission. As for pure rational analogy acting upon the evidences without this qualification, it amounts to the acceptance of the problem and the reduction of the principle in the issue. Ponder over it.

217 Editor: The elaboration of verification will be coming up in what follows.

218 Editor: This has preceded in the eighth concept.

219 Editor: He has mentioned three forms: The first is a substantive issue based upon another substantive issue, which in turn is based upon a source text. What is understood is that each one of the substantive issues has a specific source text. This leads to confusion with derivation being neglected and judgement is suspended. At other times the person is not rightly guided to the source text to which recourse can be had for some substantive issues; judgement is suspended and derivation given up. Again, the substantive issue may vacillate between two source texts and the scholar is not able to determine the preferred source, and he in fact adopts the other source text thereby leading to suspension of judgement. Illustrations for all three are not concealed from you and in all cases the fact that he is a leading scholar is not affected. Mālik suspended judgement in many cases and retracted from many views that had been preferred by him earlier due to the preceding reasons.

220 Editor: Because one of them is the basis for verification of knowledge, and this is the second, while others are consequential to it, which is the first. These traits conform to the conditions that have preceded with respect to the attainment of each, even if there is a difference in the order of consideration.

221 Editor: Perhaps, the word *fahum* is an excess or corruption of another word *minhu*. From this it is determined that the testimony in the story of ʿUmar replies upon all the other preliminaries. Among these preliminaries is his statement, "Sahl ibn Ḥunayf said" and his statement "Submission to scholars and exhibiting patience with them on occasions of ambiguity", along with his statement "Yet, they submitted and gave up their views till such time that the Qurʾān was revealed. Their confusion and perplexity was removed." Accordingly, the whole narrative becomes organised with one part removing the veil from the other. The matter was not confusing for Abū Bakr, but it was for ʿUmar; however, he showed patience till the evidence became manifest.

222 Editor: Included in a lengthy tradition mentioned in *al-Taysīr* from al-Bukhārī and Abū Dāwūd.

223 Editor: It is recorded by al-Bukhārī, "O people, take your views with caution …," and the Author will mention it in the third issue pertaining to the rules of questions and answers in the fourth volume. It is different from his narration here and also from the report of al-Bukhārī as well.

224 Editor: It is narrower than the first sign, because emulation of those from whom he has acquired knowledge and adoption of their method is part of the work with respect to knowledge. The Author's attributing Mālik with the trait as distinguished from his contemporary *mujtahids* with respect to this trait leads to the conclusion that acting upon what he has come to know does not necessarily imply that he is following the person from whom he acquired knowledge. In fact, his action is based upon what comes to be persuasive according to his own *ijtihād* even if it is not his intention to highlight some of the methods of his teacher. This can become an independent sign.

225 Editor: Recorded by al-Bukhārī and al-Tirmidhī.

226 Editor: He used to disapprove of writing and asked them not to write the opinions he was handing down to them. Perhaps, this was because his opinion would change and the writing would have spread to various regions prior to the attainment of stability in the *ḥukm*. This could cause problems for the people, for otherwise he had himself written *al-Muwaṭṭaʾ*.

227 Editor: It is recorded in *al-Taysīr* from all five Shaykhs.

228 Editor: The Author states in his book *al-Iʿtiṣām* (vol. 2, 25) as follows: "A tradition has been related for deeming unlawful sexual intercourse permissible and it is related by Ibrāhīm al-Ḥarbī from Aū Thaʿlaba from the Prophet (pbuh), who said, 'The first phase of your religion is prophethood and mercy, followed by kingdom and tyranny, followed by cruel domination in which every good and bad thing will be deemed permissible.'" He does not mention anything about the soundness of the tradition.

229 Editor: Recorded by al-Bukhārī in *Kitāb al-Iʿtiṣām bi-al-Kitāb wa-al-Sunna*.

230 Editor: Recorded by Muslim.

231 Editor: Related by al-Tabarānī and Abū Naṣr in *al-Ibāna* from Jābir ibn Sanh. On the margin of *al-Iʿtiṣām* it says: Related by al-Tabarānī with the words, "Those who set matters right when people fall into corruption." This is mentioned in *Majmaʿ al-Zawāʾid*.

232 Qurʾān 110:1.

233 Qurʾān 5:3.

234 Editor: It is recorded by Ibn Abī Shayba from ʿAntara – taken from al-Alūsi (vol. 2, 248).

235 Editor: This is linked to statements. The first means that a statement in itself, ignoring other statements that precede it or follow it, can convey different meanings varying from the sound to others. As for understanding pertaining the modes of address, it is to be examined whether it has been understood in a sound way that is required by the entire syntax without contradicting those preceding it and those following.

236 Qurʾān 4:141.

237 Editor: Some learned people have written while commenting on this topic that it is permissible to consider the verse in its apparent meaning or as a report. The meaning would then be that among the believers is a group of those who do what is required by deep faith with respect to ability, unity and strength. They said that history is witness to the fact that Muslims will not be dominated as long as they exhibit these qualities. However, this implies things that may not be conceded. Among these is that such people have been granted what even the Prophet (pbuh) and his Companions were not granted during his lifetime. You know what happened to them while they were at Mecca as individuals among the people of Abū Tālib with respect to their humiliation and migration to Abyssinia and other places. Among these is also the fact that in the history of the Crusades, which took place during the zenith of Islam that lasted for centuries, the pendulum swung sometimes towards the Muslims and sometimes towards the enemy who took their lands and dominated the Bayt al-Maqdas with the shrinking of the state, taken along with the verse, "Allah has promised, to those among you who believe and work righteous deeds, that He will, of a surety, grant them in the land inheritance (of power), as He granted it to those before them; that He will establish in authority their religion – the one which He has chosen for them" [Qurʾān 24:55]. This does not indicate the meaning that the intended interpretation says. What is in this last verse was given to the Prophet (pbuh) and his Companions during his lifetime and after his death and to Muslims after them. The reason is that establishing the authority of religion and the changing of fear to security is not what is implied by the intended meaning of the first verse. You can see that the verse of promise has qualified faith with the doing of good deeds, as against the verse mentioned, for there is only the condition of belief in the face of unbelief differing from the verse of promise in the Qurʾān. It bears the qualification of good deeds. It is known that mere belief is sufficient for the implementation of the *ḥukm* implying that the unbeliever will not gain authority over the affairs of Muslims with respect to contracts and other things. It is, therefore, necessary to say that the verse has been revealed for this.

238 Qurʾān 2:233.

239 Editor: He did not say continued, because continuity is available through both interpretations. His purpose is to show that according to the second interpretation there is no additional benefit, as it is merely a report about the customary practice of the people that exists even

without the verse. For being a benefit it is necessary that it give rise to a *ḥukm* confirming that the customary practice is a *ḥukm sharʿī*, to which recourse is to be had for determining maintenance and other things. However, the discussion of the issue of using it as an example remains as he has mentioned. Through an illustration it may be required that there is deviation from a report of Allah and His Messenger, or an obligation to do the impossible is created, or in it there is a burden that is greater than the usual. Not one of these three is to be found in this report; rather there is another thing and that is that it has not given an additional benefit. If there had been something in excess of the three things the report about Allah and His Messenger would have yielded a new benefit that was not known prior to this. If this report had sprung from such new benefit it would be meaningful.

240 Qurʾān 5:93.

241 Editor: The reason is that the preceding verse of the prohibition of wine (*khamr*) requires on the very same topic the prohibition of wine through the text, and the apparent meaning here negates this implication. Accordingly, the syntax cannot be applied, in the absence of the inclusion of *khamr*, in the general meaning, because the invalidity of the prohibition becomes binding. In the alternative, it becomes an obligation to the impossible, besides invoking negligence with respect to a cause stated in the revelation. This is explained through what they said when the prohibition of wine was revealed: "What about our companions who died and they used to drink." It was then that the verse was revealed, "On those who believe and do deeds of righteousness there lies no blame for what they ate (in the past) ..." that is, there is no burden on them for they believed, feared God, did not transgress and did not drink after the prohibition. Beyond this, there is also a clash of the text with the apparent meaning and it is known that the text has precedence. As an illustration of the fact that there should be no invalidity of the mode of address, this verse is sufficient, even when there are other factors, as has been indicated by his words "by negating the cause", and subsequent statements, and that Allah knows best, and also as we have indicated that the text has precedence over the apparent meaning and restricts it.

242 Qurʾān 5:93.

243 Editor: That is, among these is the drinking of wine for which the valid mode of address required the prohibition of wine. As long as this was included in the circumstances upon which ʿUmar was basing his view, that fear of God cannot come except by avoiding it, the prohibition was valid and it was not included in this apparent meaning. The Author uses the words "It is here" for he is not so certain as to be able to say "Therefore ʿUmar said." Ponder over this.

244 Editor: That is, by way of perfection, as his text conveys.

245 Qurʾān 5:93.

246 Editor: This amounts to extreme hardship for individuals, and the combined obligation amounts to an obligation to do the impossible. It also goes against the purposes of the law with respect to the preservation of necessities and needs and so on, as it is applied in an unsound manner.

247 Editor: The word *jumhūr* of things means most of them, and that is a claim that needs the enumeration of the issues of the *sharīʿa* case by case. Reliance upon the occurrence of disagreement among the *mujtahids* in most cases in their *ijtihād* is conceded for them, and their disagreement has been transmitted to us through a sound channel. Further, this disagreement is enumerated as he says. He will mention in the *Kitāb al-Ijtihād* that there are ten basic reasons that give rise to disagreements that are not to be taken as disagreement. Thereafter, piety after all this is in insisting upon an element or condition that has not been asserted by another, or prohibition of a thing that no one else has prohibited, or making a thing obligatory whose obligation no one else has upheld. As for the disagreements about the permissible and recommended, the *sunna* and the permissible, the requirement of precedence of a thing and its relegation, as well as other examples like them, they do not lead to

prohibition or the nullification of a worship. Thus, these are not among those that are intended to be included in piety to avoid disagreement. Now, therefore, does the fact remain that piety in all this is an extreme form of hardship? This is what requires a penetrating examination.

248 Editor: The elaboration will be coming up in the additional sections pertaining to the *mutashābih* and *muḥkam*.

249 Editor: The words to complete it are: "and the Fire becomes justified through lust." It is recorded by Muslim, al-Tirmidhī, by Aḥmad from Anas, Muslim from Abū Hurayra, and Aḥmad from Ibn Masʿūd. Al-ʿAzīzī said that it has been related by al-Bukhārī as well. In a narration from the two Shaykhs (al-Bukhārī and Muslim) the word "veiled" is used in place of "concealed" on both occasions.

250 Editor: We have recently indicated that he has claimed numerous points of disagreement and he will retract from this in his text, but a few are acknowledged as disagreements.

251 Editor: He refutes with this what can be assumed through his statement, "And it is not known if the evidences are equal." It is sometimes said that knowing the equality or similarity depends upon the *mujtahid*. Here he says that, "It is not possible for him to have recourse to the *mujtahid*."

252 Editor: Because it applies to the *mujtahid* and not to the layman, and applying it to the layman, which is the crux of the question, entails hardship.

253 Editor: A conflict of evidences for the *mujtahid* does not create a conflict for the layman. When views conflict for him, he is under an obligation to have recourse to one of the views, but he takes into account for preference apparent facts that leave no doubt like adopting an opinion of one about whom he knows that his views are followed.

Part I
The Book of *Aḥkām* (Legal Rules)

In the name of God, Most Beneficent, Most Merciful. God's peace and blessings upon our Master, Muḥammad, and peace on his family and Companions.

The aḥkām *(rules) of the sharīʿa are of two types: the first type is based on the communication* (khiṭāb) *of obligation* (taklīf), *while the second is based on the declaratory communication.*

1

The First Category of Rules

The first category of rules is restricted to five types. We shall discuss here the issues that pertain to these. The issues are several.

The first issue: the *mubāḥ* requires neither commission nor omission of an act

The *mubāḥ* (permissible) category of rules[1] insofar as they are permissible does not require the commission of an act nor does it require the avoidance (omission) of an act. Such rules do not require the avoidance of acts due to several factors:

First: The permissible category, according to the Lawgiver, grants an option between the commission and omission of an act without associating approval or blame with it, neither on the commission of an act nor on its omission. When a legal equality and option is realised, it cannot be conceived that one omitting the act can be considered as being obedient, because no demand is associated with the omission. Obedience does not take place without the existence of a demand. As there is no demand, there is no obedience.

Second: The *mubāḥ* (permissible) category is equal in strength to the *wājib* (obligatory) *mandūb* (recommended) categories insofar as none of these entails a demand for omission. Thus, as it is impossible for one omitting the obligatory or the recommended to be legally called obedient by omission, because the Lawgiver has not demanded an omission in them, it is likewise impossible for one omitting the permissible to be legally called obedient.

It is not to be said: The obligatory and the recommended differ from the permissible as they require the commission of an act. An obstacle has been established in them for the demand of omission, and the permissible is not like this, because there is no obstacle in the way of the permissible. For we would say: The permissible is just like that, and there is an obstacle in its way for the demand of omission, and that is the option granted for the omission. Thus, it is impossible to reconcile the demand for omission and the option in the same thing.

Third: When equality between commission and omission is established legally in the case of the *mubāḥ*, if it is permitted that a person omitting the *mubāḥ* is obedient by the act of omission, it would be possible for the person committing the act to be obedient by its commission. This is true insofar as these acts carry equal weight with reference to it, and that is not correct by agreement (of the scholars) nor is it comprehensible in itself.[2]

Fourth: There exists a consensus (*ijmāʿ*) of the Muslims on the point that a person who makes a vow to give up a permissible act is not bound to abide by his vow of giving up such permissible act. This is similar to a vow for committing the act. A tradition[3] says: "A person who makes a vow to be obedient to God must be obedient to Him."[4] If the omission of a permissible act had amounted to obedience, it would have become binding by virtue of the vow, but it is not binding. This text indicates that it does not amount to obedience. A tradition says, "A person made a vow that he would fast while standing erect and would not seek the shade. The Messenger of Allah (pbuh) ordered him to sit down and to do so in the shade completing his fast."[5] Mālik says, "The Prophet (pbuh) ordered him to complete what amounts to obedience to Allah, and to give up what amounts to disobedience."[6] As you can see, he (Mālik) deemed a vow for giving up a permissible act to be disobedience.

Fifth: If the person omitting a permissible act were deemed obedient by virtue of the omission – and we have assumed[7] that its omission and commission are the same for the Lawgiver – he would have a higher status with reference to the Hereafter as compared to the person who commits the act. This is certainly null and void. The agreed principle[8] is that grades in the Hereafter are based upon the affairs of this world. As equality is established with respect to grades, and as the commission and omission of a permissible act are equal in the sight of the Lawgiver, the equality in the grades of the person committing the act and one omitting it becomes necessary. If we assume their equality in terms of obedience, and the assumption[9] is that the person relinquishing the act is obedient and not the one who commits the act, it is then binding that the former has a higher grade than the latter. This is a deviation and in opposition to what the *sharīʿa* has laid down, unless the person is unjust[10] and is then given a recompense for it. If he is not obedient,[11] then there is no discussion on the point.

Sixth: If the omission of a permissible act amounted to obedience, it would become necessary to remove the *mubāḥ* (permissible) category from the *aḥkām* of the *sharīʿa* insofar as its own category is kept in view. This is invalid according to consensus (*ijmāʿ*). This notion is not opposed by al-Kaʿbī[12] for he negated it in view of what he considered to be a binding category and not by focusing on the act itself. Our discussion, on the other hand, is about the essence of the act itself, not with reference to it as a binding category.

Further, al-Kaʿbī has said what he said by focusing on the commission of the permissible act, for it requires the giving up of a prohibited act as against focusing on its omission, for its omission does not lead to the commission of an obligatory act so that it may be called obligatory nor the commission of a recommended act so that it may be called a recommended act. Thus, it is established that holding such a view leads to the absolute removal of the *mubāḥ* category. This is void by agreement.

Seventh: According to the Muḥaqqiqīn, the omission of an act is also an act that is subject to the exercise of choice. Thus, the omission of a permissible act amounts to commission of a permissible act.[13] Further, the principle is that the *aḥkām* (rules) are associated with omissions and commissions with reference to the *maqāṣid* (purposes), as will be coming up, God willing. This makes it necessary to base the omission on the exercise of the choice as is the case with the commission. Thus, if it is permitted that the person omitting the permissible act be deemed obedient through the omission itself, it is permissible that the person committing the act be deemed obedient. This is defective[14] and impossible.

If it is said: All this is contradictory due to several reasons:

The first of these reasons is that the commission of a permissible act is a cause of many injuries.

Among them is occupation with it to the neglect of what is important in this world including the performance of supererogatory commendable acts, and it amounts to a shutting out of a number of acts of obedience.

Among them is the fact that occupation with it amounts to the neglect of obligatory acts and it becomes a means to the performance of prohibited acts. The reason is that the enjoyment of this world leads to temptations, like the temptation of consuming *khamr*, and some of these acts lead to others that make the actor sink into perilous situations. We seek the protection of Allah from this.

Among them is the fact that the *sharīʿa* has condemned this world and the enjoyment of its pleasures, as in the words of the Exalted, "And on the day that the unbelievers will be placed before the Fire (it will be said of them): Ye received your good things in the life of the world, and ye took your pleasure out of them: but today shall ye be recompensed with a penalty of humiliation: for that ye were arrogant on earth without just cause, and that ye (ever) transgressed",[15] and His words, "Those who desire the life of the present and its glitter, to them we shall pay (the price of) their deeds therein, without diminution."[16] A tradition says, "My worst fear for you is that the world will be laid wide open for you like it was for those before you." It has the words, "What spring causes to grow may sometimes kill the bloated animal or cause it to suffer."[17] Such meanings are numerous and well known in both the Book and the *Sunna*, and they are sufficient for demanding the omission of the permissible act, because it is a worldly act and is not related to the Hereafter insofar as it is permissible.

Among them is the problem of the length of the reckoning in the Hereafter. It has been reported that the permissible is subjected to reckoning, while the prohibited leads to torment.[18] Someone said, "Remove from me its reckoning", that is, when he was brought something for consumption. The intelligent person knows that lengthy reckoning is a kind of torment, and that speedy departure from this station to the heavens is the greatest aim. The *mubāḥ* (permissible) stands in the way of this. Thus, its giving up is legally preferable. As this amounts to obedience, the omission of the permissible amounts to obedience.

The response is that its becoming a cause for injury has no evidence (*dalīl*) due to several reasons.

First: The discussion is about the essential issue and that is that the permissible act insofar as it is permissible has two equally balanced sides (options). There is no discussion about its being a means to other things. If it is a means to a prohibited act, it comes to be prohibited and belongs to the category of *sadd al-dharāʾiʿ* (blocking of the lawful means to an unlawful end), and not because it belongs to the permissible category. It is in this sense that the statement is to be interpreted of those who said, "We used to give up that in which there was no harm as a precaution against that in which there was harm."[19] It has also been reported as a *marfūʿ* tradition. The same is to be said of all other texts in the same meaning. The blame associated with this world is for the reason that it becomes a means for the suspension of obligations. Further,[20] certain factors may be associated with the preliminaries, dependencies and circumstances of the permissible act that convert it to other than a permissible act. For example, wealth on which *zakāt* has not been paid or horses[21] that have been tied up out of abstinence, but in which the right of God has been forgotten, as well as things similar to this.

Second: When we examine it for being a means to other things we find that giving up such an act may not be the best thing to do in the absolute sense. In fact, it is of three types. One type is a means to something that is prohibited, and by virtue of this it is required to be omitted. Another type is a means to something that has been ordered, and becomes an aid for a matter that pertains to the Hereafter. It is stated in a tradition, "How good is clean wealth for a righteous person."[22] It is further stated, "Earlier people have received rewards, high stations and lasting blessings" – till he said – "This is a blessing from Allah that He grants to whom He likes."[23] In fact, it has been stated that there is a reward for having sexual intercourse with one's wife, even though it serves lust, but it prevents falling into sin. There are many such cases in the *sharīʿa*, and as they are a means to something ordered it is as if they have a *ḥukm* that urges their commission. A third type is of those acts that are not a means to anything. This is the absolute *mubāḥ* (permissible act). On the whole, if it is assumed to be a means to something else, it acquires the rule (*ḥukm*) of that other thing. The discussion, however, is not about such acts.

Third: If it is said that "the giving up of the permissible act is obedience in the absolute sense due to the fact that it is a means to what stands prohibited", it will be countered with a statement similar to it. Thus, it will be said, "In fact, commission of the permissible is absolute obedience, because each permissible act amounts to the avoidance of the prohibited."[24] You can see that when a permissible act is permitted it amounts to the omission of all prohibited acts during the moment of commission of the permissible act; the person is involved with it away from all such (prohibited) things. The second statement is better,[25] because the universal principle appears sound in this case. It is not valid to say that each permissible act is a means towards a prohibited or a proscribed act in the absolute sense; therefore, it becomes evident that the objection raised against it does not amount to an evidence that the omission of the *mubāḥ* is obedience.

As to the statement that it is the basis for the lengthening of the reckoning process, the response is from different perspectives.

First: If the person committing the *mubāḥ* is to be held accountable, it becomes necessary that the person omitting the act be held accountable for his omission insofar as an omission is an act too. Legally omission and commission are equal in proportion. If this were not so it would cause a contradiction in the rule that assumes that there is a *mubāḥ* category, and this is not possible. Therefore, the act of commission that led to it (the prolonged reckoning) is like this act of omission. Further, if it is assumed that its permissible part leads to accountability and it is then decided that one omitting it is not held accountable, even though he has also brought about a permissible act, which is omission, the permissible becomes the basis for the lengthening of the process of reckoning and (at the same time) it does not become the basis for reckoning. The reason is that the lengthening of the reckoning is based on the assumption of the commission of the permissible and this amounts to a contradiction in the claim.

Second: If reckoning gives rise to the reason for demanding omission, it is necessary that it demand the giving up of all forms of obedience, because there will be liability for all such things. Allah, the Exalted, has said, "Then shall we question those to whom Our message was sent and those by whom We sent it."[26] Thus, He made it incumbent for the Messengers, peace be upon them, that they be asked about their mission and the propagation of the *sharīʿa*, and doing so would not prevent the reckoning. Likewise, all the subjects (will be questioned). It is not to be said: "Demanding the giving up of matters of obedience clashes with the demand to bring them about." The reason is that we will respond by saying: "So also the *mubāḥ*; the demand for giving it up clashes with the option granted in it, because its commission and omission have the same status with respect to the intention of the Lawgiver."

Third: What has been said about the reckoning on the basis of the consumption (commission?) of the permissible is related to a factor external to the *mubāḥ* itself. Thus, if the *mubāḥ* is the consumption of such and such thing, for example, then it has preliminaries, conditions and associated acts that must be maintained. When these matters are observed, the consumption is permissible, but if the conditions are not observed then bringing about the cause and consumption cannot be deemed permissible. On the whole, the *mubāḥ* – like other acts – has its elements, conditions, obstacles and associated acts that are observed. Omission of an act with respect to all these is like commission. Thus, when the cause is brought about there is liability for the cause. Likewise, if the cause of omission is brought about there is liability for that too.

It is not to be said: "Commission has a large number of conditions and obstacles, and it requires the completion of elements as against omission, for in it the requirements are few. The mere intention of omission is sometimes sufficient."

For we would say: "The reality of the *mubāḥ* arises from the preliminaries (*muqaddimāt*) whether the act is that of commission or omission even when this is through mere resolve." Further, rights are associated with omission just as they are associated with commission, whether these are rights of God or of the individual or of both combined. This is indicated by the words of the Prophet (pbuh), "Your own person has rights against you and your wife (family) has rights against you. Thus, grant the right to the owner of the right to whom it is due."[27] Ponder over this tradition of Salmān and Abū al-Dardāʾ,[28] God be pleased with both, for it will explain to you through its meaning that there is no difference between commission and omission in this context, especially in the case of the *mubāḥ*.

Thus, reckoning is related to the mode of omission just as it is related to the mode of commission. When this is so, it is established that if reckoning is based on the mode of performance of the *mubāḥ*, the acts of commission and omission are equal. If the reckoning is based on the *mubāḥ* itself, or on both act and its performance, commission and omission are again equal. Further, if there is within the *mubāḥ* something that requires omission then there is within it what requires the absence of omission, because it is on the whole what Allah has granted as favours to His subjects. Note the words of the Exalted, "It is He Who has spread out the earth for (His) creatures: Therein are fruit and date palms, producing spathes (enclosing dates); also corn, with (its) leaves and stalk for fodder, and sweet smelling plants. Then which of the favours of your Lord will ye deny? He created man from sounding clay like unto pottery, And He created Jinns from fire free of smoke: Then which of the favours of your Lord will ye deny? (He is) Lord of the two Easts and Lord of the two Wests: Then which of the favours of your Lord will ye deny? He has let free the two bodies of flowing water, meeting together: Between them is a barrier which they do not transgress: Then which of the favours of your Lord will ye deny? Out of them come pearls and coral; Then which of the favours of your Lord will ye deny?",[29] and His words, "It is He Who has made the sea subject, that ye may eat thereof flesh that is fresh and tender, and that ye may extract therefrom ornaments to wear; and thou seest the ships therein that plough the waves, that ye may seek (thus) of the bounty of Allah and that ye may be grateful",[30] as well as the words, "And He has subjected to you, as from Him, all that is in the heavens and on earth: behold, in that are Signs indeed for those who reflect",[31] and many of the verses in which the granting of favours is explicitly stated. Thus, omission is based upon intention about which questions will be raised: Why did you give it up? For what reason did you turn away from it? What prevented you from consuming what was made lawful for you? The questions will be asked for both sides. In what follows, the discussion about the "permissible act serving another purpose/act" will come up, God willing.

The majority of these responses are of the defensive type. The correct position is in the response that in the undertaking of a permissible act it is not proper that the person performing the act be subjected to reckoning in the absolute sense. He will only be held accountable when he falls short in giving thanks for it either by way of consuming it or acquiring it by way of seeking support from it in the performance of duties. Thus, if a person holds himself accountable for this and acts upon what he has been commanded to do, then he has offered thanks for the blessings granted by Allah. It is in this context that the Exalted has said, "Say: Who hath forbidden the beautiful (gifts) of Allah, which He hath produced for His servants, and the things, clean and pure, (which He hath provided) for sustenance? Say they are, in the life of this world, for those who believe, (and) purely for them on the Day of Judgement thus do We explain the Signs in detail for those who understand",[32] that is, there is no accountability here. Allah, the Exalted has said, "Then he who is given his record in his right hand, soon will his account be taken by an easy reckoning."[33] This has been elaborated by the Prophet (pbuh), who said that it is an "observation" and not the reckoning in which there will be a discussion and torment, otherwise the blessings that are permissible would not be exclusively for the believers on the Day of Judgement. It is to this that the words of the Exalted, "Then shall We question those to whom Our message was sent and those by whom We sent it",[34] refer, that is, to the questioning of those who were sent with the message. All this is verified by the undertaking of permissible acts by the worthy ancestors, as will be stated in what follows after this.

The second of these reasons is the turning away from things (*muʿāraḍa*) to the effect that what has preceded goes against the practice of the worthy ancestors from among the Companions and their Followers as well as the pious scholars. Thus, they used to abstain from many permissible things. This is reported about them through continuous reports, like those about abstaining from excess food, drink, ride and residence. The foremost in this were ʿUmar ibn al-Khaṭṭāb, Abū Dharr, Salmān, Abū ʿUbayda ibn al-Jarrāḥ, ʿAlī ibn Abī Ṭālib and ʿAmmār, God be pleased with them all. Examine what has been related by Ibn Ḥabīb in the book of *al-Jihād* as well as by al-Dāwūdī in *Kitāb al-Amwāl*, for in these is an adequate answer. The net result is that they abstained from the *mubāḥ* insofar as it was *mubāḥ*, and had the giving up of *mubāḥ* not amounted to obedience they would not have done it.

The response to this is provided from different perspectives.

First: These are, in the first instance, reports of states/circumstances. Legal reasoning based merely on such states is not appropriate, for it is not necessary that what they abstained from was because the act was *mubāḥ* due to the possibility that this could have been for some reason external to it. The discussion of narrations of states as not being suitable for legal reasoning by themselves will be coming up, God willing.

Second: It amounts to turning away from something that is equal in strength though contrary. Thus, the Prophet (pbuh) used to like sweets and honey. He used to eat meat, and especially liked the meat of the fore-leg. Water was made sweet and pleasant for him and figs and raisins were soaked in it for him. He used to wear musk as perfume and liked the company of women. Further, a number of similar reports exist about the Companions, their Followers and the pious scholars to the effect that abstention was not required in their view. The certain meaning is that had abstention been legally required, in their view, they would have undertaken this just as they undertook all other supererogatory acts and acts of piety, and they would have tried to attain a high station and grade in this too. The reason is that no one among the people has undertaken the performance of supererogatory acts of welfare, and no one has been able to share his own wealth with, or extended help to, his believing brother as they did, either in the period before them or after them. Anyone who has studied their lives knows this. Despite all this, they did not give up the utilisation of permissible things. Had this been legally required, they would have known it with a certainty, and they would have acted according to its requirements without exception, but they did not do this. This indicates that abstention is not required in their view. In fact, some of them tried to give up some of the permissible things, but were forbidden from doing so. The evidences for this concept are many. See the section on the comparison between poverty and wealth[35] in *al-Muqaddimāt* by Ibn Rushd.[36]

Third:[37] When it is established that they gave up some of the acts, seeking a spiritual reward for such abstention, then this is not merely due to the fact that such acts were permissible, and this is on the basis of evidences that have preceded. In fact, they abstained from such acts due to external factors, and this does not refute the fact that there is no demand for abstaining from such acts.

Among these is the factor that they were an obstacle in the way of worship (*ʿibāda*) and a barrier facing good deeds. Such acts were given up for attaining the ability to perform reward-bearing acts and as such would belong to the category of the means to achieve what is required. For example, ʿĀʾisha, God be pleased with her, used to receive huge amounts of wealth that gave her the ability to undertake a number of permissible acts, but she gave it away in charity consuming the least amount that would sustain life. The giving up of such facility (opportunity) does not imply that abstention is required (in such a case). This is the subject of controversy.

Among these is the fact that some permissible acts are a natural part of the noble character traits of some people and not matters that they have chosen for themselves, and they give up some permissible acts for the sake of these traits. For example, it has been related about ʿUmar ibn al-Khaṭṭāb that some people made him dismount his donkey during his journey to Syria and made him mount a horse. When the horse ambled across, he said that he felt something and dismounted returning to his donkey. Likewise, it has been related in the tradition about the embroidered cloak when the Prophet (pbuh) wore it, and he informed the people that it almost distracted him during his prayer when he looked at the embroidery.[38] The Prophet (pbuh) was infallible and he was only instructing his *umma* on how to deal with a permissible act when it leads them on to something disapproved. In the same manner, the permissible act can become a means towards the prohibited, and is to be given up insofar as it is a means, as it is said, "I will place a veil of the lawful between the unlawful and myself, but I will not prohibit it." A tradition says, "A person does not attain the status of the God-fearing until he gives up the harmless as a precaution against the harmful."[39] This is from the perspective of one who knows that if he traverses such and such path for his needs, he will come up against something forbidden or will say things that do not concern him, and the like.

Among these is the fact that some people give up acts that appear permissible to others, but when they ponder over them they find some problems and doubts about the acts and their permissibility is not obvious to them. This is a case where the giving up of the act is required on the whole without dispute, as in the case with the statement, "We used to give up the harmless as a precaution against the harmful." They did not, however, give up all harmless acts, but only those about which they were apprehensive that they would lead them to the disapproved or the forbidden.

Among these is the giving up by a person of the permissible as the resolve (*niyya*) to commit it is not present either to strengthen obedience to God or because[40] the person wishes that his acts be solely for the sake of God and he should not seek to serve his own desire insofar as it urges him on to do so. It is a characteristic of some servants of Allah that they do not wish to undertake a permissible act; rather they give it up till such time that they can undertake it as an act of worship or as one supporting worship. They may also undertake the act as a form of permission rather than as a means of satisfaction, because the former is a way of thanking the Benefactor as against the latter. Thus, such a person will relinquish the act until it becomes necessary, like eating, drinking and the like, for the act is permissible as long as there is no need for it. Accordingly, the consumption of some fruit may be given up for a time when there is need for nourishment and then it is consumed intentionally for maintaining the constitution and for supporting worship. All these are sound aims that are reported from the worthy ancestors, and they do not negate the claim in our issue.

Among these is the case where the person giving up the act is totally immersed in a certain form of worship: in the search for knowledge, reflection or in an act that pertains to the Hereafter. This person, therefore, does not find any other act to be enjoyable, nor is he inclined towards it, nor does it cross his mind. Although this is rare, the relinquishment of an act in this way resembles the neglect of the relinquished act. Neglecting the commission of a permissible act does not amount to obedience. In fact, it is obedience with respect to the act that keeps him away from this act. Something similar to this has been reported from ʿĀʾisha (God be pleased with her) when she was brought a huge amount of wealth and she distributed it without leaving anything for herself. When her inner self blamed her somewhat for this, she said: "Do not bother me. Had you reminded me of this, I would have done so." This conforms to what is the practice of the Ṣūfīs. Likewise, if a person gives up a permissible act due to a lack of desire for it,[41] it will take the rule of an act that is neglected.

Among these is the case where a person may deem the commission of a permissible act as extravagance, and extravagance is blameworthy. Extravagance has no maximum limit just like covetousness has no limit. A balance can be arrived at by undertaking *ijtihād* between the two limits. A person may view certain acts, with reference to his own circumstances, as classified under extravagance. He therefore gives up such acts. Another person, who does not consider such acts with reference to his state as extravagance may presume that it is the relinquishment of permissible acts on his part. The truth may not be as this person has presumed. Each person is a *faqīh* for his own self. The result is that the comprehension of the permissible act, with respect to extravagance or its absence, and acting upon such comprehension, is a required act. It is one of the conditions for undertaking a permissible act. Through this a permissible act does not become one whose omission is desired nor one whose commission is desired. This resembles the case of entering a mosque[42] for a permissible matter, which is permissible, but its condition is that the person not be in a state in ritual impurity (*janāba*), while the condition for the performance of supererogatory prayers is ritual purity, which is obligatory. By virtue of this, entering of a mosque or the performance of obligatory prayers do not became obligatory. So also in this case, the commission of a permissible act is contingent upon the giving up of extravagance, but the condemnation of extravagance does not make the permissible act blameworthy in the absolute sense.

If you ponder over all the narrations about the giving up of some permissible acts, out of the narrations that have preceded, you will find that they do not go beyond the explanations provided. In such case, they do not conflict with what has preceded with respect to the claim. Allah knows best.

The third objection to the claim in the first issue: the claim conflicts with what is established about piety and the relinquishment of its pleasures and temptations

The basis of the objection

The third point of conflict is based on what is established about the merit of piety in this world, the giving up of its pleasures and desires. The person who acts accordingly is praised by the *sharʿ* (law) by agreement, while one who relinquishes such acts is to be blamed in general. Al-Fuḍayl ibn ʿIyāḍ said: "All evil has been placed in a room whose key lies in the love of this world, and all blessing has been placed in a room whose key lies in piety." Al-Kattānī, the Sufi, said: "The thing that has not been opposed by a Kūfī, a Madanī, or an ʿIrāqī or a Shāmī, is piety in this world, personal generosity and sincerity to the creation." Al-Qushayrī said: "He means thereby that no one disputes the merit in these things." The evidences from the Book and the *Sunna* about this are beyond reckoning. Piety, in reality, exists in the lawful.

Piety, however, is necessary in the case of the prohibited as a fundamental of Islam, applicable to the believers generally, and its application is not confined to the elect believers alone. The practice that made them the elect was piety in the case of the permissible. As for the disapproved (*makrūh*) act, it has a dual nature. When this is established, it is not possible in practice that they adopt this approach towards something in which there is no benefit. It is, therefore, not possible to lawfully praise someone for an act when there is equality between its commission and omission.

The response to the objection

The response is covered in several points.

First: Piety in the *sharīʿa* is specific to an act whose omission is required, in accordance with what is obvious in the *sharīʿa*. The *mubāḥ* itself lies outside this, on the basis of evidences that have preceded. If some of those expressing this view have applied the word piety to the giving up of the lawful, then, it is by way of allusion taking into account the blessings that may be lost or due to other reasons that have preceded.

Second: The most pious of persons was the Prophet (pbuh), but he did not give up the good things in their totality whenever he came across them. So also the Companions and their Followers whose status in piety is confirmed.

Third: The giving up of permissible acts is either intentional or unintentional. If it is unintentional, it is not under consideration, rather it is neglect for which even the term *mubāḥ* cannot be employed and the use of the term "piety" is far-fetched. If the omission of the act is intentional, the intention is either restricted to its being permissible (*mubāḥ*), which is a point of dispute, or it is due to an external factor. If this external factor is a worldly matter, as is the relinquished act, it amounts to moving from one permissible act to one like it, and it cannot be called piety. If the external factor (act) pertains to the Hereafter, then, relinquishment is a means to the desired aim. It is, therefore, a merit with respect to this desired aim, and not with reference to mere relinquishment. There is no dispute about this.

This is the meaning elaborated by al-Ghazālī when he said: "Piety is an expression for the transferring of an inclination for a thing to one that is better than it." Elaborating this, he said, "Insofar as piety is the changing of the inclination for a desired thing on the whole, it cannot be conceived except by moving over to a thing that is dearer than it, because the giving up of a desired object for an undesirable thing is impossible." Thereafter, he mentioned various types of piety. He indicated that piety is not related to the *mubāḥ*, insofar as it is *mubāḥ*, in any form. One who ponders over the speech of the eminent will be led to this conclusion.

Sub-issue: evidences for not requiring commission of the permissible

The fact that the commission of the permissible act (*mubāḥ*) is not required is indicated by most of what has preceded,[43] because both aspects of it with respect to commission and omission are equal. He who argues that it is required seeks support from the idea that the commission of a permissible act amounts to the giving up (not-committing) of a prohibited act. As the giving up of a prohibited act is obligatory, the commission of a permissible act is obligatory. He will then continue in accordance with what the specialists in *ʿuṣūl al-fiqh* have determined. It does appear, however, that he who upholds this view concedes that the *mubāḥ*, despite what it gives rise to, has two equal sides to it with reference to commission and omission. Consequently what the jurists say is sound,[44] due to several reasons.

First: It becomes binding that permissibility is not to be found in any particular act by itself.[45] Thus, no act committed by a subject can essentially be designated with permissibility (*ibāḥa*). This is void by agreement. The *umma*, prior to this view, continued to assign the ruling of permissibility to acts, just as it assigned them the rulings of the rest of the categories of the *aḥkām*. This is true even where the commission of the *mubāḥ* leads to the binding view of giving up the prohibited. This indicates not taking into account what it leads to, because it is something external to the nature of the *mubāḥ*.

Second: If the truth lies in what such person claims, the category of *mubāḥ* will be removed altogether from the *sharīʿa*. This is void according to his own view and the views of others. The explanation is that if upon ascertainment the *mubāḥ* is not found to exist externally, its inclusion in categories of the *aḥkām* is futile. The reason is that the subject-matter of the *ḥukm* is the act of the *mukallaf* (subject), and we have assumed that it is obligatory and is not permissible. Thus, the category of *mubāḥ* becomes void with respect to its basis and details, because there is no benefit from the perspective of the *sharīʿa* in establishing a rule that does not regulate any of the acts of the subject.

Third: If the position is as this person claims, it has to be the same for all the remaining categories of rules in making it necessary to give up the prohibited. All the rules will then move out of their categories and become obligatory.

If he makes it binding in acknowledging two sides, in accordance with what is needed from him, then, this is not valid, because the aspect of necessity is considered and this negates the *mubāḥ* category. He should, therefore, take into account the aspect of necessity in the remaining four categories and negate them too. This goes against *ijmāʿ* and reason. If he acknowledges[46] the proscription in the prohibited and the disapproved, and the imperative in the recommended, like the obligatory, it will become binding for him to acknowledge the aspect of option in the permissible (*mubāḥ*) category, because there is no distinction between them with respect to their conceptual forms.

If he says that the *mubāḥ* ceases to be *mubāḥ* due to what leads to it or due to what it leads up to, then, this is not conceded. If it is conceded, it belongs to the category without which an obligatory act is not complete, and the disagreement about this is known. We, therefore, do not accept that it is obligatory. If this is conceded, then, the same applies to the other categories of rules. Thus, the prohibited, the disapproved, and the recommended will all become obligatory, when the obligatory that is obligatory from one aspect is obligatory from both aspects. All this does not yield a valid purpose in the *sharīʿa*.

The conclusion is that the *sharʿ* (law) has no inclination towards the commission of the permissible act in preference to omission or towards its omission in preference to its commission; in fact, the matter is left to the choice of the subject. The commission or omission undertaken by the subject is the intention of the Lawgiver with respect to it. Thus, commission and omission with respect to the subject are like the options in expiation (*kaffāra*): whichever one he chooses becomes the intention of the Lawgiver, but that does not mean that the Lawgiver intends its exclusive commission or its exclusive omission.

An additional difficulty arises, however, in the case of the two aspects[47] taken together as compared to one side as has preceded. This occurs in the case of certain *mubāḥ* acts where something is laid down that implies the preference of the Lawgiver for the exclusive commission of the act or its exclusive omission.

The first is witnessed in several cases: Among these is the command to benefit from good things, as in the words of the Exalted, "O ye people! Eat of what is on earth, lawful and good",[48] His words "O ye who believe! Eat of the good things that We have provided for you",[49] and His words "O ye Messenger! Enjoy (all) things good and pure, and work righteousness",[50] as well as other similar verses that indicate the meaning of utilisation. Further, the blessings are spread all over the earth for utilisation by the servants with respect to which favours are mentioned and that have been acknowledged. In all these the meaning is that of utilisation, but with the condition of thanking the Benefactor.

Among these is the rejection by God of the view of those who have prohibited anything from the good things spread out in the earth. He deemed this prohibition as one form in which they are misguided. Allah, the Exalted, has said, "Say: Who hath forbidden the beautiful (gifts) of Allah, which He hath produced for His servants",[51] that is, what has been created "Purely for them on the Day of Judgement."[52] In the consumption of these things there is neither reckoning nor sin. This is evident insofar as the meaning is that of utilisation and not relinquishment.

Among these is the fact that these blessings are a gift from Allah for His servant. Is it suitable for the servant to refuse the gift from his Master? It is not suitable on the basis of good behaviour or in the practice of the *sharʿ* (law). The intention of the donor is that his gift be accepted. The gift of Allah for His servant are the blessings He has bestowed on him. These are then to be accepted and thankfulness is to be expressed. The tradition from Ibn ʿUmar and his father ʿUmar in the case of curtailment of prayer is evident on this point. The Prophet (peace be upon him) said: "It is charity (*ṣadaqa*) granted by Allah to you, so accept His charity."[53] There is an addition from ʿUmar (may Allah be pleased with him), in which the narration stops at him (is *mawqūf*), "How will you feel if you give something by way of *ṣadaqa* and it is returned to you? Will you not feel angry?" In a tradition it is reported "that Allah wishes that His *rukhaṣ* (exemptions) be laid down for you just as His injunctions are laid down for you".[54] The most prominent of these *rukhaṣ* are found in the form of permissions granted through the relaxation of obligations like not fasting during a journey, or relaxing of prohibitions as is maintained by a group about the words of the Exalted: "If any of you have not the means wherewith to wed free believing women."[55] When love is exhibited for a permissible act preference is to be given to commission. All these cases indicate that sometimes the commission of a permissible act is to be preferred over omission.

As for the meaning that implies specific omission, it includes all that has preceded regarding the condemnation of pleasures and the inclination towards temptations of the flesh in general. In particular, there are commands that imply the linking of disapproval with certain acts whose permissibility is established, like *ṭalāq al-sunna* (prescribed form of divorce).[56] It is stated in a tradition, even though the tradition is not sound, "The most despicable of permitted acts for Allah is divorce."[57] It is for this reason that a command for divorce is not laid down in the Qurʾān, it is merely stated that "Divorce is twice",[58] "So if a husband divorces his wife (irrevocably), he cannot, after that, remarry her until after she has married another husband and he has divorced her",[59] "O Prophet! When ye do divorce women, divorce them at their prescribed periods",[60] "Thus when they fulfil their appointed terms."[61] There is no doubt that the aspect of disapproval in a permissible act will convert the *mubāḥ* into a disapproved act.[62] It has been stated in a tradition, "Every type of pleasure is void, except three";[63] however, most of forms of pleasure are permissible, and play too is permissible, though it is sometimes held blameworthy. All this indicates that the permissible act does not go against the intention of the Lawgiver, in either of its aspects of commission or omission specifically. This indicates that the demand is related equally to commission and omission and not in the manner that has preceded.[64]

The response is twofold: one is general and the other is detailed.

The general response is: When it is established that the permissible act is equal with respect to its two aspects (of commission or omission) for the Lawgiver, then, anything that prefers one of its aspects takes it out of the category of *mubāḥ*, either because it is not a true *mubāḥ*, even though the term *mubāḥ* is applied to it, or because it was originally a *mubāḥ*, but has ceased to be so due to an external factor. It is to be conceded that the *mubāḥ* becomes other than *mubāḥ*, due to the *maqāṣid* (purposes of law) or due to an external factor.

The detailed response is that the *mubāḥ* is of two types: The first type is subservient to the necessary, supporting or complementary principles, while the second type is not subservient to these principles.

The first type is to be considered in the light of what it serves and this will make its commission required or preferred. Thus, the utilisation of what Allah has made lawful out of eatables, beverages and the like makes such acts permissible in themselves with their permissibility arising out of particular rules;[65] however, these are subservient to the necessary (universal) principle, which is the preservation of life, and from this perspective the acts are required, valued and preferred insofar as this universal principle is required. The matter is, therefore, referred to its universal reality,[66] not to its particular rule. It is in this form that it is proper to accept a gift and not refuse it, and not on the basis of an ascertained particular rule.

In the second type, the act either serves something that annuls the three recognised principles or it does not serve anything. The illustration is that of divorce,[67] for it is the relinquishment of the permissible that serves the universal principle of preservation of progeny, which is necessary, or it serves in an unqualified way the bonds of affection, association and relation between the people, which is either necessary or supporting or complementary for one of these values. If divorce, in the light of this, demolishes one of these requirements and negates it, it is disapproved and its commission is not preferable to its omission, unless there is a more powerful obstacle like enmity and the non-observance of the limits imposed by Allah. Insofar as it is a particular rule in the case of the concerned individual, at that particular time, it is permissible and lawful.

It is also in this context that this world has been looked down upon, and this has preceded. If the lawful in the world is utilised and leads to the demolition of the necessary, it becomes blameworthy from this aspect. Just as *dīn* is demolished[68] by unbelief or the fear of God by the disobedient. Pleasure, play and freedom from all kinds of work, which are *mubāḥ* when they do not involve the prohibited or do not give rise to the prohibited, become blameworthy and are not approved by scholars. In fact, they disapprove the acts of a person who is neither paying attention to the improvement of his livelihood or to his Hereafter, because it amounts to the wasting of time that does not yield any benefit in this world or the next. It is stated in the Qur'ān, "Nor walk on the earth with insolence",[69] because it leads to this meaning. A tradition says, "Every act of pleasure is invalid, except three." The meaning of "invalid" here is that it is futile, or useless, as it does not yield a benefit or fruit that can be utilised, as against pleasure with one's wife for it is a *mubāḥ* that serves a necessary principle, which is the preservation of progeny. Likewise, the training of a horse or practising with arrows, for both of them serve a complementary principle, which is *jihād*.[70] If it for this reason that these three have been exempted from invalid pleasure. All this elaborates that *mubāḥ* insofar as it is *mubāḥ*, is an act whose commission or omission is not required through the particulars.[71]

The second issue: the *mubāḥ* in the wider sense includes all the other categories of the *aḥkām*

It is said: Permissibility in its universal and particular aspects absorbs the remaining *aḥkām*. The permissible act (*mubāḥ*) is permissible from the perspective of the particular, but is required from the perspective of the universal principle by way of recommendation or obligation. Further a permissible act viewed through the particular may be proscribed through the universal by way of disapproval or prohibition.

This classifies use into four types.

First: enjoying the good things

The first type covers the enjoyment of good things[72] among eatables, beverages, riding animals and clothes. This is besides what is obligatory out of these and recommended by way of requirement. It also covers what is disapproved among customary practices, for example extravagance which is permissible by the particular rule (*juzʾ*), like giving it up sometimes[73] when there is ability to undertake it, but it is permissible if undertaken. If it is given up in its entirely, it would go against what is recommended by the law (*sharʿ*). A tradition says: "If Allah has granted you ease, grant ease to yourselves. Allah loves to see the effect of His blessings upon His servant."[74] When the person to whom this was addressed improved his appearance, he said to him at the end of the tradition: "Isn't this better?"[75] Then there are his words: "Allah is beautiful and loves beauty."[76] This was stated after a person had said that one prefers that his dress be good, his shoes be good, and that he wants the same with respect to many things. Accordingly, if all the people were to give up this it would be deemed disapproved.

Second: utilising what is lawful

The second type covers eating and drinking, cohabiting with spouses, sale, purchase and employing the means of livelihood that are lawful. Allah, the Exalted, has said: "Allah has permitted *bayʿ* (exchange) and prohibited *ribā* (usury)",[77] and "Lawful to you is the pursuit of water-game and its use for food",[78] and "Lawful unto you (for food) are all beast of cattle",[79] as well as a number of other verses. All these things are permissible through particular rules; that is, if a person chooses to do one of these and not the others, it is permitted, or when a person gives up these things under certain circumstances or times, or when some of the people give up these acts,[80] it is not objectionable. If we assume that all of the people were to give up these acts, it would amount to the giving up of necessities that are required. Undertaking these acts would then become obligatory under the universal principles.

Third: relaxation and enjoyment of nature

The third type covers enjoyment in gardens (parks),[81] listening to the chirping of the birds, permissible music, permissible play with pigeons and other things. Things like these are permitted according to particular rules. If these are undertaken on some day or under certain circumstances, there is no harm in it, but if these are undertaken all the time they will become disapproved. The person doing so (always) would be deemed irrational and contravening preferred practices and extravagant in the commission of this *mubāḥ* (permissible act).

Fourth: permissible acts whose persistent commission is likely to affect probity (ʿadāla)

The fourth type pertains to permissible acts that are likely to affect *ʿadāla* (moral probity) if undertaken continuously, even though the acts are permissible. These acts are not objectionable until the person undertaking them has moved out of the limits set for those possessing moral probity, and when such a person traverses the path of the disobedient, even if he is not such a person in reality, it is nothing but a sin that he has committed under the law (*sharʿ*). Al-Ghazālī has stated, "Persistence in the commission of a permissible act converts it into a minor sin, just as persistence in the case of a minor sin converts it into a major sin." It is in such a case that it is said: There is no minor sin in the case of persistence.

The act recommended by the particular is obligatory under the universal

When an act is recommended according to a particular rule, it becomes obligatory under the universal rule.[82] Illustrations are the call to prayer in congregational or other mosques, congregational prayer, Īd prayers, voluntary charity, marriage (*nikāḥ*), *witr* prayers, morning prayers (recommended), *umra* and all supererogatory forms of worship. All these are deemed recommended under particular rules. If we assume the giving up of all these acts in their entirety, the person giving them up will become liable to censure. Do you not see that the call to prayer is an expression of the symbols of Islam. It is for this reason that the residents of a city can be subjected to war if they give it up. Likewise, congregational prayer given up in its entirety leads to censure, and the testimony of a person who does so is no longer acceptable, because its giving up is an opposition to the symbols of the *dīn*. The Messenger of Allah (pbuh) reprimanded the persons who gave up the congregational prayer in its entirety and he had almost resolved to set fire to their houses. Likewise, the Prophet (pbuh) would not carry out a raid when it was dawn. If he heard the call to prayer, he would hold back, otherwise he would attack.

The act disapproved by the particular is prohibited under the universal

When an act is disapproved according to the particular rule, it becomes prohibited under the universal rule, like playing chess and backgammon without gambling and listening to disapproved music. If such acts are undertaken occasionally, they do not affect moral probity, but if they are undertaken persistently they do affect the probity of the player. This is an evidence[83] of prohibition based on the principle highlighted by Al-Ghazālī.[84] Muḥammed ibn al-Hakam has said about the playing of chess and backgammon that if these are played excessively, so much so that they keep the player away from congregational prayers, his testimony ceases to be acceptable. Likewise, all play through which a person moves out of the category of manly virtues, so also the visiting, without excuse, of places under suspicion as well as other similar things.

Wājib *and* farḍ *distinguished*

If we maintain that the *wājib* is the same as *farḍ*, then, it must be *wājib* according to the universal as well as particular rules. The scholars have applied the term *wājib* with reference to the particular rule. If it is *wājib* according to the particular rule, it is necessary that it be *wājib* according to the universal. Does the rule differ for it according to the universal and the particular?

As for the possibility of this,[85] it is evident. If a particular *ẓuhr* prayer is *farḍ* upon a subject he will sin if he gives it up and will be considered to have committed a major sin. The consequential penalty will be implemented against him due to this, unless he seeks forgiveness from Allah. Thus, a person who gives up all *ẓuhr* prayers or other prayers will deserve the reprimand more. Likewise, a person who commits murder once, along with the person who commits it more than once and does it persistently, and other examples like these. An injury with persistence is more grievous than one that is without persistence.

With respect to actual occurrence, there have been cases that imply this, as in the case of the Friday congregational prayer, with the Prophet (pbuh) saying: "If someone does not attend the Friday congregational prayer three times in a row, Allah puts a stamp on his heart."[86] This was qualified by three times, as you see. In another tradition, he said: "Whoever takes the duty (of the Friday congregation) lightly[87] or considers it insignificant."[88] In fact, when he gives it up of his own accord[89] without taking it lightly or considering it insignificant, he is deemed to have given up a *farḍ*. The Prophet (pbuh) said this because doing so a number of times has a higher gravity with respect to prohibition and so also[90] has considering it something minor or insignificant. This was treated in *fiqh* as a basis for the rule that whoever neglects it three times will have his testimony made inadmissible. Saḥnūn said: "Ibn Ḥabīb has related from Mutarrif and Ibn Majishūn, 'If he neglects it a number of times without an excuse, his testimony is inadmissible.'" This is what Saḥnūn said.[91] The jurists (*fuqahā*ʾ) likewise say about one who commits a sin, but has not done so too often, that his testimony is not to be objected to, if it is not a major sin (*kabīra*), but if he does it continuously and a number of times his testimony will become inadmissible (for any kind of case) and he will be classified among those who are guilty of major sins. This is done on the basis of the rule that "persistence in committing a minor offence converts it into a major offence".

If, however, we maintain that the *wājib* is not the equivalent of *farḍ*, then what has preceded applies to this too. It is to be said: When the *wājib* is *wājib* according to the particular rule, it is *farḍ* under the universal rule.[92] There is nothing that works against it when we examine this rule and the examples laid down in the Hanafi School. The generalisation goes well with this method and it is said about the *farḍ*:[93] it varies in accordance with the universal and the particular, as has been elaborated at the beginning of the section.

The same is to be said about the prohibitions; that is, their grades vary in accordance with the universal and the particular, even if they are counted as falling under a rule in a single category at a certain time or in certain situations. This is not the case in other situations; rather their rule varies, as in the case of falsehood without a valid excuse and all the minor sins undertaken persistently, because persistence converts them into major sins. One sin may be added to another leading to its magnification due to this addition; however, theft of one-half of the *niṣāb* (scale) is not the same as one-fourth of the *niṣāb*, nor is the theft of the whole *niṣāb* the same as one-half. It is for this reason that the jurists deem the theft of a morsel or weighing short by a grain as a minor sin, even though theft (*sariqa*) is a major sin. Al-Ghazālī said: Whenever a major sin is committed on impulse without preparation and its preliminaries, it is to be conceived of as a minor sin. He said that if the major sin is conceived of as committed on an impulse without repetition, perhaps there is greater hope of its forgiveness as compared to a minor sin that is committed persistently throughout one's lifetime.

The rules for different acts vary according to the universal and particular

This issue is raised from the perspective that the rules for all acts vary in accordance with the universal and the particular without any correspondence between the rules.[94] The person making a counter-claim may say that there is correspondence between the rules even when there is difference between the universal and the particular. With respect to the *mubāḥ* (permissible category) the example is the killing of injurious things, undertaking *qirāḍ* (term used by Mālikīs for the *muḍāraba* partnership), *musāqāh* (irrigation contract), dealing in *ʿariyya* (a contract involving dates), relaxing after toil insofar as this is not required, and medication when we say that it is permissible (if not required). All these things, if they are undertaken always or are always given up, no sin is committed by such commission or omission, nor is there any disapproval, nor recommendation, nor obligation. The same applies if all the people voluntarily give up these acts, so also if all of them undertake these acts. With respect to the recommended category (*mandūb*) the illustration is that of medication if this is to be deemed recommended because of the words of the Prophet (pbuh), "Take medication",[95] or like swiftness in the killing of deadly animals (without causing excessive pain), due to the words of the Prophet (pbuh), "When you kill, do it properly."[96] If these acts are omitted by a person continuously, it would neither be deemed disapproved nor prohibited.[97] Likewise, if the acts are undertaken persistently. With respect to the disapproved category (*makrūh*), the illustration is the killing of ants that are not injurious, or the use of peat, bones or other things for cleaning after the call of nature, except that these are affected by the *jinn* or have a right that belongs to them. The proscription in such case is not for prohibition nor is it established that a person using such things is not injured or becomes sinful. The same applies to urinating in holes or adopting effeminate manners with drinking. The examples are numerous. As for the obligatory and the prohibited categories, the evident rule is that of equality. The *ḥudūd* are based upon equality. Thus, the person who drinks wine a hundred times is the same as one who drinks it once. The person who makes a false accusation of unchastity against one person is the same as one who makes it against a group,[98] and the murder of one person is the same as one who kills a hundred with respect to the implementation of the *ḥudūd* against him. So also the omission of one prayer and doing so persistently, and the like. Further al-Ghazālī has stated that back-biting or listening to it, spying on others, evil designs, omitting the commanding of the good and forbidding the blameworthy, the consumption of things about the legality of which there is doubt, abusing a child or a slave and beating them in anger beyond the limits of the beneficial, giving honour to tyrant rulers, laziness in providing education to one's child or family that is necessary for following their *dīn*, when undertaken persistently are similar to the avoidance of other acts. The reason is that it is these things specifically that people are likely to avoid just as they would avoid certain other things. If all this is established, the claim is settled that the rules remain the same even though the acts may differ according to the universal and the particular.

The person who upholds the first view may respond that what appears to be the same is most probably different.

First: The universal and particular differ in accordance with individual circumstances and subjects. The evidence for this is that when we examine the permissibility of omission in the killing of every injurious animal (or insect) with reference to one individual then there is leniency in the requirement, but if we assume this for all the people collaborating in their omission, they will be exposed to injury in various ways. The law (*sharʿ*) has required the repelling of injury in certain terms; thus, omission is prohibited at least at the level of *karāhat al-taḥrīm* (disapproval inclining toward prohibition) if not at a higher level. The act then becomes recommended in view of the universal even if obligation is not transmitted. The same is the case in the undertaking of *qirāḍ*, as well as other things mentioned with it. There is, thus, no equality between the universal and the particular. It is sufficient for this issue, if we say that if all the people collaborate in its omission it will become a means for demolishing a fundamental of the law. This is prohibited. Yes, we may come across cases in which the universal and particular are very close to each other,[99] but if there is a gap between them the facts are as have been stated. These cases occur with respect to the recommended and disapproved.

As for what is said about the obligatory and the prohibited, this proximity does not have any occurrence. Thus, the difference between the rules of the *ḥudūd* is evident even though there is correspondence in certain cases. What is stated by al-Ghazālī cannot be conceded on the basis of this principle.[100] If it is conceded, it is possible in the case of moral probity (*ʿadāla*) alone due to a preferred obstacle, which is that if persistence in these acts is objected to, then *ʿadāla* will become a rare thing thus preventing testimony.

Evidence supporting the distinction between the universal and the particular

Now that the picture of the operation of the universal and the particular in the five categories of rules has been formed, the evidence for its validity must be demanded. This matter is evident due to a focus on what has preceded while establishing the concept. In fact, in the consideration of the *sharīʿa* the matter reaches the level of the definitive for one who undertakes induction through its sources. If, however, further conviction and persuasion is required, then this is undertaken through the following statements.

Among these is what has been indicated already with respect to the injury caused due to what a human may do persistently, injury that may not arise if there is no persistence. This is a principle that is agreed upon by the jurists in its entirety. If persistence did not have some effect, the distinctions they draw between persistence and non-persistence with respect to the commission of acts would not be valid, but they do indeed consider this effect. This indicates that there is a distinction and that persistence in relation to an act is more severe and significant than is non-persistence. This is the concept that has been established in what has preceded with respect to the universal and the particular, and this method is sufficient for those who have acknowledged the distinction.

Among these is the agreed upon view that the Lawgiver has laid down the *sharīʿa* in consideration of interests (*maṣāliḥ*). In issues related to this, it has been established that the acknowledged interests are the universals and not the particulars, because the practices on which the *aḥkām* (rules) are based have this nature. If the particulars had not been weaker in strength during acknowledgement, this assumption would not have been valid. In fact, if this had not been the case the application of the universals would not have been continuous, like the rule about testimony and acceptance of the *khabar wāḥid* when there is a possibility of error and forgetfulness in individual narrations. The preponderant rule is that of truth. The universal rules operate on the basis of what is preponderant and usual, in order to safeguard the universals. If the particulars had been taken into consideration there would have been no distinction between the universals and the particulars, and as a result the application of the law would become confined to what was known (expressed) and all probabilities would be rejected. This is nothing but the rejection of the rule of the particular[101] by the rejection of the rule arising from the universal. It is also an evidence of the validity of the disagreement between the same act with respect to the universal and the particular, and of the fact that the significance of the particular is lesser.

Among these is also what is laid down with respect to an error by a scholar in his knowledge or in his acts insofar as it affects a person other than the scholar. If the error extends to another, the rule for that error will become different. This is nothing but a particular rule when it remains confined to the scholar and does not extend to another. If it does extend to another, it becomes a universal due to someone else following this and acting according to it. It becomes a grave error for someone following the ruling, but this is not the case when it is applied to the scholar. This applies in the same way to someone doing something that is followed. If the act is good the following is good, but if the act is bad the following is bad. It is in this regard that it is said: "Whoever establishes a good practice (*sunna*) …" and "No one is killed unjustly without imputing part of the blame to the first son of Adam, because it was he who laid down the bad practice of murder." The error made by the scholar is, therefore, considered grievous, even though it is minor in itself. The evidences for this principle reach a level of certainty due to their abundance. These evidences elaborate what we have argued for; that is, that acts are judged on the basis of the particular and the universal. This is the aim.

The third issue: two meanings of *mubāḥ*

The term *mubāḥ* (permissible) is applied in two meanings. The first meaning implies that the subject has a choice between commission and omission. The same meaning is conveyed by the statement: there is no harm in it. On the whole, it has four categories.

First: Serving an act whose commission is required.

Second: Serving an act whose omission is required.

Third: Serving an act in which there is a choice

Fourth: That the act is not related to any of the above.

The first category is *mubāḥ* (permissible) according to the particular, but is required to be committed according to the universal. The second is *mubāḥ* (permissible) according to the particular, but is required to be omitted according to the universal, in the sense that persistence in such an act is prohibited. The third and fourth categories are related to this second category.

The emerging meaning is that the *mubāḥ*, as already stated, is assessed on the basis of what it serves when it does serve something. Service here is sometimes from the aspect of omission, like giving up persistent omission of enjoyment in gardens, listening to the chirping of birds, and permissible music. This is what is required. Service is also from the perspective of commission, like the utilisation of lawful good things. The persistent omission of such things depends upon its possibility without indulging in extravagance. It is required insofar as it serves a requirement, and is a principle of the category of necessities (*ḍarūriyāt*), as against the requirement of omission, for that serves the opposite, which means not being occupied with that act. The act that serves a choice carries the same rule. As for the fourth category, insofar as it does not serve anything, it is futile, like futility according to all reasonable men. It is, therefore, an act whose omission is required, because it attempts to serve the mere passing of time without serving an interest of this world or of the Hereafter.

It thus serves the requirement of omission and is required to be omitted according to the universal. The third category is similar to it as well, because it serves it; thus it too is required to be omitted.

In summary, then, a *mubāḥ* is not a *mubāḥ* in the absolute sense, it is *mubāḥ* according to the particular alone. As for the universal, the *mubāḥ* is either required to be committed, or it is required to be omitted. It may be said that this determination amounts to a contradiction of what has preceded insofar as the *mubāḥ* has two equally balanced sides. The response is in the negative. The reason is that what has preceded was an examination with respect to itself, without the consideration of an external factor. The examination here is in the context of factors external to it. If you were to examine it exclusively it will be what is called *mubāḥ* by virtue of the particular. Thus, for example, if a certain good dress is lawful for use, such use would be the same in the eyes of the *sharʿ* (law), without there being any specific intention for one side or the other. This is reasonable and is found to be confined to the *mubāḥ* insofar as it has this form. From the perspective of protection from heat and cold, covering of the body, and adornment, however, its commission is required. Such a perspective is not confined to the particular dress alone, nor to a particular time. It is an exemption from the perspective of the universal.

The fourth issue: *mubāḥ* in which there is no harm

When it is said of the *mubāḥ* that there is no harm in it, and this is said in one of the two meanings, it does not fall under the category of a choice between commission and omission. This is due to several reasons:

First: We made a distinction between the two after we understood that the *sharīʿa* intends to distinguish between them.

The category whose commission is required according to the universal is what distinguishes between commission and omission with respect to the choice, as in the words of the Exalted: "Your wives are as a tilth unto you",[102] "And remember We said: 'Enter this town' ",[103] "And eat of the bountiful things therein as (where and when) ye will",[104] as well as other verses conveying the same meaning. Further, the matter is unqualified insofar as the command employing permissibility requires a choice in reality, as in the words of the Exalted: "But when ye are clear of the Sacred Precincts and of the state of pilgrimage",[105] "And when the Prayer is finished, then may ye disperse through the land",[106] and "Eat of the good things",[107] and other verses like these. Leaving it unqualified, when there are various implications, makes it obvious for purposes of choice in such meanings, unless there is an evidence that takes the meaning out of this context.

As for the category whose omission is required by the universal, we do not know of anything in the *sharīʿa*, based on a text, that would indicate a choice in it. It is something on which the *sharīʿa* is silent, or it is indicated partially through a statement that takes out of the meaning an express command implying choice, as in the case of calling this hair splitting and pleasure and attaching blame to the act of the person who indulges in it. Here it is indicated that idle play is not a matter of choice. It is laid down in the Holy Qurʾān: "But when they see some bargain or some amusement, they disperse headlong to it, and leave thee standing",[108] which is the beating of drums or whatever resembles it. The Exalted says, "But there are, among men, those who purchase idle tales, without knowledge (or meaning), to mislead (men) from the Path of Allah and throw ridicule (on the Path): For such there will be a humiliating Penalty."[109]

Then there are sayings from the Companions stated earlier[110] when they were bored and asked the Prophet (pbuh) for some sayings and the response was: "Allah has revealed the most beautiful Message."[111] Another tradition says: "All idle play is void."[112] There are other similar statements that do not usually incorporate choice. Thus, where some of these matters have been laid down in a determined form, or there is some room for choice at certain times or certain circumstances, then the meaning of absence of harm is to be taken in the sense of another tradition: "What has not been stated is pardonable";[113] that is, what is forgiven. This is how it is stated in practice, indicating that it consists of something that can be forgiven or what gives a similar impression in practice.

The result of the distinction is that one of these is explicit[114] in the removal of sin and fault, even though permission to undertake the act or its omission does become linked to it if expressed; however, the underlying intention of the meaning is the specific negation of sin. As for permission, it belongs to the category of "an act without which an obligation cannot be met" or it belongs to the category of "a command to do one thing is a proscription of its opposite" and "whether the proscription of a thing is a command to undertake one of its opposites". The other is explicit in terms of the choice itself, even though the absence of harm is associated with the act. The intention behind the meaning, however, is that of choice exclusively. As for the removal of harm, it belongs to these categories. The evidence for this is that removal of harm sometimes accompanies an obligation, as in the words of the Exalted: "It is no sin in them, should they compass them round",[115] while at other times it accompanies opposition to the recommended act, as in "Except under compulsion, his heart remaining firm."[116] Had the removal of harm necessitated choice in commission or omission, it would not have been valid with the obligatory, nor with the opposition to the recommended act. The choice expressly mentioned is not of this type, because it is not valid with an obligatory act in the absence of omission, nor with the recommended act or vice versa.

Second: The word *takhyīr* (granting a choice) is understood to imply the intention of the Lawgiver for the tacit approval of permission with respect to the two sides of commission and omission of an act, and that these two sides are equal with respect to such intention. Removal of harm is unexpressed. As for the term removal of sin, the meaning is that of the intention of the Lawgiver in removing harm from its commission when the act is committed by the subject. The element of permission in this act remains unexpressed. It is possible that it is the intention of the Lawgiver, but this would be a secondary intention, as in the case of exemptions (*rukhaṣ*), for they relate to the removal of harm, and this will be coming up (for discussion) God willing. Thus, what is expressly mentioned in one of these is unexpressed in the other, and vice versa.

Third: The third reason consists of what indicates that the act in which there is no harm is not a matter of choice in the absolute sense. The choice in it, insofar as it serves the commission of the act, moves out of the mere pursuit of whim. In fact, personal whim in it is restricted and is subservient to the secondary intention. Thus, whatever falls under it falls under the demand based on the universal; therefore, the choice in it does not take place except on the basis of the particular. As it is required by the universal, it falls outside the ambit of the pursuit of whim in this respect. We have already seen the concern of the Lawgiver with universals and the intention to impose them in matters of obligations (*takālīf*). The particular that does not disturb the universals does not clash with their objections nor does it oppose them; in fact, it affirms them.

In the pursuit of whim, where the act entails a choice, there is an inducement to pursue the objectives of the Lawgiver in the context of the universals. There is, therefore, no injury here in the pursuing of whim, because it amounts *ab initio* to the intention of the Lawgiver, and this pursuit of whim is serving such intention.

As for the category in which there is no harm, it resembles the pursuit of whim that is blameworthy. You will notice that it works contrary to the intention of the Lawgiver that requires a universal proscription on the whole. Due to its rare occurrence, non-persistence and participation with the external serving act, as is mentioned at its proper occasion, it is not aligned with it. It is, therefore, classified with that in which there is no harm, because the particular in it does not upset a required principle. Even though this opens a door to it in general, it is not effective insofar as it is a particular so that it does not merge with one of its own genus. Merger would mean strength and would lead the prohibitive universal to recede into the background, which would run contrary to what requires the act. If it is established that it is like the pursuit of whim and does not fall under a universal imperative, the legal rules demand that there be no choice in it. This is an expression for the aforementioned rule for the pursuit of whim and is opposed to the *sharīʿa*.

The fifth issue: *mubāḥ* is designated as such when the advantage of the subject is taken into account

The *mubāḥ* (permissible) is designated as *mubāḥ* when the advantage of the subject (*mukallaf*) alone is taken into account. When it is removed from such intention, it acquires a different rule. The evidence for this, as has been stated earlier, is that the *mubāḥ* is an act in which a choice has been granted with respect to commission and omission so that there is no intention on the part of the law as to going ahead with it or refraining from it. From this aspect, therefore, insofar as it is particular, no necessary (*ḍarūrī*) affair depends on its commission or omission, nor even a supporting need (*ḥājī*) or a complementary value. It thus refers to the securing of some immediate interest in particular. Likewise, the *mubāḥ* in which "there is no harm" is to be referred to such interest. Further, the imperative and the proscription intend to protect what is necessary, a supporting need or a complementary value. In each of these, the intention of the Lawgiver is discernible, and whatever is beyond this amounts to the mere seeking of an advantage and the satisfaction of a desire.

It may be said: What is the evidence that the *mubāḥ* is confined within the advantage of the subject and in nothing else, and that the command and the prohibition refer to the right of Allah and not to the advantage of the subject? Further, it may be true that certain types of *mubāḥ* are not undertaken from the perspective of advantage, just as it is true for certain things commanded or prohibited that they are based on advantage.

The response is that the established principle is that the *sharīʿa* has been laid down in the interest of humankind. Thus, commands, prohibitions and options are all associated with the advantage and interest of the subject, because Allah is not in need of any advantage arising from desires. Advantage, however, is of two types.

First: The first type falls under demand. The individual is to act upon it from the perspective of demand and is not to strive for his advantage. Despite this his advantage is not lost, but he secures it by acting upon the demand and not of his own accord. This is the meaning of being devoid of advantage. Insofar as it is classified under demand, it is undertaken from the perspective of demand, and the advantage is subservient to the demand. It is, therefore, associated with the former, devoid of advantage, and is called by that name. This is settled at its proper occasion in this Book. Success comes from Allah.

Second: The second type does not fall under demand, thus, the subject does not undertake it except on the basis of his own volition and choice, because the demand is removed from it on the basis of the assumption. The subject, therefore, undertakes it on the basis of his own advantage. Thus, the following is stated about the *mubāḥ*: It is an act that is permitted and its purpose is mainly specific worldly advantage.

The sixth issue: the five categories of rules are related to acts and omissions on the basis of the purposes of the law (*maqāṣid al-sharīʿa*)

The five categories of rules are related to acts and omissions through the *maqāṣid* (purposes of the Law). When the *maqāṣid* are removed the relationship is not found. The evidences for these are several.

First: It is established that acts are based upon intentions. This is a principle that is agreed upon as a whole, and the evidences for it are nothing short of definitive.[117] The meaning is that acts alone, in the physical sense, are not considered by the law (*sharʿ*) under any circumstances, except when an evidence has been adduced for their consideration, especially those in the category of the declaratory rules.[118] As for all other cases, the principle applies continuously. When these acts are not taken into account, unless the *maqāṣid* (intentions) are associated with them, taken by themselves they are the equivalent of the movements of animals or irrational things. In such a case, the five categories of rules cannot be associated with them rationally or on the basis of transmission or in any other way.

Second: The established principle is that acts issuing forth from the insane, a person asleep, the minor and one under a fit of fainting have no rule in the law so that it cannot be said these acts are "permissible", "prohibited", "obligatory" or another type, just as there is no such category for the acts of animals. The Qurʾān says, "But there is no blame on you if ye make a mistake",[119] and it says, "Our Lord! Condemn us not if we forget or fall into error."[120] The reply was "I have done so."[121] It is in this meaning that the tradition is related, "Liability has been removed from my *umma* for mistake, forgetfulness and what they have been coerced to do."[122] Even though its chain of transmission is not sound, its meaning is agreed upon for its soundness. A tradition also says, "The pen (of liability) has been lifted in three cases."[123] After this, the minor till he attains puberty and the person under a fit of fainting until he recovers are mentioned. All the persons mentioned above do not have the ability to formulate an intention. This is the underlying cause (*ʿilla*) for the non-operation of the primary rules of obligation against them.

Third: The existence of consensus (*ijmāʿ*) on the point that there is no obligation to undertake the impossible in the law (*sharʿ*). Placing a person who cannot form an intention under an obligation is asking him to perform the impossible.

It may be said: This applies where a demand (for commission or omission) is made. As for the *mubāḥ*, there is no obligation there. The response would be that if the association of an option with acts is possible, the association of demand is possible too. This implies an underlying intention in a *mubāḥ* subject to choice. Whereas we have assumed that there is no intention in this case. Accordingly, there is a discrepancy here.

The assertion above cannot be objected to on the basis of the liability of fines and *zakāt* for minors, insane persons and so on. The reason is that this association belongs to the category of declaratory rules, while we are discussing the category of obligation (*taklīf*). There is also no objection on the basis of intoxication, "Approach not prayers in a state of intoxication."[124] This is countered in *ʿuṣūl al-fiqh*. The reason is that such a person is placed under interdiction in other cases. As he has made himself intoxicated, and it was his intention to remove the operation of the rule of obligation against himself, the action will be contrary to what he intended. In the alternative, consuming liquor is the cause for a large number of evils, and his using it has caused those evils. Thus, the law takes him to task even though he has not intended those evils, just as one of the sons of Adam is assigned part of the blame for every soul killed unjustly and just as the person guilty of unlawful sexual intercourse is taken to task for mixing up the progeny (lineage) even though he is only guilty of penetration. The examples of this are numerous. The principle therefore is sound and the objections against it are misplaced.

The seventh issue: recommended category (*mandūb*) in the wider sense serves the obligatory (*wājib*)

The recommended category, when considered in a sense wider than what has preceded, will be found to serve the obligatory (*wājib*), because it is either a preliminary introduction to it or its reminder whether or not it belongs to the same genus as the obligatory act. Those that belong to the same genus are like supererogatory prayers compared to the obligatory prayers or supererogatory acts of worship pertaining to fasts, charity and *ḥajj* compared to the obligatory acts within these. Those that do not belong to the same genus are like the removal of impurities from the body, clothes and place of prayer as well as *siwāk* (brushing of the teeth), adornment and the like as compared to prayer itself, as well as prompt breaking of the fast, delaying, abstaining from talking about what is irrelevant as compared to the obligation of fasting itself and so on. If the relationship is like this, then such acts are linked to the obligation on the basis of the universal, and it is rare that a recommended act falls outside this, an act that is recommended by virtue of the universal as well as particular. This concept needs to be established; however, what has preceded leaves no need for this, by the power of Allah.

Sub-issue: the makrūḥ *serves the prohibited*

If the *makrūḥ* is considered in the same way with respect to the prohibited, it appears in the same relationship as that of the recommended with the *wājib*. Some obligations are ends in themselves, and these are the major obligations, while other obligations are a means to the ends and serve those ends, like purification from the ritual state of impurity, the covering of the private parts facing the *qibla*, the call to prayer as an identification of the appointed timings and for affirming the symbols of Islam, and all these as a means to prayer. Insofar as these are a means, their role in relation to the intended objectives are similar to the rule for the recommended category in relation to the obligatory when this obligation arises from the particular rule and not the universal. Likewise, some of the prohibitions are ends in themselves, while some are a means to such ends exactly like the obligatory, so ponder over this.

The eighth issue: obligations with a time limit

The occurrence of obligatory or recommended acts for which the Lawgiver has determined a limited time period does not entail during this time period any legal defect, reprimand or blame. Reprimand and blame are invoked when the act oversteps its determined time irrespective of this time span being narrow or wide. This is due to two reasons.

First: The limit on time is either due to a reason intended by the Lawgiver or without reason, and it is not valid that it be without reason. The only possibility left is that it be for a reason. The reason is that the act takes place during this time. If it occurs during this time, then this is the aim of the Lawgiver in fixing a time period. This implies, with a certainty, that there is agreement between the command and the act taking place during this time. Had it entailed reprimand or blame, it would be necessary that it be contrary to the aims of the Lawgiver, that is, by running within a time period that becomes a cause for reprimand and blame. We have, however, assumed that it is in complete conformity with the aim. This is inconsistent.

Second: Had it been so, it would become necessary that the segment of time in which reprimand is invoked is not the time determined for it, because we have assumed that the time determined grants a choice with respect to its various constituent segments when the time span is wide. Reprimand accompanying such choice is contradictory. It is, therefore, necessary that reprimand falls outside this time span. If, however, we assume that this time is one of its constituent time segments, it would make it incoherent and impossible. The evident nature of this concept does not need supporting evidence.

Objection to the above

It is said: The principle of requiring a hastening towards good works and surpassing others in them is established. It is a principle that is definitive, and this is not specific to some times and not others nor to some circumstances and not others. As surpassing others in good works is required as of necessity, one who falls short of this requirement is counted among the defaulters and evaders. There is no doubt that those who fall in this category are to be assigned the rule for defaulters and evaders. How then can it be said that there is no reprimand?

What includes the confirmation of this fact is the report from Abū Bakr al-Ṣiddīq, God be pleased with him, that when he heard the words of the Prophet (pbuh) "The beginning of time brings the pleasure of God, while its end brings forgiveness", he said: "The pleasure of God is preferable for us to His forgiveness, because His pleasure is for those who do good, while His forgiveness is for those who fall into error."[125]

There is an opinion in Mālik's school that also supports this. He said about travellers who ask someone to lead them in prayers, and he does so for the morning prayer when there is more light, "It is preferable in our view that a man says his prayer alone at its first appointed time as compared to one who says it in a congregation when there is more light."[126] He, therefore, gave priority, as you can see, to eagerness. He did not consider the congregation, which is a *sunna*, as better, and counted one who misses it as falling short. He was more likely to consider one who gave up eagerness as falling short. An opinion is also reported from him about the person who does not fast during Ramaḍān due to journey or illness and returns or regains health in a month of delayed performance (*qaḍā*ʾ) other than Shaʿbān and then dies not fasting on account of the missed fasts. Such a person (in his view) is liable for feeding the needy as atonement. He deems him similar to one who returns or regains health during Shaʿbān and does not fast until the next Ramaḍān. He maintains this despite the fact that (a command for) *qaḍā*ʾ does not require immediate compliance in his view. Al-Lakhmī says that he deems such a person to be waiting, neither working towards immediate compliance nor towards delayed performance. If he undertakes *qaḍā'* during Shaʿbān, having the ability to do so prior to Shaʿban, there is no feeding (as atonement) for him, because he is not in error. If he dies prior to Shaʿbān, he is in error and is liable for feeding (as atonement). The Shāfiʿīs maintain a similar opinion about *ḥajj* that it does not require immediate compliance. If, however, the subject dies prior to performance, he is a sinner. This opinion of the Shāfiʿīs too goes against the above mentioned principle.

You can see that timings are determined legally either through the text (*naṣṣ*)[127] or through *ijtihād*.[128] Thereafter, one who falls short of eagerness in these cases is subject to blame and reprimand. In fact, he is liable to sin in certain cases. This conflicts with what has preceded.

Response to the objection

The response is that the principle of competing for good works is not denied. However, should it be said for the act for which a fixed time is determined that it is to be advanced within its appointed time? In such a case, will it be said that the stated principle includes it or will it be said that it does not include it?

The first assertion is in conformity with the requirement of the evidence. The saying of the Prophet (pbuh), when he was asked about the preferred acts, is: "Prayer is to be performed in its first appointed time."[129] He meant by this the chosen time without qualification. It is indicated by the act of the Prophet (pbuh) when he was instructing the villagers about the timings, and he prayed at the beginning of the appointed timings as well as towards their ends. By doing so he determined a period of time that was not to be exceeded. He did not warn them about any shortcoming in this. He did warn them about falling into error with respect to the timings that were beyond the prescribed timings. When a person prayed at a timing when he was not required to, he said, "This is the prayer of the hypocrites."[130] He elaborated through this that the time of default was that timing in which the sun is between the horns of the Devil.[131] It is, therefore, necessary that a person who moves out of this limited timing moves out of the meaning of eagerness and competing for the good. In such a case, he will be in default, falling short, as well as a sinner according to some. Likewise, the obligations that require immediate compliance.

As for those acts that are assigned a whole lifetime for performance, insofar as their end has been limited by an unknown event, their performance and eagerness to do so is associated with the first time of possibility. The future is unknown. If the subject lives for a time in which this required act is performed, but he does not do so in the absence of an excuse, he is necessarily deemed a defaulter. Al-Shāfiʿī has considered such a person a sinner. The reason is that performance is a required act and is not the indicator that confirms the delineation between the first appointed time and the last. The end is unknown and what is known is what is being faced at the moment. This issue does not fall within the principle we have mentioned and it, therefore, does not negate it.

Further, the accompanying eagerness with respect to a determined time period cannot be denied, but in the meaning that a person postponing performance till after the first appointed time is not to be deemed a defaulter for otherwise the rule here does not apply to a wide span of time. This would be similar to *wājib mukhayyar* with respect to the choice in expiation (*kaffāra*) where the subject has a choice among several acts for this purpose, even though the recompense in these is different so that one act may bear a greater reward as compared to others, as is maintained about the expiation of Ramaḍān and the existence of a choice in the context of the tradition and (related) opinion of Mālik. The same is to be said about emancipation in the expiation of *ẓihār* (vow of continence) or homicide or other cases. The subject may choose any slave he likes although it is preferable to choose the one with the highest price and with the most value for the owners. Nevertheless, he does not violate the rule by exercising such a choice nor does he become a defaulter or evader by choosing one who is not the most valuable. Likewise, the one choosing between clothing and food in expiation of breaking an oath, as well as all similar cases of undetermined acts in which the Lawgiver has not identified some of the individual options even though there is merit in choosing the best of these, just as the performance of *ḥajj* on foot is better, but one who takes a ride is not considered a defaulter. Likewise, the greater number of steps leading to the mosque has greater merit than a lesser number of steps and the neighbour of a mosque is not considered guilty of dereliction due to the lesser number of steps leading to the mosque. The person who is a defaulter is one who falls short of what has been fixed for him, and ignores the requirements of the command directed at him. This does not affect the issue we are discussing.

As for the tradition from Abū Bakr, God be pleased with him, it has not proved to be sound. Even if we assume its soundness, it clashes with a definitive principle, and if we concede its content, it is to be interpreted for delayed performance within the entire chosen time. If it is conceded, then, the word shortcoming is to be applied in the unqualified sense to mean the giving up of the preferable eagerness to double the reward and not because delayed performance opposes the implication of the command.

As for issues decided by Mālik, perhaps the accompanying eagerness is for giving priority to prayer over congregation in consideration of the view that the morning is the time of need and the imam has delayed it for this reason. What he has said about feeding of the needy due to delayed performance in lieu of Ramaḍān is based on the view that prompt compliance is required for *qaḍā*ʾ. Thus, the main point raised in the question is not identified, and no objection is raised on this basis. God grants success.

The ninth issue: obligatory rights and the right of God

The duties imposed on the subject are of two types:[132] those that pertain to the right of God, like prayer, fasting, *ḥajj*, and those that pertain to the rights of human beings, like debts, maintenance, loyalties and moral improvement as well as those resembling them. The first are rights that have been limited by the law (*sharʿ*) and the others are rights that are not limited.

As for those that are limited and determined, these are necessary for the liability (*dhimma*)[133] of the subject and are owed by him as a debt until he has met them, like the prices of things purchased, value of things destroyed, amounts of *zakāt*, the obligations of prayer (*ṣalāt*) and whatever is similar to these. There is no difficulty in seeing that such rights are associated with his *dhimma* (liability) as a debt. The evidence of this is limitation and determination, as it indicates the intention for the performance of such a determined duty. If he does not perform such duties, the communication from the Lawgiver (*khiṭāb*) remains addressed in his case and is not extinguished (remitted) without evidence.

As for those that are not limited, he has no liability, but he is asked to perform them. These acts do not become associated with the *dhimma* due to several reasons.

First: If they were associated with the *dhimma,* they would have to be limited and determined, because an uncertain act cannot be associated with the *dhimma* and such association cannot be conceived rationally, thus, they are not like debts. It is through this argument that we reasoned for a lack of association. The reason is that these acts cannot be quantified and an obligation for us to perform acts whose extent is not known is an obligation to perform the impossible. This is forbidden on the basis of transmission as well.

The illustrations of such acts are unqualified charity, preventing poverty, meeting the needs of the indigent, providing succour to the deprived, saving those drowning, undertaking *jihād,* requiring what is good and denying what is evil. All the communal obligations fall under this category.

Thus, if the Lawgiver says, "Feed the indigent and the deprived",[134] or he says, "Clothe the naked" or "Spend in the cause of God",[135] then the meaning of this demand is to eliminate need in each case as required without fixing the extent. When the need is determined the extent of need becomes evident through examination and not the text. If a hungry person is identified, then the donor is ordered to feed him and remove his wants, due to the unqualified nature of the demand. When he feeds him in a manner that does not remove his hunger the demand remains until he does what is sufficient to remove the need due to which he was given the command initially. What is sufficient varies according to time and circumstances of this determined case. Thus, on occasions it does not do away with hunger and needs a substantial amount of food. If the person neglects him till it overwhelms him, he is in need of more. On occasions another person may feed him, removing the demand from the first person altogether. At other times another person may feed the needy in a way that is inadequate; then the first person is required to give less than what he was originally required to give. Insofar as the subject-matter of the obligation varies with circumstances and time, a determined amount is not associated with the *dhimma*, and this is exactly what an unknown amount means. It does not become known except at the relevant moment through examination and not through the requirement of the text. When that moment passes, the person is obliged to do another thing and not the first, or the obligation may be extinguished altogether if the removal of the intervening need is assumed.

Second: If such an act is associated with the *dhimma*, it is something that cannot be rationalised, because the donor is under an obligation, through each moment of the need of the indigent, to remove it. As time passes, he may be in a position to remove this person's need through a known quantity, but he does not do it and this amount becomes associated with the *dhimma*. This is followed by a second moment when the indigent person has the same need or is in greater need. Here it may be said that he is under an obligation to meet this need or it may be said that he is not under such obligation. Meeting the second need is void, because this second need does not have a priority higher than that of the first, as he is under an obligation on account of removing want, and here the obligation is removed, but the want persists. This is impossible. It is, therefore, necessary that the *dhimma* be linked with the second quantity through which his want will be removed at that moment. This will lead to the engaging of the *dhimma* with different values with respect to a single right for moments that have passed. This is incomprehensible in the law (*sharᶜ*).

Third: This duty is either universal or it is communal. It will become binding in either case if no one undertakes it. It will either be an obligation associated with an unknown *dhimma*, which is void and incomprehensible, or with all the *dhimmas* of individuals proportionally, which is also of the same nature due to the uncertainty of the instalment assigned to the *dhimma* of each individual. Then again, it may not be divided into portions where each portion is valued at one *dirham*, and a hundred thousand *dirhams* may be associated with the *dhimmas* of a hundred thousand persons. This is void, as has preceded.

Fourth: If the obligation is established against his *dhimma*, it would be futile, and futility is not acknowledged in the law. Where the purpose is the removal of need, the engaging of the *dhimma* negates this purpose, because the purpose is removal of this state, not the imposition of compensation for this state. If the *ḥukm* (rule) engages the *dhimma* in contravention of the cause of the obligation, it is futile and void.

It is not to be said that it is binding in obligatory *zakāt* and what resembles it, because its purpose is the removal of wants and this is established against the *dhimma*.

The reason is that we respond by saying that we concede the purpose as mentioned, but the need that is met through *zakāt* is undetermined on the whole. Notice that by agreement it is paid even where the need has not appeared. It therefore resembles rights that are met through compensation or donation. The law aims at compensation through a similar item or through value as against what we are discussing. The need in such cases is determined and must be removed. It is for this reason that the wealth of *zakāt* is not made specific for the need, which can be met through any type of wealth that meets the objective. Wealth is not required for itself. Thus, if the need is met without expending anything, the obligation stands removed. *Zakāt* and similar forms of wealth must be spent even though the object is not in need of it at the moment. It therefore stands identified.

It is in accordance with this mode of spending wealth for meeting needs that all the remaining rights in this category are settled.

Suppose it is said: when uncertainty becomes an obstacle in the way of association with the *dhimma*, it becomes an obstacle in the way of the obligation itself. The reason is that knowledge of the subject-matter of the obligation is a condition for the obligation, because an obligation to undertake an uncertain act is an obligation to do the impossible. If it is said to someone, "Spend an amount you do not know", or "Pray without knowing how many *rakʿahs* there are", or "Give advice to someone you do not know or identify", or the like, then this would be an obligation to do the impossible. The reason is that the subject cannot come to know of these things at all, except through revelation. If these become known through revelation they are ascertained and no longer unknown. Obligation to do known things is valid. This is unacceptable.

The response is that uncertainty that becomes an obstacle in the way of obligation is what is related to the ascertained, according to the Lawgiver. For example, if it is said, "Emancipate a slave", when the intended slave is a particular slave, but there is no elaboration, this is what becomes an obstacle. As for things that are undetermined, according to the Lawgiver, in accordance with the obligation, the imposition of the obligation in that form is valid, just as it is valid in the case of the choice between the various options in expiation (*kaffāra*), because the Lawgiver does not have a specific intention with respect to one option to the exclusion of others. The same applies here, as the aim of the Lawgiver is the elimination of want as a whole. Thus, as long as want is not identified there is no demand. When want is identified demand comes into operation. This is the meaning here; that is, an action is possible for the subject as long as a quantity is identified and not otherwise.

There is a third type that takes something of the first two types, but does not conform fully to either one, and this type is subject to *ijtihād,* like maintenance for next of kin and wives. As it resembles the other two types, people have differed about it as to whether it becomes linked to the *dhimma*. If it is established against the *dhimma*, it is not extinguished due to dire straits. The first type, then, is linked to the necessities (*ḍarūriyāt*) of *dīn* and is, therefore, supported by quantification and ascertainment. The second type is linked to the principle of refinement and adornment, and it is for this reason that it has been delegated to the *ijtihād* of the subjects. The third partakes of both sides on the basis of a strong cause. It is, therefore, necessary to examine it for ascertaining each case. Allah knows best.

Sub-issue: the first two types are organised on the basis of the demand of a universal or a communal obligation

Perhaps, the first two types are organised into rules on the basis of the demand for the universal and communal obligations. The conclusion about the first is that it is based on a demand for a quantified obligation imposing a universal on each of the subjects. The conclusion about the second is to implement the burdensome difficulties for the religion and its followers, except that this second type includes things that give the impression that these are universal obligations, but it does not become a decisive demand unless it is a communal obligation, like justice, fair-dealing and charity for relatives. When the demand is not decisive, it is treated as a recommendation. All communal obligations are recommended universal obligations. Ponder over this point. As for the third type, it partakes of both types for which reason there is disagreement about its details as has been discussed by the jurists (*fuqahā*ʾ). Allah knows best.

The tenth issue: the category of exemption between the permitted and the prohibited

It is valid if a category of *ʿafw* (pardon, exemption) is assumed between the permitted category and the prohibited, which should not be considered one of the established categories. This is so in general terms. The evidence for this is as follows.

First: What has preceded with respect to the five categories of rules: that these are related to the acts of the subject along with an intention to commit the act, and there is no intention where there is no commission. When none of these rules is related to the act along with the consciousness that it should be so related, then it gives the meaning of exemption that is being discussed; that is, there is no accountability for it.

Second: What has been laid down in the texts specifically about this category. It is related from the Prophet (pbuh) that he said, "Allah has prescribed certain obligations so do not neglect them, He has prohibited certain things so do not violate them, He has determined certain boundaries (*ḥudūd*) so do not cross them, and He has made certain exemptions as a mercy to you and not out of forgetfulness, so do not be too curious about them."[136] Ibn ʿAbbās has said: "I have never seen a group better than the Companions of Muḥammad (pbuh). They never asked him about anything other than thirteen issues until the day he died. All these are in the Qurʾān: "They ask thee concerning women's courses";[137] "They ask thee concerning orphans";[138] "They ask thee concerning fighting in the Prohibited Month";[139] and so on. They never used to ask about anything unless it would benefit them",[140] and this was usually the case with them. It is related from Ibn ʿAbbās (God be pleased with him) that he said: "What is not mentioned in the Qurʾān is what Allah has forgiven."[141] He used to be asked about a thing that was not prohibited and he would reply: "It is forgiven." He was asked about *zakāt* with respect to the Ahl al-Dhimma and he said that it was forgiven, that is, *zakāt* was not to be levied on them. ʿUbayd ibn ʿUmayr said: "Allah has permitted the lawful and has prohibited the unlawful. What He has permitted is lawful and what He has prohibited is unlawful, but that about which He has maintained silence is forgiven."[142]

Third: What points to this concept in a general way like the words of the Exalted: "God give thee grace! Why didst thou grant them exemption?"[143] This is an object of *ijtihād* with respect to permission as long as there is a text.

The meaning of exemption (*ʿafw*) in the context of mistake in the undertaking of *ijtihād* is laid down in the *sharīʿa* in accordance with what the specialists on *ʿuṣūl* have elaborated. Related to this are the words of Exalted: "Had it not been for a previous ordinance from Allah, a severe punishment would have reached you for the (reason) that ye took."[144] The Prophet (pbuh) used to look down upon excessive questions about matters on which no *ḥukm* (rule) had been laid down, and this is based on *barāʾa aṣliyya* (original rule of permissibility or no liability) as it refers to this meaning. The meaning is that when it is found things are exempted. The Prophet (pbuh) said, "The most sinful among Muslims are those who ask about things that are not prohibited, but they become prohibited because of their questions."[145] He also said: "Let me be, for as long as I leave you alone. Those before you perished because of excessive questioning and due to their disagreement about their Prophets. Abstain from what I proscribe for you, and undertake according to your ability what I require you to do."[146] The Prophet (pbuh) recited the words of the Exalted: "Pilgrimage to the House is a duty men owe to Allah."[147] A man said: "O Messenger of Allah, is it so for every year?" The Prophet (pbuh) turned away from him. The man said again: "O Messenger of Allah, is it so for every year?" The Prophet (pbuh) turned away from him again. The man persisted and said: "O Messenger of Allah, is it so for every year?" The Messenger of Allah (pbuh) replied saying: "By Him in whose hand is my life, if I were to say yes, it would become obligatory. If it were to be made obligatory you would not be able to perform it. If you do not perform it, you would be guilty of unbelief, so let me be as long as I leave you alone."[148] He then stated the meaning of what has preceded. It is with respect to such things that the following verse was revealed: "O ye who believe! Ask not questions about things which, if made plain to you, may cause you trouble."[149] The Exalted then said about such things, "Allah has forgiven them."[150] The meaning then is that of exemption (*ʿafw*). The Prophet (pbuh) disapproved the raising of issues, deeming it a failing, and he proscribed excessive questions. He stood up one day to address the people and anger could be perceived on his face. He mentioned the Last Day, indicating events to occur before it, and then said, "He who wishes to ask about things may do so now. By Allah, I will answer every question you ask for as long as I stand at this spot." Anas says that most of the people started weeping profusely when they heard this. The Prophet (pbuh) kept on repeating over and over: "Go ahead, ask me." ʿAbd Allah ibn Ḥudhāfa al-Suhmī stood up and asked, "Who is my father?" The Prophet (pbuh) replied, "Your father is Abū Ḥudhāfa." When he had said, "Ask me", many times, ʿUmar went down on his knees and said, "O Messenger of Allah, we are content with Allah as our Lord, Islam as our religion, and Muḥammad as Prophet." The narrator says that when ʿUmar said this, the Messenger of Allah (pbuh) became silent. This is when the verse was revealed, but prior to that he said, "By Him in whose hands is my life, I was offered heaven and hell a moment ago next to this wall while I was praying. I have never seen a day like this that contains both good and evil."[151] The apparent meaning in this context is that his words, "Ask me," said in anger are a rejection of excessive questions by them, and would lead them to the consequences of the questions. It was for this reason that the verse, "If made plain to you, may cause you trouble,"[152] was revealed. From all this emerges the meaning of the "forgiven" category, which is a category about which questions are not to be asked. Thus, the implication of the verse is that *ḥajj* is prescribed for God and the verse, likewise, implies that it is for the current year. When the verse is silent about repetition, it is necessary to interpret its more lenient meanings. If it is assumed that the other meaning is implied, then it belongs to the forgiven category. A similar incident is that of the owners of the cow who asked detailed questions when they were in a position to slaughter any cow that they possessed. The detailed constraints were described for them till they slaughtered it, "And they were not about to do it."[153] This makes it evident that there is a category of acts of the subjects questions about which, or about their rules, are not proper. This makes it necessary that there be a forgiven/exempted category. It also establishes that the category of exception (forgiveness) is affirmed and it is not a category falling within the five existing categories.

Sub-issue: this category is witnessed on various occasions within the sharīʿa

This category is visible on various occasions in the *sharīʿa*. Within it are cases that are agreed upon, and those that are disputed. Thus, among them are cases of mistake (*khaṭaʾ*) and forgetfulness (*nisyān*). These are agreed upon for non-accountability. Any act that issues forth from a person who is unaware, forgetful, or mistaken is excusable. It does not matter if these acts are assumed by us to be required or prohibited, because if these acts are neither prohibited, nor required, nor optional, they revert to a category for which there is no rule in the law (*sharʿ*). This is the meaning of exception (forgiveness) (*ʿafw*).

When the command and proscription are related to these acts, a condition of accountability is the statement of the command and proscription and the ability to comply with them. This is not possible in the case of a person making a mistake, and one who is forgetful and unaware. Similar to such persons are one who is asleep, an insane person, the menstruating woman and others like them.

Among them is mistake in *ijtihād* and that refers to the first type. It is laid down in the Qur᾿ān, "God give thee grace! Why didst thou grant them exemption?"[154] The Qur᾿ān says, "Had it not been for a previous ordinance from Allah …"[155]

Among these is coercion (duress) including what is agreed upon in it and what is disputed. When we uphold its permissibility, it refers to the category of *ʿafw*, irrespective of the command and proscription remaining in operation with respect to it. The conclusion in this case is that there is no harm in its commission when it is committed or in its omission when it is omitted.

Among these are all the *rukhaṣ* (exemptions) with all their variety. The texts have indicated these when they talk about removal of sin, the removal of harm and the attainment of forgiveness. There is no distinction in this respect whether the exemptions are optional or required. The reason is that if these are optional there is no difficulty, but if these are required, forgiveness becomes necessary to counter what is required. Thus, in the case of consumption of carrion, where we uphold its obligation, its negation must be through omission, which is omission that is forgiven, for otherwise the gathering together of two contraries in an obligation will become binding, and this is impossible and not imposed upon the *umma*.

Among these is preference between two evidences when they conflict and reconciliation is not possible. When one of the evidences is not preferred the implication is that the evidence not preferred takes the rule of the forgiven category. The reason is that if it is not so, it does not amount to preference. In this case, it would lead to the removal of its basis, when that is established through consensus. Further, it would lead to a communication (*khiṭāb*) that includes two contraries, which is invalid. There is no distinction with respect to the necessity of *ʿafw* whether we maintain the continued existence of the demand in the evidence not preferred, deeming it established, or whether we consider it non-existent.

Among these is acting contrary to an evidence that has not reached a person or acting according to one that has reached him but is abrogated or is not sound as a proof has not been adduced with respect to it at the moment. The evidence must reach him and he must have knowledge of it, before he can be held accountable for it, otherwise it will necessarily be an obligation to do the impossible.

Among these is also the preference between two different communications (*khiṭāb*) when they clash and it is not possible to reconcile them. It is necessary to uphold forgiveness with respect to the one that is later to be able to act according to the one that is prior, because it is not possible to act according to both for that would amount to an obligation to undertake the impossible, which is something eliminated by the law (*sharʿ*).

Among these are acts about which silence has been maintained. These are in the forgiven category. The reason is that if silence is maintained about them, with the existence of the opportunity to comment upon them, it amounts to forgiveness.

What has preceded with respect to illustration of the evidences is sound. Allah knows best.

Sub-issue: the obstacle to the category of forgiveness should be perceived from various perspectives

The obstacle to the category of forgiveness should be grasped from various perspectives.

First: The acts of the subjects, insofar as they are subjects (*mukallafūn*), either fall entirely within the communication of obligation, which is either a demand or an option, or they do not fall entirely under such communication. If they do fall entirely within it, they do not go beyond the five categories, which is required. If they do not fall under them entirely, it becomes necessary that some of the subjects be outside the ambit of the rule of the communication of obligation even though this is at a particular moment or under certain circumstances. This is not valid, however, because we have assumed that they are subjects. Thus, they do not fall outside their ambit and there is nothing that goes beyond the five types of *aḥkam*.

Second: This addition is either a legal rule (*ḥukm sharʿī*) or it is not. If it is not a legal rule, it is not to be considered as such. What indicates that it is not a legal rule is that it is being called the category of forgiveness (*ʿafw*). Forgiveness is invoked when opposition to a command or proscription is expected of the subject. This necessarily implies that the subject is faced with a rule; therefore, it is not proper to impose another rule on him due to the clash of rules. Further, *ʿafw* is a rule that applies to the Hereafter and not to this world, while we are discussing rules faced in this world. If, however, the category of forgiveness is a legal rule, it either falls within the communication of obligation or within the declaratory communication. The types of communication of obligation are confined to the five categories of rules, while the types of declaratory communications are limited to five categories as well and these have been mentioned by the specialist of *ʿUṣūl*. The category we have been discussing is not one of them; it is, therefore, that of forgiveness.

Third: If this addition is an issue of *ʿUṣūl*, like questioning the validity of the proposition that some incidents do not have a rule laid down by Allah, then the issue is disputed with respect to its proof, and is without an evidence having no priority over its negation. The evidences for this are conflicting, and it is not proper to establish it without evidence that is free from conflict or claims of conflict. Further, even if it is subject to *ijtihād*, the obvious action is that of its negation through evidences mentioned in books on *ʿUṣūl*. If, however, it does not belong to this issue, then it is incomprehensible. There is no evidence for it in the evidences that have preceded for affirming the category of forgiveness. The transmitted evidences do not imply that it should be outside the five categories due to the possibility of reconciliation between them. Another reason is that forgiveness is a category that pertains to the Hereafter. Further, if a proof is conceded for the category of *ʿafw*, then it pertains to the period of the Prophet (pbuh) to the exclusion of other periods. Due to the possibility of these apparent interpretations and due to what has been said about its types, it falls within the five categories. Forgiveness in these types belongs to the category of exception as rules of mistake, forgetfulness, duress and harm. This either implies permissibility or it implies the removal of what is the consequence of opposing rules, as in blame and the causes of punishment. This will require the imposition of command and proscription along with the removal of their consequences due to opposition. The impact of the rule, therefore, stands removed due to the category of forgiveness and it is an addition over the five categories. There are several discussions in this context.

Sub-issue: rules of the unexpressed category

In examining the rules of what falls under the category of waiver (*ʿafw*), where such need is felt, restricting such examination to the text appears to be an obvious inclination. An absolutely fragmented approach towards it is a folly that cannot be accepted. Restriction in this context to some aspects, to the exclusion of others, is an arbitrary action that is not justified rationally or on the basis of transmissions. It is, therefore, necessary to adopt an approach towards it that elaborates the issue, through the power of God. The discussion on the issue is confined to three types.

First: Abiding by the implication of the opposing evidence if such opposition is strong enough.

Second: Moving beyond its implication without a particular aim or with an aim after interpretation.

Third: Acting upon what is unexpressed from the start.

As for the first, it includes acts based upon the initial general rule (*ʿazīma*) where the rule of exemption is adopted on the basis of the apparent meaning. When the initial rule is applied on the basis of the apparent general, or unqualified, meaning a person relying upon it is relying upon an evidence applied in general terms. The exemption has been adopted in the same way. In case the rule of *ʿazīma* is adopted, the exemption extends from the principle of removal of hardship, just as the initial rule belongs to the basis of obligation. Both the application of universal principles and having recourse to the exemption amounts to relying on equally reliable evidence. As the principle of removal of hardship has been imposed as a complementary rule for the basic obligation, it is considered to be a rule pre-supposing basic obligation in some respects.

This, however, does not disturb recourse to the exemption, because the basic obligation is maintained through this complementary rule. This has been acknowledged in Mālik's school. It is stated in this school that if a person travels less than twelve miles during Ramaḍān believing superficially that the relief of not fasting is available to him and he therefore does not fast he is not liable to atonement through expiation. The same rule applies to him if he adopts the exemption on the basis of a conscious interpretation, even though the rationale is not based on sound legal reasoning. In fact, this is practised in each action that is based on judgement like the consumption of liquor thinking that it is not an intoxicant, like one killing a Muslim thinking that he was an (enemy) unbeliever, like the consumption of unlawful wealth thinking that it was lawful, like one who performs ablution with impure water considering it to be pure, and so on. Here the *mujtahid* (jurist) who has made an error in his legal reasoning resembles this person. It is recorded by Abū Dāwūd from Ibn Masʿūd (God be pleased with him) that he arrived on a Friday when the Prophet (pbuh) was addressing the people and he heard him say, "Sit down", so he sat down right at the door. The Prophet (pbuh) saw him and said, "Come here, O ʿAbd Allah ibn Masʿūd."[156] The apparent meaning here is that acting upon the mere literal meaning, even though another meaning was intended, shows eagerness in complying with his commands. ʿAbd Allah ibn Rawāḥa heard the same when he was on the street leading to the Prophet's house, and he said, "Sit down", so he sat down by the street. The Prophet (pbuh) then passed by him and said, "What are you doing here?" He replied, "I heard you saying sit down, so I sat down." The Prophet (pbuh) said, "May Allah advance you in obedience."[157] The apparent meaning of this story is that he did not actually mean "sit down" in the literal sense by this command, but when he (the listener) heard it he hastened to act in obedience. It was for this reason that the Prophet (pbuh) questioned him when he saw him sitting in an odd place. The Prophet (pbuh) said, "No one is to offer *ʿaṣr* (middle) prayer except at Banū Qurayẓa." The time of *ʿaṣr* prayer came upon them on the way, so some of them said that the prayer is not to be offered until they reach the destination, while others said that it should be prayed and he (the Prophet) did not mean this in the literal sense. This was mentioned to the Prophet (pbuh) and he did not deem any of the two groups to be wrong.[158] All the decisions of a *qāḍī* fall under this when he is deciding an issue that is based upon *ijtihād* and in which it turns out later that he made a mistake when the mistake is not based on a text, consensus or certain definitive matters. Likewise the preference of one of two evidences over the other, because it amounts to reliance upon one of two evidences and disregarding the other. If a disregarded evidence is assumed along with the preferred evidence, this is due to the reason that reliance can be placed on the disregarded evidence along with the existence of the preferred evidence. The same is the case with evidence that is abrogated or it is not valid, as it is reliance on an apparent evidence that is usually relied upon. Such evidences and those like them are classified under the meaning of *ʿafw* (waiver) mentioned above. We have stipulated reliance upon the implication of a conflicting evidence. Conflict has been stipulated here as it cannot be classified under waiver (*ʿafw*) if there is no conflict. The reason is that acting upon a command, prohibition or option on the basis of the apparent meaning of a text does not give rise to waiver (*ʿafw*), as no censure or blame is attached to it in doing so. Waiver is upheld when a strong conflict is realised. If the conflict is not strong it does not belong to this category; rather it belongs to the category that follows it as a consequence, for that is the giving up of evidence. In this case, even when it amounts to acting upon an evidence, such action is due to its strength in the eyes of the examiner or at the same time acting upon evidence that does not conflict and in which there is no waiver (*ʿafw*).

As for the second type, which is the moving beyond the implication of evidence without an intention or with intention, but after interpretation, this includes the case of the person who undertakes an act believing it to be permissible, because the evidence of its prohibition or disapproval has not reached him or he omits the act believing it to be permissible as the evidence of its being obligatory or recommended has not reached him. This would be like a person in the early days of Islam who does not know that drinking of wine is prohibited and consumes it or who does not know that bathing is obligatory after major ritual impurity and omits it. It is similar to what happened in the early phase when the Anṣār did not know that bathing is required after sexual intercourse.[159] There are many cases of this type that came up before *mujtahids*. It is related from Mālik that he did not uphold the *takhlīl* (passing through) of the toes by the fingers during ablution and he arrived at this view upon deep reflection until the report reached him that the Prophet (pbuh) used to do so,[160] upon which he withdrew his opinion. It also happened to Abū Yūsuf, along with Mālik, in the case of the *mudd* and the *ṣāʿ* until he withdrew his opinion.[161]

Within this category is acting against the rule by mistake or out of forgetfulness as is related in the tradition, "Liability has been lifted from my *umma* in case of mistake, forgetfulness and what they are coerced to do."[162] If the tradition is proved sound it applies. If it is not proved to be authentic, its content is still agreed upon (among the jurists). There is lack of intention in mistakes and forgetfulness but an underlying intention is to be found in the case of coercion in the tradition. More evident than this is the waiver in the case of erroneous excesses by decent persons. Treating them with leniency is established in the *sharʿ* (law) in the case of erroneous excesses, and they are not to be treated like other ordinary cases. It is stated in a tradition, "Treat decent persons with leniency for their erroneous excesses."[163] Another tradition says, "Avoid punishing decent and well meaning persons."[164] Acting upon this rule is reported from Muḥammad ibn Abī Bakr ibn ʿAmr ibn Ḥazm. He gave a decision in the case of a person from the family of ʿUmar ibn al-Khaṭṭāb, who had injured a person by beating him. He sent for him and said, "You are a decent person." It is reported from ʿAbd al-ʿAzīz ibn ʿAbd Allah ibn Abd ʿAllah ibn ʿUmar ibn al-Khaṭṭāb that he said, "A slave of mine called Salām al-Barīrī, whom I had injured, complained to Ibn Ḥazm, so he came to me and said, 'Did you injure him?' I said, 'Yes.' He said, 'I heard my maternal aunt ʿAmra saying, "ʿĀʾisha said, 'The Messenger of Allah (pbuh) said, "Treat decent people with leniency for their erroneous excesses."' " ' "[165] He therefore, let him go and did not punish him. This is also of concern to the Lord of Glory, praise be to Him. He says, "And He rewards those who do good, with what is best. Those who avoid great sins and indecent deeds, except lesser offences."[166] These rules, however, pertain to the Hereafter, while our discussion is about the rules pertaining this world. Close to this meaning is the waiving of the *ḥudūd* penalties on the basis of *shubhāt* (mistakes). In these cases the evidence gives a probable meaning for purposes of implementation of *ḥadd* and when accompanied by *shubha*, even if it is weak, it will take its rule and the person liable will be entitled to waiver (*ʿafw*). This category may be counted as one where the evidence is opposed through interpretation, which belongs to this type as well. The example of opposing it through interpretation, along with the identification of the evidence, is what is stated in a tradition on the interpretation of the words of the Exalted, "On those who believe and do deeds of righteousness there is no blame for what they ate (in the past)."[167]

In this tradition, Qudāma ibn Mazʿūn said to ʿUmar ibn al-Khaṭṭāb, "Had I drunk it, then, you would not have the right to apply the punishment of stripes on me." He asked, "Why?" He replied, "Because Allah says: On those who believe and do deeds of righteousness there is no blame for what they ate (in the past)."[168] ʿUmar said, "O Qudāma, you have erred in the interpretation. As you fear Allah, you will avoid what He has prohibited."[169] Al-Qāḍī Ismāʿīl said that he intended to declare such a state as a denial of drinking of wine, because he (Qudāma) was God-fearing, had a strong faith and undertook good works; therefore, he made a mistake in interpretation as against someone who would permit it. This is elaborated in a tradition from ʿAlī, God be pleased with him. Accordingly, it is not stated in Qudāma's tradition that he was awarded the *ḥadd*.

In the school (Mālik's), it is stated about the woman with irregular bleeding (*mustaḥāḍa*) that if she gives up prayer for a period, being ignorant of the required act, she is not required to undertake substitute prayers in lieu of those she gave up. It is stated that it is in the *Mukhtaṣar*, when it is not in the *Mukhtaṣar*, that if the bleeding is prolonged in the case of the *mustaḥāḍa* or in the case of one in the post-natal state, with the woman with post-natal bleeding not praying for three months and the *mustaḥāḍa* not praying for one month, they are not to perform substitute prayers for those that have lapsed. If we use interpretation here for the giving up of prayer in case of prolonged bleeding and it is said about the *mustaḥāḍa* that if she gives up prayer for a short duration after the days of her period, she may perform substitute prayers, but if this duration is lengthy substitute prayers are not obligatory upon her. In the narration of Abū Zayd from Mālik, it is stated that if she gives up prayer out of ignorance after seeking to discover her state, she is not to perform substitute prayers. Ibn al-Qāsim, however, deemed it recommended that she undertake substitute prayers. All this is in opposition to the evidence, either with ignorance or through interpretation; therefore, they deemed it to fall in the category of waiver (*ʿafw*). Included in such cases is also that of the traveller who arrives at his destination prior to the morning prayer and believes that a person who does not arrive prior to sunset does not have to fast. There is also the case of the menstruating woman who reaches the period of purity prior to sunrise and believes that her fast is not valid unless she attains purity prior to sunset. In such cases there is no expiation even where the act goes against the evidence, because it is a case of interpretation. The extinction of expiation falls within the category of waiver (*ʿafw*).

As for the third type, which is the undertaking of an act whose rule is unexpressed, it needs examination. The fact that the *ḥukm* of Allah is not applicable to some incidents is disputed. If the statement that it is not applicable is deemed valid, it needs examination in the light of the tradition, "What remains unexpressed is deemed as waiver (*ʿafw*),"[170] as well as in the light of what has preceded. If the other view is deemed valid, the meaning of the tradition becomes difficult to apply, because in such a case there is no act that can be left unexpressed whatever the case. In fact, such a case is either directly expressed or is settled through analogical extension of the text. Analogy is one of the sources (evidences) of the *sharīʿa*. Thus, there is no incident that does not have an assigned rule and the unexpressed category is, therefore, eliminated. It is also possible to construe silence with reference to this statement as the giving up of the search for details despite the possibility of their existence, to construe it as silence about customary practices despite their existence within incidents, and to construe it as silence about acts acquired earlier from the *sharīʿa* of Prophet Ibrāhīm (Abraham) (pbuh). The first is to be found in the words of the Exalted, "The food of the People of the Book is lawful unto you."[171] This general meaning includes in its apparent meaning what they slaughtered for their festivals and synagogues. When we examine this meaning, we find an ambiguity, because among the animals slaughtered for their festivals is an excess that negates the laws of Islam. Thus, there is room for examination here. When Makḥūl was asked about this issue he said that you should consume it, because Allah knew about what they say, yet he permitted their slaughtered animals. By this, God knows best, he intended that the general meaning of the verse is not restricted even when this negative particular meaning is found. Allah knew about its implication, and its inclusion within the general meaning, yet, despite this, He declared permissible that in which there is an objection as well as that in whch there is none. This He did under the rule of waiver (*ʿafw*) with reference to the negative factor. It is such a meaning that is indicated by the words of the Prophet (pbuh), "He has forgiven things for you by way of mercy and not out of forgetfulness, so do not be too curious about them."[172] The tradition about *ḥajj* has the same tenor in which a person asks, "Is it for this *ḥajj* this year or for ever?"[173] The reason is that the consideration of the syntax gives the sense that it is for every year. The Prophet (pbuh) disapproved this person's question and elaborated for him the underlying reason for giving up questions on matters such as this. Likewise, the tradition that says, "The greatest offenders among Muslims …",[174] indicates the same meaning. Questions about things not prohibited, which then become prohibited after the raising of questions, are usually those that give rise to aspects that require prohibition despite the fact that there is a principle for them to which recourse can be had for accommodating uniqueness. This occurs despite the fact that the individual cases differ among themselves or a concept is introduced that gives the impression of moving away from such a principle. There is also the tradition that says, "Let me be, as long as I leave you alone",[175] as well as others like it.

The second includes things about which there was silence in the early days of Islam, but were gradually prohibited, as in the case of wine (*khamr*). It was in habitual use during the days of the Jāhiliyya thereafter; with the arrival of Islam it was left without alteration prior to the Hijra and even for a period after it. The texts of the *sharʿ* (law) did not address it, until the following verse was revealed, "They ask thee concerning wine and gambling."[176] The verse explained that there were benefits as well as harm in it, and that the harmful effects were more than the benefits. The verse omitted the rule that was required by *maṣlaḥa* (jurisprudential interest) and which was prohibition. The reason is that the legal principle states that when the harm exceeds the benefit, the rule is based on the harm, and harm is prohibited. The meaning of prohibition thus oscillated between the two; however, as the text did not mention prohibition, even when interpretation required this, they held on to the subsisting rule that was established for them by their customary practice. The rule was classified for them under waiver (*ʿafw*), until the verse of Sūrat al-Māʾida was revealed, saying, "Avoid it."[177] It was then that the rule of prohibition was laid down and that of waiver was removed. This is indicated by the words of the Exalted, "On those who believe and do deeds of righteousness there is no blame for what they ate (in the past), when they guard themselves from evil, and believe, and do deeds of righteousness, (or) again, guard themselves from evil and believe, (or) again, guard themselves from evil and do good. For Allah loveth those who do good."[178] The verse was revealed as on the laying down of the prohibition they had asked: How about those who died when they used to drink wine? The sin was removed and that is the meaning of waiver (*ʿafw*).

Similar to this is the *ribā* (usury) that was practised during the Jāhiliyya and during early days of Islam. Likewise, sales involving *gharar* (uncertainty) that were transacted among them, like the *maḍāmin* (sale of foetus) and *malāqīḥ* (sale of stud for breeding camels) sales, the sale of fruit before its ripening and other similar transactions. All these were unexpressed, and whatever is unexpressed takes the meaning of waiver (*ʿafw*). Subsequent abrogation (*naskh*) does not remove this meaning due to the existence of all of them up until now having been confirmed by Islam, like *qirāḍ* (*muḍāraba* partnership), the rule for the eunuch with respect to inheritance and so on. There are others similar to them that have been pointed out by scholars.

The third type includes those like marriage, divorce, *ḥajj*, *ʿumrā*, and all other acts except those that were altered. They used to undertake these acts prior to Islam. They distinguished between marriage and fornication; pronounced divorce; performed circumambulation of the house every week; they used to kiss the black stone (of the Kaʿba); make the circuits between al-Safā and al-Marwā; pronounce the *ṭalbiya*; make the stay at ʿArafāt; descend at Muzdalifa; throw stones at the *jimār*; respect the prohibited months and treat them with veneration; they used to bathe after major impurity, and wash their dead, after placing them in shrouds and praying over them; they used to cut off the hands of the thief and to crucify the brigand; and they used to undertake all acts that were given to them by the nation of their father Abraham. They continued doing these things until the arrival of Islam, and they maintained the earlier rules till Islam issued the rulings that it did abrogating those that went against it.

Insofar as no new addition was made by the communication to acts that were practised before Islam, they were abrogated if they went against Islam. Those that had to be abrogated were abrogated, while those that had to be retained were retained. With this elaboration the occasions of waiver (*ʿafw*) in the *sharīʿa* became obvious and were organised. Praise be to Allah for most effectively employing the evidences that affirm it. There remains, however, the examination of the category of waiver (*ʿafw*) as to whether or not it can be deemed a category of rules. If it is asserted that it is an independent category of rules, then, does it belong to the division of obligatory rules (*taklīfī*) or to the communication dealing with declaratory rules? All this is probable, but insofar as no rule of conduct is structured upon this category, it does not necessitate elaboration. It is, therefore, better to omit it. It is Allah who guides us to the correct view.

The eleventh issue: the demand for the communal obligation and the universal rules

The specialists in *ʿUṣūl* maintain that the demand for the communal obligation is addressed to all, but if some persons undertake it the liability is removed from the remaining. What they say is true from the perspective of a demand that is collective (*kullī*). As for the particular perspective, it requires a detailed explanation and the demand is divided into several types. Perhaps, it can be split up into many branches, but the precept on the whole is that the demand is addressed to some. It is not addressed to an indeterminate group in general terms, but to those among the people who have the ability to undertake the required act.

There are several evidences supporting this.

First: The first evidence is from the texts that indicate this, like the words of the Exalted: "It is not for the believers to go forth together."[179] Here the command is restricted to a group and is not addressed to all. There are also verses like: "Let there arise out of you a band of people inviting to all that is good, enjoining what is right, and forbidding what is wrong: they are the ones to attain felicity",[180] and "When thou (O Messenger) art with them, and standest to lead them in prayer, let one party of them stand up (in prayer) with thee, taking their arms with them; when they finish their prostrations, let them take their position in the rear."[181] There are many such evidences in the Qurʾān of this type in which the demand is addressed to some and not to all.

Second: The second is what is established through definitive principles of the *sharīʿa* in support of this concept like *imāma kubrā* (leadership of the nation) or *imāma ṣughrā* (leadership for prayers). This is ascertained for those who have qualities of leadership and not for all the people. Likewise, all positions of authority of the same status; the demand is addressed, by agreement in the law, to those who are qualified to undertake these responsibilities and are not in need of such duties. So also *jihād*, insofar as it is a communal obligation, for it is ascertained for one who will undertake it with courage and bravery. The same applies to all similar legal duties as it is not proper to apply the demand to those who have nothing at all to do with the task. In such a case it would become, for the subject, an obligation to do the impossible and a futile act with respect to the interest to be secured or injury to be repelled. Both situations are not legally valid.

Third: The third evidence is found in the *fatāwā* (legal opinions) issued by the jurists as well as in the entire *sharīʿa* in support of the concept. Among these is what is related from Muḥammad, the Messenger of Allah (pbuh). He said to Abū Dharr, "O Abū Dharr, I see that you are weak. I prefer for you what I prefer for myself. Do not assume authority over two persons or over the wealth of an orphan."[182] Both acts are communal obligations and despite this he forbade him from undertaking them. If it is assumed that all the people will neglect these two duties, it would not be valid to uphold that Abū Dharr would be held liable for the injury caused by the dereliction. The same applies to all those who are like him. A tradition says, "Do not ask for authority."[183] This proscription implies that it is not for general obligation. Abū Bakr (God be pleased with him) forbade certain people from assuming authority. When the Messenger of Allah (pbuh) passed away and Abū Bakr had to assume authority, a man came up to him and said, "You forbade me from assuming authority, but now you have done so yourself." He replied, "And I, even now, forbid you from assuming it."[184] As for his own assumption of authority, he offered the excuse to the person that he had absolutely no choice in it. It is related that Tamīm al-Dārī sought permission from ʿUmar ibn al-Khaṭṭāb (may Allah be pleased with both) to relate (historical) incidents, but he forbade him doing so[185] when this was a communal obligation. I mean by this, the type of incidents that Tamim (God be pleased with him) wished to relate. A similar view is reported from ʿAlī ibn Abī Ṭālib (God be pleased with him).[186]

It was this broad road that was trodden by the scholars in settling a large number of communal obligations. It is reported from Mālik that he was asked, about the acquisition of knowledge, whether it was an obligation. He replied: For all the people, no.[187] He meant thereby what was in excess of the universal obligation. He also said: As for one who is suited for leadership, it is obligatory on him to strive in search of knowledge, while making efforts for knowledge is subject to his resolve to acquire it. Thus, he divided it into different types, as you can see. For him who has the ability to take authority, he deemed it obligatory and for him who does not have this ability he considered it recommended. This explains that it is not obligatory for all persons. Saḥnūn said: a person who is eligible for taking authority and acquiring knowledge in various fields, it is obligatory that he acquire it on the basis of the words of Exalted: "Let there arise out of you a band of people ..."[188] The reason is that one who does not understand justice will not be able to administer it, and one who does not understand injustice will not be able to forbid it.

On the whole, the meaning underlying this concept is evident and the remaining discussion of the issue is left for the discipline of *ʿUṣūl al-Fiqh*.

It may, however, be appropriate to say that it is obligatory on all in a certain meaning of permissibility. The reason is that undertaking this form of duty amounts to undertaking an interest (*maṣlaha*) that has to be secured. Thus, they are required to secure this interest as a whole. Some of them are able to undertake it directly, and these are those who are qualified to do so. The remaining, even though they cannot undertake it, are able to facilitate those who are able to do so. A person, therefore, who is eligible for assuming authority, is under an obligation to do so. The person with ability, accordingly, is to undertake the obligation, while one who does not have this ability is required to equip one who is able, because the assumption of authority by one able is not attained without the implementation of its process. This issue falls under the rule that anything without which an obligation cannot be met is itself obligatory. It is in this manner that the basis of disagreement is eliminated and no obvious reason for dispute remains.

Sub-issue: some details of the communal obligation

It is necessary to elaborate some details of this general discussion so as to bring out aspects that make its soundness evident – through the power of God.

Allah, the Mighty and Majestic, has created all creatures in a manner that they are unaware of certain aspects of their own interests (*maṣāliḥ*) whether of this world or of the Hereafter. Examine the verse: "It is He Who brought you forth from the wombs of your mothers when ye knew nothing."[189] Thereafter, He instilled in them such knowledge in phases through training. This is either through inspiration (*ilhām*), like the infant suckling at the breast and rubbing it, or through education. Mankind are, therefore, required to give and seek instruction on all matters that will help secure their interest and in all ways that will repel injury from them, relying upon all the natural instincts and inspired ideas. The reason is that there is a fundamental principle for accomplishing the details of the interest to be secured – whether it is through deeds, words, science (*ʿulūm*), beliefs and legal or other practices. During occupation with these things, all the natural powers with which one is created are strengthened. When the details of certain situations and acts are given to a person by inspiration, the effects appear in him and upon him, and he rises up with respect to such things as compared to those around him who have not been equipped accordingly. Thereafter, there is no period of rational activity in which such merits, with which he was endowed initially, do not appear in him. Thus, you will see that a certain person was prepared for the seeking of knowledge, another for statesmanship, another for the crafting in certain essentially needed professions, and yet another for fighting and combat, and likewise for all other affairs.

Even though general drives are instinctively present in each person, it is some of these tendencies that become dominant in an individual. The obligations placed on him are meant to instruct and train him according to his situation. The demand is to arouse in each subject the requirements for which he is best equipped. Those who train him are to focus on these aspects, developing them accordingly, so that at their hands these qualities can be channelled into the right path. They are to direct them to act according to their talents and develop them persistently so that each person excels in what is predominant in him and for which he has an aptitude over and above all other activity. Thereafter, the owners of these talents are to be left alone so that they can employ them as it suits them for their advancement, for these are then like natural traits and essential reflexes. This is how benefit can be derived causing the result of the training to become manifest.

Thus, for example, if we assume that there is a child who is intelligent, has good comprehension and abundant ability to memorise what he hears even though he enjoys other traits, he becomes inclined towards this goal. It is obligatory on the person who supervises him on the whole, in consideration of the expectations he has for his education, to require that he have an overall education in all the disciplines. The student must be inclined towards some, so he must focus on them, and support them, but in an order that has been specified by the scholars in education. When he begins the study of these disciplines he will feel inclined towards them and will like them more than the others. He is to be left to do what he likes and is to be associated with people adept in that field. It is obligatory on these people to prepare him in this discipline till he has acquired what is sufficient without any one of them neglecting him or giving up concern for him. If he stops at this point it is good. He may, however, wish to pursue another discipline or to work with one who is already working in the same field.

This may be illustrated, for example, by the case of a person who begins with the study of Arabic – and it deserves to be studied first – then he is to go to its teachers and become a student so that they become his supervisors. It becomes obligatory on them to take care of him with respect to what he requires in accordance with what suits him and them. If his resolve is then strengthened so that he develops a skill in the study of the Qurʾān, he will become their subject, while they will be like shepherds for him. Similar to this is his desire for the study of traditions and *fiqh* of the *dīn* as well as all the disciplines that deal with the *sharīʿa*. Likewise the training of the person who exhibits traits of advancement, courage and administration. He is to develop an aptitude accordingly and has to be taught the common disciplines. He then moves higher and higher in the art of administration like being the administrator or headman or commander or a guide or leader or takes up another office that suits him and for which excellence and enthusiasm are found in him. It is in this manner that training is to be imparted for each task that is a communal obligation for the nation. It is a journey on the common path, and just as the traveller stops and tires of that journey, he stops at the stage that is needed in general. If he has the strength, he continues to travel till he reaches the highest destination in communal obligations, in which the person reaching them becomes unique, like *ijtihād* in the case of the *sharīʿa* and statesmanship. It is through this that the affairs of this world and the acts for the Hereafter are established.

You can, therefore, see that the application of the requirement of communal obligations is not made in the same way, nor is it applicable to all, nor to some in the unqualified sense, nor is it required with reference to the ends rather than the means nor *vice versa*. It is proper to view it in a common way till details are uncovered in this way and duties are distributed among the citizens of Islam in this manner, otherwise a sound statement cannot be made about its varying meanings. Allah knows best.

The twelfth issue: *ibāḥa*, necessity and need

If something is originally permissible on the basis of need or necessity, but is affected by factors that oppose the original basis of permissibility either actually or potentially, then, do these factors attack the basis of permissibility, thereby diminishing it? This is an issue that requires examination and is complex.

The statement for the issue is that either there is a state of duress for the adoption of this permissible act or there is not, and if there is no duress for adopting it, then, is there a consequential harm in its neglect? This gives rise to three types.

The first type: *That there is a compulsion to undertake this permissible act. In such a case there is a necessity to have recourse to the permitting basis and to ignore the factors that oppose it, for various reasons.*

First reason: Among these is the reason that this act has become obligatory and is no longer relying on its permitting basis. If the act has become obligatory, then, it can only be opposed from the other side by a rule that is as strong as it or even stronger. The basic assumption of the issue does not require this, except when the obligatory aspect is stronger and it becomes necessary to have recourse to it. This necessarily leads to the absence of opposing factors.

Second reason: Those situations of duress that have been exempted in the *sharᶜ* (law). I mean those in which the implementation of the necessity is acknowledged, and the unexpected and detrimental opposing factors are exempted from the perspective of the interest to be secured. Just as the detriments of consuming carrion, blood and swineflesh and the like are exempted due to necessity of reviving life threatened with duress. Likewise, the proclamation of unbelief or falsehood for the preservation of life or wealth under coercion (*ikrāh*). What we are discussing pertains to this category. It is necessary in this case not to acknowledge a conflicting rule for the sake of an interest that is necessary.

Third reason: If we take into account the opposing factors and do not exempt these cases, it would lead to the elimination of permissibility right at its foundations. This is not valid, as will be coming up in the *Kitāb al-Maqāṣid*, to the effect that if a complementary rule assails the principle, thus diminishing it, the principle itself cannot be acknowledged. The acknowledgement of the opposing factors here belongs to this category. Thus, sale and purchase are permissible according to the original rule. If someone feels compelled to undertake them, but there are opposing factors in his path, then, the loss of the opposing factors amount to complementary factors like a group of conditions. If these are acknowledged, it will lead to the elimination of what the person is compelled to undertake. Thus, each complementary rule that attempts to assail its original rule, so as to diminish it, is void, and what we are discussing here belongs to this category.

The second type: That there is no compulsion in undertaking the act, but its neglect leads to hardship. The examination here requires recourse to the original principle of permissibility and ignoring opposing factors, because forbidden things have been declared permissible for the removal of hardship, as will be discussed with reference to the example given by Ibn al-Arabi about entering the bath, so also the increase in blameworthy acts on the highway and in market places. This does not prevent the undertaking of transactions for meeting needs when the forbidden factor in the transactions leads to an evident hardship. "And (He) has imposed no difficulties on you in religion."[190] The forbidden has been declared permissible for the removal of hardship, like *qarḍ* in which there is the sale of silver for silver when it is not from hand to hand,

and the permissibility of *ʿarāyā* (transaction in dates), and all that jurists have mentioned with respect to the obstacles to marriage and the mixing up of people, and whatever resembles these, and such cases are numerous. If there appears an apparent conflict here, then, it is due to people who have been very strict with themselves, and these are scholars who have a following. There are some among them who have clearly based their opinions on abstention and the implementation of opposing factors. Such persons have based their decisions on two considerations. First, they did not find any hardship, due to its insignificance, in their view, and that it is something normal in most obligations, and that normal hardship of the same strength in obligations has not been removed, for otherwise the elimination of all or most obligations would become necessary. This has been elaborated in the second part dealing with the types of *aḥkām*. Second, they acted upon and rendered decisions in consideration of the meanings present in *rukhaṣ* (exemptions). They held the permissible to be an exemption with an inclination towards omission and the possibility of commission even when no opposing rules cross its path. What would be the position if such an opposing rule did arise? The discussion on this point is also found in the section on *rukhaṣ* (exemptions). Perhaps, some opposing factors do cross the path of the *mubāḥ* that together require the inclination towards acknowledging them. The reason is that the detrimental factors associated with them are greater than those that will be associated with the act if it is given up. Thus, the hardship in its commission is greater than that in its omission. This too falls within the scope of *ijtihād*. It may be said, however, whether the hardship associated with the omission of the principle is the same as the hardship associated with the acceptance of the opposing factors. This is an issue that we will sketch now with the help of Allah, the Exalted. The issue is:

The thirteenth issue: balancing the hardships

We say: The only possibility is that the absence of opposing factors with respect to this principle brings them into the category of the complementary in this category or into another category, which would be a principle in itself. If it is the latter, it is either actual or likely. If it is likely, it has no effect upon hardship, because hardship through omission is actual and is a detriment. The detrimental opposing factor is expected and likely, thus there is no actual opposing factor. If, however, it is actual, it is a matter of *ijtihād* in reality. The detriment of the opposing factor in it is more than the detriment of omitting the permissible. The situation is sometimes reversed. The examination of this category belongs to the area of conflict and preference (*taʿāruḍ wa-tarjīḥ*). If it is the first, then conflict is not valid nor are the detriments equal; in fact, the detriment of the loss of the original principle is greater. The evidence in this case has various components.

First: The complementary factor and what it complements are like an attribute and the thing described. The discussion on this point has preceded. If the loss of the attribute does not lead to the loss of the thing described in the absolute sense – as against the reverse – the aspect of the described thing is stronger with respect to existence and non-existence and with respect to benefit and loss. Likewise, what is similar to this.

Second: The principle as compared to things complementing it is like the universal (*kullī*) with respect to its particulars. It has become known that when the universal is contradicted by its particular, the particular has no effect on it whatsoever. Likewise here, the detriment of the loss of the complementary has no effect on the interest being complemented.

Third: The complementary, insofar as it is complementary, provides strength to the fundamental interest and emphasises it. Its loss is the loss of one of the complementary values with the original interest remaining intact, and when it remains it is not contradicted by what does not oppose it. Just as the loss of the original interest is not opposed by what remains of complementary interests, which is evident.

The third of the first type:[191] *This is the type in which there is no compulsion for following the original principle of permissibility nor is there any hardship in giving it up.* This is a topic of *ijtihād*. There is also the influence of the principle of blocking the lawful means (*dharāʾiʿ*) to an unlawful end based on the principle of gathering support for obedience or disobedience. This principle is agreed upon with respect to its legal validity, and within it are things that are disputed like the means adopted in sales and other similar things, even though the basis of the means is also agreed upon. There is then the influence of the conflict of the principle and what is predominant, and the disagreement about it is well known. The scope of the examination of these types vacillates between affirmation and negation that are agreed upon. The basis of cooperation for righteousness, fear of God, and for sin and enmity is complementary for the thing for which support is sought. The same is the case with the principle of *dharāʾiʿ*. On the opposite side is the principle of permission, which is being complemented and is not complementary.

One who acknowledges the principle of permissibility (*ibāḥa*) here should argue on the basis of the principle of permission that relies on a necessary concept, as it is often established that the reality of permissibility that lies in choice is a reality that is associated with the necessities, and these are the foundations of all interests. They take the rule of serving them even if they are not so in reality. Thus, the acknowledgement of a rule contrary to the permissible (*mubāḥ*) is an acknowledgement of a rule contrary to the necessary in general. If this is so the aspect of permissibility is preferable to the aspect of the contrary rule that is not like it, and this is contrary to the evidence (*dalīl*). Further, if non-acknowledgement of the contrary complementary rule is assumed, the examination becomes unqualified or a suspicion is created that it will incline towards hardship that the Lawgiver has removed, as is likely, because the obstacles to the *mubāḥ* are numerous. If these are acknowledged, the method will become narrow and exit will become difficult. In this case it will turn into the type that has preceded and its contents have been discussed. As the neglect of the principle of *ibāḥa* leads to this, the desire for inclination towards it is not formed nor for turning towards it. Further, as this principle vacillates between two sides that are agreed upon and that conflict, inclination towards either one of them is not preferable as compared the other. There is no evidence in either one of them except that an evidence like it opposes it. Thus, suspension (of judgement) becomes necessary, except that we have a principle that is more general than this. The principle is that the original rule of things is either permissibility (*ibāḥa*) or waiver (*ʿafw*) and both require recourse to the requirement of permission. Thus, it is preferable.

The person who prefers the aspect of conflict would argue that the permissible interest, insofar as it is permissible, grants a choice of securing it or not securing it, which is evidence that does not reach the level of the necessities. This is so always, because when it reaches this level no choice remains in it. This is what has been assumed, and it is a discrepancy. If the subject is given a choice in the matter then this determines the absence of a detriment in securing the interest, while the aspect of the opposing factor determines the existence of a detriment or its likelihood. Both are prevented from the path of choice. Thus, it is not valid – this state – that there be a choice in it. This is the meaning of an opposing factor being less than the principle of *ibāḥa*. Further, the principle of *mutashābihāt* (ambiguities) is included within this principle. The reason is that it is verified that it relies on the principle of *ibāḥa*; however, its crossing over into other principles is what has been acknowledged by the Lawgiver and He has, therefore, prohibited its adoption. It is a principle that is definitive and is relied upon in such issues, and it negates reliance upon the principle of *ibāḥa*. Further, precaution in matters of *dīn* is established in the *sharīʿa* and when established this restricts the generality of the principle of *ibāḥa*. The issue is disputed. Those who say that things prior to the coming down of the *sharīʿa* take the rule of prohibition, therefore the opposing factors are not examined, do so because things are referred to their principles and this aspect is given preference. Those who maintain that the principle (before the *sharīʿa*) is that of permissibility or waiver (have to acknowledge) that this not applied generally by agreement; rather there are restrictions for it, but on the whole no opposing factor or principle should oppose it. The issue we are dealing with is not devoid of opposing factors and it is not to be said that they conflict due to the possibility of restriction of one by the other, just as it is not to be said that the words of the Prophet (pbuh), "No Muslim can inherit from an unbeliever" oppose the words of the Exalted, "Allah (thus) directs you as regards your children's (inheritance): to the male, a portion equal to that of two females."[192] The reason for arguing from both sides are many. The purpose, however, is to caution that these are issues subject to *ijtihād* as has been stated earlier. Allah knows best.

Notes

1 The Editor of one edition says: The Author has benefited immensely in this issue from a book written by Shams al-Dīn ʿAlī ibn Ismāʿīl al-Ṣunhājī al-Abyārī al-Mālikī (d. 616 A.H.), *Kitāb al-Warʿ*, published recently from Beirut.

2 Editor: It leads to a contradiction, as will be coming up.

3 Editor: This is the complete evidence. The result is that a vow is only valid for purposes of obedience, as stated in the tradition. They arrived at a consensus that the vow of a person undertaking not to perform a permissible act is not valid. Had such omission amounted to obedience, and was included in what is required by the tradition, they would not have reached a consensus about the invalidity of such a vow.

4 Editor: The complete tradition is that a person who makes a vow to be disobedient to Allah is not to be disobedient. It has been recorded in *al-Taysīr* from all the six *imams*, except Muslim. It has been reported in *Ramūz al-Ḥadīth* from Aḥmad, al-Bukhārī, Abū Dāwūd, al-Tirmidhī, al-Nasāʾī, Ibn Māja and Ibn Ḥibbān.

5 Editor: See *al-Taysīr* in the chapter on *nadhr*. It also includes the words "would not speak". It has been reported from al-Bukhārī, Mālik and Abū Dāwūd.

6 Editor: The Author has construed Mālik's words to mean the relinquishment of *mubāḥ*, that is, sitting and seeking shade. He therefore makes this statement. A similar sound tradition, however, conveys the meaning that the act itself amounts to inflicting pain on the body, and this is prohibited insofar as it is said, "Allah does not require such infliction of pain on oneself." This is a vow for committing directly a sinful act and not by way of giving up a *mubāḥ*.

7 Editor: There was no need for him to mention this assumption within the *dalīl*. He mentions it again under the topic of the invalidity of the binding act, by saying: "The permissible act and its relinquishment ..."

8 Editor: From where has this principle been derived when it is said that Allah, the Exalted, grants in abundance for a small act and that matters of reward are to be estimated only through bounty and not through a measure of weight? Allah, the Exalted, says: And those who believe and whose seeds follow them in faith, to them shall We join their families" [Qurʾān 52:21]. There is nothing to prevent one of two persons, who are equal in terms of obedience, being superior in status in terms of the Hereafter. In fact, one who is less obedient may be superior in spiritual status, because it all depends upon the bounty of God and not upon the scale of acts. It is, therefore, an evidence that is surrounded by doubt from different aspects.

9 Editor: The summary of the evidence is that if the person relinquishing the *mubāḥ* is obedient by virtue of the relinquishment, it becomes necessary that he have a higher grade than one who committed the act. Such a consequence is not valid, as the two are equal in status. Thus, what leads to it is not valid. You should ponder over what has emerged from his statements about the *dalīl* and know the need for doing so.

10 Editor: That is against his own body by subjecting it to undue burden and hardship by relinquishing the *mubāḥ*. He then claims that he should be rewarded for this. This no one has claimed.

11 Editor: Refers to his statement, "If he is not obedient by relinquishment", that is, if he is not deemed obedient by relinquishment, then it is not required that the *mubāḥ* be avoided. In other words, by virtue of this assumption he is discharged from it and there is no need to discuss it.

12 Editor: His opinion, evidence and the response to it will come up in the section following this issue.

13 Editor: That is, it is not required, and that is what we claim.
14 Editor: As it requires that something be the object of the commission, in the eyes of the Lawgiver, due to the preservation of an interest. Likewise, the object of the omission should also be for the preservation of such interest so that the rule for each is related to to such interest. This is required by the demand for the commission and the omission of the act in order to make the subject (*mukallaf*) obedient with respect to them.
15 Qur'ān 46:20.
16 Qur'ān 11:15.
17 Editor: The tradition is recorded in its complete form from the two Shaykhs as well as al-Nasā'ī in *al-Taysīr*. That version is slightly different from what is stated here.
18 Editor: Al-ʿIrāqī in his *Takhrīj* of the traditions of *al-Aḥyā'* has said: Ibn Ubayy and al-Bayhaqī in *al-Shaʿb* as a *mawqūf* tradition stopping at ʿAlī ibn Abī Ṭālib, God be pleased with him, and the *isnād* are *munqatiʿ*. The words in this tradition are: "the prohibited leads to the Fire". I did not find a *marfūʿ* version of this tradition. The tradition common among people is mentioned in *Tamyīz al-Tayyib min al-Khabīth* and is from Zayn al-dīn ʿAbd al-Raḥmān ibn ʿAlī ibn Muḥammad ibn ʿUmar ibn al-Shaybānī. It is the version quoted by the Author from Ibn Ubayy and al-Bayhaqī, but its *sanad* is *munqatiʿ*. In *Musnad al-Firdaws*, it is recorded from Ibn ʿAbbās (God be pleased with both) as a *marfūʿ* tradition. It is reported in *Ramūz al-Ḥadīth*, "O Son of Adam! what do you do with this world? The lawful leads to reckoning and the prohibited to torment."
19 Editor: That is, something that was not harmful in itself, as a precaution against falling into something that was leading to a thing that was harmful.
20 Editor: It is more general than what precedes it and is specific to associated things.
21 Editor: The two examples are of the same category. It is obvious that they belong to the circumstantial category or better still to the associated.
22 Editor: It is recorded by Aḥmad in *Kunūz al-Ḥaqā'iq* by al-Manāwī. Al-ʿIrāqī has said about it in *Takhrīj Aḥādīth al-Aḥyā'*: It is recorded by Aḥmad, Abū Yaʿlā and al-Ṭabarānī from the tradition of ʿAmr ibn al-ʿĀṣ with a good *sanad*.
23 Editor: It is recorded by Muslim.
24 Editor: It is not the case that the commission of the *mubāḥ* is sometimes the giving up of a *wājib*, in which case he is not one who avoids the prohibited. Ponder over this.
25 Editor: That is, this statement is stronger than the opposing evidence, as it is universal as distinguished from the original evidence.
26 Qur'ān 7:6.
27 Editor: It is recorded by al-Bukhārī and al-Tirmidhī.
28 Editor: And that is this preceding tradition.
29 Qur'ān 55:10–23.
30 Qur'ān 16:14.
31 Qur'ān 16:14.
32 Qur'ān 7:32.
33 Qur'ān 84:7–8.
34 Qur'ān 7:6.
35 Editor: The Editor of the book says: The merit of the Companions did not differ on the basis of these two attributes, but only on the basis of righteous deeds associated with each one of them. There is, therefore, no justification for the objection raised here about poverty and wealth not being included in the scale of merit, and superior merit is based on righteous conduct. The Author will discuss this at the end of the book in an excellent discourse.
36 Editor: This is Ibn Rushd, the grandfather of the well-known Averröes (Ibn Rushd).
37 The Editor says: It is to be noted that the difference between this point and the previous is not based upon the lack of, or existence of, detail within the *maqāṣid*, unless it is said that he considered them mere narrations of circumstances in the first, and these by themselves are

not considred evidences. It is necessary to check them against the *qawāʿid* of the *sharʿ*. His statement that "this could have been for some reason external to it" is what has been elaborated here, and is not the reason for what has preceded.

38 Editor: The tradition of the embroidered cloak has been reported by al-Bukhārī and Muslim, and in their reports it does not say that it distracted him.

39 Editor: It is recorded by al-Tirmidhī with the words, "The servant does not attain *taqwā* in reality ..." It is recorded in *al-Targhīb wa al-Tarhīb* from al-Tirmidhī with the words, "The servant is not among the God-fearing ..." He said it is *ḥasan*. It is also recorded from Ibn Māja and al-Ḥākam, who said its *isnād* are sound.

40 Editor: The Editor says: Alters what is prior to it insofar as his act is not always due to one of these reasons: that there is resolve for the worship or help towards what is worship; or he has adopted it due to permissibility. He gives up the act when one of these factors is present. Perhaps, the last prompts relinquishment in certain cases. The mere presence of resolve due to its being permissible is not sufficient and in fact there is need for a condition that is not easily attainable all the time. As for the first, it is agreed that he is to give it up as it does not bring about resolve for supporting worship. There is no doubt that the second is superior to the worshipper in the first case.

41 Editor: Like giving up the consumption of some eatables, because he does not have an urge for them or does not enjoy them, and another person may differ from him in this respect.

42 Editor: It is a precedent and not an example.

43 The Editor says: The first evidence applies to it, but not the second. The third applies to it with reference to his words, "It is not comprehensible in itself" and not with reference to his words, "It is not sound, but agreement", because it is a case of relinquishment that is not agreed upon. The fifth does not apply to it, but the sixth does. He has repeated it here by saying "first", because he needs to discuss it here and to refute what al-Kaʿbī has said. The last part of the seventh evidence applies to it. Accordingly, his statement "indicated by most of what has preceded" is sound. You may examine its application here.

44 The Editor says: He does not say that in such a case the dispute is verbal. The reason is that even though he argues with them, he is of the view that deeming it a *wājib* is necessary as in that there is always the giving up of the prohibited. This is different from their position in his view. There is no point in calling it the *mubāḥ* in his view. Consequently, no act can be found that can be termed *mubāḥ*, because whenever an act that is called *mubāḥ* occurs it is deemed a *wājib*. It is the basis of the refutation according to the first interpretation. He will not construct the second interpretation, which is that placing this category within the *aḥkām sharʿiyya* is futile. He does not maintain this, however, like the others.

45 Editor: That is, in any particular act.

46 Editor: In order that the four categories of the *aḥkām* are retained and not negated so that the view opposing reason is not faced. This is done by taking into account the proscription and the command and not the obligation.

47 Editor: That is, the equality of commission and omission in the *mubāḥ*. The previous problem was about the relinquishment not being required. Here, it is based on each being "not required". It is, therefore, said: How is it when the commission is demanded and the omission too is demanded? Can it be said then that the two sides of the *mubāḥ* are equal?

48 Qurʾān 2:168.

49 Qurʾān 2:172.

50 Qurʾān 12:51.

51 Qurʾān 7:32.

52 Qurʾān 7:32.

53 Editor: It is recorded in *al-Mishkāt* from Muslim by dropping the words, "It is". Likewise, it is mentioned in *Nayl al-Awṭār*, without the words "It is", from the *Jamāʿa*, except al-Bukhārī (*Jamāʿa* in technical terminology means all the six sound compilations as well

as Aḥmad).
54 Editor: It is recorded by Aḥmad and al-Bayhaqī from Ibn ʿUmar (God be pleased with both), and by al-Ṭabarānī from Ibn ʿAbbās (God be pleased with both) as a *marfūʿ* tradition, as well as a similar tradition from Ibn Masʿūd (God be pleased with him). Ibn Ṭāhir has stated in *al-Jāmiʿ al-Ṣaghīr* that considering it *mawqūf* is correct.
55 Qurʾān 4:25.
56 Editor: It is a form described by the *Sunna* where the husband is to pronounce a single repudiation in one period of purity in which he has not cohabited with her. *Talāq bidʿa* is not *mubāḥ* and cannot be employed as an example.
57 Editor: It is recorded by Abū Dāwūd.
58 Qurʾān 2:229.
59 Qurʾān 2:230.
60 Qurʾān 65:1.
61 Qurʾān 65:2.
62 Editor: That is, it makes it disapproved, just as the linking of preference with a *rukhṣa* that is permissible makes the *mubāḥ* preferred.
63 Editor: It is recorded by Ibn Khuzayma and has been declared sound by al-Ḥākam.
64 Editor: It is besides this category; the one that is by way of obligation. That is, it is in fact preferred for the permissiblity. Thus, the responses that have preceded do not apply.
65 The Editor says: That is, the eatable as it is an eatable and the dresses as well as beverages are *mubāḥ* due to particular rules, but as they serve a necessary universal, which is the preservation of life, they are required. This is not from the perspective of the particular, but from the perspective of the universal. The command, therefore, is not laid down because a thing is an apricot or apple or bread at a certain time, but in a general way. It is in this context that the words of the Exalted are to be understood, "O ye messengers! Enjoy (all) things good and pure, and work righteousness: for I am well-acquainted with (all) that ye do" [Qurʾān 23:51]. "O ye who believe! Eat of the good things that We have provided for you, and be grateful to Allah, if it is Him ye worship" [Qurʾān 2:172]. There are other such commands as well.
66 Editor: This is not the obligation or the external factors that have been discussed earlier by way of response to al-Kaʿbī.
67 Editor: Divorce is the giving up of lawful marriage, which in turn serves a universal necessity, which is the preservation of progeny. Divorce is, therefore, promoting something that negates a universal principle as well as a supporting need, as he will be stating shortly.
68 Editor: Wealth and its acquisition are permissible in themselves, but they may become a trial in the case of an individual becoming the cause of unbelief or continuing in that state. This is the case of one who does not believe. It may become the cause of the elimination and demolition of of *taqwā* in the case of a disobedient Muslim.
69 Qurʾān 17:37.
70 The Editor says: He has considered it here as a supporting need, but he will deem it a necessity in the *Book of Maqāṣid*. There is no conflict between the two situations, as there is no problem in considering it necessary in one situation and complementary in another situation. The first situation is where giving it up leads to injury and corruption and the demise of life in this world and the next. The second situation is where need requires the prominence of Islam, or the restraining of aggression against Muslims depends on it.
71 Editor: This is the benefit of the problem and the response to it that is not available from the initial issue nor from all the previous discussions. It is from this that he has qualified and refined the earlier statement, that is, we must add the statement "through the particulars".
72 The Editor says: Concerning the enjoyment of good things when it is not obligatory (like being required by necessity to preserve life or repel harm), not recommended (as being part of what is considered a meritorious practice) nor reprehensible (insofar as there is the

elimination of preferred practice in it, like extravagance in certain situations), we would say that if the enjoyment of such good things is not one of these three, then, it is *mubāḥ* by virtue of the particular and recommended by virtue of the universal. Thus, if all the people were to give it up it would be disapproved and commission of the act would become recommended in the *sharīʿa* on the basis of the universal.

73 The Editor says: The implication, along with the tradition, is that it is *mubāḥ* on the basis of the particular and recommended on the basis of the universal for an identified individual. His statement that "if the people give it up completely it would be disapproved" means that it is required as a communal duty so that if some perform it the duty is removed from the rest. Thus, if he is able to perform it and does not do so at all, it would not be disapproved. Perhaps, the first is acted upon. This is supported by his statement in the second: If he chooses one or gives it up in certain situations or when some people give it up.

74 Editor: The first part of the tradition is reported from Abū Hurayra by al-Bukhārī. The second part is recorded by al-Tirmidhī and al-Ḥākam.

75 Editor: It is recorded by Mālik with the words, "Is this not better?"

76 Editor: It is recorded by Muslim, Abū Dāwūd and al-Tirmidhī, and the words, "Allah is beautiful and loves beauty" have been reported through other channels.

77 Qurʾān 2:275.

78 Qurʾān 5:96.

79 Qurʾān 5:1.

80 The Editor says: This applies either to eating or to drinking, but not to both. The statement that applies to both is "if some people give it up under certain circumstances". As to his statement, "If we were to assume that all of the people were to give up these acts", it amounts to the statement, "If we assume the giving up of eating and drinking completely ..." Although he mentions numerous situations, it would be sufficient to mention some leaving the general rule to apply to the remaining situations assumed. It is also possible to say that its parallel is found in the first part. It is as if he has said in those parts: If we assume that a certain individual gives it up always and completely, he would be relinquishing a recommended act in the first case and an obligation in the second insofar as this applies to eating and drinking.

81 Editor: In this section and the one that follows, he has applied the discussion to a single individual both in terms of the particular and the universal, so please note.

82 Editor: Either as a communal obligation like *adhān* and the observance of the congregation by way of a universal obligation, as in the case of the remaining examples, except those coming up later like *nikāḥ*, because the communal aspect of its obligation extends to the realisation of the purposes of the Lawgiver.

83 Editor: This persistence, that is, in disapproved acts, demolishes probity and disqualifies such a person from being a witness, as it is an evidence that his person has committed a sin.

84 Editor: That persistence in the performance of a *mubāḥ* amounts to a minor violation and it is better than persistence in the performance of some permissible acts.

85 Editor: That is, the permissibility of this and the possibility of its legal occurrence. Its opposite will be mentioned, that is, its actual occurrence as evidenced by his statement: "As for its occurrence."

86 The Editor says: The narration recorded according to the compilers of the *Sunan*, as stated in *al-Taysīr* is: "If a person gives up three Friday congregational prayers with disdain, Allah places a stamp on his heart." The version in *al-Taysīr* is reported in *al-Targhīb* from the compilers of the *Sunan* – Ibn Māja, Ibn Khuzayma in their *Ṣaḥīḥs* and from al-Ḥākam. The Author says that it is *Ṣaḥīḥ* according to the conditions stipulated by Muslim. It is also reported from Aḥmad with *isnād* that are *ḥasan*. It is reported from al-Ḥākam too. He said that the *isnād* are sound: (If a person gives up the Friday congregation three times without necessity, Allah will place a stamp on his heart.) There are other narrations with different

words, but these are not related to the report here.

87 Editor: He has quoted this narration of the tradition to convey the meaning that the Lawgiver has provided the same consequences for persistence in the order as He has for disdain and neglect. The gravity of the offence of disdain should not be ignored. It indicates that persistence is more grievous an offence than doing it a single time. You should also be aware of the wisdom behind it, because persistent relinquishment is without an excuse even if there is no disdain and it does not cross his mind. It is in fact necessary that the individual persisting be conscious of it as that is the real cause of persistence, as is indicated by his statements that follow. Refer to the two traditions for they are in words on which we need to ponder. Thus, it is stated in *al-Taysīr*: If a person gives up three Friday congregations with disdain, Allah places a stamp on his heart.

88 See the note before the previous note.

89 Editor: That is, a single time. He will be relinquishing a *farḍ* (definitive obligation) and this does not lead to the stamping of the heart.

90 Editor: Perhaps, the correct words would be "just like". It contains the elaboration of the wisdom in quoting the second tradition.

91 Editor: What is the point in repeating it here? Perhaps, it is an error of the scribe.

92 The Editor says: That is, the *wājib* descends to the level of the *mandūb* in what has preceded; its particular rule implies a *wājib*, while its universal rule denotes a *farḍ* (definitive obligation). This is superior to the *mandūb*. Accordingly, the *wājib* is not different with respect to the method elaborated for the *mandūb*, the *makrūh* and the *mubāḥ* in terms of the difference between the particular and the universal acquiring a rule different from the particular.

93 The Editor says: Likewise what is said about the *wājib* and the categories prior to it, but according to the method stated in the section, because the offence of repetition is greater than that of omission. It is the same for what has preceded it, and it is not that it acquires a title that is different from the five *aḥkām*, one that it did not have earlier in terms of the particular. The same is to be said about the prohibited (*ḥarām*).

94 Editor: That is, a correspondence of rules between the particular and the universal. This is deemed a universal rule that applies invariably. His statement, "The person making a counter-claim", means one who disputes the application of the rule saying that the rule for the universal and the particular is the same. This is seen in the examples that he has mentioned and that are found in each of the five categories.

95 Editor: Part of the tradition has been recorded by Abū Dāwūd from Abū al-Dardāʾ (God be pleased with him). He said, "The Messenger of Allah (pbuh) said, ʿAllah has sent down both remedy and disease. For each disease He has sent a remedy, so use medicine, but do not use *ḥarām* as medicine.'"

96 Editor: Part of the tradition has been recorded by the five *imams* other than al-Bukhārī. The version as reproduced in *al-Taysīr* is: "Allah has prescribed fair treatment of all things; therefore, when you kill do it properly, when you slaughter perform proper slaughter. You should sharpen your knife and handle the slaughter animal with care."

97 Editor: In the context of what has preceded, he should have said, "Not prohibited." Further, what he intends to deny is the claim that it is obligatory according to the universal, that is, its total relinquishment should be prohibited in the context of what has preceded. As for its not being disapproved, it is from the perspective that the opposite of recommended is disapproved.

98 Editor: Review these rules in the *furūʿ*.

99 The Editor says: That is agreement of the rules for the universal and the particular in these cases, and this is when the universal has very few incidents and is weak in terms of generality. Perhaps it can be said that if a person gives up the killing of venomous insects or practising of *qirāḍ* or *musāqāh* during his entire life, he has not moved beyond the rule of *mubāḥ*. The same

can be said about the rest of the cases. When the generality is wide, the rule will not be the same. You should know that conceding something leads to the weakening of the general universal rule, and this is what the Author established earlier in this section.

100 Editor: This is the difference in the grades of the prohibited categories according to the universal and the particular, as has preceded.

101 The Editor says: Even though this pertains to the declaratory rules and not to the five *taklīfī aḥkām* that are being discussed. The reason is that testimony and its acceptance are declaratory rules, unless it is said that practices include *taklīfī aḥkām* as well. You can see that these three evidences indicate merely the essential difference between a single act from the perspective of the universal and the particular (but does this apply to all the five *aḥkām* as they are?), that is, to the essence of the claim or to part of it.

102 Qurʾān 2:223.

103 Qurʾān 2:58.

104 Qurʾān 2:35.

105 Qurʾān 5:2.

106 Qurʾān 62:10.

107 Qurʾān 7:160.

108 Qurʾān 62:11.

109 Qurʾān 31:6.

110 Editor: It is recorded by Abū ʿUbayd in *Faḍāʾil al-Qurʾān*, 22, No. 13.

111 Qurʾān 39:23.

112 It is recorded by al-Ḥākam in *al-Mustadrak,* vol. 2, 95.

113 It is recorded by al-Ḥākam in *al-Mustadrak,* vol. 2, 357.

114 Editor: The one in which there is no harm.

115 Qurʾān 2:158.

116 Qurʾān 16:106.

117 Editor: This is based upon a well-known tradition that says, "Verily, all acts are to be judged on the basis of intentions." The tradition is treated as a universal principle; however, there is a disagreement among the majority of the schools and the Ḥanafīs about the application of the tradition to the issues of the Hereafter. The Ḥanafīs maintain that the tradition applies to affairs of the Hereafter and not to matters like contracts, for example, where the objective theory of contracts is applied and the inner intention is not probed.

118 Editor: The declaratory rules do not focus on the intention of the subject; rather they declare a relationship between various acts for the legal significance of such acts insofar as they are valid or void and so on.

119 Qurʾān 33:5.

120 Qurʾān 2:286.

121 Editor: This is part of a lengthy tradition recorded by Muslim, *Ṣaḥīḥ*, vol. 1, 116, Tr. No. 126.

122 Editor: It is recorded by Ibn ʿAddī in *al-Kāmil*, vol. 2, 573.

123 Editor: It is recorded by Abū Dāwūd, *Sunan*, vol. 4, 558, Tr. No. 4398.

124 Qurʾān 4:43.

125 It is recorded by al-Dārʾquṭī, *Sunan*, vol. 1, 249; it is also recorded by al-Tirmidhī, *al-Jāmiʿ*, Tr. No. 272.

126 Editor: The source of the statement is not known.

127 Editor: As in the tradition quoted above.

128 Editor: This refers to opinions from Mālik's school.

129 It is recorded by al-Bukhārī, *Ṣaḥīḥ*, vol. 2, 9, Tr. No. 527.

130 It is recorded by Muslim, *Ṣaḥīḥ*, vol. 1, 434, Tr. No. 622.

131 Editor: When the sun appears red on the horizon.

132 Editor: The Author is providing another way of looking at the classification of rights into the

rights of God and the rights of the individual.
133 Editor: The concept of *dhimma* may be considered equivalent to the concept of "personality" in law. Here it means liability.
134 Qur'ān 22:36.
135 Qur'ān 2:195.
136 It is recorded by al-Dār'quṭnī, *Sunan*, vol. 1, 249; it is also recorded by al-Ṭabarānī, *al-Kabīr*, vol. 2, 221–22, Tr. No. 589.
137 Qur'ān 2:222.
138 Qur'ān 2:220.
139 Qur'ān 2:217.
140 It is recorded by al-Ṭabarānī, *al-Kabīr*, vol. 11, 454, Tr. No. 12228.
141 It is recorded by Abū Dāwūd, *Sunan*, vol. 3, 354, Tr. No. 3800.
142 See ʿUbayd ibn ʿUmayr ibn Rajab, *Jāmiʿ al-ʿUlūm*, vol. 2, 152.
143 Qur'ān 9:43.
144 Qur'ān 8:68.
145 It is recorded by al-Bukhārī, *Ṣaḥīḥ*, vol. 13, 264, Tr. No. 7289.
146 It is recorded by al-Bukhārī, *Ṣaḥīḥ*, vol. 13, 251, Tr. No. 7288.
147 Qur'ān 3:97.
148 Editor: This is from the previous tradition.
149 Qur'ān 5:101.
150 Qur'ān 5:101.
151 It is recorded by al-Bukhārī, *Ṣaḥīḥ*, vol. 13, 265, Tr. No. 7294.
152 Qur'ān 5:101.
153 Qur'ān 2:71.
154 Qur'ān 9:43.
155 Qur'ān 8:68.
156 It is recorded by Abū Dāwūd, *Sunan*, vol. 1, 286, Tr. No. 1091.
157 It is recorded by al-Bayhaqī, *Dalā'il al-Nubuwwa*, vol. 3, 256.
158 It is recorded by al-Bukhārī, *Ṣaḥīḥ*, vol. 2, 436, Tr. No. 946.
159 It is recorded by Muslim, *Ṣaḥīḥ*, vol. 1, 272, Tr. No. 349.
160 See al-Zaylaʿī, *Naṣb al-Raya*, vol. 1, 26–27.
161 Editor: This is mentioned by Ibn Taymiyya and Ibn al-Qayyim.
162 It is recorded by Ibn ʿAddī in *al-Kāmil,* vol. 2, 573.
163 Editor: A tradition from ʿĀ'isha. See the tradition coming after the next tradition.
164 It is recorded by al-Taḥāwī, *al-Mushkil,* vol. 3, 130.
165 It is recorded by Aḥmad, *al-Musnad*, vol. 6, 181; it is also recorded by al-Taḥāwī, *al-Mushkil,* vol. 3, 129.
166 Qur'ān 53:31–32.
167 Qur'ān 5:93.
168 Qur'ān 5:93.
169 It is recorded by al-Bayhaqī, *al-Kubrā*, vol. 8, 315.
170 It is recorded by al-Ḥākam in *al-Mustadrak,* vol. 2, 375.
171 Qur'ān 5:5.
172 It is recorded by al-Dār'qitnī, *Sunan*, vol. 4, 183–84.
173 It is recorded by al-Bukhārī, *Ṣaḥīḥ*, vol. 3, 606, Tr. No. 1785.
174 This tradition has been quoted earlier. It is recorded by al-Bukhārī, *Ṣaḥīḥ*, vol. 13, 264, Tr. No. 7289.
175 It is recorded by al-Bukhārī, *Ṣaḥīḥ*, vol. 13, 251, Tr. No. 7288.
176 Qur'ān 2:219.
177 Qur'ān 5:90.
178 Qur'ān 5:93.

179 Qurʾān 9:122.
180 Qurʾān 3:104.
181 Qurʾān 4:102.
182 It is recorded by Muslim, *Ṣaḥīḥ*, vol. 13, 251, Tr. No. 7288.
183 It is recorded by al-Bukhārī, *Ṣaḥīḥ*, vol. 11, 516–17, Tr. No. 6622.
184 It is recorded by ʿAbd al-Razzāq in *al-Muṣannaf*, vol. 11, 321.
185 It is recorded by Aḥmad, *al-Musnad*, vol. 3, 449.
186 And also from ʿUtmān (God be pleased with him), as recorded by Ibn Wahb in *al-Jāmiʿ*, vol. 1, 88.
187 Editor: A similar report is found in Ibn ʿAbd al-Barr, *Jāmiʿ Bayān al-ʿIlm.*
188 Qurʾān 3:104.
189 Qurʾān 16:78.
190 Qurʾān 22:78.
191 Please note that the thirteenth issue is actually a sub-issue of the twelfth, and the first type here refers to the first type of that issue.
192 Qurʾān 4 :11.

2

The Second Category of Rules: The Declaratory Rules

This category of rules is based on the declaratory communication (*khiṭāb al-waḍʿ*). It is covered by: causes (*asbāb*); conditions (*shurūṭ*); obstacles (*mawāniʿ*); validity and nullity (*siḥḥa wa-buṭlān*); and initial rules and exemptions (*ʿazāʾim wa-rukhaṣ*). These are five types.

The first type of declaratory rules: causes

In the first type a number of issues are examined.

The first issue: the ability of the subject to perform the act

Acts that actually come into existence and that are required for various affairs for which laws are made, or that are given up and also require laws, are of two types on the whole: first, those that are beyond the ability of the subject; and second, those that properly fall within his ability.

The first type are sometimes causes, sometimes conditions, and sometimes obstacles. The cause is like the existence of duress as a cause for the permissibility of consuming carrion, the fear of falling into sin as a cause for the permissibility of marriage or for having an *umm al-walad*, *salas* (incontinence of urine) as the cause of suspending the obligation of ablution prior to each prayer despite the emergence of urine, the declining of the sun or its setting or rising in the morning as the cause for the obligation of the respective prayers, and so on. The condition is like the existence of a year (its passage) as a condition for the obligation of *zakāt*, puberty (*bulūgh*) as a condition for the existence of legal capacity in the absolute sense, the ability to deliver as a condition for the validity of sale, discretion (*rushd*) as a condition for delivering the wealth of the orphan to him, the sending of Messengers as a condition for the assigning of reward (spiritual) (*thawāb*) and punishment, and whatever is of this nature. Obstacles are like the existence of menstrual bleeding as an obstacle to sexual intercourse, divorce, the circumambulation of the house, the obligation of prayer and the undertaking of fasting, and insanity as an obstacle to the performance of worship, the undertaking of transactions and other similar things.

As for the second type, it is viewed from two perspectives. The first is from the perspective that it belongs[1] to what falls under the communication of obligation (*khitāb al-taklīf*), whether prescribed or proscribed or permitted, insofar as these are required by the interests to be secured or injuries to be repelled, like sale (*bay*ʿ)[2] and purchase for utility, marriage for reproduction, compliance (*inqiyād*) in obedience for the attainment of success,[3] and similar things. This is evident. The other perspective is that it falls[4] under the declaratory communication (*khiṭāb al-waḍ*ʿ) either as a cause or as a condition or as an obstacle. As for the cause, it is like marriage as a cause of mutual inheritance between the spouses, prevention of certain other marriage relationships, and the permissibility of intercourse, and like slaughter as a cause for utilisation as food, journey as a cause for the permissibility of curtailment (of prayer) and not fasting, homicide and wounding as the cause of retaliation (*qiṣāṣ*), unlawful sexual intercourse, drinking wine, theft, false accusation of unchastity as causes for their prescribed punishments and things that resemble these. These things have been declared as causes giving rise to their consequences.

As for the condition, it is like the existence of marriage as a condition for the validity of divorce or for the legality of taking back the divorced woman divorced three times,[5] the existence of *iḥsān* (marriage) as a condition for awarding the penalty of stoning to the fornicator, purification as a condition for the validity of prayer, *niyya* (resolve) as a condition for the validity of worship. These states and those similar to them are not causes, but are conditions taken into account for the validity of these requirements.

As for the obstacle, it is like marriage to one sister as a prohibition from marrying other sisters, marrying a woman as an obstacle to marrying her paternal or maternal aunt, faith as an obstacle to conceding the right of retaliation to the unbeliever, unbelief as an obstacle to the acceptance of (ritual) obligations, and things similar to these. Sometimes a single command gathers within it the cause, condition and obstacle. The example is faith which is a cause for spiritual reward, condition for the obligation of ritual obligations or of their validity, and an obstacle to granting the right of retaliation to the unbeliever. Such examples are numerous, except that these three cannot be gathered together for a single act. If one thing is a cause for a legal rule (*ḥukm shar*ʿ*ī*), it cannot be a condition for the same thing nor can it be an obstacle to it insofar as they exclude each other. It can only be a cause for one *ḥukm shar*ʿ*ī*, a condition for another, and an obstacle to a third. It is not proper that all three gather within one *ḥukm* or even two of them in a single rule, just as this is not proper for the rule flowing from the communication of obligation (*khiṭāb al-taklīf*).

The second issue: legality of causes does not necessarily imply the legal validity of the consequences

The legality of the causes (*asbāb*)[6] does not necessarily mean the legality of the result even if the necessary relationship is usually found between them. The meaning is that if a *ḥukm shar*ʿ*ī* is related to the causes, like permissibility, recommendation or prevention or other rules of obligation, it is not necessary that these *aḥkām* be related to the consequences as well. Thus, a command to bring about the cause does not necessarily mean a command for the consequences, and if the prohibition is issued about the cause, it does not necessarily mean the prohibition of the consequence. The illustration for this is that a command to undertake sale, for example, does not mean the permissibility of benefiting from the sold commodity. A command to undertake marriage does not necessarily mean a command about the lawfulness of sexual intercourse. The command pertaining to execution in the case of retaliation does not necessarily mean a command to take a life (cause death). Prohibiting about premeditated homicide does not necessarily mean prohibiting causing death. Prohibiting dropping things in the well does not necessarily mean prohibiting concealing things in the well. Prohibiting throwing a dress in the fire does not necessarily mean prohibiting burning it. Such examples are numerous.

The evidence for this is what is established in the discipline of *Kalām* that it is up to the subject to bring about the causes, but the effects are an act of God and His Command, (and) the subject has no influence over them. This is elaborated in another discipline, and the Qurʾān and the *Sunna* provide evidence for it. What indicates this is what requires the guarantee of sustenance, like the words of the Exalted, "Enjoin prayer on thy people, and be constant therein. We ask thee not to provide sustenance",[7] and His words, "There is no moving creature on earth but its sustenance dependeth on Allah",[8] and His words, "And in heaven is your sustenance, as (also) that which ye are promised",[9] and His words, "And for those who fear Allah, He (ever) prepares a way out",[10] as well as other verses that express the guarantee of sustenance. The meaning here is not the causation of sustenance, but sustenance that will be caused. Had the meaning been causation itself, there would have been no obligation on the subject of striving first under any circumstances, even though it can be deemed the placing of a morsel in the mouth and chewing, the sowing of grains, the gathering of edible vegetation and fruits, but this is absolutely invalid. It is, therefore, established that it means the effect itself. It is stated in a tradition, "If you place your trust in Allah as He deserves, He will provide for you as He provides for the birds."[11] Related to this is another tradition: "Tie it up (your camel)[12] and then place your trust in Allah."[13] In this and other evidences like it is an elaboration of what has preceded. Further, the texts that elaborate this are the following verses, "Do ye then see? The (human seed) that ye emit – is it ye who create it, or are We the Creators?"[14] "See ye the water which ye drink?"[15] "See ye the seed that ye sow in the ground?"[16] and "See ye the fire which ye kindle?"[17] And He ruled for all this, "Allah is the Creator of all things"[18] and "But Allah has created you and your handiwork."[19] He attributed the act to them so that they could undertake it, but thereafter the command for the effect belongs to Allah alone. This meaning derived through induction from the *sharīʿa* is definitive. If this is so, the causes obligated fall under the generality of this meaning, which is indicated by rational and transmitted evidences. The gains made by the subjects become linked to the causes and not to the effects. Thus, the obligation and its communication are not related to the end result. The effects[20] are excluded from the obligation creating communication, because these are not within the ability of the subject. If the effects had been related to the communication of obligations, it would be an obligation to do the impossible, which does not exist as is discussed in the discipline of *ʿUṣūl.*

Objection: An objection may be raised saying that necessity exists here. Do you not see that the permissibility of the contracts of sale and hire and others necessarily leads to the specific utilisation of each one of them? If prohibition is linked with them as in the sale involving *ribā*, *gharar*, and uncertainty, it necessarily leads to the prohibition of utilising what results from them. Further, there are the examples of torts, usurpation, and theft and so on, and so also the slaughter of animals, that are permissible in conformity with the law, which leads necessarily to the permissibility of their utilisation. If these animals are not lawful their utilisation is prohibited. The examples of this type are numerous. How then can it be said that the command to bring about the causes, or the prohibition, does not necessarily lead to the command to bring about the effects, or to prohibit them? The same is the case with permissibility (*ibāḥa*).

We say in response. All this does not indicate such necessity for two reasons.

First: The examples that have been provided at the beginning of the issue indicate the absence of a consequential necessity, and an evidence has been provided to show this. What is laid down in opposition is a matter of evidence and not that of necessity.

Second: There is no necessity in what has been stated on the evidence of its being apparent in certain cases. Sometimes the cause is permissible (*mubāḥ*), while the effect is required. Just as we say that the utilisation of the sold commodity is permissible, we say that it is obligatory to provide maintenance if it is an animal when maintenance is an effect of a permissible contract. Likewise, the preservation of owned wealth is an effect of a permissible cause, but it is required. Similar to this is slaughter of animals, because it is not described in terms of prohibition when it applies to animals that cannot be consumed like swine, habitual predators, dogs and so on, when the utilisation of all such animals is prohibited or in some cases it is prohibited and in other cases it is disapproved. This is in causes that are lawful. As for causes that are prohibited their case is easy,[21] because the meaning of their prohibition is that these are not causes at all in the *sharīʿa*. If they are not causes, they do not have effects. The effect then remains based on its original rule of prohibition and not that prohibition[22] is the cause of the occurrence of prohibited causes. All this is evident and the principle is continuous and everything goes well with the rule. Success comes from God. This principle is to be built upon.

The third issue: the subject in bringing about the causes does not intend the effects

In bringing about the causes, the subject on his part need not necessarily turn to the effects nor should he intend them; rather the intention should be to act according to the *aḥkām* that are laid down and nothing more, whether the *aḥkām* have causes or otherwise and whether they have underlying causes or require ritual obedience.

First: The evidence for this is what has preceded in that causes refer to the *Ḥākim*, who is the Cause, and that they are not within the power of the subject.[23] As the effects do not refer to him, his concern should be for what refers to his gain. This is binding and it is the cause. Whatever is beside this is not binding. This is what is required.

Second: Further,[24] the legal requirements pertain to those things in which a person has an interest, and towards which he is inclined, and these prevent him for complying with the requirements of the demand. The Prophet (pbuh) did not appoint a person for an (official) task if he asked for it.[25] All authority under the *sharīʿa* is required either through the demand of obligation or that of recommendation, but he (pbuh) took into account the consequences related to personal interest. The nature of desiring personal interest in such things is that the person may undertake acts that are disapproved, as will be coming up due to the power of God. On occasions, the Prophet (pbuh) considered such acts to be permissible (*mubāḥ*). He said, "Whatever wealth comes to you when you do not desire it, take it."[26] The condition for accepting it is the absence of personal desire. This indicates that taking it with a desire for it is different. The elaboration is found in another tradition, "One who takes wealth rightfully receives the blessings of Allah with it, but one who takes it without a lawful right is like the person who eats and is never satisfied."[27] Taking something on the basis of a right is that the person does not forget the right of Allah in it, which is the sign of a lack of control over the self. Taking something without a lawful right is different from this. This meaning is explained by another tradition, "That companion of a Muslim is good[28] who gives of his wealth to the needy, the orphan and the wayfarer",[29] or as he said, "He is one who takes it without right, and is like one who consumes but is never satisfied; this wealth will testify against him on the Last Day of Judgement."[30]

Third: The third reason is that the servants of Allah, like those considered here, have taken it upon themselves to cleanse their acts of the ills of desire so much so that they reckoned the inclination of the self towards some good acts as part of its baggage of tricks. They formulated a rule upon which they constructed further, regarding the clash of acts and the preference of some over others, to prefer those for which the self had no desire or those that proved burdensome for it. This left them with acts that went against the inclination of the self. They are authorities in what they permitted, because their agreement amounts to consensus. This is an evidence for the validity of turning away from the effects of causes. The Prophet (pbuh), when Jibrīl asked him about *iḥsān*, said, "That you worship[31] Allah as if you can see Him even if you do not see Him, for He can see you."[32] Any act of the servant (*ʿabd*) that falls under the rule of the *sharʿ* is a form of worship. If someone worships Allah while under control of his desire, things are concealed from him for he mixes up with worship the interests of his own desire. It is the requirement of continuous practice that everything other than his desire is concealed from him. This meaning has been elaborated by those qualified to do so like al-Ghazālī and others. Thus, it is not a condition for undertaking lawful causes to turn to the effects. The rule applies to prohibited causes just as it applies to lawful causes. Not turning to the effects does not affect reward and punishment.[33] This refers to one who is likely to prefer the effect over the cause when it is the cause that is guaranteed for him. Thus, he does not lose anything except a condition or the original or the complementary fragment with respect to the cause in particular.

The fourth issue: the determining of causes implies the intention of the lawgiver to bring about the effects

The determination of the causes requires that the determiner has an intention to bring about the effects. I mean, the Lawgiver. The evidence for this is made up of different factors.

First: All reasonable persons are certain that causes are not causes for themselves insofar as they are entities but for reasons that they give rise to other factors. If this is the case, the intention to determine them as causes necessarily implies the intention to bring about the effects that arise from them.

Second: The *aḥkām sharʿiyya* (legal rules) have been legislated for the securing of interests and the repelling of injuries and these are definitively the effects (of the causes). If we know that the causes have been legislated for their effects, it is necessary that aiming for the causes implies aiming for the effects.

Third:[34] If the effects are not intended through the causes, their determination would not have been as causes, but this is what has been assumed. Thus, it is essential that they have been determined as causes and they cannot be causes other than as causes of their effects. The determiner of causes, therefore, intends that the effects come into being through them. If this is established and the causes are intended as determined, it is binding that the effects be the same.

If it is said: How is this possible with the existence of what has been said previously that the effects are not intended by the Lawgiver through the command requiring the causes?

The response is in two parts.

First: The two intentions are identical. What has preceded means that the Lawgiver does not intend the creation of obligation (*taklīf*) through causes, the necessity to bring about the effects as well. The effects are beyond the power of the servants as has been said earlier. Here the meaning is that the effects come into being through their causes, and it is for this reason that He has determined them as causes. In this meaning there is nothing that requires that it be included under the communication of obligation. The meaning in this requires the intention for the mere occurrence of the effects in particular. Thus, there is no contradiction between the two principles.

Second:[35] If the convergence of the two intentions upon a single thing is assumed, it is not impossible that these be from two different perspectives, just as the command and the proscription for prayer upon usurped land have converged from two different perspectives. The conclusion is that the two principles do not repel each other in any absolute sense.

The fifth issue: the right of the subject in intending the effects

If it is established that the intention (of the servant) to bring about the effects is not binding, the subject should relinquish absolutely the resolve to bring about the effects, but he has the right to intend the effects. The first view is explained by what has preceded.[36]

If it is said to you: Why do you work for your livelihood through agriculture or trade or other means? You will say that is because the Lawgiver has recommended these acts, and I act according to the requirements of what I have been ordered to do, just as He has commanded me to pray, to fast, to pay *zakāt*, to perform *ḥajj* and to do other acts that He has imposed on me as obligations. Suppose it is said to you that the Lawgiver has commanded and proscribed things for you to secure interests. You would say: Yes, but that is for Him, not for me. What I am obliged to do is to bring about the cause, and the realisation of effects is not up to me. I direct my intention towards what is determined for me and I leave what is not for me to Him.

What also indicates this is that the cause does not act on its own; the effect is found at its occurrence and not because of it. When the subject tries to bring about the cause, it is Allah who creates the cause, while the subject attains it. "But Allah has created you and your handiwork",[37] "Allah is the Creator of all things, and He is the Guardian and Disposer of all affairs",[38] "But ye will not, except as Allah wills; for Allah is full of knowledge and wisdom",[39] and "By the self, and the proportion and order given to it; and its enlightenment as to its wrong and its right; truly he succeeds that purifies it, and he fails that corrupts it!"[40] There is the tradition of ʿAdwā that the Prophet (pbuh)[41] said, "Who then infected the first (camel)?"[42] There is the statement of ʿUmar in the tradition of *ṭāʿūn* (plague), "We run from the *qadr* of Allah towards the *qadr* of Allah." He said this in response to the question of ʿAmr ibn al-ʿĀṣ. "Is it running away from the decree of Allah?"[43] A tradition[44] says, "The pen has gone dry after writing what is to happen. If the entire creation were to come together to give you something that Allah has not written down for you, they would not have the power to do so, and if they were to prevent something that Allah has written down for you, they would not be able to do so."[45]

The evidences of this end up in certainty. If this is so, then turning to the effect in promoting the act of the cause is the same[46] as not turning to it. The effect may sometimes come into being and sometimes it may not. This is the case when the usual cause of events would require that it come into being, because it is within the power of Allah and that requires that it may or may not come into being. The negation[47] of the usual course of events is an evidence indicating this. Further, there is no evidence in the *sharīʿa* that explicitly demands the forming of an intention for the effect.

Suppose it is said[48] that the intention of the Lawgiver is to bring about the effects and turning towards them is evidence that it requires an intention from the subject (as well). (We say:) The meaning of obligation is nothing more than the conformity of the intention of the subject with the intention of the Lawgiver. If his intention goes against that of the Lawgiver, obligation itself is not valid, as has been elaborated at the proper occasion[49] in this book. When it does conform it is valid. If we assume that a subject has not intended the coming into being of the causes, when we have assumed that the Lawgiver has intended this, it would be like going against Him, and any obligation in which the intention opposes[50] the intention of the Lawgiver is invalid, as is explained. So also here.

The response is that this becomes necessary if we assume that the Lawgiver has intended the occurrence of the effects through obligation (*taklīf*) imposed with respect to it, just as He has done with respect to the causes. It is, however, not so. It has preceded that the effects are not the object of obligation. He has intended the occurrence of effects in accordance with the usual practice in creation, which is that the creation of effects is the effect of the subject's bringing about the causes so that the fortunate attain fortune and the unlucky face misfortune. The intention of the Lawgiver for the occurrence of the effects is in no way linked with the intention that pertains to obligation. Thus, it is not necessary that the intention of the subject be directed towards the effects, unless there is an evidence for this, and there is no such evidence. In fact, it is not valid,[51] because an intention directed towards this is an intention directed towards the act of another, and it is not binding for anyone to intend the occurrence of the act of another. The reason is that the subject is under no obligation for the act of another, but he is under an obligation for what constitutes his own act and that is the cause exclusively. It is this towards which the directing of intention is binding, or he is required to direct his intention towards it. In this the intention of the Lawgiver is acknowledged.

Sub-issue: the intention of the subject and effects – As for the subject having an intention for the bringing about of effects, it is like saying to you: why do you seek a livelihood? You would say: To maintain my strength, to maintain my life and that of my family, or for the securing of other such interests that are based on causes. This intention, if it is associated with an effect, is valid, because it is based on the accepted practices of the people. Allah, the Exalted, has said, "And He has subjected to you, as from Him, all that is in the heavens and on earth:

behold, in that are signs indeed for those who reflect",[52] and He said, "And among His signs is the sleep that ye take by night and by day, and the quest that ye (make for livelihood) out of His Bounty: verily in that are signs for those who hearken",[53] and He said, "And when the prayer is finished, then may ye disperse through the land, and seek[54] of the bounty of Allah: and celebrate the praises of Allah often (and without stint): that ye may prosper."[55] Insofar as this expresses the intention towards the cause, which is the seeking of livelihood, through the intention to seek His bounty, and the adoption of a course of gratitude without denial, it is known that such intention is valid. This works for affairs related to the Hereafter as well as for those pertaining to this world, as in the words of the Exalted, "And those who believe in Allah and work righteousness, He will admit[56] to gardens."[57] Similar to this are cases where the formulation of an intention directed towards the effects through the cause is permitted. Further, the conclusion from this is that he seeks what Allah has prepared for him through this cause, and this refers to reliance on Allah and turning to Him insofar as He feeds him through the effect through which his needs are met and his situation is improved. There is no denial of this in the *sharʿ* (law). The reason is that it is known about the *sharīʿa* that it has been laid down for securing the interests of the servants. Obligation in its entirety is either for the repelling of injury or for the securing of an interest or for both at the same time. Anything that falls within its fold requires that for which the *sharīʿa* is laid down. There is no opposition in this, then, of the intention of the Lawgiver. The prohibited factor is to form[58] an intention in opposition to what the Lawgiver intends, and this is when such intention does not lead to an act that is not intended by the Lawgiver nor does an opposing transaction become binding. Thus, the act[59] is compatible with it and so is the intention, and the collection of these is compatible too.

Suppose it is said: Are these two[60] aspects suitable for all the rules pertaining to practice and rituals? What appears *prima facie* is that the intention directed at the effects in transactions in general is due to the obvious interests in them. This is different from acts of worship as these are based on the absence of rational meanings. In these, not turning towards the effects is suitable, because the rational meanings refer to the genera of interests or injuries, which are obvious in normal acts, but not so in rituals. If this is the case, turning to the causes and intending them is acknowledged in usual (non-ritual) acts. This is especially so in the case of the *mujtahid*. The *mujtahid* expands the scope of his *ijtihād* by applying the underlying causes and turning to them. If this is not the case, the application of laws (*aḥkām*) in conformity with interests is not possible, except through the text or through consensus. *Qiyās* is, therefore, nullified, and this is not valid. It is, thus, essential to turn to the underlying meanings for which the laws have been laid down, and these meanings are the effects of the laws. As for ritual practices, insofar as they are dominated by the absence of meanings specific to them and reliance is upon the requirements of the text, not turning to the meanings is in the line with the purposes of the Lawgiver. Both cases, as far as the subject, who merely follows (a *muqallid*), is concerned, are similar, as he is not obliged to turn to the effects except in things that are within his usual comprehension and information in *sharʿī* (legal) transactions.

The response is: Both cases, with respect to turning to causes and not turning to them, are the same. The reason is that when the *mujtahid* examines the underlying cause (*ʿilla*) of the *ḥukm*, he extends the *ḥukm* through it to an object that is related to it on the basis of an interest for which the *ḥukm* is laid down. This is a specialised view.[61] What remains is his intention to attain it through acts or the absence of an intention that is not expressed with respect to it. He intends it sometimes when he is the actor and sometimes he does not intend it. In both situations nothing is lost in his *ijtihād* and his position is the same as that of the *muqallid*. When he hears the saying of the Prophet (pbuh),[62] "The *qāḍī* (judge) is not to render decision when he is angry",[63] he examines the underlying cause for the prohibition of rendering decision, and he finds it to be anger. The wisdom (*ḥikma*) behind it is that being mentally perturbed prevents appreciation of the arguments of the litigants. Accordingly, he links excessive hunger, overeating, pain and other such things to anger, things that lead to mental disturbance. If he finds himself in any of these states – when he is a *qāḍī* – he refuses to render judgement in accordance with the requirements of the proscription. If he directs his intention to the termination of the decision by virtue of the proscription alone, without turning to any of the meanings of the underlying wisdom due to which the handing down of the judgement is prohibited, then the purposes of the Lawgiver are attained even if these were not intended by the *qāḍī*. If he intends the obvious injury of not absorbing the arguments of the litigants, as intended by the Lawgiver, the purposes of the Lawgiver are also attained. Thus, the presence of the intention of the *qāḍī* with respect to the effects as well as its absence is the same. The same is the case of the *muqallid* insofar as the wisdom underlying his acts is understood. In cases where such underlying wisdom is not understood, the issues are in the nature of *ʿibādāt* (rituals) with respect to all. It is known that acts of worship have been prescribed for the interest (*maṣlaḥa*) of the servants in this world or in the Hereafter, but in general even if the details (of such interests) are not known. It is, therefore, proper to direct the intention towards these general worldly and other-worldly interests. Thus, formulation or non-formulation of such intention is as has preceded.

The sixth issue: the two grades of causes

If what has preceded is affirmed, then the undertaking of causes is in grades that are of two types. Turning to the effects, through the causes, has three grades.

First: To undertake the cause as if it is the causation factor behind the effects or the factor giving birth to them. This amounts to polytheism or something similar to it and we seek refuge with Allah against it. The cause is not the moving factor on its own, "Allah is the Creator of all things",[64] "But Allah has created you and your handiwork."[65] A tradition says, "The morning saw those who believe in me as well as the unbelievers."[66] One who has faith in the stars has no faith in Allah, and he is one who considers the stars to have causative powers of their own. This issue has been examined by those who specialise in *ʿIlm al-Kalām*.

Second: That he undertake the cause on the basis that in practice the effect is found at the time of its occurrence. This is what has been discussed earlier, and the net result is that the effect is to be sought from the cause not on the belief of independence, but in the meaning that its existence implies that it is the cause of the effect. Thus, it is a must that the cause be the cause of the effect for that is its rational meaning, otherwise it would not be a cause. Accordingly, turning to the effect in this meaning does not lie outside the ambit of the requirements of Allah's way with His creation, nor does it negate the occurrence of the cause taking place through the power of Allah, with the power of Allah being visible at the time of existence of the cause and the time of its absence. The existence of the cause, therefore, does not negate the fact that He is the Creator of the effect. Yet, it is here that one usually turns towards the cause in a manner that the absence of its effect is deemed effective along with its denial. The reason is that in practice it is usually the cause that is examined by virtue of its being a cause and is not seen as being a cause by determination and not as one being required on its own. This is the predominant state of the creation in undertaking the bringing about of causes.

Third: That he bring about the cause on the belief that the effect is from Allah, the Exalted, as He is the real Cause. The predominant state for the person in this grade is the belief that the effect has come about through the power of God and His will, without a decision as to its being a cause. The reason is that if its existence as a cause is valid, it is not taken back just like rational causes. When it is not so, he inclines towards divine causation on the evidence of his being the First Cause. It is here that it is said to one who gives a ruling for it:[67] "What caused the First Cause?" It was for something like this that he (pbuh) said, "Who then infected the first (camel)?"[68] If the causes, along with the effects, are governed by the power of God, then He is the (real) cause and not these, because there is no partner with Him in His authority. All this is elaborated in *ʿIlm al-Kalām*. The conclusion is based on not considering the cause as acting on its own in producing the effect; rather it is understood in the meaning that Allah is the (real) cause. This is sound.

Sub-issue: not turning to the effects – Not turning to the effects has three levels as well.

First: That he bring about the cause with the intent that it is a trial for the servants and a test for them to see how they fare, and he brings it about without turning to any other meaning. This is based upon the idea that causes and effects have been laid down in this world as a trial for servants and a test for them, and it becomes the path towards happiness or misfortune. This is of two types.

First: What is laid down as a trial for reason, and that is because the entire world[69] insofar as it is visible and created indicates what is beyond it.

Second: What is laid down as a trial for the self, and that is also because the entire world insofar as it is within reach of the servants constitutes benefits and harms, and insofar as it has been harnessed for them and is available to them for what they want to do with it. This is to bring out their actions under the rule of *qaḍāʾ* and *qadr*, to so submit their actions to the rule of the *sharʿ* (law) as to lead some to fortune and others to misfortune, to bring out the requirement of preordained knowledge and binding decree that cannot be reversed. Allah is independent of the need of this world and is free of the need of causes and means in what He does. He has laid them down for His servants so that He can test them through such causes and effects. The evidences indicating these ideas are numerous. Such as these:

> He it is who created the heavens and the earth in six days and his throne was over the waters that he might try you,[70] which of you is best in conduct. But if thou wert to say to them, ye shall indeed be raised up after death, the unbelievers would be sure to say, this is nothing but obvious sorcery.[71]

> He Who created death and life, that He may try which of you is best in deed: and He is the Exalted in Might, Oft-Forgiving.[72]

> Then we made you heirs in the land after them, to see how ye would behave![73]

> Then we roused them,[74] in order to test which of the two parties was best at calculating the term of years they had tarried.[75]

> Such days (of varying fortunes) We shift among mankind by turns: that Allah may know those that believe, and that He may take to himself from your ranks martyr witnesses (to truth). And Allah loveth not those that do wrong. Allah's object is to purify those who have believed and to obliterate the unbelievers. Did ye think that ye would enter heaven without Allah testing those of you who fought hard (in his cause) and remained steadfast?[76]

> But (all this was) that Allah might test what is in your breasts and purge what is in your hearts. For Allah knoweth well the secrets of your hearts.[77]

> Then did He divert you from your foes in order to test you.[78]

There are other verses as well that indicate that the determination of causes is by way of trial. If this is the case, one who accepts them in this meaning has taken them in the meaning that they have been determined along with affirmation of such meaning. This is correct. The person who has this intention is the servant of Allah in whatever he seeks out of the various causes. The reason is that if he has sought the cause with permission from among these that are permitted, his subservience to Allah becomes visible in it, without having turned to the effects even if they follow the causes. He is then like one who seeks the causes of all forms of pure worship.

Second: That he brings about the cause with the intention of shedding the desire to turn towards causes insofar as these are created acts, let alone the desire to turn to effects. This is based on the fact that the uniqueness of the worshipper in his worship is that he does not admit anything in his intention besides Him, and relying on the fact that joining others in this goes against pure *tawḥīd* (unity of God) in worship. The reason is that the subsistence of the desire to turn towards all such things amounts to the subsistence of association with all created things and reliance upon others. This is precision in the negation of partnership. This too is valid where applicable. It is supported in the *sharīʿa* with texts depicting denial of partnership, as in the words of the Exalted, "Whoever expects to meet his Lord, let him work righteousness, and, in the worship of his Lord, admit no one as partner",[79] and His words, "So serve Allah, offering Him sincere devotion. Is it not to Allah that sincere devotion is due?"[80] as well as other verses on the subject. Likewise, the evidences requiring truth in turning attention towards Allah, the Lord of the worlds. All this indicates this derived meaning with respect to devotional attention and sincerity in worship. The person who operates at this level has submitted himself to Allah, the Exalted, through the laid down causes by rejecting an examination of such causes from his own side let alone the examination of their effects. He turns to them insofar as these are the means to their effects, and hence to their Originator, and he strives for advancement towards a station of nearness to Him. Thus, he acknowledges in all this the Originator in particular.

Third: That he brings about the causes on the basis of legal permission (*al-idhn al-sharʿī*)[81] to the exclusion of all other factors. His focus in his intention towards the cause is compliance to the command for attaining the station of the worshipper. The reason is that when He permitted him to undertake the cause or commanded him to do so, he complied with His command insofar as he formulated the intention to undertake the cause – for it is obvious to him that it is He who is the real cause and that things operate according to His ways, and if He likes they may not operate in this way, just as He may reorder them sometimes if He likes – that this is a trial and examination, and it requires sincere devotion to Him. He undertakes all this, therefore, and his intention becomes an intention that includes all that has preceded. The reason is that he resolved to follow the intention of the Lawgiver without turning to anything else. He came to identify His intention in all these affairs, thus achieving all that is included in such seeking of the cause, all that is known and all that is unknown. He seeks the effect by way of the cause knowing that it is Allah who is the true cause and He is the one who subjects him to a trial, and who grants the ability for sincere devotion to Him. His intention, therefore, is unqualified even if it incorporates the intention of the true cause, but all this is devoid of association with others and free of all impurities.

The seventh issue: prohibited causes

The bringing about of causes may either be prohibited or it may not be prohibited. If it is prohibited, then there is no problem in demanding the elimination of seeking the cause, irrespective of the seeker having intended the occurrence of the effect. This leads to two situations. It may be that he intends through intentional homicide the loss of life and this occurs, and he may intend through usurpation the utilisation of the misappropriated thing and this takes place in the usual manner and not as required by the *sharʿ* (law); however, all this may not take place at all. On occasions the intent towards the effect or turning towards it may be concealed due to an opposing factor affecting it other than the opposing factors that have been mentioned earlier,[82] and this factor is not taken into account. If the cause is not prohibited, then, the elimination of seeking the cause is not demanded at any of the levels mentioned.

As for the first, if we assume that the seeking of the cause is permissible (*mubāḥ*) or is required on the whole, the belief of the believer, that the basis for the existence of the cause is the person acting, is a sin that accompanies what is permissible or required, but it does not annul it, unless it is stated that such type of accompaniment is a vitiating factor and that whatever is linked to a sin becomes prohibited, like prayer in a usurped house or slaughter with a usurped knife. All this is explained in the discipline of *ʿUṣūl.*

As for the second case, it is obvious that bringing about the cause is valid. The reason is that if the person acting upon it relies upon the normal course of events, the usual consequence being the occurrence of effects due to their causes, and this is what is expected, the giving up of the cause amounts to initiating an act of destruction or actually committing it. Likewise, if in practice it reaches the level of certainty, it becomes obligatory to bring it about. It is for this reason that they stated in the case of a person under duress that if he fears that he will die, it becomes obligatory for him to seek help, or to borrow, or to consume carrion and the like. It is not permitted to him to neglect himself till he dies. Accordingly, Masrūq has stated that if a person in a state of duress needs something that Allah has declared prohibited, but he does not eat it or drink it till he dies, he will enter the Fire.

As for the third case, the bringing about of the cause is obvious here too, except that an issue remains to be discussed: whether the person bringing it about has the same status[83] as that of the person in the second grade. This is what needs to be examined. The unqualified nature of the statements of the jurists indicates that there is no distinction between the two persons. The states of those who uphold *tawakkul*, and can be described as Ṣūfīs, indicate that these two persons are different. Despite this the apparent meaning in al-Ghazālī's writing is that the two persons are the same as it appears from the method of the jurists in all its details. There is another aspect of the problem that is visible and that is that the status pertains either to knowledge or to a state of existence. The distinction between knowledge and a state is well known to those who deal with this discipline. If it pertains to knowledge, then it is the second grade,[84] as it is obligatory for each believer to have the belief that causes do not act on their own, and the mover in them is the True Cause, Allah Almighty, but His practice for this creation is that it requires the usual events and when He likes He may go against these for whoever He likes. Insofar as it is a question of events, the requirement is to bring about the causes, but insofar as the causes are in the hands of the Creator for bringing about the effects, the requirement is that the person act with or without the effects. One of these two views comes to dominate (the attitude of) the subject. If the first view is predominant, which is that of usual events, the position is as has preceded. When the second view is predominant, the person concerned is in the same state with or without relation to the causes. Thus, for example, when he is hungry and has a craving (for food), then it is the same for him whether or not he brings about the cause, for he is certain that the cause and effects are equally in the hands of Allah. In such a situation the predominant thought in his mind is not that the giving up of the cause amounts to the initiation of events leading to death, rather his belief in both situations is the same. He therefore does not fall under the impact of the verse, "And make not your own hands contribute to (your) destruction."[85] He is, thus, under no obligation to bring about a cause to eliminate this, because his knowledge[86] that the cause is in the hands of the One who moves the cause has removed his need for bringing about the cause on his part. In fact, the existence and non-existence of the cause are the same for this purpose. Just as bringing about the cause does not amount to initiation (of the process leading to death), if he is relying upon the cause, so also in the case of giving up the cause. If it is assumed that bringing about the cause is the bringing about of the termination of his reliance upon the mover of the cause, it would amount to the initiation of the process leading to destruction, because he has here relied on the cause itself, when there is nothing in the cause that can be relied upon, for he has relied upon it from the perspective of its being declared as a cause. Accordingly, there is nothing else when the cause is given up.[87] The existence and non-existence of the cause in both situations is the same for the affirmation of faith and the realities of conviction, for each person here is a *faqīh* (jurist) for himself. The evidence for this has preceded.[88] It is stated in the tradition,[89] "The pen has gone dry after writing what is to happen. If the entire creation were to come together to give you something that Allah has not written down for you, they would not have the power to do so and if they were to prevent something that Allah has written down for you, they would not be able to do so."[90] It is related by ʿIyāḍ from al-Ḥasan ibn Naṣr al-Sūsī, a Maliki jurist, that his son in a year in which prices had risen said to him, "Father, buy wheat as I think the prices are going to rise." He ordered that the wheat in his house be sold. Thereafter, he said to his son, "You are not one of those who place their trust in Allah, and you have little conviction. Is it possible that the wheat in your father's possession will protect you from what Allah has decreed for you? Allah is sufficient for one who relies on Him."[91]

A parallel for the issue we are discussing is found in *fiqh*. It is the case of the warrior attacking an army of the unbelievers all by himself. The jurists distinguish between the situations where he is convinced of his safety or of his death. In the case in which he is convinced of his safety, it is permitted to him to do what he is doing. If, on the other hand, he is convinced that he will die without any advantage, he is forbidden from this act. They argue for this, on the basis of the words of the Exalted, "And make not your own hands contribute to (your) destruction."[92] The same is the case of the person who takes off into the desert with or without provisions. If he is convinced of his safety, it is permitted to him to do so, but if he is sure that he will die he is not permitted. Likewise, if a person is convinced that he will reach a place with water in time, he is ordered to wait and not perform *tayammum*. The same applies to one travelling by sea,[93] for which reason it is permitted to him to perform *tayammum* (rubbing his hands and face with dirt) despite the availability of water during his journey, but if he is convinced of reaching a place that has water, he is not allowed to do so.

If a person who is ill is convinced that his illness will worsen or recovery will be delayed or he will face hardship due to a fast, he may not fast. The examples are numerous in which the decision is based upon personal conviction. Even though what gives rise to conviction may vary, this fact does not affect this principle. Our issue falls under this principle. Thus, whoever verifies that giving up a cause is the same as bringing it about with respect to the guarantee given by Allah for the provision of sustenance, for him it can be rightfully said that bringing about the effects is not obligatory upon him. It is for this reason that we find people in various circumstances facing terrifying things, rushing into dangers and taking up things that for others amount to destruction. Things are not like this, however, on the basis that what they take up of hazards and causes of destruction are similar for them to what in our reckoning are situations of security and safety. ʿIyāḍ has narrated from Abū al-ʿAbbās al-Ibbiyānī that ʿAṭiyya al-Jazarī al-ʿĀbid visited him and said to him, "I have come to visit you and to receive your farewell for Mecca." Abū al-ʿAbbās said to him, "Do not exclude us from the blessings of your prayer", and then he began to weep. This was a time when ʿAṭiyya did not even have a cooling pot or even a haversack. He then moved out with his companions and immediately thereafter another man came to him and said, "May Allah bless you, I have five *mithqāls* (weight, *misqāl*) and a mule. Do you think I should undertake a journey up to Mecca?" He replied, "Do not make haste until these *dīnārs* increase." The narrator says that he was surprised by the difference in the two responses to the two men, keeping in view the difference in their (financial) circumstances. Abū al-ʿAbbās said, "ʿAṭiyya came to me for being bid farewell and not for consultation, and he had placed his trust in God, but this other person came to consult me stating what he possessed. I, therefore, came to know of the weakness of this resolve and gave him the advice as you witnessed."[94] Here then is a leader among scholars giving a verdict to one weak in resolve for garnering his resources and securing them, while he conceded to one strong in faith to shun all care for assets based – God knows best – on the preceding principle in matters of faith and conviction with respect to safety and destruction. These are conclusions of a legal (*fiqhī*) investigation that differ with respect to the ruling for different persons on the same issue, as has preceded.

Suppose it is said: What is better for a person of this level, the involvement with causes or their relinquishment? The response is from two perspectives.

First: The causes apply to him just as they do to another person. If unusual practices (supernatural) operate in his case, then these are causes in themselves, but these are strange causes. Bringing about the causes is not confined to well known causes. Thus, for example, one departing for *ḥajj* without provisions is fed by Allah from sources that are not reckoned: either vegetation on the land, or from the people in deserts and villages, or from the animals in the desert or from other sources. Even if this descends upon him from the sky or emerges from the land through unusual means that are experienced by the elect in this field, such a person cannot be exempted from acting to bring about the causes. Among these is prayer (*ṣalāt*), due to the words of the Exalted, "Enjoin prayer on thy people, and be constant therein."[95] It is related that the Prophet (pbuh) "used to direct his family to pray when there was no food".[96] If this is the case, the question does not apply.

Second: Assuming that the question does apply, the Companions of the Messenger of Allah (pbuh) knew definitively that they had attained this level, and they were convinced of this through their state and conduct. Even then the Prophet (pbuh) deemed it recommended for them to undertake the bringing about of the causes that were required for worldly interests just as he recommended the bringing about of causes required for the next world. He therefore did not let them be despite the level they had attained. This indicates that it is preferable to do what he indicated for them. The reason is that this state is not one that can be reckoned as stationary. Note the saying of the Prophet (pbuh), "Tie it up and then place your trust in God."[97] Further, those who possess this state are those acquainted with unusual happenings, but despite this they do not give up the bringing about of the causes in conformity with the practice of the Messenger of Allah (pbuh). This is so when they were those who possessed knowledge and would not relinquish the acts that were better for those that were not so.

As for the fourth case, and this is the case of trial, the bringing about of causes here too is obvious. The causes, for a person at this level, have become an obligation for which he is obligated in the absolute sense and this obligation is not specific to causes pertaining to worship to the exclusion of practices. Just as it is not proper to relinquish causes pertaining to worship by placing reliance upon One who has deemed them causes insofar as they are devoted to such worship, so also the causes pertaining to practices.

It is in this context that the Prophet (pbuh) said, "There is no breathing self who is created without his place being known in heaven and the fire." The people said, "O Messenger of Allah, why then should we act, why not just place our trust in Allah?" He replied, "No. Because the causes have been provided in accordance with what one is created for."[98] The Prophet (pbuh) then recited the verse, "So he who gives (in charity) and fears (Allah), and (in all sincerity) testifies to the best, We will indeed make smooth for him the path to bliss, but he who is a greedy miser and thinks himself self-sufficient, and gives the lie to the best, We will indeed make smooth for him the path to misery; nor will his wealth profit him when he falls headlong (into the pit). Verily, We take upon Ourselves to guide, and verily unto Us (belong) the End and the Beginning, therefore do I warn you of a fire blazing fiercely; none shall reach it but those most unfortunate ones who give the lie to Truth and turn their backs. But those most devoted to Allah shall be removed far from it, those who spend their wealth for increase in self-purification, and have in their minds no favour from anyone for which a reward is expected in return, but only the desire to seek for the Countenance of their Lord Most High; and soon will they attain (complete) satisfaction."[99] Likewise, the general practices for these two are (like) *ʿibādāt* (worship) as they work in accordance with laid down *aḥkām*. The approach of the person at this level towards the causes is the same as his approach towards those for the *ʿibādāt*, only the causes are taken into account and the effects are left to the One who creates them.

As for the fifth level, the bringing about of causes is sound in this too. The reason is that even if the person at this level does not turn to the cause, insofar as it is a cause, and better still to the effect, it is necessary for him to do so from the perspective that it is preferred for him and suitable for the effect to do so, on the argument that this is what he does for the causes of worship. The reason is that these causes have become a source of satisfaction for him in as much as they are a ladder leading to the aspect of worship. Thus, there is no distinction between practices and worship, except that the person at this level is compelled to isolate these causes on the whole. Accordingly, he may cast aside some causes that are not necessary and confine himself to those that are necessary, not finding the ability within himself to undertake the others as an escape from the pressure they create on his person, and so that his orientation remains focused. As far as the causes are a means towards the object, there can be no doubt about their adoption at this level, because it is through these that the object is attained.

As for the sixth level, insofar as it gathers together divergent things that have been mentioned before it, it stands as an evidence for those that have preceded, except that this attribute in it is acknowledged from the perspective of submission and obedience to a command and not due to some other factor. It is the same for it whether or not the obligation is based upon an obvious interest, for all this falls under the intention of the worshipper obeying the command of Allah. If the object of obligation is one that ties up some of the things that exist or all of them, the intention to do it in obedience to the command encompasses them all. Allah knows best.

The eighth issue: the occurrence of the cause is equivalent to the occurrence of the effects

The occurrence of the cause amounts to the same thing as the occurrence of the effects whether or not the subject has intended the effects. The reason is that as it is deemed to be the result in normal practice, he is deemed to have caused it directly. This is supported by the principle of practice in due course, because the effects are attributed to the causes under the principle, just like the attributing of hunger to food, thirst to water and burning to fire, emaciation to diarrhoea as well as all effects to their causes. Likewise, the acts that result from our acts: they are attributed to us, even when they are not in reality due to our acts. As this is the customary and known practice, the practice of the *sharᶜ* (law) has been to associate results with their legal causes on the same pattern.

There are many evidences for this in the *sharīᶜa*, that is, with respect to the lawful and unlawful causes. For example, in the words of the Exalted, "On that account: We ordained for the Children of Israel that if anyone slew a person – unless it be for murder or for spreading mischief in the land – it would be as if he slew the whole people: and if any one saved a life, it would be as if he saved the life of the whole people."[100] A tradition says, "When a person is killed unjustly, part of the responsibility falls on the first born of Adam for he was the first to set the precedent of homicide."[101] In this are the words, "He who lays down a good precedent has its reward and the reward of one who acts according to it",[102] as well as the words, "He who lays down a bad precedent ..."[103] In this context are the words, "The child is a protective barrier for his parents against the Fire", and "If a person plants something then: what is eaten of its fruit is charity in his favour and so also what is stolen from it, what is eaten by animals, or what is afflicted by calamity."[104] The same applies to cultivation. The scholar spreads knowledge; thus, he has the reward of whoever benefits from such knowledge. To this category belong things that are beyond reckoning, even though the consequences that yield benefit or harm are not the act of the originator of the cause.

If that is the case, then the effective factor for the cause is what is included in what is required by the consequence; it is required generally and for its details even if it does not cover all the details. Sometimes, however, it is required generally and not for its details. Accordingly, what God has commanded is required by way of an interest (*maṣlaḥa*) that He wants to be secured, and what He has prohibited is due to an injury (*mafsada*) that is associated with the act. Thus, when the act is brought about (or omitted) the condition is that the interests or injuries implied by the cause will be secured or repelled. His lack of knowledge about the interest, injury or their standards does not remove it from the application of this condition. The command implies that bringing about what is commanded secures an interest that is in the knowledge of God, and it is for this reason that He has commanded the commission of the act. A prohibition implies that bringing about the prohibited act amounts to an injury that is known to God and it is for this reason that He prohibited it. The person under the obligation is bound by whatever results from such a cause, whether interests or injuries, even though he is ignorant of the details.

Suppose it is said: Is he rewarded or punished for what he has not done?

The response is that reward and punishment are based on what he has done or performed, and not on what he has not done. The act, however, is considered legally in the context of the benefits and the injuries resulting from it. The law has elaborated this and has distinguished between the more important acts, by deeming them essential elements, and injuries, by deeming them grave sins, as well as between those that do not fall in these categories by calling the interests *iḥsān* (good deeds) and by calling injuries minor sins. In this way a distinction is made between those acts that are considered the essential elements or fundamental principles and those that are secondary issues and sub-issues. From among these, grievous sins are identified and so are minor offences. What the law has given importance, from among the acts commanded, are considered the fundamentals of the religion (*ʿuṣūl al-dīn*), while those other than these are considered the branches and complementary issues. Those considered important from among the prohibited things are considered grievous sins, while those outside them are considered minor acts of disobedience. All this is based upon the standard used for interests and injuries (*maṣāliḥ* and *mafāsid*).

The ninth issue: effects not in control of the subject

What has been mentioned in these issues, about the fact that the effects are not in control of the subject, but rather the cause is the object of the obligation, leads to the following sub-issues.

First: The person bringing about the cause, when he brings it about with all its conditions[105] when the obstacles are absent, and he then intends that the effects do not occur is intending the impossible, and is striving to remove what he has no right to remove, and to prevent something whose prevention is not in his hands.

Thus, if a person who concludes a contract of marriage in a manner in which it has been formulated in the *sharīʿa*, or concludes a sale or other contract but thereafter intends that the subject-matter of the contract should not be made permissible, then his intention is futile, and the legal effects will take place as a consequence of the cause. Likewise, if he undertakes divorce or emancipation intending thereby what is required by the *sharīʿa*, but then intends that such requirement should not be met, his intention is void. Similar to this are acts in forms of worship. If he prays, fasts or performs *ḥajj* as commanded, or anything that resembles these, but then makes an inner intention that the worship that has taken place should not be considered valid or should not bring about nearness to Allah, his intention is redundant.

The same is the case with causes that are prohibited. It is with respect to these that words were revealed, "O ye who believe! Make not unlawful the good things which Allah hath made lawful for you, but commit no excess: for Allah loveth not those given to excess."[106]

Consequently, the prohibition of what Allah has declared permissible is void. This pertains to edibles, beverages, clothing, marriage, when a man does not marry at all or intends the stipulation of conditions in a particular case[107] as distinguished from the general, as well as to what is similar. All this is redundant. The reason is that where Allah has authorised the permissibility of a thing without the subject bringing about its obvious cause is like the cause that the subject brings about. This is illustrated by the saying of the Prophet (pbuh), "The *walāʾ* (clientage) belongs to the one who emancipates",[108] and his saying, "If someone stipulates a condition that is not in the Book of Allah, the condition is a nullity, even if these were a hundred conditions."[109]

And [**Second**] the Lawgiver intends the occurrence of the effects as a result of the causes, as has preceded; therefore, this person making an intention is opposing the intention of the Lawgiver. Each intention that contradicts the intention of the Lawgiver is a nullity. Accordingly, this condition is a nullity and the issue is clear.

If, however, it is said: This is difficult from two perspectives:

First: The choice of the subject and his intention is a condition in the formulation of the causes.[110] Thus, where his choice negates the requirements of the causes with respect to their effects, it would mean that the subject has not brought about causes completely, rather that these lack the condition of choice; therefore, they are not valid due to the loss of the condition. Consequently, it is necessary that the effects do not arise from the causes that have not occurred due to the absence of a choice.

Second: The intention contradicting the intention of the Lawgiver annuls the act in accordance with what is mentioned at its own location in this book. The bringing about of permitting causes, for example, with the intention that they do not create permissibility, is obviously contradicting the intention of the Lawgiver insofar as the intention of the Lawgiver was permissibility by means of these causes. Thus, the bringing about of these causes is null and prohibited, like the person praying intending through his prayer something that will not bring him a reward due to it, so also the person undertaking ritual purity intending that it should not permit prayer, and so on. Combining this principle with the previous principle amounts to the combination of two contradictory rules, which is a nullity.

The response to the first is: The assumption in the case of one making the cause was to occur with a choice so that it becomes a cause, but without choosing the effect. The discussion is not about the one making the cause to occur without a choice. Combining the two is conceptually possible, as in the case of intending intercourse and choosing it, but disliking the creation of a child, or choosing to sow seeds in the earth and disliking their sprouting, or shooting an arrow by aiming at a man and then disliking that it strike him, and all that resembles such acts. Just as it is possible to combine[111] these in usual acts, it is possible to combine them in those ordained by the *sharīʿa*.

The response to the second is: The actor bringing about the cause in our issue intends that what the Lawgiver intends to bear a result should not bear a result, and what has been determined to be a cause that he has acted upon here should not have an effect. This does not lie in his power, for his intention with respect to it is redundant as distinguished from what is mentioned in the principle of the intentions of the Lawgiver. The actor bringing about the cause intends it to be a cause for an effect, which the Lawgiver has not determined to be its effect, like the marriage to a *muḥallil*,[112] later so she can marry in the view of one who forbids it. The reason is that he intends through his marriage that it create permissibility for another, but the Lawgiver has not determined *nikāḥ* (marriage) to have this effect. When this intention accompanies this contract, it does not become a lawful cause; the woman is not lawful for the *muḥallil* nor for the *muḥallal*, (because) it is a nullity.

The conclusion in the matter is that one of these two persons took the cause to be something that is not a cause, while the other took it to be a cause that does not lead to a result. The first does not give rise to any result, but the second creates a result for him, because the creation or the absence of the result is not for him to choose. This person did not oppose the intention of the Lawgiver in the cause insofar as it is a cause; rather, he thought that it would not lead to the occurrence of the effect, which is a lie or a wish that is not desired. The first brought about the cause thinking that it was not a cause determined by the Lawgiver. Thus, know the difference between the two, for it is profound.

To make it evident, the intention in one of these accompanies the act and affects it, while it does not affect the other, for the act is subjected to it after it is established.

Suppose it is said: Why is it not like the rule of refusal in acts of worship, because it is in reality the refusal to accept it as a legal cause? Thus, purification, for example, is the cause for the removal of ritual impurity, but if he has the intention that it will not remove impurity, then it is in the meaning of refusal of *niyya* (intention) in it. The jurists have said that refusal of *niyya* becomes a cause for annulling worship. The discussion, therefore, comes back to the point that all this amounts to the nullifying of the causes themselves and not the nullifying of effects.

The response is that the matter is not like this. Refusal within acts of worship is valid when the intention is to act in compliance of the legal directive. Completing it later in a different manner, rather with a different intention that is not laid down for his worship, is like the person performing purification with an intention to remove ritual impurity, but later abrogating this intention with another intention of cooling himself down or for cleanliness, that is, matters for cleaning the body. If after the worship is over and is completed with all its conditions, he forms an intention that it should not be taken as worship and that it should not give rise to legal effects (of validity) or of spiritual reward or the seeking of permissibility or something else, then such intention is not effective in relation to the worship. It retains its rule as if the intention was not even formed. The difference between them is apparent.

This does not conflict with the statement of the person discussing refusal (of intention), where he says that it has an effect without going into details about his statement.[113] The statements of the jurists about the rejection of ablution and their disagreement about it does not fall outside the ambit of this principle. The reason is that purification here has two meanings from different perspectives. The person who looked towards its performance as an act that is necessary said that the making permissible of prayer through this act is essential and it is a result of this act; therefore, its removal is not valid without another intervening factor. The person who looked towards its legal rule – I mean the rule for making prayer permissible with the accompanying intention, which is a matter that will be coming up – stipulated the existence of the first intention that accompanied purification. This intention is abrogated through a negating abrogating intention; therefore, the making permissible of the prayer following it is not valid, because it amounts to the rejection of the accompanying act. Had it occurred with the commission of the act it would have been effective, so also in this case (later). If the worshipper rejects the *niyya* of purification after the performance of prayer with its rule being complete, it is not valid to say that it is obligatory upon him to perform purification as well as prayer again. Likewise the case of the person who rejects such prayer after offering salutation at its end, when he had performed it as he was commanded to do. If someone were to say something like this, then the apparent principle goes against what he said. Allah knows best and it is He who grants success.

This is the rule for causes when they are brought about completely with their conditions and with the absence of obstacles. If, however, the causes are not brought about as they should be, if their conditions have not been fulfilled, and the obstacles are not absent, then the effects will not occur whether the subject desires them or rejects them. Their occurrence or non-occurrence is not a matter of choice for him.

Further, the Lawgiver has not deemed them required causes without the existence of their conditions and the absence of their obstacles. If all these are not found, the cause is not complete in the form of a legal cause irrespective of our saying that the existence of conditions and the absence of obstacles are components of the causes; the result is the same.

In addition to this, if the causes were to require their effects when they were incomplete according to the wish of the subject, or their requirements stood removed after their completion, there would be no use in their formulation as causes by the Lawgiver; indeed their formulation would be futile. The reason is that the meaning of their being legal causes is that their effects occur as required by law, while the meaning of their being non-legal causes is that their effects do not occur in a manner that is not required by law. If the choice exercised by the subject alters the facts taken into account by law, they cease to have a form that was known for them in the law, and we have assumed that they were assigned a form by the law that is known. This is a contradiction that is impossible, and so is the conclusion that it leads to. This validates the statement that the choices exercised by the subject do not have any effect on the *sharʿī* (legal) causes.

If it is said: How does this go with the statement that the prohibition does not indicate invalidity (of the thing prohibited) or that it indicates validity or that it distinguishes between what is prohibited for itself and what is prohibited due to an external attribute? All these opinions indicate that the effect is the thing prohibited, which is something that was not completed with its conditions and negation of obstacles, and it conveys the meaning of attaining these effects. There is in Mālik's opinion[114] something that indicates this. Thus, vitiated sales, in his opinion, convey from the start the meaning of a semblance of ownership at the time of possession of the sold commodity. In addition, ownership is found due to the fluctuations in the market and other transactions that do not cause a loss of the thing that is the subject-matter. Likewise usurpation and similar acts convey the meaning of ownership in different issues even though the usurped property is not lost, where usurpation and other matters are not the basis for such transfer of ownership. This shows that a cause that is prohibited can give rise to the effects, except when the rule is upheld that the prohibition conveys the invalidity of the prohibited thing in the absolute sense.

The response is that the principle is general and the passing of ownership in these examples is due to other factors that are external to the original contract. The elaboration of this is not possible here, and it will be mentioned in what follows this, God willing.

Sub-issue: the actor is not to focus on the effect – Among the issues that are structured on what has preceded is if that a person bringing about the cause knowing that the effect is not in his control places his trust in the Actor (the Almighty) and does not focus on the effect, then he is at a higher level: in terms of sincerity, commitment and trust in Allah, the Exalted; in terms of contentment in commencing the causes that are commanded and avoiding the prohibited causes; in terms of being grateful; and other laudable states and pleasing circumstances. This will be elaborated by mentioning a few cases, because the issue is manifest.

As for sincerity, the subject – when he abides by the commands and prohibitions with respect to the cause without looking at what is outside these commands and prohibitions – is beyond personal gain, rendering the rights of his Lord, and standing firm in the state of worship. This is different from the case where he turns to the effect and keeps an eye on it. By such turning he is giving only part attention to his Lord, and his attention is through the cause by means of the attention given to the effect. There is no doubt about the difference between the two states of sincerity.

As for commitment, the reason is that when he knows that the effect does not fall under what he is obliged to do, nor does it lie within his power, he has recourse to the One who has such power, that is, Allah the Exalted. He therefore becomes one who places his trust in, and leaves everything to, Him. This is the case with most obligations pertaining to practice and worship, but the attitude is enhanced with respect to obligations of worship, for he continues, even after the causation, to remain fearful and devoted.[115] If he is one[116] who turns to the effect, by bringing about the cause, he acquires expectations and is on the lookout for what his moving the cause will bring to him. This may sometimes lead to turning away from the completion of causes as a result of being in haste for what they will yield. His attention then is turned to something he is not obliged to do, and he does not give attention to what he was required to attend to. It is here that the narration applies about the person who heard that "one who sincerely devotes forty mornings to Allah will find the fountains of wisdom gushing from his heart on to his tongue", and then adopted devotion, according to what he came to believe, so as to acquire wisdom. When the period was over and he did not acquire wisdom, he asked about it. He was told that he had adopted devotion for wisdom and not for Allah. This occurs mostly by considering effects in the case of causes. Perhaps, the consideration of effects becomes greater and becomes a barrier between the person bringing about the causes and the concern for causes. Through this the worshipper is compelled to go to extremes in his worship, the scholar loses his knowledge, and the like.

As for patience and gratitude, the reason is that when the worshipper turns only to the command of the One commanding with the belief that it is He alone who has control over effects and their causes, while he himself is merely a servant, then he comes to abide by the command of the One commanding, and there is no turning away from this or reluctance. He has made it binding upon himself to be patient, for he is within the bounds of anticipation, worshipping as if he is being seen by the Creator. When the effect comes into being, he is one of the most grateful, for he did not concern himself with the beginning or end of causation, nor does he demand any benefit or harm for himself. If it is a usual sign or cause, then it is a cause with an effect and will occur in the usual manner.

If he were to concern himself with the effect, then the cause sometimes yields a result and at other times it is fruitless. If it does yield a result, he is happy, but if it does not he is not satisfied with the distribution by Allah nor with His decree. He then considers the cause to be nothing and may become frustrated, giving up the cause. At other times he may fall into a trial because of it and the cause becomes burdensome for him. This resembles the case of the person who worships Allah with moderation as distinguished from the practice of one who goes to extremes in worship. One who ponders over the remaining laudable cases will find them to be in the lack of concern for effects. Probably this is the main benefit of miracles and the supernatural.

Sub-issue: focusing on the effect may lead to ignoble traits – Among these issues is one where the person who does not concern himself with the effect, on the basis that the command in this belongs to Allah, is more concerned with the cause that he has brought about. He is more concerned with preserving the cause, guarding it and being sincere, because the consequences are not delegated to him. If his intention were the effect attained through the cause, it would give rise to the suspicion of adopting the cause in a manner that goes against its original nature, and without the intention of worship. This can lead to disharmony when he is not aware of it, or is aware of it but has not given much thought to what he is about. It is from here that a number of irregular things spring up. It is the basis of deception in usual acts, both personal and those of worship. In fact, it is the basis for fatal traits.

As for acts pertaining to practice, it is obvious. He does not indulge in deception, except for gaining profit that he hopes to derive from his trade, or the income that he expects will accrue from his profession. This applies to other similar matters. As for matters of worship, the situation of the person whom Allah loves is that he be accepted in this world as well, after having been loved by those in the heavens. Thus, seeking nearness through supererogatory worship is the cause of the love of Allah, and thereafter the love of the angels, which is followed by a status in this world. Perhaps, the worshipper turned to the cause, the supererogatory worship, for this effect, after which he sought to hasten and interfere with what was not in his ability. This cause then becomes for eye service only, which is hypocrisy. The same applies to all ruinous things that have led to considerable corruption.

Sub-issue: the inner state of such an actor is peaceful – A significant point in all this is that such a person is full of contentment, peaceful, balanced, the least affected by the burdens of this world, and calm as well as collected. He therefore has a clean life that is rewarded in the Hereafter. Allah, the Exalted, has said: "Whoever works righteousness, man or woman, and has faith, verily, to him will We give a new life, a life that is good and pure and We will bestow on such their reward according to the best of their actions."[117] It is related from Jaʿfar al-Ṣādiq (God be pleased with him) that he described the good life as: knowledge about Allah, being truthful in the relationship with Allah, and obeying the command of Allah in truth."[118] Ibn ʿAṭāʾ has described it as: Life with Allah and turning away from all that is other than Allah. Moreover, in this there is sufficiency with respect to all concerns, and that is by gathering all concerns into a single concern. This is distinguished from the case of the person who focuses on effects of causes, for he waits for each effect of each cause that he has brought about, and these are various and wide ranging. Further, in waiting to see whether or not the cause yields an effect, there is considerable consternation. Even when it bears a result, it is not of the same type. The actor, therefore, is constantly in a state of concern, preoccupied, wondering what would have happened if the effect had been better than it was. You will see him blaming the cause sometimes, expressing dissatisfaction with the effect, or other matters, at other times. It is this meaning that the saying of the Prophet (pbuh) indicates: "Do not blame Time,[119] for Allah Himself is Time."[120] There are other sayings too.

The person who focuses on the cause alone, turning away from other things, is occupied with one thing alone, which is obedience in respect of the cause, whatever cause that may be. There is no doubt that a single concern is much lighter on the mind than multiple concerns. In fact, a sound concern is lighter on the mind than a single wavering and multi-pronged concern. It is related that "whoever turns his concerns into a single concern, Allah is sufficient for him for all his concerns, and if he is concerned about the Hereafter, Allah is sufficient for his affairs in this world."[121] Closer to this is the saying of one who said, "If a person seeks knowledge for the sake of Allah, then a little knowledge is sufficient for him, but if he seeks knowledge for the people, then the people have many requirements." The pious people have been enthusiastic in this field, and are happy to compete with each other in this, so much so that some of them said: "If the kings were aware of what we are about, they would have fought with us with their swords." It is reported in a tradition that "renouncing this world brings peace to the mind and body".[122] Renouncing this world does not mean the absence of physical labour, rather it is a state of mind that is expressed – if you like – that comes into existence by obediently pursuing the causes without turning to the effects through the causes. This is an illustration to point out to you all that falls under this principle.

Sub-issue: the mean path – Among the issues is the point that concern[123] with the effect is sometimes balanced, as will be coming up, God willing,[124] and that is when he takes it in the usual course of events, and this is the safest course for one who is concerned with effects. In some cases, this concern is excessive, over and above what the human being can easily bear. This results in excessive burden for the actor or causes him to abandon what he was obliged to do towards what he is under no obligation to do.

As for excessive burden, it may happen in many cases that it is the same for most persons in control of the effect, but sometimes it may happen that the person in control of the effect is over-anxious or afraid of losing the effect. The basis for this is Allah cautioning his Prophet (pbuh) in the noble Book – when he was over-anxious in inviting people to the religion – that it is preferable for him to have recourse to a balanced approach. This is in the words of the Exalted, "We know indeed the grief which their words do cause thee: It is not thee they reject: it is the Signs of Allah, which the wicked deny. Rejected were the messengers before thee: with patience and constancy they bore their rejection and their persecution, until Our aid did reach them: there is none that can alter the Words (and Decrees) of Allah. Already hast thou received some account of those messengers. If their spurning is hard on thee, yet if thou wert able to seek a tunnel in the ground or a ladder to the skies and bring them a Sign – (what good?). If it were Allah's Will, He could gather them together unto true guidance: so be not thou among those who are swayed by ignorance (and impatience)!"[125] In addition to this there are the following verses.

> "It may be thou wilt kill thy self with grief, that they do not become Believers";[126]

> "O Messenger! Let not those grieve thee, who race each other into unbelief";[127]

> "Perchance thou mayest (feel the inclination) to give up a part of what is revealed unto thee, and thy heart feeleth straitened lest they say, 'Why is not a treasure sent down unto him, or why does not an angel come down with him?' But thou art there only to warn! It is Allah that arrangeth all affairs!";[128]

> "And do thou be patient, for thy patience is but from Allah; nor grieve over them: and distress not thyself because of their plots."[129]

There are other verses that convey the same meaning, and indicate a recommendation to confine himself to a middle path, and to have recourse to reliance on what has been commanded which is the bringing about of the cause. Allah guides whom He wishes to the straight path.[130] "But thou art truly a warner, and to every people a guide."[131] "But thou art there only to warn! It is Allah that arrangeth all affairs!"[132]

All this indicates that what is required from you is the bringing about of the cause, it is Allah who brings about the effect and is its Creator: "Not for thee, (but for Allah), is the decision: Whether He turn in mercy to them, or punish them."[133] This indicates to you the pains that the Prophet (pbuh) took in his concern for their faith, as well as his excessive efforts in inviting them, desiring that his invitation bear fruit, and that was their faith through which they would attain salvation. This is reflected in the verse of the Qur'ān: "Now hath come unto you a Messenger from among yourselves: it grieves him that ye should suffer, ardently anxious is he over you: to the believers is he most kind and merciful."[134]

Nevertheless, it was recommended to the Prophet (pbuh) to undertake something that was more compatible with and suitable for a balanced approach, with a lower level of burdens and hardships, capable of being implemented at levels that are less than prophethood. This is so despite the fact that no one having a position lower than a prophet is qualified for the noble status of prophethood, yet it does not negate its validity to undertake legal reasoning from its principles that is beneficial for the *umma* for the grades that are lower in status. This is what was decided by the experts in *sharīʿa* with respect to the validity of reasoning from the circumstances of the life of the Prophet (pbuh) to derive rules for the *umma*, unless an evidence is offered that these were exclusively for him.

Turning from what is obligatory to what is not obligatory is based on the reason that if he intends the consequence itself, that it may or may not come into being, it goes against the purposes of the Lawgiver, for it became manifest that the consequence is not in the control of the subject and he is under no obligation to bring it about, rather it is Allah Almighty who controls it. Thus, the person who intends it is dominated by the idea of bringing it about in accordance with his specified purpose, when the consequence depends upon the will of Allah and does not conform in all respects to the specific intention of the individual. The purpose of the individual and his intention, therefore, come to oppose in their very formulation what was intended by the cause. This is beyond the requirement of the rites and in opposition to what is determined, or whatever is of this nature.

A caution has been recorded in the sound compilations about this idea through the words of the Prophet (pbuh):

> The powerful believer is better and favoured by Allah as compared to the weak believer. In both there is a blessing. You concern yourself with what is beneficial for you and seek the support of Allah, but do not become helpless. If some calamity befalls you, do not say, "Had I acted the result would have been different." Say rather, "Allah has determined what He wished." The reason is that the word "if" opens the door for Satan.[135]

Thus, you have been cautioned that "if" opens the door for Satan, because it leads to focusing on the consequence through the cause, as if it is born out of it or is conceptually inevitable. In fact, this is the determination by Allah, who does what He wills. The existence of the cause does not help Him nor does its absence hinder Him in any way.

The conclusion is that the execution of the determination is what is obtained from it. The cause remains as it is: if he is under an obligation to bring it about, he should act upon it as is required by the obligation. If he is not under an obligation to bring it about, not being within his capacity to do so, he should submit like the person who knows that all control is in the hands of Allah. This way the door will not be opened for Satan against him. It is often that a human being acts in this meaning, through prodding by Satan and opposition to the decree of Allah, so that he turns to what is legally reprehensible.

Sub-issue: examining the effect – Among these issues is that the one who relinquishes a focus on the consequence has a higher status and is pure in deed, if he is performing acts of worship and compensates adequately in transactions. The reason is that he is giving up a return (for his act) as compared to one who always turns to the consequences, for he is always looking for a return. The basis for this is that the results of acts are of benefit for human beings even though they are a creation of Allah. These are the benefits or harms that go back to them, as is stated in the tradition of Abū Dharr: "Verily, these are your deeds that I have reckoned for you, which I will return to you in full."[136] The basis is in the Qurʾān: "Whoever works righteousness benefits himself; whoever works evil, works against himself: nor is thy Lord ever unjust (in the least) to His servants."[137] Thus, he who turns to the consequences is working for his own reward, while the one who turns merely to the command and the prohibition is working for the relinquishment of the rewards, which is the view of the leaders in the field, and for this there is an explanation elsewhere.[138]

Suppose the question is raised: in what way is the relinquishment of a focus on the consequences to be understood, and what rule is to be framed for distinguishing what is included in this meaning and what is not?

The response is that the relinquishment of rewards is sometimes manifest in the meaning of the mind not inclining towards them at all, but this is rare. Usually it is witnessed exclusively among the leading *ṣūfīs*. The *ṣūfī* will undertake the cause in the absolute sense without concerning himself with whether or not it has a consequence. At other times it is not manifest in the meaning that the reward is not altogether missing from the mind, except that the inclination towards it is from behind the command and proscription with the belief that Allah will do what He will. At other times it is with the request that the consequence emerge from the cause, that is, he request from the Creator of the consequence the result of the cause. It is as if he is requesting the Creator with hands spread out the consequence of the cause, just as he would spread out the hands of need to request something, or is leaving the consequence to One who can bring it about. These people have relinquished the consequence resulting from the cause.

Turning to the consequence in the meaning of being the natural consequence of the cause, like one demanding the consequence from the cause itself, or the one believing that it is the cause itself that will give birth to the consequence, is the fearful state that is loaded with the injuries mentioned. Between these two states there are links that are the subject-matter for examination by the *mujtahids*. The state will take the rule of of the two sides to which it is closer. A similar discussion is undertaken under the topic of rewards.[139]

The tenth issue: the effects are legally based on causative acts

It has been said that legally the consequences are structured upon the bringing about of the causes,[140] and that the Lawgiver takes the consequences into account in His communication through the causes. This leads to a number of significant points with respect to the subject.

Sub-issue: causes may have unexpected consequences – Among these issues is that if the consequence is legally attributed to the Creator, it requires that the subject, in bringing about the cause by inclining towards the consequence, expect that it results in what is not in his reckoning. The bringing about of the cause may be commanded and it may be proscribed, but the bringing about of the cause in worship can result in blessings that are beyond the worshipper's expectations. This is evidenced in the words of the Exalted, "If any one saved a life, it would be as if he saved the life of the whole people."[141] There is also a tradition from the Prophet (pbuh), "Anyone who lays down a good practice has his reward for it, and the reward of whoever acts upon it",[142] as well as his saying, "When a person says something to please Allah, he cannot even imagine the loftiness of the status to which it will raise him."[143]

Likewise, the commission of an evil cause can result in a consequence not intended, due to the words of the Exalted, "if any one slew a person – unless it be for murder or for spreading mischief in the land – it would be as if he slew the whole people."[144] It is also supported by the saying of the Prophet (pbuh), "Whenever a person is killed unjustly, the son of Adam, the First, bears a burden for it."[145] And his saying, "Anyone who lays down an evil practice bears its burden",[146] as well as his saying, "When a person utters a statement that offends Allah ..."[147] There are other traditions too.

Al-Ghazālī has elaborated this concept in his book *Iḥyāʾ* as well as in others to an extent that is sufficient. He says in *Kitāb al-Kasb*, "Exchanging of a sound *dirham* with counterfeit *dirhams* during a spot transaction is gross injustice, because by this the person undertaking the transaction is harmed even though he is not aware of it. If he knows of it then he is passing it on to another. Likewise the second and the third, and it continues to move through many hands, spreading the injury and widening the corruption. The burden and the torment suffered by all comes back to him, for he was the one who opened this door." Thereafter he supported it with the tradition, "Anyone who lays down a good practice ..."[148]

Thereafter, he has narrated that the spending of a counterfeit *dirham* is an offence more grievous than committing a theft of one hundred *dirhams*. He said, "The reason is that theft is a single evil deed that is committed and ends. The introduction of a counterfeit coin is an innovation in religion, and the laying down of a practice that will be followed by those who follow. It is this person who will bear the burden of its evil even one hundred years after his death, and for two hundred years, till such time that this false *dirham* is destroyed. He will be liable for the loss in the wealth of the people as a result of it. The person is fortunate who dies and with him die his sins, and there is curse on the one who dies, but *his* sins last for a hundred years or two hundred years; he will be tormented in his grave for he will be questioned till the destruction of the coin. Allah, the Exalted, has said, 'Verily We shall give life to the dead, and We record that which they send before and that which they leave behind, and of all things have We taken account in a clear Book (of evidence)' ",[149] that is, We record the effects of the deeds that they leave behind just as we record what they have sent ahead. Similar to this are the words of the Exalted, 'That Day will Man be told (all) that he put forward, and all that he put back.'[150] What he has put back are the effects of his deeds, for he who lays down an evil practice is acted upon by others."[151]

This is what he said in that text. I have already explained the principle that the occurrence of the cause is equivalent to the occurrence of the effect.

His statement in *Kitāb al-Shukr* is even more severe than this. In this book, he has divided blessings into genera and classes. He has gone into great detail. Thereafter he said: "Rather I would say that one who disobeys Allah, even though that is by a single glance, that is, by opening his eyes where it was obligatory to close them, has denied all the blessings of Allah that exist within the heavens and the earth. All that Allah has created even the angels, the skies, animals, vegetation, all in their entirety are blessings whose utilisation comes to an end with this act."

He then mentions some of the blessings that pass on to the eyes from the eyelids. He says: "He has denied the blessings of Allah that are found in the eyelids. The eyelids do not survive without the eye, nor the eye without the head, nor the head does without the whole body, nor the body without food, nor food without water, soil, air, rain, clouds, sun and the moon. None of these things can exist without the skies, while the skies cannot exist without the angels. The whole is like a single body, one part is linked to the other part, like the link between the limbs one to another." He says that it is stated in a tradition that "a piece of land where people gather curses them when they disperse or seeks forgiveness for them".[152] It is also in a tradition that "each thing in the universe seeks the forgiveness of Allah, even the whale in the sea".[153]

In this there is an indication that the disobedient person by a single glance has committed an offence against all that exists within the universe. He has destroyed himself through an evil deed by avoiding a good deed that erases the evil effects, and converts curses into pleas of forgiveness, so that Allah may forgive him and overlook his bad deed. He then narrates other traditions and goes into details.

If the person bringing about the cause ponders over the consequences of such causes, it might act as the reason for avoiding such things, for they will appear before him on the day of judgement in ways that are beyond his comprehension. May Allah protect us.

Sub-issue: problems in undoing the causes – Among these is the issue that when the subject takes the consequences into account along with the causes, some of the confusions that occur in the *sharīʿa* will most likely be removed for him. These confusions arise due to the clash of the rule for the earlier cause with the rule for the later present cause.[154] The reason is that the rule stays with the person who brought about the cause even if he retraces the cause or repents for bringing it about. He may think that the rule for the consequence has been lifted, but it may not be so in reality.

An illustration for this is where a person occupies the usurped land, but repents thereafter and wishes to withdraw from the land. It is obvious that if at this time he is directed to vacate the land, and he obeys, then he is not disobedient or blameworthy, because it is not possible for him to be obedient and disobedient in the same state, nor can he be subject to a command and a proscription at the same time for this would be an obligation to do the impossible. Thus, it is necessary to be under an obligation to vacate the land in whichever state it is possible; however, this will not be possible with there being a proscription with respect to the same vacation. It is, therefore, essential that the application of the rule of proscription be removed from him.

Abū Hāshim[155] has said that he will still be deemed disobedient, and he does not move out of the application of this rule except by his complete separation from the usurped land. This was opposed by the earlier as well as the later jurists. Imam al-Ghazālī refers to *al-Burhān* (*The Proof*) for this concept and its validity on the basis of the first cause, which was disobedience. The rule of the consequence continues to overshadow him even though it was removed with his repentance.[156] He considers parallel cases by referring to this issue, and such a reference is sound on the basis of the earlier principle. The first cause that he brought about gave rise to consequences that lay beyond his comprehension. If the majority of the jurists had examined this issue they would not have negated the combining of obedience with the presumption of continuity till his separation from the usurped land. This case then is also based upon the principle that resulting consequences lie beyond the anticipation of the subject.[157] Had he taken this into account, he would have considered vacation of the land to have two aspects.

First: Vacation is the cause for undoing the transgression of occupation, and this is his act.

Second: His act of vacation being the result of his earlier occupation, it is not his own act from this perspective, for he does not have the power to undo its consequence.

A similar issue is of the person who repents after shooting an arrow from the bow, prior to its hitting the target. Likewise one who repents for creating an innovation prior to its reaching the people and their adoption of the practice, or after it but prior to their relinquishment of the practice. There is also the case of a person who retracts his testimony after the decision, but prior to its execution. On the whole, after the bringing about of the cause in the complete sense, but prior to its effect and coming into existence of its injury, or after its existence yet prior to its removal if its removal is possible, in these cases, the rule combines for the subject the acknowledgement of obedience and the continuation of the rule of disobedience. If these are combined in the first example, then the person is disobedient-obedient, except that the command and the prohibition do not conceptually come together for him, because he is not under an obligation with respect to disobedience,[158] because it is a consequence over which he has no power. Thus, there is no proscription here. He is under a duty with respect to obedience, for that lies within his power, for he is commanded to vacate the land and is able to obey. This is the meaning that the imam intended. The objection raised against his view and that of Abū Hāshim, if you ponder over it, is not valid when this method is adopted.[159] Allah knows best.

Sub-issue: effects follow causes – There is also the issue that Allah, the Exalted and Glorious, has deemed the consequences to flow naturally from their causes in practice, and in conformity with the causes with respect to soundness and distortion. If the cause is complete and the one bringing it about sound, the consequence will naturally be sound. The reverse is also true.

Accordingly, if there is a problem with the effect, the jurists will look to see whether the cause has been brought about completely. If the cause is complete, there is no blame attached to the person bringing about the cause. If the cause is not complete, blame and liability are associated with the person. You will notice that they hold the physician, the cupper, chef and others liable for compensation when negligence on their part is established. He has either deceived himself and is not the real actor or he has committed negligence. This is distinguished from the case where he is not guilty of negligence. In such a case there is no liability for compensation, because error in bringing about the causes or their occurrence in a manner that goes against the standards laid down for causes is rare; therefore, he is not held liable. This is also distinguished from the case where he has not put in the required effort, in which case mistakes are numerous and he has to be held liable.

The jurist who focuses on effects insofar as they are the signs of causes with respect to validity and vitiation, and not from another perspective,[160] has derived a strong rule through which the operation of causes is regulated in accordance with the stipulated standards, even when there is a violation. It is on this basis that the external forms of acts have been treated by the *sharīʿa* as an indication of internal intentions. If the external act is distorted the internal intention will be the same, and when it is sound the internal intention is also deemed sound. This is a general principle in *fiqh* as well as in all practices and experiments. In fact, deeming it so is highly beneficial in the *sharīʿa* as a whole, and there are numerous evidences that support it. It serves as a basis for issuing a ruling about the faith of the believer, the *kufr* of the unbeliever, the obedience of the obedient, the disobedience of the disobedient, the justice of the just, and the wound caused by the offender. It is through this that contracts are concluded and agreements formed, along with many other acts.[161] This is a universal principle in the *sharīʿa*, and a standard with respect to the *ḥudūd* (bounds, fixed penalties), which are a symbol of the Islamic *sharīʿa* both general and particular.

Sub-issue: general and particular effects – Among the issues is that the effects are sometimes particular and sometimes general. The meaning of their being particular is that they occur in conformity with the cause. It is like sale that leads to the effect of the permissibility of utilising the sold commodity, like marriage through which is attained the right of access, like slaughter through which food is made permissible, and so forth. The same applies to the perspective of prohibition, like the intoxication of the one who consumes *khamr* (wine), and the departure of the soul of the one who is slain.

As for general effects, it is like obedience, which is a cause for success in attaining blessings, and disobedience, which is the cause for entering hell. Likewise, the different types of disobedience through which corruption reigns on earth: the deficiency in measure and weight that leads to the cutting off of sustenance;[162] authorising unjustified killing that gives rise to claims of blood-money; the breach of truce that leads to occupation by the enemy; deception that does away with authority; and so forth. There is no doubt that the opposite of such causes will give rise to the opposite effects.

When the actor examines what blessings or evils are resulting from his acts, he will strive to avoid the prohibited acts and perform what is prescribed in the hope of seeking nearness to Allah and out of fear of Him. It is for this reason that reports exist in the *sharīʿa* about compensating acts through the effects of causes. Allah is well aware of the interests of His servants. The benefits that are based upon these principles are numerous.

Sub-issue: examining of effects based on interests – Suppose it is said: It has been settled in a previous issue that focusing on effects gives to the acquisition of injuries, and it flows from this that one should not focus on the effect in causation, but now it has been elaborated that focusing on the effects gives rise to the securing of interests, thus, it flows from this requirement that one should focus on them. If this is an unqualified proposition then a contradiction has arisen. If it is not absolute then it is necessary to identify the occasions that give rise to securing of interests and those that give rise to injuries. This should be done through a standard on which one can rely or a rule to which recourse can be had.

The response is: This concept has been made plain in another location,[163] but the rule for it is that if focusing on the effect lends strength to the cause, complements it, or an inducement to go further in its completion, then it is one that secures an interest. If it is one that it amounts to an attack on the cause leading to its annulment, weakening or degradation, then the cause is one that gives rise to injury.

These two types can be divided into two other types.

First is the type that is absolute in the sense that it strengthens or weakens the cause with respect to every subject. It also does so with respect to all times, and all circumstances in which the subject may find himself. **Second** is the type that is not applied in the absolute sense, rather it applies to some of the subjects and not others, or it applies in certain times not others, or it applies to some of the circumstances of the subject not others.

Again, it may be divided into two from another perspective: **First** the type that is certain with respect to strengthening and weakening. **Second** is the type that is probable or doubtful, and is thus a matter of examination and scrutiny. The ruling for it is based upon probability, or the ruling is suspended when there is a conflict of two probabilities. This type becomes ambiguous on the whole and is not elaborated, but when it is referred to what has preceded and what is to come, its essence becomes apparent and its meaning elaborated with the power of God.

From this division, the scrutiny by the *mujtahid* emerges. It is the duty of the *mujtahids* to examine the causes and the effects for the *sharʿī* rules that are structured upon them. The division that has preceded applies to the subject who undertake the acts. From Allah belongs all success.

Sub-issue: conflict of principles for the mujtahid – On occasions two principles conflict with each other during the examination of the *mujtahid*, and each principle is inclined towards what has come to dominate his mind.

Thus, the jurists said about the intoxicated person when he pronounces a divorce, emancipates a slave, commits an offence liable to *ḥadd* or *qiṣāṣ*, he is to be dealt with on the basis of the second principle[164] as if he was a sane (rational) person, and there are details that they go into as mentioned in *fiqh*. They also disagree about the granting of an exemption[165] to the disobedient as a result of his journey, and that on the basis of two principles. They also disagreed about voluntary fasting, the cutting off of consecutive fasting due to a voluntary journey in which he breaks the fast if the excuse applies to him. Likewise, they disagree about the consumption of carrion by a person under duress due to a journey that makes him a disobedient person.[166] It is also on the basis of these two principles that the issue stated earlier regarding the disagreement between Abū Hāshim and others regarding the person who stays on in usurped land is decided.

The eleventh issue: prohibited causes are injurious and permitted causes are beneficial

Prohibited causes are causes for injuries and not the securing of interests. Likewise, permitted causes are causes for the securing of interests and not the acquisition of injuries.

An illustration for this is commanding the good and forbidding evil (*al-amr biʾl-maʿrūf wan-nahy ʿanʾl-munkar*). It is a command that is legal for it is a cause that leads to the establishment of *dīn*, raising the symbols of Islam, and the elimination of all forms of falsehood. It is not a cause, in its legal form, for the destruction of property and life, nor the acquisition of goods, even though this may come to pass on the way. Likewise, *jihād* has been formulated for spreading the word of God, even though it leads to the loss of property and life. The repelling of brigands is legal for the elimination of killing and fighting, even though it leads to slaying and fighting. The demanding of *zakāt* is legal for the affirmation of one of the pillars of Islam, even if it leads to war, as was done by Abū Bakr (God be pleased with him) and all the Companions (God be pleased with them) agreed to this. The implementation of *ḥudūd* and *qiṣāṣ* has been prescribed for acting as a deterrence against corruption, even though it leads to the destruction of life and the spilling of blood, which are in themselves a type of corruption. The execution of the decree of the judge is legal[167] in the interest of putting an end to litigation, even though it gives rise to a command that is not legal. All this is in the case of causes that are lawful.

As for causes that are prohibited, these are like: vitiated marriage contracts that are prohibited, even though they lead to the validity of paternity, affirm the right to inherit, and other legal effects, for these are interests to be secured;[168] usurpation (*ghaṣb*) that is prohibited due to the consequential injury to the owner,[169] even though it leads to the interests of economy as a whole when the property grows in the possession of the usurper; or other cases that lead to loss.

What must be understood by way of obligation is that these irregularities arising from lawful causes, or the benefits arising from unlawful causes, do not in reality arise from such causes but from other causes that are compatible with them.[170]

The evidence for this is manifest. If the causes[171] are lawful, they are legalised for the securing of interests, or for the acquisition of injuries, or for both together, or even for reasons other than these. It is not proper that they be legalised for the securing of harm, because the transmitted revelation rejects that. The *sharʿī* evidence has been established that the *sharīʿa* came down with commands that are meant to secure interests, even though this is not obligatory rationally.[172] It was, however, established through transmitted evidences. Likewise, it is also not proper, on the basis of this evidence, that they be legalised for both at the same time. It is also not valid that they be legalised for something other than the securing of interests, for this too has been established through an evidence.[173] Thus, it becomes manifest that they have been made lawful for the securing of interests.

The same idea runs through all causes that are prohibited. A cause may be prohibited either because bringing it about leads to an injury, to the securing of an interest, to both at the same time, or to some other state. The evidence is applicable here too. Thus, there can be no lawful cause that is not permitted for the securing of an interest; it is for this interest that the cause has been made lawful. If you examine the consequence and find an injury arising from it, then know that it has not arisen from the lawful cause itself. Further, there is no unlawful cause that does not lead to an injury for which it has been prohibited. If you find that a benefit is arising from what it has led to, then know that it has not arisen from the prohibited cause itself. From both causes arises what has been assigned to them: if the cause is declared lawful it leads to the lawful and if it is unlawful it leads to what it was prohibited for.

The elaboration of this is that *al-amr biʾl-maʿrūf wan-nahy ʿaniʾl-munkar* (commanding the good and forbidding evil), for example, is not intended by the Lawgiver to lead to loss of life or property. These are consequences that follow the lawful cause, which is laid down for the raising high of the truth and demolishing falsehood. It is like *jihād* whose purpose is not the destruction of life, rather it is the spreading of the word of Allah; however, on the way it leads to loss of life, because human beings place themselves in a position that leads to conflict between two groups, the picking up of weapons, and clashing through warfare. *Ḥudūd* and similar provisions lead to the securing of an interest in which there is loss of life too, because the interest cannot be secured without such loss. The judgement of the judge is the cause for the avoidance of controversy and the settling of disputes, according to the apparent meaning, so that it is an obvious interest. The errors of the judge relate to other causes like inadequate examination of the issue or the fact that the obvious differed from an inner *ratio*, and he did not have an evidence for it, but making such errors is not the objective of the judge's ruling.[174] The judgement cannot be set aside, until there is a substantial reason for doing so, and the basis is that reversing the decision leads to the opposite of the basis for which the judge was appointed, that is, settlement of disputes and removal of controversy, because reversal is the opposite of settlement.

As for the prohibited causes, the proof of the legal effects arises from the validation of such a marriage contract after its (irregular) occurrence, and not because it is vitiated, according to what has been elaborated at its proper occasion.[175] *Fāsid* (irregular) sales fall in this category. The reason is that physical possession here is assigned the ruling of compensation (*ḍamān*) according to the law. The person in possession is like the owner of the commodity as a result of *ḍamān*, and not on the basis of the contract. If the commodity is destroyed, a similar or its value has to be paid. If the commodity survives without alteration or any probability of loss, then the proscription of the cause requires the rule of vitiation. If some alteration or the like (mesne profits) takes place that does not amount to a loss in the chattel, the views of the jurists vary: is it to be assigned the rule of total loss due to the alteration? What remains is the rule for requiring revocation, except that in the demand for revocation a burden has been placed upon the owner of the goods,[176] for example, when these are returned to him in an altered form. Likewise, a burden is placed upon the buyer insofar as he is paid back the price, but he is not given what he spent by way of expenses for the growth in the goods. Justice requires that both aspects be considered, thus in the case of loss fluctuations in the markets are to be considered as well as the changes that did not cause a loss in the property, along with the passage of title and other things mentioned in the books of the jurists. The conclusion is that the absence of revocation and the authority of the buyer to utilise the goods do not have as their cause the proscribed contract, but external factors that operate later.

Ghaṣb (usurpation) falls in this category as well. The usual possession is assigned the rule of *ḍamān* in the law. *Ḍamān* gives rise to the ascertainment of a similar or the value attached to the *dhimma* (liability). In this sense the usurper is in the same position as the owner in some respects; therefore, a semblance of ownership (*shubhat milk*) arises for him. If a change occurs in the usurped property despite which the property survives as a whole, it becomes subject to *ijtihād*. This happens by examining the rights of the owner of the usurped property and the rights of the usurper, for his usurpation has not damaged the property so that it may invoke damages by way of penalty.[177] Likewise, the person whose property was usurped is not to be treated unjustly by diminishing his rights. The resulting *ijtihād* should come to rest somewhere in between. The cause for passing ownership to the usurper of property is not the act of usurpation itself, but holding him liable for compensation combined with what occurs later in the usurped property. In this form, or what is similar, is the examination of these cases.

The purpose is to show that lawful causes do not become causes for injuries, while prohibited causes cannot be causes for the securing of interests, for this would not be valid under any circumstances.

Sub-issue: views of the Mālikī school – It is in this way that the rules for a number of cases are understood in Mālik's school as well as in others. In the school there is a case where a person makes a vow that he will divorce his wife if he cannot meet the debt due to another by a certain time. Thereafter, he fears breaking his vow due to lack of the means to satisfy the debt. He, therefore, concludes *khulʿ* (a form of divorce) with his wife till the due date is over. When the vow is broken she is not his wife. After that he takes her back through a retraction. In this case, the breaking of the vow does not apply to him, even though his intention was blameworthy and his act was blameworthy as well, because he created a legal fiction through which he tried to annul the right of another. Thus, the *khulʿ* was prohibited as well even though it led to the absence of the breach of vow. The reason is that the absence of the breach was not caused by the *khulʿ*, rather it was caused due to the fact that he broke his vow when he had no wife, thus the breach had no corresponding subject-matter.

In the same category is the view of al-Lakhmī about the person who intends through his journey to obtain an exemption of not fasting. He has the right not to fast even though it is considered disapproved for him to form such an intention. The permission not to fast is caused by the necessary hardship[178] arising from the journey, and not due to the cause of the disapproved journey itself. If the permission not to fast is associated with the cause of *safar*, it is so because it includes hardship within it and not journey alone. It is, therefore, verified that disapproval for this person is due to his journey, which is his personal act, while hardship is external to his act; therefore, hardship itself is not disapproved for him, rather it is the cause; the consequence is the cause here for not fasting.

If we assume[179] that a prohibited cause does not give rise to something that becomes a cause for securing an interest, or that a permitted cause does not give rise to something that can become a cause for an injury, then legally an injury cannot be intended through a permitted cause nor can an interest be legally intended through a prohibited cause. This is illustrated through a legal fiction invented by those who uphold the contract of *ʿīna* (buy-back agreement) that deems some goods a link between the sale of one *dīnār* for two *dīnārs* with a delay.[180] There are two aspects of this issue along with a link. From one aspect it does not give rise to an established cause under any circumstances, as in the *hīla* (legal fiction)[181] mentioned above. From the other aspect it includes a cause by way of certainty or probability, like the changes occurring in the usurped property in the possession of the usurper, who owns it according to the details that are known. Then there is the link through which the cause is not negated nor is it established with a certainty. This is subject to examination by the *mujtahids* (independent jurists).

Sub-issue: issues examined in the light of this principle – All this takes place when we examine these detailed issues in the light of the established principle. If it is viewed from a different perspective, it gives rise to a different rule. Those who examine it move between these two views, because it has become a vacillating issue.

The reason is that it is established that the bringing about of the causes by the subject is the bringing about of the consequences. If this is the case, it requires that the consequences in the case are a result of his choice. Thus, the legal cause will not occur nor will what is required through it. Consequently, a person going on a journey to evade the rules is not to curtail his prayers nor is he to give up fasting. It is as if he has invoked the hardship arising through the journey himself, because it is arising from his personal cause. The person creating the fiction of seeking *khulʿa* for his wife in order to avoid the consequences of breaking his vow is not absolved of his liability; rather it occurs if he has recourse to his wife. Likewise, a person who takes his wife back through the device of *ḥalāla*. The same applies to other similar cases. In such cases when recourse is had to two such independent principles, the issues will become the subject-matter of *ijtihād*. The jurist who prefers one of these principles will issue a ruling according to it. Allah knows best.

Sub-issue: examining effects for validity – What has been said[182] about this principle is an examination of the consequences of causes insofar as the causes are legally valid or invalid, that is, from the perspective of the *sharīʿa* and not from the perspective of natural causes for natural consequences. If they are examined from this perspective the examination will be different. If a person intends a cure through the intention to kill, he is bringing about a cause that in his view secures an interest or repels an injury. The same is the case of the person who gives up obligatory acts of worship, for he is avoiding them due the physical burden, intending thereby rest and recreation. From the perspective of his committing the act or omitting it in the absolute sense, he intends the consequence to repel an injury to himself or to secure an interest, just as people do in times of fatigue. The injuries and interests here are considered from the perspective of their compatibility or incompatibility with temperaments. The discussion here does not concern such issues.

The twelfth issue: effects are interests that are to be secured

Causes – insofar as they are legal causes for consequences – have been prescribed for attaining consequences, and these are interests to be secured and injuries to be repelled. Consequences from the perspective of their causes are of two types.

First: Consequences because of which causes have been legally prescribed.[183] They are prescribed either through a primary intention, and this pertains to the primary objectives or the first objectives, or through a secondary intention, and this pertains to secondary objectives. Both types have been elaborated in the *Book of Maqāṣid.*[184]

Second: Those consequences that are other than the above. These are consequences about which it is known or thought that causes have been prescribed for them or it is not known nor is it conceived that consequences are prescribed or not prescribed for them. This converts the types to three.

First: **Those about which it is known or thought that causes have been prescribed for them.** The act of the person bringing about such a cause is valid, because he has done something within this category. He has attained the consequence through what has been permitted by the Lawgiver as a means of such attainment and also what it leads to. The reason, for example, is that we have assumed that the Lawgiver in the case of marriage primarily intends procreation[185] and secondarily the setting up of a household, establishing relations with the wife's family due to their nobility and honour, care, securing other interests, benefiting from what Allah has permitted through contact with women, security through the wealth of the woman, inclination towards her beauty, envy for her religion, avoiding what Allah has prohibited, or other reasons in accordance with what is implied by the *sharīʿa*. What this person intends becomes the purpose of the Lawgiver as a whole, which is sufficient. It has been elaborated in the *Book of Maqāṣid* that an intention that is compatible with the intention of the Lawgiver is valid. There is no way of asserting that bringing about such a cause is not valid.

It is not proper to say: The intention to (physically) benefit from the woman is not sufficient as a primary intention to make physical contact lawful through the contract, for it is this contract on which the intention is structured. The Lawgiver primarily intends permissibility through the contract, and utilisation is then based upon this. Consequently, the intention formed to merely benefit through physical contact is not valid. This is elaborated through the case where a person intends to obtain physically utilisation with such and such woman in whatever way that is possible, whether it is through contract or otherwise, since this is not possible for him except through a legally prescribed contract, though his intention was to obtain his objective even through unlawful sexual intercourse. Consequently, if he concludes a contract with her when this is his intention, then he has not intended permissibility. If he has not intended permissibility then he has opposed the intention of the Lawgiver through such contract, which is void. The rule for each commission and omission runs such a course.

The reason why it is not proper to say this is because we will respond by saying: In fact, the contract is valid even on the basis of what is assumed in the question. The reason is that this person cannot form an intention that is not valid; he has followed the path that the Lawgiver has laid down to reach it. His intention in the formation of the contract is not that it is not a contract, rather he intended the conclusion of the contract of marriage with the permission of one whose permission is required, and he met the obligations that are supposed to be met. He had recourse to the contract; therefore, by bringing about this valid cause he is entitled to what is demanded by this contract. What remains is his intention to seek the prohibited, which is not in his power. If at the time of forming the intention for sin, he was able to commit it, he has committed a sin according to the jurists.[186] If he has such a thought without forming an intention, then this is forgiven as in the case of all evil thoughts. Such a thought is not associated with the contract so as to render it void, because it has been brought about with all its elements, the completion of the conditions, and the absence of any obstacles. The intention of a person to commit a sin that is within his power falls outside the ambit of his intention[187] to seek permissibility in a manner intended by the Lawgiver. This latter intention[188] is present in his case without fail, and it conforms with the intention of the Lawgiver through the appointment of the cause. Thus, bringing about the cause is valid. As for the imposition of the obligation to form an intention of permissibility, it cannot be imposed, and it is sufficient if the intention to bring about a valid cause is formed, even though he forgets to seek permissibility through it. The reason is that the permissibility arising from the cause is not included[189] in the obligation imposed on him, as has preceded.

Second: **Those about which it is known, or thought, that the cause has not been primarily prescribed for them.**[190] The evidence requires that bringing about such a cause is not valid, because the cause has not primarily been prescribed for such an assumed consequence. If it has not been prescribed for it, its rationale does not lead to the securing of an interest or the repelling of an injury with respect to what is intended by the cause. It is, therefore, void. This is one interpretation.

The second interpretation is that this cause with respect to this assumed intention is not valid, thus it turns into a cause that is not prescribed in the first instance. If the cause is essentially not valid, it is void. Likewise what is prescribed when it is adopted for what is not legal.

The third interpretation is that the very fact the Lawgiver has not prescribed this cause for this identified consequence is an evidence pointing out that in such a consequence there is an injury, not an interest. In the alternative, a lawful interest has a cause that negates this consequence and to such an extent it becomes futile. If the Lawgiver has prohibited this particular causation, then the matter is clear. If he intends, for example, an act in which there is an element of invalidity like the marriage that attempts to validate remarriage for another, or intends a sale that leads to *ribā* along with an element of invalidity of the sale, or other similar matters in which it is known or believed that the Lawgiver has not intended them, then this act will be null and void due to its clash with the intention of the Lawgiver in legalising marriage and sale. The same applies to all the remaining acts and consequences that pertain to practice or worship.

If it is said: How is this possible? The marriage in this example, even though it is intended to reverse the marriage through divorce, so that the woman becomes lawful for the first husband, is an intention that is secondary to the intention of marriage. The reason is that the right to divorce is not possessed except after the ownership resulting from marriage. He has intended marriage that is undone through divorce, because the marriage contract by its very legal form is one that can be undone through divorce, but is permissible in itself and, therefore, valid. His having intended, through this initial permissibility, another act is condemnable in itself, having linked two conflicting purposes, neither of which has any effect on the other due to their independence from each other, like prayer on usurped land. In *fiqh*, there are parallel issues that support this claim.

Thus, both Mālik and Abū Ḥanīfa agreed on the validity of stipulations[191] in the case of divorce prior to marriage, and also in emancipation prior to ownership. Consequently, if a man says to a strange woman:[192] "If I marry you, you stand divorced", or he says to a slave, "If I buy you, you stand emancipated", then divorce is binding on him if he marries her, and emancipation if he buys him. It is well known that both Mālik and Abū Ḥanīfa permit this man to marry the woman or to buy the slave. A view is narrated in *al-Mabsūṭa*[193] from Mālik about a person who makes a vow to divorce each woman that he marries in the next thirty years, but then is apprehensive of deprivation. He said, "I hold that it is permissible for him to marry, but when he does so she stands divorced from him." This is the case when this marriage and this purchase do not have any element of what the Lawgiver has primarily intended through this contract nor what He has intended through a secondary intention. The only intention is that of divorce and emancipation. Marriage has not been prescribed for divorce nor purchase for losing possession; they have been prescribed for other matters. Divorce and emancipation are secondary matters not intended in the validation of these contracts. These contracts are validated only because the occurrence of divorce and emancipation are secondary to the attainment of the state of marriage or ownership and due to the intention to attain these. Thus the person contracting marriage intending divorce through marriage, and the buyer intending emancipation through his purchase, when the obvious meaning of these intentions is the negation of the intention of the Lawgiver. Despite this, the contracts are valid according to these two imams. If this is the case, then one of the two things is valid: either the permissibility of causation through lawful acts of consequences for which the cause is not prescribed or the invalidity of these issues (opinions).

There are numerous cases like this in Mālik's school. In *al-Mudawwana* there is the issue of a person who marries and at the same time intends separation.[194] It is stated that this does not amount to *mutʿa* (temporary marriage).[195] If a man is to marry a woman as a consequence of a vow, it becomes obligatory for him to marry her. The jurists framed this issue (to show the intention of divorce). Mālik said, "The marriage is lawful. If he likes he can keep her, but if he wishes to divorce her he may do so." Ibn al-Qāsim said that this is an issue about which there is no disagreement according to what we have heard or has been transmitted to us. He said, "In our view, it is an established marriage." The man who marries wishes to be absolved of his vow. His case is similar to the man who marries a woman seeking pleasure from her, but does not want to keep her confined nor does he intend this, then his intention is implied accordingly. The two cases are similar. If they wish to continue the state of marriage they may, because marriage is in its essence lawful. This explanation has been mentioned in *al-Mabsūṭa*.

It is stated in *al-Kāfī* about the man who visits a land and marries a woman when his intention is to divorce her at the end of the visit, "The majority opinion is that of permissibility."[196] Ibn al-ʿArabī has noted the strict views of Mālik in prohibiting the *mutʿa* form of marriage. He does not permit it when there is the accompanying intention that he will marry her with the purpose of staying with her for only a period, even though he does not give expression to this intention. He then adds that the rest of the jurists permit it, illustrating it with the example of those travelling to other lands. He adds, "In my view, intention is not effective in this. The reason is that if we make it binding[197] that he intend in his heart a perpetual marriage, it would amount to a Christian marriage. If the words he uses are sound, his intention is not harmful. Do you not see that a man marries for peaceful living and availability of sustenance. He either finds them or separates through divorce. Likewise he marries for maintaining security; if he finds it he remains united otherwise he separates." This is his statement in his book *al-Nāsikh wa-al-Mansūkh*. Al-Lakhmī has narrated from Mālik that if a person marries due to his estrangement or for a desire, then if his purpose is attained and he separates there is no harm in this.

These are issues that indicate a disagreement about the principle mentioned from which reasoning was undertaken. More acutely[198] it is the issue of being absolved from a vow, because he has not intended marriage due to his inclination towards it; rather he has formed an intention so that he can be released from his vow. The contract of marriage has not been permitted for a situation like this. There are many similar cases, and all of them are valid along with an intention that goes against the intention of the Lawgiver. This is nothing more than having a primary intention for marriage and a secondary intention for divorce. These are two intentions that are not interrelated. If they are deemed interdependent in the first issue[199] so that one intention is effective for the other, then all that has preceded[200] on the issues is null and void. On the whole, then, it is necessary that either all this be void or all that has preceded be void.

The response is based upon two interpretations: one is at the general level and the other at the level of details.

As for the general interpretation, we say: The issue is sound in principle due to the evidences that have preceded. The objections that have been raised do not fall under it nor are they relevant to it on the evidence of their opinion about its permissibility and validity. What they have agreed about with respect to permissibility is due to protection from the requirement of the principle of the issue. What they have disagreed about is due to its falling under its scope according to those who do not permit it, and due to its soundness according to those who permit it. The reason is that the statements of the jurists are not contradictory, and it is not required that they be interpreted in this manner when there is another solution to the problem. This answer is sufficient for one who is a *muqallid* with respect to his *fiqh* and *ʿuṣūl*. From the scholar[201] is expected a sound approach towards these ancestors. He should stop, ponder over the issue, and seek out a solution, and he should not go astray by rejecting it outright.

As for the response referring to the details, we say: These issues do not demolish what has preceded. As for the issue of prior stipulations, al-Qarāfī has said, "These are difficult cases settled by the two imams. Where one declares the validity of marriage in the case of stipulations prior to ownership, then he has made its validity binding despite the negation of the rationale that is legally taken into account." He said, "It was essential that the contract be declared invalid in the case of the woman, but it is valid on the basis of consensus (*ijmāʿ*). This indicates that relying on the attainment of the *ḥikma* (wisdom) underlying the contract, divorce should not be binding." He adds: "As we arrived at consensus about its permissibility, it indicates the survival of its underlying wisdom, which is the survival of the contract of marriage with the force of all its objectives." Here his statement ends.

This supports what has preceded, but reflecting upon it leads to another principle that we state within this issue due to the need for it. This principle is:

The thirteenth issue: causes based on rationale (wisdom)

The principle is that in the case of a cause made lawful due to an underlying wisdom, its underlying wisdom may be known or believed to have occurred or be known or believed not to have occurred. If it is known or believed to occur then there is no confusion about its permissibility, but if it is not known or believed to occur then it is of two types: The first is the non-acceptance by the subject-matter of this underlying wisdom, or (second) it may be due to an external factor.

If it is the first, then its legal validity is removed *ab initio*. In this case the cause will have no effect at all with respect to this subject-matter, like deterrence for an insane person when he commits an offence, the contract for *khamr* (wine) and *khinzīr* (swine), divorce in the case of a stranger,[202] and emancipation with respect to another's slave.[203] The same is the case with acts of worship and the capacity to enter into transactions for the insane, as well as other similar cases.

The evidence for this consists of two things.

First: The cause is based upon the assumption that it is made obligatory due to some *ḥikma* (wisdom), and this is based on the principle of securing interests, as is explained at its proper occasion. If its validity is formulated despite the absence of wisdom as a whole, it is not proper that it be lawful, while we have assumed that it is lawful. This will be a contradiction.

Second: Had this been so, it would necessarily follow that the *ḥudūd* have been prescribed without the objective of deterrence, and the *ʿibādāt* without the purpose of devotion to Allah. Likewise all the remaining *aḥkām*. This is a nullity according to all those who uphold that the *aḥkām* have underlying causes.

If, on the other hand, the legal effect of the cause is prevented – and these are the consequences – due to an external factor, while acceptance of the wisdom by the subject-matter itself is found, then does this external factor affect the lawfulness of the cause, or does the cause remain lawful maintaining its original validity? This is probable, and the disagreement exists. The person who permits it may reason in several ways.

First: A universal principle is not demolished by individual decisions nor rare opposing cases. The description of this concept will be coming up at its proper occasion,[204] God willing.

Second: This is specific to this situation: that the wisdom is considered in the light of its subject-matter, being compatible with it, or it is considered to exist within it. If it is considered due to the acceptance by the subject-matter alone, then this is the claim. In the case of stipulations, the woman about whose divorce an oath has been taken is eligible to enter into a marriage contract with the deponent or someone else. This is not to be prevented except by some specific prohibiting evidence, which does not exist. If it is considered on the basis of its existence[205] within the subject-matter it becomes necessary that in the case of prohibition it be absent without qualification, and this due to an obstacle or without an obstacle. For example, if in the case of an affluent king there is no hardship during journey or he gives the impression of there being no hardship, then curtailing of prayer and not fasting are prevented in his case. Likewise the exchange of a *dirham* with one similar to it, despite the fact that there is no benefit in this contract. There are other issues too in which we find the *ḥukm* (rule) to be based upon initial legality when the wisdom does not exist.

It is not to be said[206] that journey is the basis for hardship in the absolute sense, and the exchange of a *dirham* for a *dirham* is the basis of conflicting objectives in the absolute sense. Likewise the remaining issues that convey the same meaning. Consequently, causation is permitted without qualification. This is distinguished from marriage of the woman with one deposing about a woman's divorce in an unqualified sense, for she is not the basis of the wisdom, and such meaning is not found in her at all.

The reason, we say,[207] is: the parallel for the absolute meaning in the case of journey is the absolute meaning in the case of marrying a strange woman. If you claim absolute permissibility without taking into account the existence of an underlying interest in the restricted issue, then you have to assert the validity of the marriage of the woman whose divorce was the object of the deposition. The reason is that it is a qualified case among all the unqualified cases of marriage with strange women, as distinguished from marriage in the prohibited category due to proximity of kin relationship, like a mother or daughter for example, for they are prohibited in the absolute sense. Thus, the subject-matter is ineligible in the absolute sense. This belongs to the first category. If, however, it is not like this (not ineligible),[208] it is necessary to uphold it in these issues, because there are some causes that are lawful even if the wisdom or the basis is not apparent. The subject-matter in itself is lawful, and the acceptance of the subject-matter in itself is the basis for the underlying wisdom, even though it is not seen to occur. This is acceptable rationally.

Third: The assumption that the wisdom exists in the corpus of the subject-matter is not established, because the wisdom is found only after the occurrence of the cause. Prior to the occurrence of the cause we are ignorant about its occurrence or non-occurrence. There are so many divorces that follow as a consequence of the occurrence of marriage, and so many marriages are annulled due to external factors or obstacles. Thus, if we do not come to know about the occurrence of the underlying wisdom, it is not proper to rely on the lawfulness of the cause as a sign of the underlying wisdom, because the wisdom does not become apparent, except after the occurrence of the cause. We have, however, assumed the occurrence of the cause after the occurrence of the wisdom, which is circular and impossible. Consequently, it is necessary to move towards the consideration of the basis of acceptance of the subject-matter as a whole,[209] and deem it sufficient.

The person who denies this may also argue on the basis of three interpretations.

First: The acceptance of the subject-matter may be considered lawful because it is acceptable to reason exclusively,[210] even though it is assumed that it is not acceptable due to external reasons. What is not acceptable[211] is not to be deemed lawful for causation, or because its underlying wisdom is found due to an external factor. A subject-matter whose underlying wisdom is not found in an external factor is not to be deemed lawful at all irrespective of its being rationally compatible with the wisdom. If it is the first, it is not valid, because the causes have been deemed lawful for the interest of the subjects, and these are lawful rationales. Thus, what does not consist of an interest or is not the basis of an externally existing interest becomes equivalent to what does not accept[212] *maṣlaḥa* (interest) either rationally or due to an external reason with respect to the objectives of the law. If they are equivalent, they are either both permitted or are both denied, but their permissibility leads to the permissibility of what has been agreed upon with respect to its denial. It is, therefore, necessary to deny them in the absolute sense, and that is our purpose.

Second: If we act upon the cause here with the knowledge that an interest (*maṣlaḥa*) cannot arise from this cause and is not to be found due to it, it would amount to the negation of the intention of the Lawgiver in declaring the validity of underlying rationales. The reason is that causation here has become futile, and what is futile is not declared legal, on the basis of the view that upholds interests (*maṣāliḥ*). Accordingly, there is no difference between this and first category. This is the meaning of the statements of al-Qarāfī.

Third: The permissibility of those issues out of these that have been declared permissible is due to the consideration[213] of the underlying wisdom. The absence of hardship for an affluent king is not realised; however, the probability of this being so is predominant, except that hardship differs from person to person and does not remain constant. The Lawgiver has, therefore, provided the underlying cause as the basis in place of the *ḥikma* for the application of the rules of the *sharīʿa*, just as He has determined the meeting of the private parts for the effectiveness of the known causation, even if the sperm does not flow, because this is the apparent basis. Likewise, He has deemed ejaculation to be the basis for the attainment of mental maturity leading to capacity for obligations, because it cannot be ascertained on its own. The cases that resemble these are many.

As for the exchange of a *dirham* for one like it, complete similarity cannot be conceived rationally. There are no two similar things in which a difference does not exist even if it does not appear in their ascertainment, just as there are no two dissimilar things in which a similarity cannot be found, though it is negated in all the remaining characteristics. If similarity is assumed in all respects, then it is rare and such similarity is not taken into account. In general *dirhams* and *dīnārs* do differ, but in terms of precision,[214] therefore, absolute permission has been granted in such cases. If this is the case, then there is no evidence in this case for our issue.

Sub-issue: stipulations (taʿlīq) – Within[215] the response for this issue a response with respect to stipulations has been realised.

As for the issue of marriage of a person attempting to fulfil an oath and what has been said about other issues with it,[216] it is a situation in which there is a possibility of disagreement, though the aspect of validity is stronger. Those who consider that the marriage was contracted by one who had the capacity to conclude it with respect to subject-matter that was eligible – as has been elaborated earlier – did not prohibit it. Those who focused on the fact that he had the intention to separate or that was the basis of the marriage, held it to be similar to temporary marriage and thus did not permit it. This is so despite the fact that Ibn al-Qāsim did not narrate a disagreement about marriage with an oath bearing a stipulation. He and others raised the issue that such a marriage does not lead to *iḥṣān* (married for purposes of the *ḥadd* penalty). This is sufficient to create a case of doubt. The issue is one that offers an opportunity for examination by the *mujtahids*.

When we examine Mālik's opinion, we find marriage with a stipulation bearing oath to be a marriage that is intended for its objectives, but in a manner that will lead to release from an oath. For the intention to seek release from the oath it is sufficient that he intended a valid marriage through which a woman becomes lawful for physical access and other purposes, except that it includes within it release from an oath. This does not adversely affect it. Likewise a marriage intended to fulfil a wish, because the fulfilment of a wish is part of the objectives intended in general, while the intention to separate thereafter is a factor that is external to it insofar as he possesses the right to pronounce divorce as determined by the *sharīʿa*. It may so happen that he will not proceed with the separation. This is the vital difference between this and the *mutʿa* form of marriage. The contract of *mutʿa* is clear with respect to the stipulation of a temporary union.

The same is the case with the contract of marriage for *taḥlīl*,[217] because in that he did not intend what is intended in a usual marriage. He intends thereby making the woman lawful for the first divorcer, who has to fall back on the contract of marriage with another husband, and not a contract of marriage in reality. It does not include any of the purposes for which it was made lawful. Further, as the contract is undertaken for another, it is not possible for him to perpetuate the relationship with her by way of custom or stipulation. Consequently, it is not possible for this contract to last. In addition to this, the text readily prohibits it and this is to be relied upon. Nevertheless, if there is no agreement or stipulation in the contract of the *muḥallil*,[218] and the husband intends this, then some jurists declare it to be valid in consideration of the fact that he intends, as a whole, physical access by this, and thereafter divorce. Accordingly, he has intended in general the main purpose out of the purposes of marriage. It does, however, include the understanding that she will return to the first husband if he agrees. This is so according to one view. According to another view, it does not include this understanding; rather it follows in due course. Even though this is one of the views that has not been preferred, it does contain aspects that are worthy of examination.

Among the things that indicate the legal validity of the oath when the intention is marriage, and that it is not objectionable, is that if he makes a vow or oath for seeking nearness to God, like prayer, pilgrimage, *ʿumra*, fasting or some similar act of worship, then he has a right to do so and it would be valid. This case is similar to these. Had this been effective in causing a defect in the core of the contract, it would be effective in causing a defect in the acts of worship too. The reason is that the condition for worship is devotion to God with the intention of seeking nearness to Him. Just like an act of worship, which is an object of a vow or oath even though the intention is release from the oath, and without this act he would not be released; so also here, rather this has a higher priority. Likewise the person who makes an oath to sell a commodity if he comes to own it. The contract of sale would be valid even if he had no other intention here except release from the oath. Add to this the oath that he will hunt or slaughter such and such a goat or whatever resembles it.

All this is to be referred to two principles.

First: In the *aḥkām* that have been laid down for securing interests, it is not stipulated that the interests exist in each individual subject-matter; what is considered is that such interests be the basis for them.

Second: In normal affairs what is considered for their validity is that they do not go against the intention of the Lawgiver, but the manifestation of compatibility is not stipulated.

Both principles shall be coming up God willing.

Sub-issue: unknown purposes – The third category of the first type[219] is that the individual, while bringing about the cause, intends objectives about which it is not known whether they are or are not intended by the Lawgiver. This is a matter that requires examination and it is a matter of confusion and ambiguity. The reason is that if we bring about a cause, it is possible that this cause is not meant for the assumed effects, just as it is possible that it is meant for such consequences or for other consequences. According to the first, bringing about the cause is unlawful, but according to the second it is lawful. If the act vacillates between being lawful and unlawful, taking steps to bring about the cause is unlawful.

It is not to be said: The cause is assumed to be lawful in general; therefore, why should we not bring it about?

The reason, we will say, is: it has been assumed to be lawful in relation to some specific known assumed thing, and not in the undetermined sense. Bringing about the cause is valid in the undetermined sense if it is known that all that it gives rise to is lawful in the unqualified and general sense. What we have assumed in our statement does not pertain to this; rather we came to know that on many occasions causes are made lawful for matters that they give rise to, while they are not lawful for some consequences that arise from them. For example, in the case of the marriage contract, for it is lawful for matters like reproduction and its associated things, but it is not lawful for purposes of *taḥlīl* nor for what resembles it. Thus, when we come to know that it has been made lawful for specific things, the things whose legality is not known remain suspended with respect to a ruling. Consequently, steps taken to bring it about are not lawful, unless the *ḥukm* is known.

It is also not to be said that the initial rule is that of permissibility.

The reason is that this rule is not applied in an undetermined sense. Thus, the initial rule for sexual activity is prohibition, except through measures that are deemed lawful. Likewise, the original rule with respect to the consumption of animals is prohibition until lawful slaughter is accomplished. The same is true for other lawful things, after the fulfilment of conditions, and the rule is not absolute. If this is established and it becomes obvious that we do not know about the consequences whether these are or are not what have been intended by the Lawgiver through the lawful act, it is necessary to suspend judgement till the rule is known (discovered). For determining this there is a principle through which the intention of the Lawgiver is established for the consequences of the causes whether they are permitted or not permitted. This principle is mentioned in the *Book of the Purposes of Law*. All help is sought from Allah.

The fourteenth issue: rules associated with invalid causes

Just as laws are based indirectly on lawful causes, so are laws based indirectly on unlawful causes. Thus, wounding fatally leads to retaliation (*qiṣāṣ*), while blood-money (*diya*) is based on the wealth of the offender or on that of the *ʿāqila*.[220] Compensation up to the value is paid if the victim of homicide is a slave. Then there is expiation too. Likewise, destruction and transgression lead to liability for compensation as well as punishment, while theft leads to compensation and amputation of the hand. There are other causes that resemble these unlawful causes in the obligation creating communication from the Lawgiver (*khiṭāb al-taklīf*), which are deemed consequences of these unlawful causes in the obligation creating communication, while the consequences are causes in the declaratory communication (*khiṭāb al-waḍʿī*).

Sometimes this prohibited cause gives rise to an interest (*maṣlaḥa*),[221] but from another aspect this is not the cause for the interest. For example, homicide leads to inheritance by the heirs, the execution of bequests, emancipation of the *mudabbar* slaves,[222] freedom of slave-mothers and even the children. Likewise, destruction of property through transgression leads to the ownership of the destroyed property by the aggressor, as a consequence of his compensating its value. Usurpation (*ghaṣb*) leads to ownership of the property by the usurper when the property alters in his possession, according to known details based upon compensation. There are other cases similar to this.

As regards the first category, a reasonable person does not intend the consequences that it leads to, for there is no interest in it, but it is in its nature that it be intended.

In the second category, where he forms an intention, the intention is viewed in two perspectives.

First: That the offender intends only that element because of which the cause is prohibited and nothing else, like satisfaction in the commission of homicide, and like utilisation of the usurped or stolen property in the absolute sense. This intention does not affect the operation of subsidiary rules that bear interests. The reason is that causes when they have been achieved lead to their consequences, except when we employ the blocking of lawful means to an unlawful end (*sadd al-dharāʾiʿ*), as in the denial of inheritance to the murderer even when he has not intended satisfaction, or when the homicide is manslaughter, according to those who uphold denial in this case as well. They said: If the usurped property changes in the possession of the usurper or he destroys it, then the rules of such change are excessive, then the owner does not have an option, that is, it is permitted to the usurper to utilise it on payment of compensation, along with disapproval on the part of some of the jurists and lack of disapproval on the part of others.

The reason for this is that the intention for this consequence does not negate the intention of the Lawgiver in the operation of these rules, because they came into operation on compensation of the value and change or a combination of the two. It is negated by the intention for bringing about the prohibited cause. The intention to bring about the cause so that the objective is attained in the absolute sense is different from the intention for this consequence, which arises from compensation or value or both. There is a distinction between the two. The distinction is that usurpation is followed by the obligation of *ḍamān* on the assumption of change in the property. Thus, the value becomes due on the basis of change arising from usurpation. When the value becomes due and is determined, the usurped property moves into the ownership of the usurper to preserve the property of the usurper so that the illegality be removed in the absolute sense. It becomes his property as a consequence of the obligation of paying of value by him, and not as a result of usurpation itself. The two intentions thus separate. The intention of the killer to attain satisfaction is different from his intention to inherit property, while the intention of the usurper to utilise the property is different from bearing the liability of paying value and removal of property from the ownership of the owner. When this is the case, the operation of the subsidiary rule, which the killer or usurper had not intended, runs its course. The negation of his intention[223] necessarily follows insofar as he had intended its negation. This amounts to punishing him, as it does in the case of the usurped property by its taking or compensation. This is obvious, except where the unlawful means are blocked.

Second: That he intends the secondary consequences of the cause, and these are consequences that support interests indirectly. The examples are of the heir who kills the ancestor so as to inherit from him, the usurper who wishes to own the property of the owner and alters it so that he may pay its value and own it, and so on. This causation is null and void, because the Lawgiver has not included these means in the obligation creating communication so that an interest can be secured through the declaratory communication. Thus, it is not lawful through such causation. It remains, however, to examine whether this specific causation negates the intention of the Lawgiver itself so that the intended consequences are not allowed. From this arises the principle of a "transaction contrary to its objectives". The rule is applied in it if this assumed intention is realised. This is the aim of the tradition[224] that prohibits inheritance for the murderer. It is also the aim of the rules of *fiqh* in the case of addition and deletion of assets to work out *zakāt*, the inheritance of the wife divorced during terminal illness, and the permanent denial of inheritance for one who marries during the waiting period, along with a host of other rules. It may also be considered that the Lawgiver has deemed it a cause for the resulting interest (*maṣlaḥa*) and the intention of the actor is not effective in this; therefore, it is assigned the same rule as the first. This is the area for *mujtahids* for in this is the widening of the inquiry. There is no way of being certain on either of these paths; therefore, we rein in our discourse.

The second type of declaratory rules: requisite conditions

The first issue: condition is a complementary attribute

The meaning of *sharṭ* (condition)[225] in this book is an attribute that completes its object insofar as it is required by such object or is required by its governing rule. Thus we say: The *ḥawl* (year) or the potential for growth completes the requirement of ownership to the rationale of being wealthy; *iḥṣān* (being married or once married) is a characteristic that completes the offence of *zinā* (unlawful sexual intercourse) insofar as it invokes the penalty of stoning (*rajm*); equality in protection completes the penalty of retaliation (*qiṣāṣ*) or the rationale of deterrence; ritual purification, facing the *qibla*, and covering of the private parts complete the act of prayer for the underlying meaning of establishing spiritual contact and devotion; and like them other acts too. It is the same for us whether the condition is an attribute of the cause, the underlying *ʿilla* (cause), the consequence of the act, associated circumstances, or other things beside these to which the requirement of the obligation creating communication is related. It is an attribute of the object of the condition. It follows necessarily from this that it distinguish it so that the object becomes identifiable despite ignorance about the conditions, even though the reverse is not true. This is just like the remaining attributes of actual or conceptual things that are described. There is no benefit in lengthening the discussion here for it merely establishes a term.

The second issue: terms related to conditions

The condition as a technical term has been mentioned for this book; therefore, the other terms of the book may also be mentioned, like *sabab* (cause), *ʿilla* (*ratio legis*), and *mānīʿ* (obstacle).

As for the *sabab* (cause), the meaning is what is determined[226] as such by the *sharīʿa* due to the underlying wisdom demanded by such rule. It is like the attainment of the *niṣāb* as a cause for the obligation of *zakāt*; the declining of the sun as the cause for the obligation of prayer; theft as a cause for the obligation of the amputation of the hand; contracts as causes for the utilisation or transfer of property; and the like.

The meaning of *ʿilla* (*ratio legis*) is the underlying wisdom and interests to which the commands are related or the permissible and vitiated acts to which prohibitions are related.[227] Thus, hardship is the *ʿilla* for the curtailment of prayer and breaking of the fast during a journey when the journey is the cause determined for permissibility. On the whole, the *ʿilla* is the interest (*maṣlaḥa*) or injury (*mafsada*) itself and not its cause, whether or not it is apparent, stable or unstable. It is on this basis that we say about the saying of the Prophet (pbuh), "The *qāḍī* is not to render judgement when he is angry." Here anger is the cause, the resulting confusion in the mind for assessing arguments is the *ʿilla*.[228] The word cause (*sabab*) here can be applied to the *ʿilla* itself due to the bond between them. There is no doubt in this terminology.

The term *māniʿ* (obstacle) is the required cause on the basis of an *ʿilla* that negates the prohibiting *ʿilla*.[229] The reason is that it is applied with respect to the cause requiring the rule arising from the *ʿilla*. Thus, when the obstacle appears it requires an *ʿilla* that negates the other *ʿilla*, thus removing the application of the rule and annulling the *ʿilla*. A condition for the existence of the obstacle is that it upset the *ʿilla* of the cause to which the obstacle is attributed, thus removing the *ḥukm*. If it is not so then its appearance alongside what is an obstacle leads to a clash between two causes or conflicting rules. This belongs to the topic of conflict and preference. Accordingly, if we say that debts are an obstacle for the imposition of *zakāt*, it means that it is a cause that requires the debtor to be deemed poor till his debts are paid off, and this has been ascertained through the *niṣāb*. When the claims of the creditors are related to the *niṣāb* the underlying rationale of the existence of the *niṣāb* is negated. This rationale is affluence, which is the *ʿilla* of the obligation of *zakāt*. Thus, the claim for *zakāt* is extinguished. We say the same in the case of fatherhood, which becomes an obstacle for the imposition of *qiṣāṣ* (retaliation). It contains within it an *ʿilla* that upsets the rationale for premeditated and malicious killing. There are many cases that are similar to these.

The third issue: three types of conditions

Conditions are of three kinds.

First: Those that are rational like life for knowledge and understanding for meeting obligations.

Second: Natural, like contact of fire with a flammable substance for igniting fire, the coming of a visible object before sight, the recording of a clear image within the eye, and other similar things.

Third: Legal (*sharʿiyya*): like ritual purification for prayer; passage of a year for imposition of *zakāt*; being married (or once married) for (the imposition of *rajm* – stoning) in unlawful sexual intercourse.

The purpose is to mention the third type here. If a condition from the first two types arises then it does so with respect to its relationship with the legal rule (*ḥukm sharʿī*) within the declaratory communication or the obligation creating communication. In such a case it becomes a legal condition in the light of such a relationship; thus, it enters the third category.

The fourth issue: conditions are like attributes

We need to elaborate that the relationship of the condition to the thing it affects is that of qualification of a thing qualified, and is not part of it. The reliance in this is on induction of the conditions in the *sharīʿa*. Do you not see that the passage of a year is complementary to the rationale of completing the *niṣāb*, which is affluence? If the subject comes merely to possess it, the rule is not established against him unless he is enabled to utilise it in the service of his interests. The Lawgiver has, therefore, deemed the passage of a year as the basis for such a facility through which his affluence becomes apparent. The breaking of a vow is the completion of its requirement. Thus, expiation is not prescribed unless the violation in the vow is against the name of God, although they have differed about its determination. According to all the jurists, determination of requirement of the violation is not realised except through the breaking of the vow. With this the requirement of the oath is completed. The departing of life completes the requirement of carrying out killing that leads to retaliation or payment of blood-money.[230] It also completes the establishment of the rights of the heirs in the wealth of the person in apprehension of death.[231] *Iḥṣān* (being married or once married) completes the requirement of the offence of unlawful sexual intercourse that leads to stoning (*rajm*). Likewise all the remaining conditions in the *sharīʿa* in relation to acts they affect.

This formulation may become ambiguous when it is stated that reason is a condition for *taklīf* (obligation) and faith is a condition for the validity of acts of worship and for the seeking of nearness to God. Thus when reason is not found, meeting obligations becomes impossible on the basis of rational and transmitted proofs, like placing duties on animals and inanimate matter. How then can we say that it amounts to completion? In fact, it is the basis for the validity of meeting obligations. Likewise it is not proper to say that faith completes acts of worship. Thus, the worship of an unbeliever has no reality that can be completed with faith. The same is true of a number of other issues.

This ambiguity is removed[232] with two things.

First: These belong to the category of rational, and not legal,[233] conditions, while we are discussing legal conditions.

Second: Reason in fact is a condition that completes the subject-matter of obligation, and that is a human being, not the obligation itself. It is known that with respect to a human being it is a complementary attribute. As for faith, we do not accept that it is a condition, because acts of worship are based upon it. Do you not see that the meaning of acts of worship is the directing of oneself towards the object of worship with devotion and reverence through the acts of the mind and the limbs? This is an offshoot of faith. How then can the foundation of a thing and the base on which it has been erected be a condition for it? This is not understandable. Those who have applied the term here have done so in the wider meaning of the expression.

Further, if it is conceded that it is a condition for faith, then it is a condition for the subject and not one for the obligation. It is a condition of validity according to some, while it is a condition of obligation according to others – in matters other than the obligation of faith – in accordance with what has been mentioned by the ʿUṣūlīs under the issue of whether the unbelievers are addressees for the detailed rules.

The fifth issue: the cause cannot be implemented without a condition

The principle well known in *ʿuṣūl al-fiqh* is that if the cause is dependent upon the condition for effectiveness, then it is not valid that the cause come into operation without it. In this, complete and partial operation are the same. Thus, the rule cannot be applied with completion while the cause is waiting for the condition, just as the rule is not valid with partial operation on the assumption of its dependence on the condition. This is obvious from their discourse. If the cause associated with the condition could occur without its condition, it would not be a condition for it, and it has been assumed that it is. This is the logical conclusion.

In addition to this, had this been deemed valid, it would be dependent upon its condition and at the same time not dependent upon it for occurrence. This is impossible. Further, the condition, insofar as it is a condition, requires that the contingent cause should not come into operation except on its existence. If its occurrence was deemed possible without it, the contingent cause would have occurred and not occurred at the same time. This is impossible. The matter is obvious without lengthening the discussion.

Another principle, however, has been established from the discussion of a group of jurists. This has been attributed to Mālik's school. When the cause of the rule has appeared, the attainment of the consequences depends upon the condition. Is it valid that they come into being without the condition? There are two views about this based upon the requirement of the cause and the delaying of the condition. Those who gave priority to the cause that is bound to give rise to its consequences, gave preference to its requirement without making it dependent upon its condition. Those who gave prominence to the condition, deeming the cause to be dependent upon its condition, considered it to be an obstacle for the occurrence of the consequences. They did not accept the existence of the cause on its own. It could only occur when the condition was present and made the cause rise up according to its requirement.

Perhaps some of them applied the disagreement about the principle in an unqualified way. They gave examples of this, and among these are (the following.)

- The attainment of the *niṣāb* (minimum amount of wealth) is a cause for the obligation of *zakāt*, while the passage of a year over this wealth is a condition. It is possible to give precedence to it (by advance payment) prior to the passage of a year, with views differing about it.
- A vow is the cause for expiation, while its violation is a condition. It is possible to give precedence to the violation according to one view.
- The fatal piercing of the body is the cause in the case of retaliation (*qiṣāṣ*) and blood-money, while departure of life is a condition for this. It is, however, possible to forgive prior to the departure of life and after the wounding. The jurists did not narrate a disagreement about this.

In Mālik's school a case is discussed where a husband grants the right of divorce with respect to a woman he is marrying to his existing wife, so that she may if she likes divorce the woman. He then seeks permission from his existing wife to marry that woman, and she grants such permission. After he had married the woman, the existing wife decided to divorce her. Mālik said: She does not have the right to do so. This is based on the reasoning that she relinquished such right after the cause, which is granting the right of ownership, came into being, even though it occurred prior to the attainment of the condition, which is marriage.

When the heirs grant permission to a person who is ill and expects to die to make a bequest in excess of one-third of his property it is valid, even though their ownership will be established only after his death. Illness is the cause for their passing on ownership, while death is a condition. Their permission is executed according to Mālik, even though the condition has not occurred as yet, with Abū Ḥanīfa and al-Shāfiʿī disagreeing with Mālik. There are jurists who have considered the execution of their permission to be valid in sickness or in health. The cause according to these jurists is being near of kin. It becomes necessary for them to say that death is a condition.

In Mālik's school there is an issue that one who has intercourse and derives pleasure but does not ejaculate, but does ejaculate when he takes a bath, then about his bathing again there are two views. There is no obligation to do so based upon the reasoning that the cause of the movement of fluid from its location is bathing, and he has already had a bath. Accordingly, he is not to bathe again. This is the argument of Saḥnūn and Ibn al-Mawwāz. The cause is separation (of the fluid) and ejaculation is the condition, which is not taken into account. There are many issues that revolve around this principle.

This principle obviously clashes with the first. The first principle requires that the occurrence of the contingent cause is not valid in the absolute sense without its condition. The second requires, according to some jurists, that it can validly occur. Perhaps, it is valid by agreement, as in the case of pardon prior to departure of life. It is not possible, however, that both principles be valid at the same time in an unrestricted sense. The validity of the first principle, however, is well known. It is, therefore, essential to examine their reasoning about the second principle.

First: The clash itself between the two principles is sufficient to indicate the absence of validity with the knowledge that the first principle is valid.

Second: We do not accept that these issues have been settled by ignoring the condition. Accordingly, we say:

Those who permitted advance payment of *zakāt*, without restriction, prior to the passage of the year – from among jurists outside our school – did so on the reasoning that it is not a condition for obligation; rather it is a condition for incidence. Thus, the entire year becomes the time of payment, according to these jurists,[234] for the payment of *zakāt* as a *wājib muwassa*ᶜ (obligation with a time span), but it becomes final at the end of the period like all obligations of this nature. As for payment prior to the passage of the year, it is easy, in our school, based upon the reasoning that what is close to a thing is deemed to take the same rule. Thus, the condition of the obligation is attained.

Likewise the reasoning with respect to violation of oath as a condition. Those who permitted the payment of expiation prior to it, did so on the basis that it is a condition of incidence without an a choice, but is not a condition of its obligation.

As for the issue of departure of life, it is a condition for the obligation of retaliation and payment of blood-money, but is not a condition for the validity of pardon. This is agreed upon, because forgiveness after death is not possible.[235] Accordingly, it is necessary that it occur prior to it if possible. It cannot be valid as a condition for in that case it would be a condition of validity when validity requires the right of the wounded, which is not linked to wealth. Consequently, unrestricted forgiveness[236] is allowed just like forgiveness in all other cases of wounding. This applies to his reputation as well when subjected to *qadhf* and to other similar cases. The evidence is that the *ratio* for the rule of forgiveness is not what they claimed, to the effect that it is not permitted by agreement to the wounded nor the heirs to claim *qiṣāṣ* or take the entire blood-money for life prior to departure of life. Had it been as they said, it would have led to two views on this issue.[237]

In the case of granting the ownership of the right of divorcing the woman, the reasoning is that when she relinquished her own right stipulated for the husband prior to marriage, nothing related to it remained with her afterwards. The reason is that what was granted to her to own was relinquished by her[238] after the cause had come into being. Consequently, his subsequent marriage could not be linked effectively to what was relinquished. This is *fiqh* that is obvious.

The issue of permission of the heirs is evident. Death is the cause for the validity of ownership, not in linking their right to property. Illness is the cause of linking the right of the heirs to the wealth of the ancestor, but not the cause for owning it. Thus, these are two causes with each one of them requiring a rule that is not required by the other. Insofar as illness is the cause for linking the right, even though it is not ownership, their permission has an effect on the subject-matter. The reason is that when their right becomes linked to the wealth of the ancestor there arises for them in it a semblance of ownership. Thus, if they relinquish their right in it, they cannot subsequently have a claim that as they became like strangers during the time when the transaction of the sick person was given effect, when death occurs they do not have such a right, like insisting on the operation of the bequest up to a third. The view of the jurist who denies execution is valid along with the view that death is a condition. The basis is that they granted permission prior to the transfer of ownership and prior to the attainment of the condition. Consequently, it is not executed like all the other conditions along with their contingent objects.

As for the issue of ejaculation, it is valid based[239] upon the fact that it is not a condition for this bath or that it does not take a rule, because it is ejaculation without deriving pleasure.

On the whole, reasoning in these matters cannot be pinned down without the consideration of the condition.

The sixth issue: conditions stipulated with two types of purposes

Conditions acknowledged with respect to their objects are of two kinds in the *sharᶜ* (law).

First: Those that are linked to the obligation creating communication. The attainment of these may either be demanded like ritual purification, prayer, adornment for it, purification of clothes, and the like, or they may be proscribed, like the marriage to facilitate a remarriage as it is a condition for the woman's return to the first husband, the combining of two differing assets or separating those to be combined due to fear of imposition of *zakāt*, which is a condition for reduction in *zakāt*, and the like. This kind elaborates the intention of the Lawgiver. In the first it is the commission of the act, while in the second it is its omission. Likewise the condition in which there is a choice, when there is agreement.[240] The intention of the Lawgiver in this is to leave it to the choice of the subject: if he likes he may bring it about so as to attain the object of the condition, and if he likes he may not, in which case it will not be attained.

Second: Those that pertain to the declaratory communication. These are like the passage of the year for *zakāt*, *iḥṣān* for unlawful sexual intercourse, and place of safe-custody for the amputation of the hand. In these kinds of conditions, the Lawgiver does not have an intention for their attainment insofar as they are conditions, nor is there an intention for not bringing them about. Thus, the survival of the minimum scale (*niṣāb*) for a year until *zakāt* becomes obligatory in it is not required with respect to its occurrence so that it may be said that the owner must hold on to it till *zakāt* is imposed. It is also not required that he eliminate it like saying that he should spend it out of fear of the obligation of *zakāt*. Likewise *iḥṣān*: it is not to be said that the act be committed so that *rajm* can be imposed when unlawful sexual intercourse is committed, nor that he should avoid it so that *rajm* is not imposed when unlawful sexual intercourse is committed.

Moreover, if it was required, it would not belong to the obligation creating communication, and we have assumed that it is. This is the logical conclusion and the rule for it is obvious.

When the intention of the subject is directed to the commission of the condition or its omission, insofar as it is an act that is within his power, it is necessary to examine it. This is done as follows.

The seventh issue: condition may be given up

He may commit it or omit it insofar as it is within his power to do so, whether it is required or proscribed, and in this case it will lie within the obligation creating communication. If it is so, there is no confusion about it. The rules required by the causes will be based upon it when the cause arises, and they will be removed in the absence of the causes. This is like the minimum scale of wealth (*niṣāb*) when he spends it due to his need prior to the passage of the year, or when he retains it due to the need for retaining it. He may also mix up his flock of cattle with another person's flock due to the need for such mixing or separate his flock due to the injury arising from partnership or for another reason. He may demand the state of *iḥṣān* through marriage for its prescribed purposes or relinquish it for any reason that a human being may have. There are other cases like it.

If its commission or omission,[241] insofar as it is a condition, is intentional aimed to annul the rule required by the cause so that it has no legal effect, then this act is not valid and is an effort that is a nullity. This is indicated by both rational and transmitted evidences.

Among these is a tradition, a saying of the Messenger of Allah (pbuh), "Differing types of wealth are not to be combined nor similar types to be separated for fear of the imposition of *ṣadaqa* (*zakāt*)."[242]

He (pbuh) said: "The seller and the buyer have an option until they part (in the session of the contract), unless it is a bargain in which an option is stipulated. The seller is not to move away in haste for fear that the buyer will ask him to take back the goods."[243]

He (pbuh) also said: "One who releases a horse among two horses when he is not sure that it will win the race, then this is not gambling, but if he releases a horse among two horses knowing well that it will out-race the rest, then this is gambling."[244]

In the tradition of Barīra, when her owners stipulated the condition of *walāʾ* (clientage) for themselves, he (pbuh) said, "If someone stipulates a condition that is not in the Book of Allah, then such condition is void even if there are a hundred conditions."[245]

The Prophet (pbuh) prohibited "sale and a condition, sale and a loan, two conditions in one sale",[246] as well as other traditions of conditions that proscribe some conditions.

Among these traditions is, "One who deprives another of his wealth through his oath ...",[247] as well as the tradition, "The oath depends upon the intention of the person making it."[248] It is in this context that the following verse was revealed: "As for those who sell the faith they owe to Allah and their own plighted word for a small price, they shall have no portion in the Hereafter: Nor will Allah (deign to) speak to them or look at them on the Day of Judgement, nor will He cleanse them (of sin): They shall have a grievous penalty."[249] In the Qurʾān we also have the verse: "It is not lawful for you (men), to take back any of your gifts (from your wives), except when both parties fear that they would be unable to keep to the limits ordained by Allah."[250] The verse on perjury also belongs to this category.

Allah, the Exalted, has said: "O ye who believe! Eat not up your property among yourselves in vanities: But let there be among you traffic and trade by mutual good-will."[251] There are traditions on this point as well.

He said: "So if a husband divorces his wife (irrevocably), he cannot, after that, remarry her until after she has married another husband and he has divorced her."[252] In this connection there are also traditions about the *muḥallil* and the *muḥallal* that they are cursed, as well as about the borrowed billy goat. There is then the tradition about *taṣriyya* (blocking the udder) in which a goat is purchased under the impression that it gives a lot of milk. To these may be added all the traditions in which the proscription pertains to fraud, deception, misrepresentation and *najsh* (competing offers). There is also the tradition of Rifāʿa al-Quraẓī when he divorced his wife and ʿAbd al-Raḥmān ibn al-Zubayr married her.

The evidences are more than can be recorded here.

Further, this type of act renders the *sharʿī* rule, which is based on a cause that requires the acquisition of benefits and the repelling of injury, futile, devoid of wisdom, and there is no benefit in it. This runs contrary to what is established under the principle of interests, that is, it is to be acknowledged in the framing of rules.

In addition to this, it runs contrary to the intention of the Lawgiver from the perspective that the cause when it is established and comes into existence legally requires its consequences, yet it is suspended till the attainment of the condition,[253] which amounts to completion of the cause. Consequently, this actor, committing or omitting the act, intending to evade the rule emanating from the cause, is acting contrary to the intention of the Lawgiver in the determination of the cause. It has been elaborated that opposition to the intention of the Lawgiver is a nullity. Accordingly, this act is null and void.

Suppose it is said: The issue assumes a cause, whose requirement of the rule is dependent upon a condition. If the condition is absent due to the formulation of an intention for its absence, then it is as if he does not intend this, and the intention will have no effect. It has been made evident that if the condition is non-existent the cause is not activated so as to have a requirement, as for the passage of a year in the case of *zakāt*, because of the presumption that it is a condition without which *zakāt* does not become obligatory. It is known about the intention of the Lawgiver that the cause is to amount to a cause with requirements upon the existence of the condition, and not with its absence. If the cause is not activated, the issue is reduced to one where a person spends the wealth for some form of utilisation prior to the passage of a year; therefore, *zakāt* does not become obligatory for him. The reason is that the cause did not require obligation due to its dependence upon that condition, which has been acknowledged by the law. Thus, how can it be said about it that it is contradictory to the intention of the Lawgiver? It is to be said that it is compatible. Likewise all the remaining issues.

The response is: This meaning applies to it if he does not intend the evasion of the rule arising from the cause. If he does intend it, then it is a meaning that is not acknowledged. The reason is that the law has provided evidence for its rejection in certain terms. This became evident from the evidences recorded above when the issue was judged through them. Thus, the combining of differing assets or the separation of similar assets was proscribed when the intention was to annul the rule arising from the cause,[254] by associating it with a condition that negates it and diminishes the right of the poor. Thus, forty goats are liable to one goat when reckoned independently, but to one-half goat when they are mixed up with another forty, for example. If he combines them with the intention of paying half, then this is what is proscribed. Likewise if they were a hundred mixed up with another hundred plus one, and he separates them with the intention of paying one. This too is proscribed. What is this other than his bringing in a condition or removing a condition with which the requirement of the first cause is evaded? The same applies to the person who spends his *niṣāb* with the intention of evading the obligation of payment. This falls under the statement: "It is not lawful for him to separate (during the session) fearing return of goods by the buyer." He was forbidden from formulating an intention of evading the stipulated option that was established for the buyer through the contract as a cause. He was also forbidden to bring about the condition of the validating horse with the intention of acquiring it when his intention was not to indicate swiftness. The issues pertaining to conditions are like these, because these are conditions through which the intention is to evade the rules of causes that have occurred. Thus, contract of *kitāba*[255] requires that it is a contract for all its legal effects, and among these is *walāʾ* (clientage). If someone stipulates for the buyers that *walāʾ* is retained by him, then he intends a condition that has the effect of removing the legal effects of the cause. The consideration of all that has preceded you will find to be similar. Consequently, the bringing about of conditions or their evasion with such an intention is proscribed. If these are proscribed,[256] then they run contrary to the intention of the Lawgiver and are thus null and void.

Sub-issue: does this act imply nullity – Does this act require nullity in the absolute sense or does it not?

The response is: There is some detail in it, which does, and we say: The condition brought about either conveys the meaning of actual removal or it conveys removal in meaning alone, or it does neither.

If this is the case, then the rule that is demanded by the cause is maintained prior to the commission of this act. The act in such a case is a nullity having no benefit at all, nor does it have a rule. It is like his gifting away wealth prior to the passage of the year to one who collaborates with him to return it to him after the passage of the year through a gift or another mode. It may also be like the person who combines two types of differing animal wealth into one till such time that the official arrives and thereafter he separates them, or it is like the person who separates two similar types of wealth in the same way, but later returns them to the status they were in earlier. Another example is of the person who marries so that the condition is fulfilled and then returns the woman to the one who divorced her thrice. Likewise other similar cases. The reason here is that this condition that operates on it has no meaning nor benefit that can be intended from the perspective of the law.

If this is not the case, then the issue becomes probable, and its examination demands three interpretations.

First: That it be said: The mere occurrence of the cause is sufficient, for that is the moving cause for the rule, while the condition is an extraneous factor that completes it. If it is not interpreted like this then the condition becomes a part of the underlying cause (*ʿilla*), when the presumption is otherwise. Further, the underlying intention has become unlawful, and the act has come to oppose the intention of the Lawgiver. It then acquires the rule of an act that is not to be committed; thus, it comes to be classified with the first type with respect to the rule. This act does not lead to legal effects. An example of this is the person who spends wealth prior to the passage of a year for some of his needs, or gifts it through a conclusive gift that will not revert to him, or combines differing assets, or separates similar ones, and all this with the intention of evading *zakāt* with the status not changing thereafter to what it was prior to the passage of the year, or whatever is similar. We have come to know that when the Lawgiver determined this cause for the rule, He intends the establishing of the rule through it. If this person then removes the cause when it has been activated as a cause, he opposes the intention of the Lawgiver. This is null and void, and the condition, when it is removed or applied, in the manner that the Lawgiver acknowledges it in general, has been subjected to an invalid intention. It is not valid that he activate it as a lawful condition for it is non-existent in the absolute sense and is linked to the first type.

Second: That it be said: The mere occurrence of the cause is not sufficient, and even though it is a moving cause, it has been deemed in the law as restricted by the existence of the condition. The cause, therefore, is not a moving cause in certain terms as being one that the Lawgiver has meant to lead to its consequences.

If someone, then, intends to remove the cause of the rule, for example through an act lifting the condition, his intention does not oppose the intention of the Lawgiver in all respects. In fact, he has formed an intention that the intention of the Lawgiver should not emerge in this case either by way of occurrence or non-occurrence, which is the existence of the condition or its non-existence. Accordingly, as this intention reverts to the negation of the intention of the Lawgiver in general and not in specific terms, it does not amount to an obstacle in assigning the rules of conditions to it.

Further, as this act is effective, attained and has come into being, the preventing intention within it is not effective in its application as a lawful condition or as a lawful cause. It is like the alteration of the usurped property acting as a condition or a cause in preventing the owner from taking and in transferring ownership to the usurper, and his act with the intention of committing evil does not amount to a cause in the lifting of such a rule.

On the basis of this principle, the validity of what al-Lakhmī says is structured in the case of a person who gives part of his wealth in charity so that *zakāt* does not become obligatory for him, or one who travels during Ramaḍān with the intention of not fasting, or delays his prayer while resident from its flexible time so that he can offer two *rakʿas* when he will travel, or a woman delays her prayer when its time commences in the hope that she will menstruate thus extinguishing the obligation from her. He says: All this is disapproved (*makrūh*), but it does not lead to an obligation for this person to fast, to pray four *rakʿas*, nor does it lead to the obligation of delayed performance for the woman who has started menstruating. This applies to the case of a person making an oath to the effect that he will definitely pay so and so his due by the end of the month. It also applies to one making a vow to divorce (his wife) thrice, but fearing violation enters into a contract of *khulʿ* with his wife so that he will not violate his vow, and when the period is over he has recourse to her. This arrangement implies that he will not violate his vow when the time comes as she is not his wife at that time, because *khulʿ* has lawfully occurred even though he intended a wrongful act through it.

Third: That a distinction be made between the rights of God and the rights of individuals. Consequently, the condition stipulated within the rights of God will stand nullified, even though an independent legal rule is assigned to it, as in the case of the person separating wealth that has to be combined, and in the case of the marriage of the *muḥallil* according to one opinion that it is executed and past and does not make the woman lawful for the first husband. The reason is that *zakāt* is a right of God and so also the prohibition of the marriage of the *muḥallil* is a right of God due to the predominance of the right of God in the case of marriage over the rights of humans. The requirement of the condition takes effect in the case of the rights of individuals, as in the case of travelling for curtailment, or not fasting and so on.

All this applies as long as a specific evidence does not indicate the contrary meaning. If the specific evidence does convey the opposite meaning, the rule changes to conform to it, and it does not amount to a negation of the principle mentioned. The reason is that it indicates the association of this particular act with the right of God or with the right of the individual. This leaves the case where the two rights are mixed. This is a case of examination and *ijtihād*, during which one right is given predominance in accordance with what appears appropriate to the *mujtahid*. Allah knows best.

The eighth issue: three types of rules for which conditions are stipulated

Conditions with respect to their objects[257] are of three types.

First: That the condition completes the underlying wisdom of the object and strengthens it so that it does not amount to its negation in any way. This is like the stipulation of fasting during *iʿtikāf* (seclusion in a mosque) according to those who stipulate the condition, like the stipulation of proportionality, fair treatment and compassion in the contract of marriage, the stipulation of collateral or a surety or cash or credit in the case of the price of the sold commodity, the stipulation of allegiance for the emancipated slave, the stipulation of wealth of the subject, fruit existing on trees, or whatever is similar to this. Likewise the stipulation of the passage of a year in the case of *zakāt*, *iḥṣān* in the case of unlawful sexual intercourse, the absence of procrastination in the marriage of female slaves, a place of safe-custody in the case of amputation of the hand. This category has no confusion about it with respect to its validity in the law, because it completes the rationale of each cause that requires a rule. As *iʿtikāf* is seclusion in a mosque for worship due to a suitable reason, the effect of fasting on it is obvious. When the lack of proportionality is the basis for discord and scorn on the part of one of the partners and their antagonism, while proportionality is closer to the strength of the union of the parties and better living, its stipulation is compatible with the objects of marriage. Likewise fair treatment. All the remaining conditions out of those mentioned are construed in this manner; therefore, their affirmation in law is evident.

Second: That it is not compatible with the purposes of the objects of the conditions nor does it complement the underlying wisdom, rather it is the opposite of the first. It is like stipulating in prayer that the worshipper may talk during it if he wishes, the stipulation in *iʿtikāf* that he come out of the mosque whenever he likes, according to Mālik's opinion,[258] the stipulation in marriage that the husband not spend on the wife or that he not have intercourse with her when he is neither impotent nor lacking the organ, the stipulation in sale that the seller not utilise the sold commodity or when he does use it to do so in a limited way, the stipulation by the artisan that the orderer should not hold him liable for loss to the property, or to deem him truthful in a court claim for destruction, as well as similar cases. In this category too there is no confusion that the stipulations are null and void, because they run counter to the purposes of the cause, therefore, they should not be combined with it. Thus, the statement about prayer negates the purpose for which it is prescribed like devotion to God, turning to Him and seeking forgiveness from Him. Likewise the stipulation in the case of *iʿtikāf* about going out of the mosque negates the essence of *iʿtikāf* with respect to seclusion. Stipulating for the groom that he should not spend on her negates the seeking of compassion required by the contract. If it is stipulated that he should not cohabit with her then this negates the primary purpose of marriage, which is reproduction, and inflicts an injury on the wife. It does not amount to the required fair treatment, which is the basis of perpetual relations and companionship. The same is to be said of the remaining stipulations mentioned. The question arises that if these are void, do they affect the object of the stipulation? This is a matter of examination that emerges from the issue that is prior to this.

Third: That neither negation nor compatibility are evident in the condition. This is a matter of inquiry. Is it to be linked with the first from the perspective of the lack of negation or with the second from the perspective of lack of apparent compatibility? The principle applies to the illustrations of this distinction between acts of worship and transactions. In the case of worship, it is not sufficient that there be an absence of negation; compatibility must be obvious. The reason is that the principle in this is ritual obedience rather than the consideration of meanings. The rule is that he should not overstep in this without permission, because reason has no role in innovating in the case of acts of worship. The same applies to the conditions related to this. In the case of transactions it is sufficient if there is an absence of negation, because the principle in this is reliance on rational meanings rather than ritual obedience. The rule for transactions is permission unless an evidence indicates the contrary. Allah knows best.

The third type of declaratory rules: the obstacles (defences)

In this there are several issues.

The first issue: obstacles are of two types

Obstacles are of two types: first are those in which it is not possible to combine them with the demand (for the commission of an act); and second are those in which it is possible. This second type is again of two kinds: first those that remove the original demand; and second are those in which it is not removed, but lessens its strength. This too is of two kinds: first in which removal means that the subject, who has the capacity, is granted a choice about it;[259] and the other in which the meaning is that there is no blame for the one opposing the demand. This leads to four types.

First: This is like the loss of reason due to sleep, insanity, or other reason. This is an obstacle in the way of the demand altogether. The reason is that the condition for the relationship of the communication to conduct is its understanding, because it is an obligation that gives rise to an obligation. It is not possible to place one who lacks reason under an obligation, just as it is not possible in the case of animals and inanimate matter. The relationship of the link created by the demand requires the acquisition of an interest (*maṣlaḥa*) or the repelling of an injury. This pertains to another, like giving exercise to animals and their training. The discussion of this issue is elaborated in *ʿuṣūl al-fiqh*.[260]

Second: This is like menstruation and post-natal bleeding. They remove the original demand even if it is possible to carry out the act with it. This type of demand, however, is removed to the extent of not being demanded with it, like prayer, entering into a mosque, touching the *muṣḥaf* (Qurʾān), and the like. As for those that are demanded because of it,[261] after the removal of the obstacle, their discourse among the specialists in *ʿuṣūl* is well known and we have no need to mention this here. The evidence that they are not required during the existence of the obstacle is that had it been so then two contradictory things would stand combined. The reason is that the menstruating woman is prevented from praying, and those with postnatal bleeding likewise. Had she been commanded to perform it too, she would be commanded during her state of prohibition with respect to a single act, which is not possible. Further, if she had been commanded to do it and forbidden from doing it, then by law she would be obliged to do it and not to do it, which is not possible. In addition to this, there is no benefit in an act whose commission is not valid with respect to her while the obstacle exists nor after its removal. The reason is that she is not commanded to perform it as delayed performance by agreement of the jurists.

Third: This is like slavery and being a female with respect to the *jumuʿa* prayer, the two *īds* as well as *jihād*.[262] The reason is that to such persons an obstacle is attached despite the definitive nature of these acts of worship, which for them are applied according to the category of complementary values and adornment, because they are not the object of the divine communication in this respect, except as a secondary rule. If they are able to carry them out then the same rule will apply to them as in the case of those to whom the communication is addressed, and these are male freemen. Here the meaning is that of a choice with respect to them along with the stipulation of the ability to carry them out. As for the lack of capacity for performance, the prior rule will apply.

Fourth: This pertains to the acquisition of exemptions (*rukhaṣ*), which are obstacles with respect to definitive requirements, in the meaning that there is no harm in relinquishing the original rule when there is an inclination towards an exemption, like the curtailment of prayer for the traveller, not fasting, and the giving up of the Friday congregational prayer, as well as other similar cases.

The second issue: obstacles are not intended by the Lawgiver

Obstacles are not intended by the Lawgiver in the meaning that He does not intend that the subject attain them or remove them. This means they are of two types.

The first type falls under the obligation creating communication whether it is commanded, prohibited or permitted. There is no ambiguity in this from this perspective. It is like the raising of a loan that becomes an obstacle in the way of activation of the cause of obligation affecting the payment of *zakāt*, even if the *niṣāb* (minimum amount of wealth) is found. Payment depends upon the absence of the obstacle. Likewise unbelief is an obstacle for the validity of performance of prayer and payment of *zakāt* or in the creation of their obligation.[263] It is also an obstacle in reckoning the number of repudiations in divorce. There are other legal issues too in which unbelief acts as an obstacle. Islam too is an obstacle in the way of the damaging of the protection given to life, property and reputation, except when (legally) justified. Inquiring into these matters and their parallels from the perspective of the obligation creating communication lies outside the objectives of this issue.

The second type is intended, and it falls under the declaratory communication insofar as it is intended. The Lawgiver does not intend its attainment insofar as it is an obstacle, nor does He intend its absence. Thus, the debtor is not addressed in the meaning of removal of the debt, when he possesses the *niṣāb*,[264] so that *zakāt* can be imposed on him, just as the owner of the *niṣāb* is not addressed to raise a loan so that the obligation can be waived. The reason is that it is a declaratory communication and not an obligation creating communication. The intention of the Lawgiver is that if the loan is created the requirement of the cause is removed.

The evidence for this is that the formulation of the cause with complete conditions bears the intention of the declarant requiring the creation of the consequences. If this is not the case, then it has not been declared to be a case, and we have presumed that it is a cause. This is conclusive. If the intention of the declarant is established for the attainment of the consequences, then the assumption regarding the obstacle is also intended by Him in the meaning of the removal of the consequences arising from the cause, and it has been established that He does intend the consequences. This too is conclusive, (for intending the cause itself would make) the two intentions contradictory. He also does not intend the removal of the cause, for had He intended that, it would not be possible to establish an obstacle in the law. The elaboration of this is that had He intended its removal insofar as it is an obstacle, its attainment would not be acknowledged by the law. If it is not acknowledged it cannot be an obstacle for the operation of the cause, but it has been assumed that it is. This is the essence of the contradiction.

When the intention of the subject is directed towards the occurrence of the obstacle or towards its removal, there are details about it. These are (as follows.)

The third issue: obstacles may be given up

The subject may either bring it about or relinquish it insofar as it falls under the obligation creating communication, whether commanded, prohibited, or permitted.

If it is the first, then the matter is evident, like a person possessing the *niṣāb*, but raising a loan for his needs. The rules will be applied according to the attainment of the obstacle.

If it is the second, that is, he brings it about, for example, insofar as it is an obstacle, with the intention of evading the rule required by the cause so that the consequences do not flow from it as required. This act is not valid. The evidences for this on the basis of transmission are several. Among these are the words of the Glorious and Lofty, "Verily We have tried them as We tried the People of the Garden, when they resolved to gather the fruits of the (garden) in the morning."[265] This includes within it the report of their punishment for intending legal fictions for the suspension of the right of the needy, through the seeking of an obstacle. This was their arrival in the morning at which the needy usually do not come.[266] The punishment, however, was for the act that was prohibited. There are then the words of the Exalted, "Do not treat Allah's Signs as a jest."[267] It was revealed due to the causing of injury to wives through recourse so that they could not ever seek another husband,[268] and that their waiting period should not end except after a prolonged period. The recourse was made with this intention, for it was an obstacle in the way of making them lawful for other husbands.

A tradition says, "May Allah cause the Jews to perish. Fat was prohibited for them, but they melted and mixed it up thereby selling it." In some traditions the words are: "They consumed its price."[269] The Prophet (pbuh) is reported to have said, "People from my *umma* will drink liquor (*khamr*) and call it by another name."[270] One report says, "There will be people in my *umma* who will declare lawful unlawful intercourse, silk, wine and musical instruments."[271] Another report[272] says, "A time will come over the people when they will declare five things lawful through five things: they will legalise *khamr* by assigning different names to it; bribery calling it a gift; murder by calling it awe; unlawful sex by calling it marriage; and *ribā* by calling it sale."[273] It is as if the person legalising considered the name to be an obstacle and transferred the object to another name so that the obstacle be removed making the thing lawful.

Allah, the Exalted, has said, "After payment of legacies and debts."[274] He exempted injury from this. If a person acknowledges a debt in favour of an heir, or makes a bequest for more than a third of the estate intending thereby to deprive an heir or to reduce part of his entitlement by creating this obstacle in the way of his complete right, then it amounts to an injury. Causing of injury is prohibited by agreement of the jurists.

Allah, the Exalted, has said, "And break not your oaths after ye have confirmed them."[275] Ahmad ibn Ḥanbal said: I am amazed at what they say about legal fictions and oaths. They annul oaths through legal fictions when Allah has said, "And break not your oaths after ye have confirmed them."[276]

A tradition says, "Surplus water is not to be denied so as to prevent the growth of vegetation."[277] In another tradition it is said, "When you hear of it, that is, infectious disease, in some land, do not go there, and when it afflicts a land when you are there, do not go out, to avoid it."[278]

The evidences from the Book and the *Sunna* on this issue are many along with the statements of the noble ancestors.

The meaning of evidences that have preceded along with the questions and responses in the case of conditions applies to obstacles as well. It is from there that its rules are understood and whether or not an act is a nullity. From this perspective the issue is divided into two types. In the removed rule, the obstacle is acquired or is not acquired. If it is like this, then the rule is clear, as in the case of the owner of the *niṣāb*, who raises a loan so that *zakāt* is waived for him intending thereby that when the year is over he will return the loan without utilising it. If it is not like this, rather the obstacle has occurred in a lawful manner, like the person repudiating for fear of violating his vow. This is subject to examination in the light of what has preceded in the case of conditions. There is no benefit in repeating it here.

The fourth type of declaratory rules: validity and nullity

There are several issues in this.[279]

The first issue: the meaning of validity (two meanings)

This issue is about the meaning of *ṣiḥḥa* (validity). The word *ṣiḥḥa* is used in two senses.

First: The term means the legal effects of the act in this world, like our saying in an act of worship: it is valid in the meaning that there will be reward for it, the obligation has been met, and the obligation for delayed performance is extinguished, that is, if the act has delayed performance built into it. This is the meaning along with other statements that are indicative of its full meaning. We say in the case of transactions: They are valid, in the meaning of there being a legal interest (*maṣlaḥa*) being secured for purposes of ownership, permissibility for cohabitation, permissibility for utilisation, or other statements that convey these meanings.

Second: The term means the legal effects of the act for purposes of the Hereafter. It is like the act leading to spiritual reward. Thus, we say: This act is valid, in the meaning that reward in the Hereafter is to be hoped for.

In the case of worship it is obvious, while in the case of transactions it depends on how far obedience to the commands of God is intended, and whether he intended through it what is required by the commands and prohibitions. The same applies to an act subject to choice as well, that is, whether he acted in accordance with the choice granted to him by the Lawgiver, not intending merely his share of utilisation being oblivious of its basis in the *sharīʿa*. This too is deemed a valid act in this meaning, even though it is an unknown meaning of the term and is not employed by the scholars of *fiqh*. It has been employed, however, by scholars of ethics like al-Ghazālī and others, and it is this meaning that the earlier ancestors sought to preserve. Ponder over this meaning in the light of what al-Ghazālī has said in his *Kitāb al-Niyya wa-al-Ikhlāṣ*.

The second issue: the meaning of nullity (two meanings)

This issue is about the meaning of *buṭlān* (nullity).

First: The meaning is the absence of legal effects in this world, like our saying about an act of worship that it does not carry a reward, or absolve one of liability, nor extinguish the liability for delayed performance. Thus we say that it is a nullity in this meaning; however, there is some examination required here. The act of worship is a nullity as it has opposed the intention of the Lawgiver in it, as has been elaborated at its proper location. The opposition though may sometimes refer back to the act of worship itself and the word *buṭlān* is applied to it in the absolute sense, as in the case of prayer without *niyya* (intention), or one with a defective *rakʿa* or prostration. Likewise other things of the same type that undermine the fundamental element. On occasions the nullity refers to an external factor that is independent of the real act of worship even though it qualified it, like prayer on usurped land,[280] for example, thus leading to the occurrence of *ijtihād*: (a) that acknowledges separation, in which case the prayer is valid for it has taken place in conformity with the directives of the Lawgiver, while opposition with respect to an external attribute does not vitiate it; (b) that acknowledges the external attribute, in which case it is rather it is assigned the legal rule of nullity[281] from the perspective that prayer proper must be devoid of such an attribute. Prayer in a usurped house is not assigned such a rule, like all prayer in similar circumstances.

In the case of practice (transactions) we say the same, that is, they are a nullity in the meaning of the absence of their benefits according to law, like the transfer of ownership, permissibility for cohabitation, and utilising the object desired. As human practices in general are linked to interests of this world, the examination takes place from two perspectives: First, from the perspective that these are acts that are permissible or are legally required; and second, that they pertain to human interests.

As for the first, some jurists acknowledged them in the absolute sense, neglecting the perspective of interests deeming opposition to His command as opposition in the absolute sense, like treating pure acts of worship equally as if they were inclining towards ritual obedience. An elaboration will be coming up in the *Book of Maqāṣid* about all things that are understood in the meaning of ritual obedience. If this is the case then confronting the command of the Lawgiver with opposition implies going beyond this act with respect to the requirement of the communication. Going beyond the acts contained in the communication of the Lawgiver is given the ruling of illegality, and an illegal thing is a nullity. This is of this nature, and is like the acts of worship that are invalid outside the ambit of the communication of the Lawgiver.

As for the second, a group of jurists acknowledged it, not with the neglect of the first type, but by deeming the matter to be steeped in human interests, in the meaning that the underlying reason due to which the act is nullified is to be examined. If it is attained or is attained in legal form so that there is no likelihood of removing the external factor,[282] the act is nullified in essence. This is the basis due to which the law has proscribed it. The proscription requires that there be no interest of the subject in it. Even though an interest appears on preliminary examination, Allah knows that there is no interest in undertaking the act even if the actor considers it to be so. If it is not attained, nor is it attained in legal form, but if it is possible to remedy the situation, the act is not assigned the rule of nullity. This is what Mālik says about the sale of the *mudabbar* slave,[283] that is, he is to be returned, unless the buyer emancipates him in which case he is not to be returned. The sale, therefore, is forbidden in lieu of the right of the slave with respect to emancipation, or in lieu of the right of Allah in emancipation whose cause was originated by the master through the declaration of *tadbīr*. The sale usually causes a loss of freedom to him after the death of the master; thus, if the buyer sets him free the objective of the Lawgiver with respect to emancipation is attained; therefore, he is not returned. Likewise in a vitiated *mukātaba* contract he is returned as long as the *mukātab*[284] has not attained emancipation. Similarly, the sale of the usurped property by the usurper is suspended subject to ratification by the owner or it is returned to him. The reason is that the prohibition is associated with him; therefore, if he ratifies it the sale becomes valid. Resembling these is sale with a loan, which is forbidden. If the person stipulating the condition relinquishes the condition of loan, the contract they have concluded becomes valid, and is executed according to some views. In some cases the remedy is found in relinquishing the offending condition, as was done in the tradition of Barīra. In accordance with its requirement, the Ḥanafīs have upheld the rectification of irregular contracts, like *nikāḥ al-shighār*,[285] the exchange of two *dirhams* for one, and the like. They do so in other types of contracts that are void in some respects, so that the void aspect is dropped and the contract is executed. The meaning of such an interpretation is that the prohibition by the Lawgiver was due to an offending factor, and when this factor is removed the prohibition is lifted converting the contract to one that is compatible with the intention of the Lawgiver. This is done either through the rule of prior validation where it is possible to refer the validity to the original contract or through novation when we say that the rectification has occurred now and not before this. This interpretation is based on the fact that the interests of the individual overcome the rule of ritual obedience.

Second: The second application of the term: That the term *buṭlān* means the absence of the legal effects of the act in the Hereafter, which is spiritual reward. This is conceived in the case of worship as well as practices.

Worship is nullified according to the first consideration, and no reward follows it, because it does not conform to its command. It may be valid in the absolute sense according to the first application of the term, but no reward follows it either.

In the first case it is like the worshipper who worships to be known among people (for his piety). Such an act of worship is not reckoned for waiving the liability and no reward follows it. The second is like the person giving in charity, but follows it up with claims of generosity and harassment. Allah, the Exalted, has said: "O ye who believe! Cancel not your charity by reminders of your generosity or by injury – like those who spend their wealth to be seen of men."[286] He also said, "If thou were to join (gods with Allah), truly fruitless will be thy work (in life), and thou wilt surely be among the losers."[287] A tradition says, "Convey it to Zayd ibn Arqam that his *jihād* alongside the Messenger of Allah (pbuh) stands annulled if he does not repent."[288] This amounts to nullity according to the interpretation of those who consider nullity to be a reality here.

The acts pertaining to practice are also nullified in the meaning of the absence of consequential spiritual reward, and it is the same for us whether or not these are nullified in the first sense. The first are like contracts that have been lawfully revoked. The second are like acts that the one undertaking them has done on the basis of his whims and desires without turning to the communication of the Lawgiver with respect to them. These are like eating, drinking, sleep and the like. The concluded contracts are based on whim, but they have conformed to the command or permission of the law as a matter of coincidence not through a conscious intention. These are acts that are maintained by the law due to their conformity with a command or permission insofar as a worldly interest has been secured. It is only to this extent that they are taken into account for having conformed to the intention of the Lawgiver. The aspect of the intention to obey continues to remain lost. Thus, its consequential effects with respect to the Hereafter are lost as well. The reason is that all acts are dependent upon intentions. The conclusion is that these acts whose basis was merely whim, even though they have (accidentally) conformed with the intention of the Lawgiver, continue to be maintained for the life of the actor. As soon as he departs from this world, they are destroyed with the destruction occurring in the world and are nullified: "What is with you must vanish; what is with Allah will endure";[289] "To any that desire the tilth of the Hereafter, We give increase in his tilth, and to any that desire the tilth of this world, We grant somewhat thereof, but he has no share or lot in the Hereafter";[290] and "Ye received your good things in the life of the world, and ye took your pleasure out of them."[291]

There are other evidences besides these whether explicit or apparent in meaning, and in them we find an indication of the concept. It is from these texts that earlier writers have taken the idea that to strengthen the acts pertaining to practice an intention be associated with them so that the actors may find their acts rewarded in the Hereafter. Look up this idea in *al-Iḥyāʾ* and other works.

The third issue: elaborating the second meaning of nullity

What has been mentioned with respect to the application of the term *buṭlān* in the second meaning above implies a division, but one pertaining to acts of human practices. When a normal act of practice is devoid of the intention of ritual obedience, it may be undertaken with some intention or without an intention. The act with an intention may either have an intention based upon mere whim and desire without concern for compliance with the intention of the Lawgiver or opposition to it, or it may be with concern for compliance, in which case it is undertaken, or for opposition, in which case it is relinquished, and again this may either be voluntary or under duress. This yields four types.

First: That he undertake the act without intention, like one who is not in his senses or is asleep. It has preceded that the demanding communication is not linked to it nor the communication granting a choice. Thus, there is neither reward nor punishment in it, because recompense in the Hereafter is consequent upon acts that fall under the obligation creating communication. Accordingly, an act not related to the obligation creating communication does not lead to fruition.

Second: That he undertake the act to attain merely his own objective. In this too there is no spiritual reward, as with the first, even when the obligation creating communication is linked to it, or it becomes obligatory, like the payment of debt, the return of deposits and trusts, spending on children, and the like. The relinquishment of prohibited things also falls under this category at the secondary level, because acts are dependent upon intentions. The tradition[292] says, "Whoever moves over (migrates) towards Allah and His Messenger has moved over to Allah and has His Messenger, but he who moves over to this world for gain or to a woman he wishes to marry has moved over to what has moved over to."[293] The meaning of the tradition is agreed upon (by the two Shaykhs) and definitive in the *sharīʿa*.

This category, and the one preceding it, are null and void according to the second meaning of *buṭlān*.

Third: That he undertakes the act with awareness of compatibility, but under compulsion, like his intention to seek pleasure from a certain woman, and when this is not possible through unlawful sexual intercourse due to her refusal or prevention by her family, he enters into the contract of marriage so that he can attain what he intended. This too is a nullity within the second meaning of *buṭlān*, because he has not relied upon the rule of compatibility (of intentions) except under compulsion, insofar as he attained his goal in a manner not permitted by the law, and even though it is not a nullity according to the first meaning of *buṭlān*. Similar to this is the payment of *zakāt*[294] acquired under coercion. It is valid according to the first meaning, as it absolves him from payment and removes the liability, but it is a nullity according to this second meaning. Likewise, the giving up of prohibited things under fear of sanctions in this world or fear of being shamed before people, as well as other reasons. It is for this reason that the *ḥudūd* penalties are merely forms of expiation, and the Lawgiver has not communicated that there will be some consequential spiritual reward for them in any case. The principle for this is that acts are dependent upon intentions.

Fourth: That he undertake the act with the awareness of compatibility (of intentions) by his own volition, like the person committing a permissible act after knowledge that it is a permissible act, so that he would not have committed it had it not been permissible. This category requires an inquiry for identification of the permissible act. As for an act commanded, he commits it with the intention of compliance, or a prohibited act that he omits, which he also does with the same intention. This act is sound according to both meanings. Just as he would commit a required act, or one forbidden, with the intention of opposition, as that would be a nullity according to both meanings. This leaves inquiry in the commission or omission of the permissible (*mubāḥ*) act alone insofar as the Lawgiver has communicated a choice here, and he chooses one or the other, act or omission, merely for his gain. Three interpretations are implied in such inquiry.

First: That it be sound according to the first meaning, and a nullity according to the second. This is the application of the preceding principle about the concept of *mubāḥ* when it is examined in itself (*bil-juzʾī*), and not on the basis of what it implies as a whole.

Second: That it is sound according to both meanings taken together, on the basis of his inquiry for acquiring personal gain to the extent that it is permitted to him, and excluding what is not permitted. It is according to this that the tradition has communicated the reward for having intercourse with the wife.[295] They said: Does he first satisfy his lust and is then rewarded? He said: What do you think if he were to leave her to commit what is forbidden? This is elaborated in the *Book of Maqāṣid*, within this book.

Third: That it is sound according to both meanings taken together in the case of the *mubāḥ* whose commission is required at the general level, but it is valid according to the first meaning and a nullity according to the second in the case of the *mubāḥ* whose omission is required at the general level. This rule is applied according to what has preceded in the first category out of the two categories of the *aḥkām*. It is, however, linked to what is before it when a factor external to the essence of the permissible act is considered, and with the first when it is considered on its own.

Sub-issue: elaborating the second meaning of validity – As for what is mentioned about the application of the term *ṣiḥḥa* according to the second meaning, it may either refer to an act of worship or to a practice. If it applies to an act of worship then there is no division in this as a whole. If it applies to a practice, then it is either accompanied by an intention for ritual obedience as well as seeking an interest or it is not so. In the first the intention of personal interest is either predominant or is dominated. This gives rise to three types.

First: One that is not accompanied by personal interest. There is no ambiguity about its validity.

Second: This is the same, because the predominant is assigned a rule, and what is beside this is something external.

Third: In which there is a probability of both. (1) It is valid when considered in the second meaning as well, acting upon the side that is dominated, considering that the side of personal interest is not objectionable for practices but it is for acts of worship. (2) It is valid when considered on the basis of the first meaning and not the second, acting upon the rule of predominance. The elaboration of this division and its evidence is mentioned in the *Book of Maqāṣid* in this book. Praise be to Allah.

The fifth type of declaratory rules: *ʿazīma* and *rukhṣa* (initial rules and exemptions)

The first issue: ʿazīma *is a rule imposed initially*

ʿAzīma is what is laid down as a general rule of law initially.[296] The meaning of the word "general" here is that it is not confined to some of the subjects, insofar as they are subjects, to the exclusion of others, nor is it confined to particular circumstances to the exclusion of others. It is like prayer (*ṣalāt*) for example, for it is a rule that is laid down in the absolute sense and applies generally to each person and to every circumstance. Likewise the rules of *ṣawm*, *zakāt*, *ḥajj*, *jihād*, as well as all the remaining general symbols of Islam. Under this meaning are classified those rules that have been laid down for a cause serving the principle of securing interests, like those prescribed acts through which one attains the securing of interests of the two worlds, including sale, hire, and all the commutative contracts. Likewise the rules for offences, retaliation, liability, and as a whole all the general rules of the *sharīʿa*.

The meaning of "rule of law initially" is that the intention of the Lawgiver in laying it down is the declaration of the obligation creating *aḥkām* for the servants in the first instance; thus, no legal rule (*ḥukm sharʿī*) preceded it, and if it did, it stands abrogated by this later rule, which becomes the initial rule, so as to pave the way for general universal interests. The general rules that affect causes are not excluded from this meaning. The causes were unknown prior to this, and when they are found they required the rules. This is so in the words of the Exalted, "O ye of Faith! Say not (to the Messenger) *rāʿnā*, but say *unthurnā* (i.e. say not words of ambiguous import, but words of respect); and hearken (to him)";[297] "Revile not ye those whom they call upon besides Allah, lest they out of spite revile Allah in their ignorance";[298] "It is no crime in you if ye seek of the bounty of your Lord (during pilgrimage)";[299] "Allah knoweth what ye used to do secretly among yourselves";[300] "But if any one hastens to leave in two days, there is no blame on him, and if any one stays on, there is no blame on him";[301] as well as others like these. This amounts to paving the way for the *aḥkām* that are laid down gradually in accordance with the need for them. The term *ʿazīma* includes all these meanings, because they have been laid down as rules in the first instance. Likewise the exceptions to the general rules as well as universal particular rules are laid down in the first instance. This is like the words of the Exalted, "It is not lawful for you (men) to take back any of your gifts (from your wives), except when both parties fear that they would be unable to keep the limits ordained by Allah. If ye (judges) do indeed fear that they would be unable to keep the limits ordained by Allah …";[302] "Nor should ye treat them with harshness, that ye may take away part of the dower ye have given them – except where they have been guilty of open lewdness";[303] and "Then fight and slay the Pagans";[304] however, he (pbuh) prohibited the slaying of women and children.

These and other similar rules are *ʿazāʾim* (initial rules), because they refer to general initial rules.

As for *rukhṣa* (exemption), it is a rule laid down for a substantial excuse, as an exception to the general rule requiring prevention (of the application of the general rule) along with confinement to the extent of the need for the purpose. "Laid down for a substantial excuse" is a characteristic that has been mentioned by the *ʿulamāʾ* of *ʿuṣūl*.[305]

The meaning of "substantial excuse" is that the excuse is sometimes based upon mere need without hardship being present. This is not called *rukhṣa*, like the legalising of *qirāḍ* (the *muḍāraba* partnership) for example. This is due to an essential excuse, which is the inability of the owner of capital to undertake a journey in the land, and it is permitted even when there is no excuse and no inability. Likewise *musāqāh*, *qarḍ*, and *salam* for all these are not termed *rukhaṣ* even though they are exceptions to prohibiting principles.[306] Such contracts fall under the universal needs, and *ḥājiyāt* are not called by the name of *rukhṣa* by the *ʿulamāʾ*. The excuse sometimes refers to a complementary value, and this too is not called *rukhṣa*. Thus, a person who is not able to offer prayers in the standing posture, or can do so with some hardship, is then permitted to adopt the sitting posture, even though it disturbs a basic element (*rukn*) of prayer. If this person claiming the exemption is the *imām*, then this case is mentioned in a tradition: "The *imām* has been appointed so that he is followed." Thereafter it is said, "If he prays in the sitting posture, all of you should also pray while seated."[307] Their prayer then in the sitting posture would occur due to an excuse, except that the excuse in their case brings no hardship; rather it is required for compatibility with the *imām* and the absence of opposition to his acts. Thus, such a case is not called *rukhṣa* even though it has been turned into an exception due to an excuse.

The fact that this legal rule based on an excuse is an exemption from a general principle elaborates for you that *rukhaṣ* are not laid down as initial rules. It is for this reason that they are not treated as general rules in the legal sense, even if they have been presented as such. Thus, from the perspective of presentation, when we permit the traveller to shorten his prayer and not fast, this is after the rules of prayer and fasting have been established. This is so when the verses of fasting have been revealed all at once. Here the exception comes only after the establishment of the rule as a whole for which an exception has been created. Likewise the consumption of carrion for one under duress in the words of the Exalted, "But if one is forced by necessity, without wilful disobedience, nor transgressing due limits – then is he guiltless."[308]

The meaning of "confined to the extent of the need" is a characteristic of the *rukhaṣ* that must be stipulated. It is the distinctive element between what has been prescribed as part of universal needs and what has been provided by way of a *rukhṣa*. The legality of the *rukhaṣ* is at the level of the particular; it is confined to the point of need. The worshipper offering prayers is under an obligation to revert to the original rule of offering the full prayer and fasting when his journey is over. The person who is ill is not to pray in the sitting posture when he is able to offer it in the standing posture. If the worshipper is able to touch water, he is not to perform *tayammum*. The same is to be said about the rest of the *rukhaṣ* as distinguished from *qarḍ*, *qirāḍ*, *musāqāh* and other matters like them that resemble exemptions. These are not *rukhaṣ* in the true meaning of the term, because they remain legal even if the excuse is over.[309] Thus, it is permitted to a person to take a loan even if he is not in need of borrowing, and to enter into a contract to irrigate his grove even if he is able to do so himself or to hire someone to do it. He is also permitted to give his wealth to another by way of *qirāḍ* (*muḍāraba*) even if he is able to trade on his own or to hire someone to do it. Likewise transactions resembling these.

The conclusion then is that *ʿazīma* refers to a general initial principle, while *rukhṣa* refers to a particular rule that is an exemption from this general rule.

Sub-issue: rukhṣa is an exemption from a prohibition – The term *rukhṣa* is sometimes applied to mean what has been exempted from a general principle requiring absolute prohibition, without taking into account substantial hardship. Under this meaning fall *qarḍ*, *musāqāh*, returning a *ṣāʿ* of wheat in the issue of *muṣarrāt*, the *ʿariyya* contract in the case of sale of dates by estimate, the imposition of *diya* (blood-money) on the *ʿāqila*, as well as other cases. This is indicated by the saying, "He (pbuh) proscribed the sale of what you do not have",[310] and "he made a *rukhṣa* (exemption) in the case of *salam*".[311] All this is related to the principle of *ḥājiyāt*, which participates in the first meaning of *rukhṣa*. Thus, the rule is applied to it for purposes of the term, just as its rule is applied to it as an exemption from the prohibiting principle. Under this is also classified the preceding issue of the followers of the handicapped *imam* being seated, and prayer in fear prescribed for the *imām* is the same. Yet, these two issues arise from the principle of complementary values (*taḥsīnāt*) and not from the principle of needs (*ḥājiyāt*). Consequently, the word *rukhṣa* is applied to them even though they are not classified along with it under a single principle. It is in the same way that the term *rukhṣa* is applied even though the issue arises from the principle of necessities (*ḍarūriyāt*), like the worshipper who is not able to stand up. The exemption in his case belongs to the necessary and not needs. It becomes a rule of needs if he is able to stand up with hardship or as a result of it. All this is evident.

Sub-issue: rukhṣa in the sense of hardship not imposed – The word *rukhṣa* is sometimes applied to burdensome obligations and difficult acts that have not been imposed on this *umma*, which is indicated by the words of the Exalted, "Our Lord! Lay not on us a burden like that which Thou didst lay on those before us",[312] and His words, "He releases them from their heavy burdens and from the yokes that are upon them."[313]

The word *rukhṣa* in its literal meaning implies gentleness and it is this meaning that is attributed to what has been mentioned in some traditions,[314] "When the Prophet (pbuh) did something he adopted gentleness (*rukhṣa*) in it."[315] Its meaning may be referred to another tradition, "Allah wishes that His exemptions be acted upon just as his initial impositions are acted upon."[316] The elaboration will be coming up soon, God willing. Thus, whatever magnanimity and gentleness has been exhibited for this *umma* is *rukhṣa* with reference to what was borne by earlier nations in terms of strict rules.

Sub-issue: rukhṣa in the sense of absolute leniency – The term *rukhṣa* is also applied to mean the leniency for individuals in the absolute meaning with respect to the prescribed rules, and which pertains to the acquisition of their interests and the fulfilment of their wants. The first initial rule (*ʿazīma*) indicated by the words of the Exalted is: "I have only created Jinns and men, that they may serve Me",[317] as well as His words, "Enjoin prayer on thy people, and be constant therein. We ask thee not to provide sustenance."[318] The texts like these indicate that the servants are in the broader and narrower sense owned by Allah, and it is their duty to turn to Him striving in His worship. The reason is that they are His servants and have no right over Him, nor an argument against Him. Thus, when he grants a gift to them, they take it. The same is the case with a *rukhṣa* granted to them for it is turning to something other than the One worshipped and concern with what is required by servility.

ʿAzīma according to this interpretation is obedience to commands and the avoidance of things forbidden in the absolute and general sense – irrespective of the commands giving rise to obligations or recommendations and the prohibitions giving rise to disapproval or prohibition – and the relinquishment of those permissible acts that divert one away from such obedience. The reason is that the command of One who commands is meant to be obeyed in general, while permission for the acquisition of a personal gain on the part of the servant is a *rukhṣa*. From this perspective everything granted by way of leniency and concession for the subject falls under the meaning of *rukhṣa*. The *ʿazāʾim* are the right of Allah over the subjects, while the *rukhaṣ* are the share of the subjects through the generosity of the Creator. The permissible things share common attributes with the exemptions in this arrangement insofar as both create a facility for the servant, remove hardships and grant a gain to the individual. In this meaning, the permissible things on occasions come to clash with those recommended, with the apportionment in the Hereafter coming to dominate the share in this world; that is, the right of the Creator comes to be preferred over his personal right. This removes completely the rule of permissibility from authorised domain, which means the servant comes to adopt the rule containing the right of Allah. His right then becomes secondary and subservient to the right of Allah where the right of Allah is primary and is the main objective. For the servant has the duty to expend his effort, while the Sustainer rules as He pleases.

This interpretation is acknowledged by the saintly from among the spiritual. It is also acknowledged by those who have attained spiritual advancement, and it is on this basis that they train the students. Notice that among their rules is the adoption of the *ʿazāʾim* from religious knowledge and the relinquishment of the *rukhaṣ* as a whole,[319] until they reach the stage where they begin to reckon all, or most of, the *ḥājiyāt* as *rukhaṣ*, and this includes all those things that secure the interest of the individual. This will be obvious to you in this last application of the term, and also coming up will be the view of those who uphold the affirmation of this category, Allah, the Exalted, willing.

Sub-issue: the general and the specific in these four meanings – When these four meanings are established, it becomes evident that some of them are specific to some individuals, and there are those that apply generally to all persons. As for the meaning with a general application for all the people, this is the first application of the term, which gave rise to further refinements. As for the second application, there is no discussion about it here, because there is no further branch coming out of it; it became obvious through it that it was a technical term of the law. Likewise the third application. As for the fourth application, because it is specific to a specialised group, it is not employed except for that meaning; however, the meanings coming out of the first application elaborate the applications of this term; therefore, by the power of God, there is no need for the specialised meanings.

The second issue: rukhṣa *implies* ibāḥa

The rule for *rukhṣa* is permissibility in the absolute sense insofar as it is a *rukhṣa*.[320] The evidence for this is adduced in different ways.

First: The occurrence of texts about it. These are like the words of the Exalted: "But if one is forced by necessity, without wilful disobedience, nor transgressing due limits – then is he guiltless";[321] and His words, "But if any is forced by hunger, with no inclination to transgression, Allah is indeed Oft-forgiving, Most Merciful";[322] and His words, "When ye travel through the earth, there is no blame on you if ye shorten your prayers";[323] and His words, "Anyone who, after accepting faith in Allah, utters Unbelief: except under compulsion, his heart remaining firm in faith."[324]

There are other texts like these that indicate the removal of hardship alone, because of His words, "Then is he guiltless."[325] and His words, "Allah is indeed Oft-forgiving, Most Merciful."[326] In all these texts there is nothing that requires the adoption of a *rukhṣa*; rather what is mentioned is that which negates the expected consequence of relinquishing an initial general rule (*ʿazīma*), and that is sin and accountability. This negation has been mentioned in many of the permissible acts within the context of the principle, as in the words of the Exalted: "There is no blame on you if ye divorce women before consummation or the fixation of their dower";[327] "It is no crime in you if ye seek of the bounty of your Lord (during pilgrimage)";[328] "There is no blame on you if ye make an indirect offer of betrothal";[329] as well as other texts that expressly mention the removal of blame and permit the commission of a *rukhṣa* in specific terms.

Allah the Exalted has said, "But if any one is ill, or on a journey, the prescribed period (should be made up) by days later."[330] A tradition says, "We used to travel with the Messenger of Allah (pbuh) when among us were those curtailing prayers and those offering full prayers, but they did not object to one another."[331] This is supported by a number of evidences.

Second: The basis of *rukhṣa* is leniency for the subject and the removal of hardship for him, so that he moves from the burden of the *ʿazīma* towards facility and has a choice between adopting the *ʿazīma* or adopting the *rukhṣa*. The basis of this is permissibility after enumerating a number of blessings, as in the words of the Exalted, "It is He Who hath created for you all things that are on earth";[332] "Say: Who hath forbidden the beautiful (gifts) of Allah, which He hath produced for His servants, and the things, clean and pure, (which He hath provided) for sustenance?"[333] and "A provision for you and your cattle."[334]

The basis of *rukhṣa* is facility, and the root of the word (*rā*, *khāʾ* and *ṣād*) stands for facility and gentleness. Likewise its various derivatives that imply inexpensive things and inclination. All the words derived from the root convey this meaning.

Third: If the exemptions were commanded by way of recommendation or obligation, they would have amounted to initial general rules and not exemptions, when the reality is opposite of this. The obligatory (*wājib*) is final and binding, there is no choice in it. The *mandūb* (recommended) category is similar from the perspective of the unqualified command. It is, therefore, not proper to say that rules of recommendation have been laid down by way of ease and facility insofar as they are commanded. If this is so, it is established that reconciling the command and the exemption is a reconciliation between two things that negate each other. This elaborates that *rukhṣa* is not commanded as long as it is a *rukhṣa*.

If it is claimed as such, it is objected to from two perspectives.

First: The evidences that have preceded do not point to the objective of the issue, because it does not follow from the absence of blame and sin, with respect to the person committing an act, that such an act is permissible, as it may be obligatory or recommended. With respect to the first, Allah the Exalted has said, "Behold! Safa and Marwa are among the Symbols of Allah. So if those who visit the House in the Season or at other times, should compass them round, it is no sin in them."[335] These are the two locations between which circuiting is obligatory. Allah the Exalted has said, "And if any one stays on, there is no blame on him, if his aim is to do right."[336] Delay is demanded by way of a recommendation, and the one who does so is said to have undertaken a better act as compared to one who hastens.

There are other instances (in the texts) where a similar meaning is found. It is not to be said that such revelation was due to causes where sin was presumed, as has been established in the tradition from ʿĀʾisha (God be pleased with her).[337] The reason is that we will say that even occasions of permissibility have been revealed on the basis of causes where sin is presumed, as in the words of the Exalted, "It is no sin for you if ye seek of the bounty of your Lord (during pilgrimage)";[338] His words, "Nor in yourselves, that ye should eat in your own houses, or those of your fathers, or your mothers, or your brothers, or your sisters, or your father's brothers or your father's sisters, or your mother's brothers, or your mother's sisters, or in houses of which the keys are in your possession, or in the house of a sincere friend of yours: There is no blame on you, whether ye eat in company or separately";[339] and His words, "It is no fault in the blind nor in one born lame, nor in one afflicted with illness";[340] as well as "There is no blame on you if ye make an indirect offer of betrothal."[341]

In all these and those texts that are similar, sin and harm have been presumed. If the two occasions are equivalent, there is no specific indication in the texts conveying removal of sin, hardship, and fault about the rule of permissibility. It, therefore, becomes necessary to take the rule from somewhere else and from an external evidence.

Second: The jurists have written about exemptions that have been commanded. Thus, a person under duress and fearing death is under an obligation to consume carrion or other prohibited nourishing things. They also said that combining prayers at ʿArafa and Muzdalifa is demanded and is a *sunna* (recommended act). About the curtailment of prayer by a traveller, it is said that it is an obligation, emphatic *sunna* or recommended. A tradition says, "Allah wishes that the exemptions granted by Him be acted upon."[342] Our Lord, the Exalted, has said, "Allah intends every facility for you; He does not want to put you to difficulties",[343] and there are a number of other texts in the same meaning. Thus, it is not proper to say, in absolute terms and without going into details, that the rule for *rukhaṣ* is permissibility.

The response to the first is: It is not to be doubted that removal of hardship and sin in literal forms, when there are no supporting evidences, imply permission to consume and use. If we find them separated and the word refers to the meaning of permission with respect to commission of the act as a whole, and if there is a specific cause for the removal of blame and hardship, then we may construe the text in its literal meaning and not in relation to the specific cause. It may be presumed in what is legally permissible that it contains an element of sin based upon a preceding established practice or an opinion held, just as some of them believed that there was sin in circuiting the house when clothed as well as the belief in the case of some edible things, until the following verse was revealed: "Say: Who hath forbidden the beautiful (gifts) of Allah, which He hath produced for His servants, and the things, clean and pure, (which He hath provided) for sustenance?"[344] Likewise eating in the houses of fathers, mothers and all those mentioned in the verse as well as proposing marriage during the waiting period along with other such matters. The same is the case with the verse, "There is no sin on them if they circuit between them",[345] which conveys the meaning of permission. As for its obligation, it is derived from the His words, "Behold! Safa and Marwa are among the Symbols of Allah",[346] or from another evidence. The signal here about mere permission implies obligation from the perspective of mere commission without going into the issue of permissibility of relinquishment or of its absence.

We may construe the text in terms of its particular cause, and His words in a verse like "among the Symbols of Allah"[347] become the surrounding circumstance that transfer the meaning of the word required by the original application. As for those that have a cause but are in themselves permissible, they are similar to those that do not have cause in the meaning of permission. There is no ambiguity in this. It is according to this arrangement that the view about the other verse, and all those bearing a similar meaning, is to be expressed.

The response about the second has preceded in the context of reconciling the command and the *rukhṣa*, that is, it is reconciliation between two negatives. In such case, it is necessary that the obligation or recommendation be referred to the original initial general rule (*ʿazīma*) and not to the *rukhṣa* itself. This is illustrated by the case of the person under duress who does not find anything lawful with which to save himself. He has been granted the permission to consume carrion with the intention of removal of hardship and the elimination of the pain of hunger. If he apprehends death when it is possible for him to survive by consuming carrion, he is commanded to keep himself alive on the basis of the words of the Exalted, "Nor kill (or destroy) yourselves."[348] In the same way, he is commanded to keep alive others if that is possible. In fact, it is like the person who has reached the mouth of a ditch and fears falling into it. There can be no doubt that removing himself from there is required and letting himself fall into it is prohibited. A state such as this is not called *rukhṣa*, because it is based upon a universal initial principle. Likewise the case of the person who fears death if he relinquishes the consumption of carrion; he is commanded to keep himself alive. It is, therefore, not to be called *rukhṣa* from this perspective, even though it has been called *rukhṣa* from the perspective of eliminating pressure upon his person.

The conclusion is that maintaining life as a whole is required by way of a demand of an initial general rule. This is a particular instance of this principle.

There is no doubt that *rukhṣa* is allowed for the removal of hardship, and this is one instance of this principle. The two aspects cannot be unified. When the aspects are multiplied, opposition is eliminated and negation disappears, making reconciliation possible.

As for the combining of prayers at ʿArafa and Muzdalifa and so on, we cannot concede that it forms a *rukhṣa* according to one demanding it; rather it is an initial general rule requiring ritual obedience in his view. This is indicated by the tradition of ʿĀʾisha (God be pleased with her) pertaining to curtailment of prayer, "Prayer is made obligatory in units of two *rakʿas* ..."[349] Considering the underlying cause of curtailment to be injury and hardship does not make it a *rukhṣa*, because not everything that is to be removed due to injury is not called *rukhṣa* in this meaning of this general term. If this were so, it would become obligatory to consider the entire *sharīʿa* as *rukhṣa* due to its leniency in comparison to earlier scriptural laws. Thus, the law of five daily prayers would amount to *rukhṣa*, because they were initially prescribed as fifty in the heavens. *Qarḍ*, *musāqāh*, *qirāḍ*, imposition of blood-money on the *ʿāqila* would all amount to *rukhṣa*.[350] This is not the case as has been discussed earlier. Thus, all things that go beyond the parameters of permissibility are not *rukhṣa*.

As for the words of the Prophet (pbuh), "Allah wishes that His exemptions be acted upon just as his initial impositions are acted upon,"[351] its elaboration will be coming up, Allah, the Exalted, willing. Further, there are some permissible things that are desired, while there are others that are shunned, according to the discussion that has preceded under the category of obligation creating rules. Thus, there is no negation here.

As for His words, "Allah intends every facility for you; He does not want to put you to difficulties",[352] as well as other texts like it, they are to be interpreted in the same way. The reason is that the legality of prescribed exemptions (*rukhaṣ*) is based upon facility and the removal of injury. All success lies with Allah.

The third issue: rukhṣa *is an additional element*

Rukhṣa is a secondary and not a primary rule in the meaning that each person in adopting it is his own jurist, as long as no legal limitation is placed upon it, in which case he is to suspend judgement. The elaboration of this is from different perspectives.

First: The basis of *rukhṣa* is hardship. Hardship differs in intensity according to circumstances, in accordance with the strength and weakness of the initial general rules, in accordance with the time, and in accordance with the nature of the act. Thus, the journey of a human being on a ride, for a day and night, in favourable environment, in a secure land, at easy pace, in the winter season of shorter days, is not like a journey with opposite characteristics for purposes of fasting and curtailment. The same can be said about tolerance that differs with the severity of the journey and its hardships. It is possible that an environment hardened person, thoroughly accustomed to the undertaking of missions, who does not feel the hardship of travel nor feel uncomfortable as a result of it, to have the strength to undertake his acts of worship in their complete form at their appointed times. There may be a person who is the exact opposite of this person. The same applies to tolerance for hunger and thirst as well as being faint-hearted and courageous along with other traits that are beyond his control. Likewise the person who is ill, who is obliged to undertake fasting, prayer, *jihād* and other acts.

If this is the case, then there is no specified rule for the hardship legally acknowledged for granting concessions, nor a prescribed limit that covers all the people. It is for this reason that the *sharīʿa* has linked most of them to the cause rather than to the underlying *ʿilla*. Thus, the *sharīʿa* acknowledged journey because that is the most obvious indication of hardship, leaving each subject to his own discretion; that is, if it is curtailment or not fasting it has to be during the journey. The relinquishment of most of these exemptions is left to *ijtihād*, as in the case of illness. There are many people who are able to do during illness what other ill persons cannot do. The *rukhṣa* is in such a case lawful for one person and not for the other. There is no doubt about this.

Consequently, the causes of *rukhaṣ* are not classified under the original initial rule nor can a general rule be formulated for them. In fact, they are secondary with respect to each addressee within his personal context. Among those under duress, if a person is accustomed to bearing hunger and he does not lose his balanced state as a result of it, as were the Arabs, and as has been said about saintly persons, then the permissibility of consuming carrion is not based on the same standard as is to be used by a person who has different traits. This is one interpretation.

Second: It may happen sometimes that the subject actor has the strength to carry out the act so that it is easy for him as compared to other people. You have enough reports about those who love God, who patiently bear privation. They voluntarily bore the burdens of hardship to the extent of extinguishing their life as well as other acts. They continued to do so for prolonged periods, eagerly persisting in their acts, attaching great value to them, and seeking to please those whom they loved. They acknowledged that these privations and hardships were easy for them. In fact, they were a source of pleasure and blessing for them. For others these were acts of inflicting torture and extreme pain. This is the most obvious proof that hardships vary with reference to association and affiliations. The proof requires that the rule based upon them differ with respect to associations and affiliations.

Third: The indication in the *sharīʿa* laid down about continuous fasting and prolonged periods of devotion to worship. The Lawgiver has commanded leniency and mercy for the servants, which is what those coming after the Prophet (pbuh) did, knowing that the basis of the prohibition was injury and hardship that is missing in their case. It is for this reason that they reported of themselves that continuous fasting does not keep them away from their normal needs nor does it cut them off from carrying out their tasks, thus causing no hardship in their case. Hardship, they maintained, affects those who feel the hardship keeping them away from their necessities and needs. This idea is the basis of the *rukhṣa* being an additional element. It follows necessarily from this that *rukhṣa* is like this. The interpretation, however, amounts to reasoning from the genus of hardship to one of its instances, which is not sound, unless it is included in the level preceding it. Reasoning on the basis of the combined norm is valid, in accordance with what is stated under the discussion of generality in the *Book of Adilla*.

Suppose it is said: The injury acknowledged in the legality of *rukhṣa* is either effective in the case of the subject so that he cannot be free for worship or practice because of it, or it is not possible for him to undertake what he has commanded to do, or it may not be effective for him, rather it overpowers his tolerance and demolishes his determination. If it is the first, then it is obvious that it is a case of *rukhṣa*, except that he is required in this case to adopt the *rukhṣa* by way of obligation or recommendation in accordance with the total avoidance of the act or not completing it. If he is commanded to undertake such an act then it is not *rukhṣa* in the meaning that has preceded, rather it is an initial general rule (*ʿazīma*). If it is the second, then there is no injury or hardship in the act, except what is experienced in normal acts. This negates the fact that it is an injury that gives rise to the *ʿilla* of *rukhṣa*. If the subject-matter of the *rukhṣa* is negated in both types, there being no third, the rule of *rukhṣa* is removed *ab initio*, when the agreement about its existence is known. This is conclusive; therefore, what is structured on this is like it.

The response is given in two ways.

First: This question stands converted to another form, because it requires that the exemptions should all be commanded by way of obligation or recommendation. The reason is that there is no *rukhṣa* in which this discussion does not run. As it implies an ambiguous demand, it does not stand up as an evidence, and cannot be acknowledged for purposes of binding arguments.

Second: If this is conceded, then it does not remain binding due to two reasons.

First: The reliance on the fact that there are two divisions has no evidence to support it, because of the possibility of a third division in between the two, which is that the injury is not effective for the act. In this case the subject will not be occupied due to its existence. Each person finds within himself, during journey or illness, the feeling of an injury during fasting, although this injury will not lead him to terminate his journey, disturb his illness, or lead to a disruption in the act itself. Likewise all the other *rukhaṣ* presented; this division runs through them. The third is the subject-matter of permissibility, because there is no force pulling it towards either of the two sides.

Second: The demand of the law for leniency, when it makes such a demand, is not from the perspective that it is a *rukhṣa* but rather from the perspective of the initial general rule (*ʿazīma*), which the subject is not able to comply with, or it is from the perspective that it will lead to disturbance in affairs of the Hereafter or of this world. The demand conveys a proscription of disturbance in the act and is not that the act itself is a *rukhṣa*. It is for this reason that prayer in the presence of food is disapproved as well as the suppression of the two calls of nature,[353] and so on. The *rukhṣa* then continues to be based on its original rule of permissibility in as much as it is a *rukhṣa*. It does not amount to the removal of the act in the absolute sense. The explanation about the two aspects of demand and permissibility has preceded. Allah knows best.

The fourth issue: ibāḥa *associated with* rukhṣa

Does the permissibility attributed to the *rukhṣa* imply permissibility in the meaning of removal of injury or does it imply the meaning of choice between commission of the act or its relinquishment?

What appears evident from the texts pertaining to the *rukhaṣ* is that it implies the removal of injury and not the other meaning. This is evident from the words of the Exalted, "But if one is forced by necessity, without wilful disobedience, nor transgressing due limits – then is he guiltless",[354] as well as His words in the verse, "But if any is forced by hunger, with no inclination to transgression, Allah is indeed Oft-forgiving, Most Merciful."[355] He does not mention in this whether the subject has the option of committing the act or omitting it. He merely mentions that sin is removed in the case of consumption (of the unlawful) in a state of duress. Likewise the words of the Exalted, "But if any of you is ill, or on a journey, the prescribed number (should be made up) from days later."[356] He did not say that he is entitled not to fast, he should abstain from fasting, or that it is not permitted. He mentioned the same excuse and pointed out the fact that if he does abstain from fasting then he has to fast for the same number of other days. A similar meaning is found in the words of the Exalted, "There is no blame on you if ye shorten your prayers, for fear the unbelievers may attack you."[357] This is so according to the view that it means reducing the number of *rakʿas*. He did not say that you must curtail it or that if you like curtail it.

Allah, the Exalted, has said in the case of the person coerced, "Anyone who, after accepting faith in Allah, utters Unbelief – except under compulsion, his heart remaining firm in faith – but such as open their breast to unbelief, on them is wrath from Allah, and theirs will be a dreadful chastisement."[358] The meaning is that there is no wrath for one who is coerced. There is no chastisement for him if he utters unbelief when his heart is firm in faith. He did not say that he may speak or if he likes he may speak.

A tradition says, "Should I lie to my wife?" He replied, "There is nothing good in lying." The person asked, "Should I make a promise to her and say this to her?" He replied, "There is no blame on you."[359] He did not say "Yes" to him, nor did he say, "Do it if you like."

The evidence that a choice is not intended in these matters is that the majority of all the jurists uphold the view that a person who does not utter unbelief despite (life threatening) coercion is rewarded and has a lofty status. Choice negates the preference of one side over the other. The same is to be said about the other occasions mentioned and some not mentioned.

As for permissibility that is within the meaning of a choice, it is mentioned in the words of the Exalted, "Your wives are as a tilth unto you; so approach your tilth when or how ye will."[360] This means from the front, back or side. This is evident choice.[361] Likewise His words, "And eat of the bountiful things therein as (where and when) ye will."[362] There are other verses similar to these. The difference between the two types of the permissible (*mubāḥ*) has preceded in the division pertaining to the obligation creating communication.

If it is said, "What are the consequences of this distinction? " it will be said:

A number of benefits are structured upon this. The difficulty in our issue, however, is that if we say, "The *rukhṣa* presents a choice in reality", then it becomes necessary to say that it becomes a requirement like the initially imposed general rule that pertains to the obligatory category that gives a choice (*wājib mukhayyar*). This is not the case when we say, "It is permissible in the meaning of removal of hardship from the actor." The reason is that the removal of hardship does not convey a choice. Do you not see that it is present in the *wājib* (obligatory)? If such is the case, it becomes evident that the initial general rule is maintained in its original position with respect to the determined obligation intended by the law. If he brings it about then there is no difference between the person who is handicapped and another person. Yet, the excuse removes sin from the person who moves away from it if he chooses such transference for himself. This will be made plain, Allah the Exalted willing.

The fifth issue: valid rukhṣa *of two types*

Lawful exemptions are of two types.

First: Those that are in lieu of hardship that becomes unbearable. These are natural, like illness that creates an inability to bring about the basic elements of prayer, for example as they are required or in the case of fasting due to the apprehension of death. They may be legal like fasting that leads to the lack of ability to be present for prayer or complete its elements as well as other things resembling this.

Second: Those that are in lieu of hardship, which the subject can bear. The examples for this are evident.

The first pertains to the right of God. Acting upon the exemption in such a case is required. It is in this context that the tradition was laid down: "It is not piety to fast during journey."[363] The same meaning is indicated by the proscription about prayer in the presence of food or the suppression of the call of nature,[364] and the tradition, "When food is brought and prayer is to be performed, begin with food",[365] as well as others like it. The *rukhṣa* (exemption) in such a case is linked to this principle (of the right of God). There is no discussion here that the *rukhṣa* in such cases resembles the initial general rules. It is for this reason that the jurists have upheld the consumption of carrion when there is apprehension of death. If a person does not do so and dies, he goes to the Fire.

As for the second, it pertains to the rights of the individuals so that can benefit from the mercy of God and the facility provided by Him. This, however, is of two types.

First: That it is linked to a demand so that the state of hardship, with respect to presence and absence, is not taken into account, like the combining of prayers at ʿArafa or Muzdalifa. In this case too there is no discussion that it is linked with initial general rules insofar as its commission is demanded in the manner that the commission of *ʿazāʾim* (initial general rules) is demanded, so that the jurists treat this as a *sunna* and not a *mubāḥ*. Despite this it remains in the category of *rukhṣa*, because a demand of the law does not negate the fact that it is a *rukhṣa*, just like what the jurists say about the consumption of carrion by one under duress. Consequently, it is a *rukhṣa* insofar as it conforms to the definition of *rukhṣa*, and it is an *ʿazīma* insofar as it has been demanded in a form meant for initial rules.

Second: That it is not linked to a demand but rather remains within the principle of leniency and removal of hardship, which is the principle of permissibility. The subject then has the choice to adopt the initial general rule even though there is hardship in this and he has the choice of adopting the *rukhṣa*.

The evidences for the validity of the rule for these types are evident, therefore, there is no need to repeat them here. If someone is seeking to be reminded about this, then we say:

As for the first, when hardship leads to the disturbance of the universal principle, it becomes necessary not to acknowledge an initial general rule within it, because the completion of the act of worship and performing it in its required form leads to its removal from its foundation. Thus, performing it to the fullest extent of its performance – which is the requirement of the *rukhṣa* – is what is demanded. The affirmation of this evidence is mentioned in the *Book of Maqāṣid* within this book.

As for the second, when the determined *rukhṣa* is assumed to be specific to an evidence that demands the commission of the act in a particular manner, from this perspective it is now outside the rules of *rukhṣa* itself, just like the evidence established, according to Mālik, for the demand of combining prayers at ʿArafa and Muzdalifa.

As for the third, what has preceded with respect to the evidences is evident for purposes of permission of adopting the *rukhṣa* or for the removal of sin for the actor.

The sixth issue: rukhṣa *and option*

In other words, this pertains to what is said about the choice between the adoption of the *ʿazīma* and the adoption of the *rukhṣa*. There is a vast scope for preference between the two and this is the subject-matter of examination. We will mention statements that are related to evidences for each side.[366]

As for the adoption of the *ʿazīma* it is said that this is the best thing to do.

First: *ʿAzīma* (the initial general rule) is a principle that is established, agreed upon and definitive.[367] For the imposition of the *rukhṣa*, even though that too is definitive, it is necessary that its cause be definitive too with respect to its occurrence. This assertion is is not realised for each exempted act, except for the preceding category. It is not realised for those other than them and these are cases for *ijtihād*. The extent of the hardship, because of which the exemption has been made permissible, is not fixed. Do you not see that the term journey has been applied to three or more miles, just as it has been applied to three days including the nights. The underlying cause for curtailment of prayer is hardship, yet it has been acknowledged for less than what is covered by the term hardship. It has also been acknowledged in the case of illness for less than what is covered by the term. Thus, there were those among them who did not fast due to a pain in their fingers, some curtailed prayer for less than three miles, while others acknowledged a greater distance. All this falls within the category of conjectures and certainty has nothing to do with it. These conjectures conflicted and thus became the object of preference and caution. The requirement of all this is that the *rukhṣa* is not to be undertaken as long as its cause is probable.

Second: *ʿAzīma* (initial general rule) is based upon an obligation creating principle that is universal, because it is absolute and general in its application to all the subjects. *Rukhṣa*, on the other hand, is based upon a particular rule that applies to some of the subjects who have an excuse, in accordance with some circumstances and certain times relevant to such persons. It is not available under all circumstances and at all times, nor does it apply to everyone. It is like a temporary obstacle affecting the universal. The rule affirmed at its location is that when a universal claim clashes with a particular claim, it is the universal that is given priority, because the particular claim imposes a particular interest, while the universal imposes a universal interest. The social system of the world is not disrupted by disturbance of a particular interest, as distinguished from the adoption of the particular interest, for then the universal system based on the universal system will be demolished. Our issue is similar to this. It has become known that *ʿazīma* with respect to each subject is a universal requirement established as an obligation for him, while the obligation of the *rukhṣa* is by way of the particular, insofar as the obligation is established. In what we are discussing this is not realised in every situation that has been assumed and a universal obstacle clashes with it. Thus, there is no way of release from this requirement except by having recourse to the universal, which is the *ʿazīma*.

Third: There are numerous evidences for what is laid down in the *sharīʿa* about the requirement of not exercising a choice regarding a command or prohibition, and of exercising patience with respect to their harshness or sweetness, even when a *rukhṣa* has become available. Among these are the words of the Exalted, "Those to whom men said: 'A great army is gathering against you, so fear them!' But it (only) increased their Faith: They said: 'For us Allah sufficeth, and He is the best Guardian.'" This was an occasion for exemption, but they adopted patience and had recourse to Allah. The consequence of this was what Allah said. The words of the Exalted are:

> Behold! They came on you from above you and from below you, and behold, the eyes swerved and the hearts gaped up to the throats, and ye imagined various (vain) thoughts about Allah!
>
> In that situation the Believers were tried: they were shaken as by a tremendous shaking.
>
> And behold! The Hypocrites and those in whose hearts is a disease (even) say: "Allah and His Messenger promised us nothing but delusion!"
>
> Behold! A party among them said: "Ye men of Yathrib! Ye cannot stand (the attack)! therefore go back!" And a band of them ask leave of the Prophet, saying, "Truly our houses are bare and exposed," though they were not exposed: they intended nothing but to run away.
>
> And if an entry had been effected to them from the sides of the (City), and they had been incited to sedition, they would certainly have brought it to pass, with none but a brief delay!
>
> And yet they had already covenanted with Allah not to turn their backs, and a covenant with Allah must (surely) be answered for.
>
> Say: "Running away will not profit you if ye are running away from death or slaughter; and even if (ye do escape), no more than a brief (respite) will ye be allowed to enjoy!"
>
> Say: "Who is it that can screen you from Allah if it be His wish to give you punishment or to give you Mercy?" Nor will they find for themselves, besides Allah, any protector or helper.
>
> Verily Allah knows those among you who keep back (men) and those who say to their brethren, "Come along to us", but come not to the fight except for just a little while.

> Covetous over you. Then when fear comes, thou wilt see them looking to thee, their eyes revolving, like one who faints from death: but when the fear is past, they will smite you with sharp tongues, covetous of goods. Such men have no faith, and so Allah has made their deeds of none effect: and that is easy for Allah.
>
> They think that the Confederates have not withdrawn; and if the Confederates should come (again), they would wish they were in the deserts (wandering) among the Bedouins, and seeking news about you (from a safe distance); and if they were in your midst, they would fight but little.
>
> Ye have indeed in the Messenger of Allah an excellent example for him who hopes in Allah and the Final Day, and who remembers Allah.
>
> When the Believers saw the Confederate forces, they said: "This is what Allah and His Messenger had promised us, and Allah and His Messenger told us what was true." And it only added to their faith and their zeal in obedience.
>
> Among the Believers are men who have been true to their covenant with Allah: of them some have died, and some (still) wait: but they have never changed (their determination) in the least.[368]

He praised them for their constancy despite there being a cause for extreme apprehension and hardship that made the hearts come up to their throats. The Prophet (pbuh) made this recommendation to the Companions (God be pleased with them) that the confederates be given something from the crops of Madina in order to restrain them making matters easy for them, but the Companions did not accept this. They sought strength from Allah and Islam. This was the basis for their praise and appreciation.

Some of the Arabs became apostates after the death of the Prophet (pbuh). The opinion of the Companions (God be pleased with them) – or of some of them other than Abū Bakr (God be pleased with him) – was to appease them by relinquishing the charging of *zakāt* from those who had refused to pay till such time that the affairs of the Umma could be set straight after which it would be seen what was to be done. Abū Bakr refused saying, "By Allah, I will fight them even if I have to do it alone." The story is well known.[369] Allah, the Exalted, has also said, "Any one who, after accepting faith in Allah, utters unbelief – except under compulsion, his heart remaining firm in faith – but such as open their breast to unbelief, on them is wrath from Allah, and theirs will be a dreadful chastisement."[370] He permitted the uttering of unbelief even though avoiding such a statement is preferred according to all the jurists, or the majority at least. The idea runs through the principle of commanding the good and forbidding the evil that the command is a recommendation when the primary rule is to remain firm even though it leads to the loss of wealth and life. The moment of decision will be over and what will remain is the receiving of reward as a consequence of Patience.

Among the evidences are the words of the Prophet (pbuh), "The best among you is one who does not ask anything of another."[371] The Companions (God be pleased with them) construed this text in its general meaning. It is necessary that one who abides by this requirement has to face a number of unbearable hardships. They interpreted it only in its general meaning so that saintly people followed this directive. Among them was Abū Ḥamza al-Khurāsānī about whom al-Qushayrī and others have written and the incident pertains to his falling into a well. It is such acts that are suitable for being exempted from this principle.

There is the story of the three Companions who came to the Messenger of Allah (pbuh) and stated everything without stating an excuse for an occasion that was suitable for an excuse. They were praised for this and Allah sent down their forgiveness and praise in the Qurʾān after the earth had shrunk for them despite its vastness, and their life had become unbearable for them. They came to realise that there was no recourse for them other than turning to Allah. The door of forgiveness was opened for them. They were called the true ones due to their adoption of the *ʿazīma* and not *rukhṣa*.

There is the story of ʿUthmān ibn Maẓʿūn and others as well who embraced Islam in the early days. They could not enter Makka except under the protection of someone. Thereafter they relinquished this protection and relied on the protection of God even though they acquired numerous hardships as a result. The matter became easy for them in the protection of God and they patiently bore them for their faith, as is stated in the words of the Exalted, "Say: O ye My servants who believe! Fear your Lord, good is (the reward) for those who do good in this world. Spacious is Allah's earth! Those who patiently persevere will truly receive a reward without measure!"[372] Allah, the Exalted, has said: "Ye shall certainly be tried and tested in your possessions and in your personal selves; and ye shall certainly hear much that will grieve you, from those who received the Book before you and from those who worship partners besides Allah. But if ye persevere patiently, and guard against evil – then that will be of great resolution."[373] Allah said to His Prophet, "Therefore patiently persevere, as did (all) messengers of firm resolution; and be in no haste about the (unbelievers). On the Day that they see the (punishment) promised them, (it will be) as if they had not tarried more than an hour in a single day. (Thine but) to proclaim the Message: but shall any be destroyed except those who transgress?"[374] He said, "But indeed if any do help and defend himself after a wrong (done) to him, against such there is no cause of blame."[375] Thereafter He said, "But indeed if any show patience and forgive, that would truly be an affair of great resolution."[376]

When the verse, "Whether ye show what is in your minds or conceal it, Allah calleth you to account for it",[377] it was hard for the Companions (God be pleased with them). It was said to them: Say: We have heard and we obey. They did say it and Allah strengthened their hearts with faith. The verse, "The

Messenger believeth in what hath been revealed to him from his Lord, as do the men of faith. Each one (of them) believeth in Allah, His angels, His books, and His messengers. 'We make no distinction (they say) between one and another of His messengers.' And they say: 'We hear, and we obey: (we seek) Thy forgiveness, our Lord, and to Thee is the end of all journeys,'"[378] was then revealed.

The Prophet (pbuh), just prior to his death, prepared a military expedition with Usāma at its head. The departure was delayed due to his illness, and he died thereafter. The people said to Abū Bakr, "Restrain Usāma and his army so he can help you against those neighbours who are ready to wage war on you." He replied, "Even if dogs were to play with the anklets of the women of Madina I would not recall an expedition that the Messenger of Allah (pbuh) has despatched." He then asked Usāma to leave Umar behind for him, and Usāma did accordingly. The expedition left for Syria and caused heavy losses to the enemy. The Byzantines said that the death of their Prophet had not weakened them. This created awe in their hearts.

Examples of these cases are numerous where the demand is to abide by the initial general rule (*ʿazīma*) and to give up the exemption (*rukhṣa*). The reason is that the people knew they were being tried, and that is (as follows.)

Fourth: The temporary obstacles and things that resemble them are those that propel the subject into varying states of hardship, and it is these that the Lawgiver primary intends in laying down the law. I mean by this that the purpose of the Lawgiver in legislating laws runs through the usual conduct of people. They become difficult for some, or it does so in certain situations that become unusual, but that does not exclude them from the ambit of the intention of the Lawgiver. The reason is that particular cases do not overturn universal principles. In fact, they are considered to be exempted, whenever they are exemptions, on the basis of the principle of need (*ḥājiyāt*) in accordance with *ijtihād*. The first reliance of the *mujtahid* is on the principle that arises from the *ʿazīma*, and he does not move beyond it except for a strong reason. It is for this reason that the jurists did not act upon (extend) the requirement of the particular exemption of journey for other cases like difficult crafts in extreme conditions despite the existence of hardship, which is the underlying cause for the justification of a *rukhṣa*. Consequently, it is not necessary to move beyond the rule of the *ʿazīma* due to the existence of hardship creating obstacles that are not continuous or perpetual, because this runs through most worldly beneficial activities, and they do not cease to be termed normal activities. Thus, the obstacle of hardship – when it is not excessive or perpetual – is to be governed by the principle of absence of hardship, just like normal activities. Accordingly, it remains within the ambit of this principle.

It is not to be said: How can this be subject to *ijtihād* when there are numerous texts about it, like the verse, "But if someone is forced by necessity, without wilful disobedience, nor transgressing due limits – then is he guiltless",[379] as well as

His words, "But if any of you is ill, or on a journey, the prescribed number (should be made up) from days later."[380] Then there is the tradition, "Allah wishes that His exemptions be acted upon just as his initial impositions are acted upon",[381] as well as other evidences, in the same meaning, that have preceded.

The reason is that we will respond by saying: The state of duress, it became evident, is a state in which there is apprehension of loss of life. This happens only after the inability to perform acts of worship and other normal acts. This state becomes an excuse in itself. Anything else is construed to mean the occurrence of hardship that creates an inability to perform religious and worldly duties, so that the initial general principle is interpreted to mean a type of duty to perform the impossible. This is not heard of, and the other hardships are in need of an evidence that indicates their classifications under these texts. It is in these that the inquiry of the examiner becomes confused, as has preceded. Consequently, there is no conflict between the preceding texts and the issue we are occupied with. The cause of this – which is the essence of the argument – is that these temporary obstacles are encountered by the servants by way of ordeal and trial for the faith of the believers, and the vacillation of the doubters till such time that it becomes manifest who believes in his Lord with conviction and who remains in doubt. If all the governing universal principles of obligations could be overturned by their conflicting hardships, all the universal principles would be overturned as has preceded. Nothing of the sort has become evident for us, and the bad has not been separated from the good. Trial in obligations is a fact and it does not exist without the survival of the initial general rule (*ʿazīma*). A person is subjected to trials to the extent of his faith. Allah, the Exalted, has said: "That He may try which of you is best in deed";[382] "Alif. Lām. Mīm. Do men think that they will be left alone on saying, 'We believe', and that they will not be tested? We did test those before them, and Allah will certainly know those who are true from those who are false";[383] "Ye shall certainly be tried and tested in your possessions and in your personal selves; and ye shall certainly hear much that will grieve you, from those who received the Book before you and from those who worship partners besides Allah. But if ye persevere patiently, and guard against evil – then that will be of great resolution";[384] "And We shall try you until We test those among you who strive their utmost and persevere in patience; and We shall try your reported (mettle)";[385] "Allah's object also is to purge those that are true in Faith and to deprive of blessing those that resist Faith";[386] and "Be sure We shall test you with something of fear and hunger, some loss in goods or lives or the fruits (of your toil), but give glad tidings to those who patiently persevere, who say, when afflicted with calamity: 'To Allah We belong, and to Him is our return.' They are those on whom (descend) blessings from their Lord, and Mercy, and they are the ones that receive guidance."[387]

He praised them for having patiently borne them and not departing from the principle to something else. The words "We shall test you with something ..."

indicate that this trial occurs rarely as compared to the majority of the circumstances, as has preceded in the facts surrounding obligations. If it is known from the law (*sharʿ*) that the requirement in such matters is to bear them patiently and to remain firm till such time that obligation has run its original course, then an exemption (*rukhṣa*) is like something running counter to the intention of the Lawgiver with respect to the completion of the act, in its original form, for the completion of the reward.

Fifth: If the adoption of the exemption from wherever it comes is undertaken in the absolute sense, it becomes the means for the dilution of the determination of the subjects in complying with obligations in the absolute sense. When the initial general rule is adopted it will amount to firmness in compliance and its acceptance with conviction.

The explanation of the first is that there is blessing in habitual compliance and evil in obstinacy. This is something that is witnessed and felt, and it is in no need of supporting evidence. For a person who persistently performs an act, the act becomes easy when it is not easy for another person irrespective of its being light or burdensome in itself. If a person makes a habit of adopting facility (*rukhṣa*) then each initial general rule becomes hard and painful for him. This is obvious. This person then makes inroads into the universal principles and detailed rules. It is like the issue that is settled on the basis of whims when the jurists are in disagreement, as well as the case of issuing a unqualified ruling of permissibility when the jurists differ with respect to the permission and prohibition. There are other cases like these that have been pointed out within this book and those that have not been pointed out.

The explanation of the second is also evident from what has preceded, which is the opposite of the first.

The basis for all this is that the causes of exemptions are more often estimated and conjectural and not verified. They may sometimes be counted as harsh when they are in fact light. This leads to invalid compliance, and the act of the subject goes to waste, not being based upon some rule. Human beings witness this quite often. They may consider matters to be difficult when they are not actually so, except by way of unfounded apprehension. Note that the person performing *tayammum* (substitute ablution) out of fear of bandits or wild animals if he finds water within prayer time has to repeat the prayer according to Mālik, because he counts him as someone in default. The reason is that in such cases it is mere clash of conjecture for which there is no evidence. This is distinguished from the situation where the bandits or animals actually prevent him from reaching the water. In such an event there will be no repetition of prayer, and the person will not be considered to be in default. If a person persistently pursues conjecture it will cast him into some remote abyss, and most of his deeds will by nullified. This applies to all acts of worship and conduct as well as to all transactions.

The hardship can sometimes be intense, but a human being is required to show patience with respect to Allah and act according to His wishes. It is stated in a sound tradition that "If someone shows patience Allah grants him patience."[388] It is stated in a verse of Surat al-Anfāl that one person is able to confront two, after the rule of one person being equal to ten was abrogated, "Allah is with those who patiently persevere."[389] Some of the Companions (God be pleased with them) observed that "the capacity for patience stands reduced in the same proportion".[390] This is the meaning of the report, which conforms with the tradition and the verse.

Sixth: The regulations of the *sharīʿa* run counter to whims in all respects, as has been determined in the *Book of Maqāṣid* within this book. In many cases it is these whims that work into hardships and are magnified with respect to opposition to whims, when the pursuit of whims is the opposite of following the *sharīʿa*. For the person who follows his whims everything becomes difficult irrespective of its being difficult in itself, because it prevents him from pursuing his fancies, making him vacillate between the difficulty and his own goals. When the subject casts away his whims denying himself his desires and focuses on the act that he is under a duty to perform, the task becomes easy for him. Following the rule of practice he will start liking it too, thus turning the sourness of the act into sweetness: so much so that opposing it will become burdensome for him when the situation earlier was contrary to this. The existence of the hardship and its absence are now additional factors that are subservient to the purpose of the subject. The difficult may become easy in compliance with the purpose and the easy may become difficult in its defiance.

Hardship in the absolute sense at one stage is what is impossible to perform whether or not the subject performs it according to the laws of nature governing human beings. There is no discussion about this; rather the discussion is about other types that are relative. About such a hardship it cannot be said that it is a hardship in the absolute sense, nor can it be said that it is not a hardship in the absolute sense. When it vacillates between the two extremes, when the initial general rule is an established reality (in comparison), then recourse to the initial general rule is the correct action, while recourse to the exemption (*rukhṣa*) is to be examined with reference to each person and with reference to each obstacle. If there is no certain ruling about it with the strongest argument being conjecture, which is not devoid of contradiction, the interpretation is to rely on the principle until it is established that the exemption being considered in the case of a particular person is a reality. If it cannot be a reality in the absolute sense, that is, in that he cannot bring about the act, it will be linked to the first type that is not being discussed here. This is the case when no external evidence is adduced for acknowledging the exemption or leniency in the absolute sense. The illustration is when the Prophet (pbuh) did not fast during a journey when the people refused to abstain from fasting and fasting was very difficult for them. This and other cases like it are to be referred to the classifications that have preceded, but the discussion here is about something else.

It is established that abiding by the initial general rules (*ʿazāʾim*) is better and adopting them during the duration of the exemption is appropriate.

Suppose it is said: Is abiding by the initial general principle by way of an obligation or a recommendation in the absolute sense? Or is there a further subdivision? The response is that this is elaborated through the various circumstances surrounding hardships, and these are (as follows.)

The seventh issue: hardship and facility

The hardships, which become an occasion for leniency in the eyes of the examiner, are of two types.

First: Those that are actual, and these are the majority of the cases during which exemptions occur, like the existence of a hardship arising from illness or from a journey, as well as similar things for which a determined cause occurs.

Second: Those that are merely conjectural insofar as the exempting cause is not found for it nor is the underlying rationale present,[391] which is hardship, and even if something is found it does not extend beyond the normal course of events.

As for the first type, it may survive as an initial general rule that is affected by a vitiating factor so that it is not possible for him to perform the act physically or legally. This should be real and not conjectural or imagined. In the alternative the situation may not be like this. If it is the first situation then having recourse to the *rukhṣa* is required, and it is referred to the category about which there is no discussion. The reason is that the *rukhṣa* here pertains to the right of God. If it is the next, that is, conjectural, then conjectures vary, and the primary rule is to follow the *ʿazīma* (initial general rule). When the conjecture is strong enough the requirement of the *ʿazīma* is weakened, and it becomes stronger when the conjecture is weak. It is like the person who assumes that he is not able to fast with illness in which abstaining from fast is permitted. This assumption, however, may rely on a determined cause, like his commencement of fasting without being able to complete it, or praying without being able to stand up and then sitting down. This belongs to the first category, as he is not under an obligation that he cannot perform. The assumption may rely on a cause that has been derived from the majority of the cases when the cause exists in fact in the meaning that the illness is present, when there is usually no ability with such illness to fast, pray in the standing posture or to use water in the normal manner, without having personally experienced such things. This situation is linked with the one preceding it, but it does not add to its strength. As for linking it with it, it is from the perspective of the existence of the cause. Its separation from it will be due to the fact that the absence of ability is not found in his case. The reason is that such ability becomes apparent at the time of being occupied with the act of worship. He has not performed it in the manner that is required by the initial general rule so that it may become obvious to him whether or not he has the ability to perform the act of worship. In such a case it is preferable to abide by the initial general rule till such time that a condition arises on which he can base the decision.

As for the second type, which is where the hardship is conjectural insofar as the cause is not found nor is the underlying rationale, normal practice will reveal its cause or it will not. If it is the first the cause will exist or not exist. If it does exist then the *rukhṣa* occurs at its proper occasion. In this there is a disagreement. I mean in assigning a reward to the *rukhṣa*, not the permissibility of undertaking it in the first place. The reason is that it is not proper[392] to base the rule on a cause that has not come into existence as yet. In fact, if it is not proper to base a rule upon a cause whose condition has not materialised even though the cause exists, which is a requirement for the rule, what then is to be said about the situation where the cause itself has not come into being? The discussion is about a case like that of a person who assumes that the next day he will be down with fever, premised upon his recurring fever. He, therefore, does not fast prior to the fever. Likewise, a woman in a state of ritual purity who does not fast under the assumption that she will start menstruating that day. All this is based upon very weak assumptions. Some of the jurists have argued about the validity of waiving the expiation in her case due to the words of the Exalted, "Had it not been for a previous ordainment from Allah, a severe punishment would have reached you for what ye took."[393] This was for waiving the penalty due to the knowledge[394] that the spoils will be made permissible for them, but this is not what we are occupied with here. Our discussion is about the consequences that emerge for the subject out of the *sharʿī* rules, and the resulting penalty in the Hereafter is not referred to *sharʿī* consequences. It is, in fact, a divine command like all the remaining punishments coming to human beings from Allah, the Exalted, on account of their sins, based upon the words of the Exalted, "Whatever misfortune happens to you, is because of the things your hands have wrought, and for many (a sin) He grants forgiveness."[395]

If the cause does not continuously recur then there is no problem here.

The conclusion here with respect to this division is that assumptions and estimates that are not affirmed pertain to the category of conjectures, and they vary. Likewise the whims of human beings, for they estimate things that have no reality. The correct thing to do then is to abide by the initial general principle, except for a hardship that is perturbing and intense. Thus, patience is better[396] as long as it does not interfere with the reason of a person or his religion, for then he cannot bear it patiently. The reason is that only that person is asked to be patient for whom it is possible to bear it. You will note that conjectures do not affect an intense hardship, rather their effects are weak based on the fact that conjectures are not true in many situations; as a result the hardship is not real. Real hardship is one that is the underlying cause laid down for the exemption.[397] When it is not found the rule is not binding unless the basis is found, which is the cause, and is substituted for the underlying rationale. In such a case the cause gives rise to permissibility and not a binding rule, because the likelihood does not necessarily invoke the underlying rationale, which is the *ʿilla* in its complete form. It is, therefore, better by way of caution to maintain the original rule. Further, hardship that is estimated is related to real hardship that is based on caution. Reality does not have a single pattern. Consequently, the structuring of the rule upon it is not stable.

As for that related to human whims in particular, it is the opposite of the first, because it has been established that the purpose of the Lawgiver in laying down the laws (*sharāʾiʿ*) is to bring the subject out of his whims and desires. Thus, anything that the self desires cannot be acknowledged for ascertaining the legality of the exemption. Notice how Allah, the Exalted, has blamed one who creates an excuse on the basis of inner whims so that an exemption can be claimed. This is found in the words of the Exalted, "Among them is (many) a man who says: 'Grant me exemption and draw me not into trial.' Have they not fallen into trial already? and indeed hell surrounds the Unbelievers (on all sides)."[398] The reason is that Jadd ibn Qays said: Permit me to stay away from battle, and do not make it a trial for me with respect to my young daughters. I am not able to bear separation from them.[399] Allah, the Exalted, said, "They said, 'Go not forth in the heat.' Say, 'The fire of hell is fiercer in heat.' If only they could understand!"[400] He followed this with the explanation in the verse, "There is no blame on those who are infirm, or ill, or who find no resources to spend (on the cause), if they are sincere (in duty) to Allah and His Messenger: no ground (of complaint) can there be against such as do right: and Allah is Oft-forgiving, Most Merciful."[401] Here the persons with an excuse are mentioned, and these are those who are not able to undertake *jihād*. They are invalids, minors, old people, the insane, the blind and so on. There are also those who do not have their maintenance expenses and cannot find one who will bear this burden. About such persons He said, "Who find no resources to spend (on the cause), if they are sincere (in duty) to Allah and His Messenger."[402] Being sincere as a whole to Allah and His Messenger means that they do not keep any part of their selves detached from their obedience to Allah. Take note of the words of the Exalted, "Go ye forth, (whether equipped) lightly or heavily, and strive and struggle, with your goods and your persons, in the Cause of Allah. That is best for you, if ye (but) knew",[403] and also, "Unless ye go forth, He will punish you with a grievous penalty, and put others in your place; but Him ye would not harm in the least. For Allah hath power over all things."[404] What then do you think about one whose only excuse is his personal whim?

Yes, the *sharīʿa* was laid down so that personal whims would be subservient to the intention of the Lawgiver. Allah, the Exalted, has provided in such abundance for His servants where their desires, condition and enjoyment are concerned that if the subject were to partake of these in a reasonable way he would not be led towards disharmony, subjected to a hardship, or prevented from enjoying the blessings. It is for this reason that He prescribed right at the beginning the exemption of *salam* (advance payment), *qirāḍ* (Mālikī term for the *muḍāraba* partnership), *musāqāh* (irrigation contract), as well as other things that create a facility for the subject, even though there was a prevention of all these in another rule.[405] He permitted to him from the goods of this world numerous things. When his base desires overwhelm his self leading him to follow his whims, then the *sharʿ* has provided a way out of this too so that he does not follow their path. Such urges are satanic and it is obligatory on him to shun them. For the one prone to committing sin there is no exemption however, because an exemption here would mean the very essence of opposition to the *sharīʿa*, as compared to the exemptions that have preceded, which have compatibility with the *sharīʿa* when measured with their specific standards.

From all this it becomes evident that in the hardship of opposition of whims there is no exemption, when there is an exemption for true hardship through the meeting of some conditions. When the conditions are not found, then for one who wishes to be absolved of liability and to redeem himself it is appropriate to have recourse to the initial general rule (*ʿazīma*). Such a precaution, however, is sometimes based upon the rule of recommendation and on obligation at other times. Allah knows best.

Sub-issue: preventive action – Among the results of this method is the adoption of precaution in the avoidance of exemptions, within the division that is being discussed here, and to be careful in adopting them. The reason is that this is an occasion of confusion, and from this arise the snares of the Devil and the deceptions of the self, as well as the pursuit of whims in clear deviation from the straight path. It is for this reason that the Sufi Shaykhs instruct their disciples to avoid exemptions altogether. They have deemed their basic principle to be the adoption of the primary initial general rules (*ʿazāʾim*).[406] The result that they (God bless them) made manifest (through their method) was that this is a vital and sound principle. Only those exemptions are to be adopted that are definitive in nature, those that the Lawgiver has required by way of ritual obedience, or those that have been prescribed initially[407] like *musāqāh* and *qarḍ*, because they pertain to the category of needs. In the case of exemptions besides these recourse is to be had to the initially imposed rule.

Among them is the result that the evidences for the removal of hardship are to be understood according to their grades. The words of the Prophet (pbuh) "Allah wishes that His exemptions be acted upon just as his initial impositions are acted upon",[408] are understood to mean that the prized exemptions are those for which a demand has been established. If it is interpreted to mean that burdensome hardship, which is illustrated by the words of the Messenger of Allah (pbuh), "It is not piety to fast during a journey",[409] then it conforms with the words of the Exalted, "Allah intends every facility for you; He does not want to put you to difficulties."[410] It also conforms with His words, "Allah doth wish to lighten your (difficulties)."[411] This He said after having said, "And it is better for you that ye fast, if ye only knew"[412] for the former and "But it is better for you that ye practise self-restraint"[413] for the latter.

The person examining the texts should try to penetrate these delicate meanings so that he is on firm ground regarding the method of the laws. To one who follows up the evidences of the *sharīʿa* in this context, it will become evident to him that what has preceded is a complete elaboration. With Allah lies success and this is the statement of the interpretation from this perspective.

Sub-issue: claim that adopting ʿazīma is not the best thing – It is sometimes said that the adoption of the initially imposed rules is not the best option due to several reasons.

First: The initially imposed rule, even though it is definitive, faces a definitive rule granting exemption. When we find the basis we consider it to be definitive or probable. The Lawgiver has determined that the probable evidence will lead to the rules in the same manner as the definitive. When the existence of the cause of the rule is found to be probable, the cause becomes entitled to consideration. A definitive evidence has been established to show that probable evidences are treated in the same way for the derivation of the rules of the *sharīʿa* as are the definitive evidences.

It is not to be said that when the definitive conflicts with the probable the consideration of the probable is relinquished, because we will respond by saying that this belongs to the category of the conflict of evidences where one comes to completely remove the rule arising from the other. If, however, the two are treated in the manner in which the general is treated with the particular or the absolute with the determined, then it does not remove the rule. Our issue belongs to this latter category and not the former. The reason is that the initially general rules are imposed on the subject with the condition that there is no hardship.[414] If there is a hardship, its consideration becomes valid and acting upon the exemption becomes required.

Further, predominant probability can sometimes set aside the definitive prior rule, for example when there is a rule for prohibition of a certain thing, but then a probable cause permitting that thing arises. Thus, where a predominant probability arises in the mind of the hunter that the hunted animal has died due to his shot, though there is a possibility that it died due to another reason or that another factor has contributed to it, then acting upon the requirement of the probable cause is valid. This is the case here, as the principle, even though definitive, cannot continue to be presumed along with the conflicting probable factor. The reason is that a definitive prohibition cannot persist along with the presence of a probable reason; rather it will persist with doubt. The same is the case with what we are discussing. The reality of the matter is that persuasive probability does not legally permit the survival of a prior certainty. As persuasive probabilities are acknowledged, they should also be acknowledged in the case of exemptions.

Second: The rule for an exemption is a particular case that is added to the initial general rule. This makes it ineffective, otherwise it would necessarily demolish the command from which it is an exemption.[415] In fact, as the particular case is an exemption from the universal, it is considered to stand on its own for it belongs to the category of the restriction of the general with the particular, or to the category of the qualification of the absolute. The issue of the validity of restricting the definitive with the probable has preceded in *ʿuṣūl al-fiqh*. Here it has a greater priority.[416] It also applies to the case where the rule is to have recourse to the restriction, which is based upon the probable, and not to the rule of generality, which is definitive. The same is the case here, just as it has been determined at its proper occasion in this book that the universal is not demolished when some of its particulars have been demolished. This too applies here, otherwise it would become necessary that the initial general rule be demolished through exemptions that are required, and that would be invalid. The same applies to things that follow necessarily.[417]

Third: The evidences for the removal of hardship for this *umma* have reached the level of the definitive. This is seen in the words of the Exalted, "He has chosen you, and has imposed no difficulties on you in religion",[418] as well as in all the other verses that convey the same meaning. These are like: "Allah intends every facility for you; He does not want to place you in difficulties";[419] "Allah doth wish to lighten your (difficulties): For man was created weak (in resolution)";[420] "There can be no difficulty to the Prophet in what Allah has indicated to him as a duty";[421] and "He releases them from their heavy burdens and from the yokes that are upon them."[422]

This religion has been called al-Ḥanīfiyya al-Samḥa (the True Religion) insofar as there is ease and facility in it. In earlier issues preceding this the evidences for the permissibility of the exemptions have been recorded. All those evidences, and others like them, apply here. Restriction in the case of some exemptions and not others is an arbitrary ruling without an evidence.

It is not to be said that when the hardship is definitive it is to be acknowledged and not when it is probable. Definitiveness and probability are equal for purposes of the rule. The difference can only lie in conflict, but there is no conflict here when they are considered together. Accordingly, it is not to be said that it is better to adopt the initial general rule; rather it is to be said that adoption of the exemption is better. The reason is that it includes both the right of Allah and the right of the servant. The act of worship required does occur, but as required by the exemption; it is not considered to have been suspended altogether. It is distinguished from the initial general rule (*ʿazīma*) for that includes the right of Allah alone where Allah, the Exalted, is free of any wants of the world. The act of worship is based upon the reward of the servant in this world and the next; therefore, it is appropriate that the *rukhṣa* combine both factors within it.

Fourth: The intention of the Lawgiver in prescribing exemptions is to create ease for the subject in bearing hardships. Adoption of the exemption then is in conformity with the intention of the Lawgiver in the absolute sense. This is distinguished from the other course of action that becomes the basis for rigidity, pretension and intensity that is prohibited in verses and traditions, as in the verse,

"Say: 'No reward do I ask of you for this (Qurʾān), nor am I a pretender' ",[423] and His words, "He does not want to place you in difficulties."[424]

In pursuing hardships there is pretension and difficulty. It is in this regard that Ibn ʿAbbās (God be pleased with him) has elaborated the story of the cow of Banī Isrāʾīl. He said, "If they had slaughtered any cow, He would have rewarded them, but they went to extremes and God was strict with them."[425] A tradition says, "Those who exaggerate are in grave loss."[426] The Prophet (pbuh) forbade cutting oneself from society due to devotion to God and said, "He who deviates from my *sunna* does not belong to me."[427] For the person who decides to fast during the day, pray during the night and avoid women, along with other forms of extreme behaviour that was practised by some nations, Allah created a facility through His words, "He releases them from their heavy burdens and from the yokes that are upon them."[428]

The Messenger of Allah (pbuh) granted various kinds of exemptions to be adopted in private and even in front of the people, like curtailment of prayer and not fasting during journey[429] as well as prayer in the sitting posture. He indicated this when his side was injured (after riding)[430] and when his body became heavy he prayed at his house in the sitting posture. When he had to adopt the bowing posture, he stood up, recited something from the Qurʾān and then went into *rukūʿ*.[431] His Companions (God be pleased with them) adopted similar exemptions without there being any objection or blame, as in the statement that "none of us objected to each other". The evidences in support of this are many.

Fifth: The relinquishment of exemptions on the basis of their causes being conjectural leads to the termination of enthusiasm for good deeds, weariness, boredom, dislike for acts of worship, and absence of persistence. Support has been provided in the *sharīʿa* through a number of evidences for this view. When a human being conceives something as hardship or is asked to undertake it, his natural reaction is one of dislike and he feels bored, and he may even be unable to undertake it on occasions. He may bear it on some occasions and under certain circumstances, but not in others. Obligation, however, is perpetual. If the door of exemptions is not opened for him, in matters other than those that are impossible to perform, and the other burdens are not blocked for him, he will consider the *sharīʿa* to be burdensome. In such cases he will come up with wrongly conceived evidences for the removal of hardship, be convinced of this and bring up what is disapproved in the *sharīʿa*. Allah, the Exalted, has said, "And know that among you is Allah's Messenger: were he, in many matters, to follow your (wishes), ye would certainly suffer."[432] He also said, "O ye who believe! make not unlawful the good things which Allah hath made lawful for you, but commit no excess."[433] It is said that this was revealed for going to extremes in prohibiting for oneself the good things that Allah has permitted. It is for this reason that it was named "transgression". It is stated in a tradition, "Adopt those acts that are possible for you. Allah does not tire of giving rewards, it is you who will become weary."[434] Another tradition says, "Whenever the Prophet (pbuh) had to choose between two things he chose the lighter one, unless doing so would amount to sin."[435] He proscribed *wiṣāl* fasting, but when they did not abstain he kept the fast with them for one day and the next. The new moon appeared then and he said to them, "Had the moon come out later I would have added to the fasts with you."[436] It was like a denial for them when they refused to stop fasting, and he said, "Had the month been longer I would have kept so many *wiṣāl* fasts that those who go to extremes would have given up their extremism."[437] ʿAbd Allah ibn ʿUmar ibn al-ʿĀs, when he grew old, said, "If only I had accepted the exemption granted by the Messenger of Allah (pbuh)."[438] A tradition records that it was Khawlāʾ bint Tuwayt about whom it was thought that she did not sleep during the night. The Prophet (pbuh) said, "You do not sleep during the night? Adopt those acts that it is possible for you to perform."[439] He disapproved her act as you can see.

The tradition about the leading of prayers by Muʿādh (God be pleased with him) is also relevant. The Prophet (pbuh) said, "Are you one who invokes trials for people, O Muʿādh?"[440] A man said, "By Allah, O Messenger of Allah, I am late for the morning prayer because of so and so for he prolongs the prayer for us." The narrator said that he had never seen the Prophet (pbuh) so angry as he did on that day, and he then said, "Among you are those who drive people away."[441] There is another tradition about the rope tied between two pillars. When he (pbuh) inquired about it he was told that it was for Zaynab (God be pleased with her) so that when she became tired she could hold on to it. He (pbuh) said, "Untie it. Whoever prays should pray in a state of alertness. When he feels tired or weak, he should adopt the sitting posture."[442]

Cases similar to these are numerous. Thus, the relinquishment of an exemption (*rukhṣa*) belongs to this category. It is for this reason that the Prophet (pbuh) said, "It is not piety to fast during a journey."[443] When this is the case, it is established that the adoption of the exemption is better. If it is conceded that it is not better, then adoption of the initial general rule (*ʿazīma*) is not better either.

Sixth: The regulations of the *sharīʿa*, though they oppose whims as has been elaborated in this book at the proper occasion, yet they attempt to secure the interests of the servants in this world and the next. Human whims are not blameworthy unless they conflict with the regulations of the *sharīʿa*, and our discussion is not about this issue. If they are compatible with them, they are not blameworthy. Our issue pertains to this. If the law has determined a cause for an exemption, and this cause comes to dominate the mind, after which we act upon it and adopt the exemption, then where is the pursuit of whims in this? Just as the pursuit of exemptions leads to abandoning the requirement of the commands and prohibitions, the pursuit of extreme acts and the giving up of exemptions leads to moving beyond the ambit of commands and prohibitions. One of these is not better than the other. The following of lawful causes with respect to exemptions and initial general rules is the same. If the predominant probability in the case of initial general rules is legally acknowledged, so are the causes of exemptions. One is not more appropriate than the other. A person who makes a distinction between the two goes against the rule of consensus. This is the settled rule in this issue.

Sub-issue: priority in giving up exemptions – The logical outcome for priority here is that when the cause of exemptions is identified, whether through probability or certainty, it is sometimes better to adopt the exemption, while at other times the two are equal. If, however, there is no persuasive probability then there is no difficulty giving up the exemption.

Further, the evidences indicating the adoption of leniency are interpreted in the general or absolute sense, without being restricted by one or the other source. The scope of the inquiry by the two sides is that the party following the first method takes into account the *ratio legis*, which is hardship, without examining the cause, which is the basis, while the other party takes into account the basis, which is the cause, like journey and illness.[444] Consequently, if the *ratio legis* is unstable and no stable basis is found for it, then the issue is overcome by ambiguity. In many such cases the principle of precaution is adopted, because this is established and acknowledged as was elaborated at its proper occasion.

Sub-issue: conflict of evidences – If it is said that the net result of what has preceded is the employment of conflicting evidences, which has caused ambiguity in the issue, is there a solution to this issue then?

The answer is yes, and it has two aspects.

First: That the matter be left to examination by the *mujtahid*. Here the reasoning of each side has been recorded without showing a preference for either side. The matter, therefore, remains suspended till such time that one view is preferred in the unqualified sense, or one is preferred for certain occasions and the other for other occasions, or the preference is according to circumstances.

Second: To reconcile this discussion with what has been said in the *Book of Maqāṣid* about the categories of hardship and their rules, when the two positions are pondered over the correct view will become apparent,[445] Allah the Exalted willing. From Allah comes all success.

The eighth issue: each hardship has a facility

The Lawgiver has provided a way out for the subject in each matter that is burdensome. The intention of the Lawgiver in providing such a way out is that the subject exercise a choice in it if he likes. It is in this context that the lawful exemptions provide a release from hardship. Thus, when the subject intends a release from such hardship in the manner prescribed, he is acting in compliance with the command of the Lawgiver, with a firm resolution to carry out His command. If he does not do this, he will become involved in two types of prohibitions.

First: Going against the intention of the Lawgiver, whether this opposition is for the obligation, recommendation or permission.

Second: The blocking of the doors of facility for him, and the loss of the way out of a burdensome matter when he desires release in a manner that is not prescribed for it. The elaboration of this takes place in several ways.

First: After the Lawgiver established that He brought down a *sharīʿa* for securing the interests of His servants, and the laws laid down as initial rules are affected by obstacles like illness and burdensome factors that lie outside the usual, He also prescribed supplementary and complementary rules as well as ways out through which these obstacles are removed for the subject. Obligation of performance then becomes something normal and easy for him. Had this not been so there would have been no addition to the initial rules. One who ponders over obligations can notice this with the minimum of reflection. If this is the case, then the subject, in seeking ease, is commanded to demand it in a manner that is lawful. The reason is that the facility demanded is available through this method with respect to the situation and the outcome by way of overall certainty. If he demands it through means other than this method, then the facility he demands is neither certain nor probable either for the present situation or the outcome, neither in general nor in its details. Had it been so, it would have been lawful too, but it is assumed that it is not lawful. It is, therefore, established that the demand for a facility through other than lawful means cannot lead to a way out.[446]

Second: If the person demanding the facility does so through lawful means, the facility available to him will be adequate and his intention will be accorded favour and blessings. Likewise the person demanding it in a manner that is not lawful will not attain his objective and his intention will be met with unfortunate consequences. This is indicated in the Qurʾān through the words of the Exalted, "And for those who fear Allah, He (ever) prepares a way out, And He provides for him from (sources) he never could imagine."[447] The condition associated with the meaning is that one who does not fear Allah will not find a way out.

Ismāʿīl al-Qāḍī has recorded from Sālim ibn Abī al-Jaʿd that he said, "A man from the Ashjaʿ tribe came to the Prophet (pbuh) and mentioned his hardship. The Prophet (pbuh) said to him, 'Go and wait patiently.' His son was a prisoner in possession of the Polytheists. He escaped from their control and came to the share of this man in the form of spoils. He came to the Prophet (pbuh) and informed him of this. The Prophet (pbuh) congratulated him and this verse was revealed:[448] 'And for those who fear Allah …' ".

It is reported from Ibn ʿAbbās (God be pleased with him) that a man came to him and said that his uncle had divorced his wife thrice. He said to him, "Your uncle has been disobedient to Allah and Allah has caused him to feel perturbed. He followed Satan, who does not provide a way out." He said, "What do you think if another person were to make her lawful for him (through marriage and subsequent divorce)." He replied, "One who attempts to deceive Allah is deceived by Allah."[449]

It is recorded from al-Rabīᶜ ibn Khuthaym about the words of the Exalted, "And for those who fear Allah, He (ever) prepares a way out", that it means "From everything that pressurises man."[450] It is recorded from Ibn ᶜAbbās (God be pleased with him) that the fear of Allah provides salvation from each suffering in this world and the next.[451] It is said that it means that for one who avoids the unlawful and sin a lawful way out is provided. Al-Taḥāwī has recorded from Abū Mūsā, who said, "The Messenger of Allah (pbuh) said: "For three persons who call upon Allah a response is not given: a person who gives his wealth to the prodigal, because Allah the Exalted has said, 'To those weak of understanding give not your property which Allah has assigned to you to manage';[452] a person who gives credit to another in sale, but does not take witnesses; and a person who has a wife with vile nature, but does not divorce her."[453] The meaning here is that when Allah has commanded the taking of witnesses in a sale contract, proscribed the handing over of wealth to those weak in understanding as a means of protecting them, and has informed us that divorce has been made lawful for need, then the person relinquishing these directives of Allah will fall into circumstances that he deems reprehensible, and consequently his prayer will not be answered as he has failed to follow the directives.

Reports that indicate this through their literal or implied meanings are numerous. It is related from Ibn ᶜAbbās (God be pleased with him) that he was asked about a man who had divorced his wife thrice, so he recited, "O Prophet! When ye do divorce women, divorce them at their prescribed periods, and count (accurately), their prescribed periods: and fear Allah your Lord ... And for those who fear Allah, He (ever) prepares a way out."[454] He then said: "You did not fear Allah, therefore, I cannot find a way out for you."[455]

Imam Mālik has recorded something indicating this meaning in *al-Balāghāt*. A man came to ᶜAbd Allah ibn Masᶜūd (God be pleased with him) and said, "I have divorced my wife through eight consecutive repudiations." Ibn Masᶜūd said, "So what did the people say to you." He replied, "They say that she is now irrevocably separated from me." Ibn Masᶜūd said, "They spoke in truth. If a person divorces as commanded by Allah, Allah has elaborated the way out for him, but one who mixes up the matter for himself, He makes it mixed up for him. Do not make things doubtful for yourself for He will make you bear what you say."[456] Ponder over the story about Abū Yazīd al-Bustāmī when he resolved to ask Allah that desire for women be removed from him. He was reminded that the Prophet (pbuh) did not do so. He then refrained from doing so. The desire was removed from him so that he was no longer able to distinguish between a woman and a stone.

Third: The person demanding a way out in the prescribed manner demands what has been guaranteed by the Lawgiver as the path to success, but the one demanding it in a manner that is not prescribed is intending transgression from the way out, and is, therefore, aiming at the opposite of what he demands insofar as he was prevented from such a method. The opposite of what is intended cannot bring about anything other than what is intended. He is, therefore, demanding the absence of the way out. This is the implication in the meaning of the verses stated above, that is, mockery, scheming and deception, as in the words of the Exalted:

> And (the unbelievers) plotted and planned, and Allah too planned, and the best of planners is Allah.[457]

> Allah will throw back their mockery on them, and give them rope in their trespasses.[458]

> Fain would they deceive Allah and those who believe, but they only deceive themselves, and realise (it) not![459]

> Those are limits set by Allah: and anyone who transgresses the limits of Allah, does verily wrong his (own) self.[460]

> Then anyone who violates his oath, does so to the harm of his own self, and any one who fulfils what he has covenanted with Allah – Allah will soon grant him a great reward.[461]

> Whoever works righteousness benefits his own self; whoever works evil, it is against his own self: nor is thy Lord ever unjust (in the least) to His servants.[462]

There are other texts that convey the same meaning. All these meanings stand verified as has preceded. The person transgressing against the method of securing lawful interests is striving against such interests, and that alone is our claim.

Fourth: The interests on which the development of the servant is based are known in the true sense only to the One who created them and laid them down. The servant cannot identify them except from certain aspects. What is concealed from him is more than what is apparent to him. He therefore works for his personal interest in a manner that does not enable him to attain them. He may attain them in the short term, but not in the long term, or he may attain them in a defective not a complete form. Again, there may be an injury flourishing inside that may be heavier in the scales than the interest; therefore, the blessings cannot survive along with the evil. There are so many managers of affairs who cannot complete them at all nor can they reap any fruits of their endeavours. This is well known and evidenced by those who possess intelligence. It is for this reason that Allah sent prophets, givers of good tidings, and warners. If this is the case, then having recourse to the way that has been laid down by the Lawgiver is a recourse to the attainment of interests and facility in the perfect sense. This is distinguished from having recourse to what opposes this. This issue as a whole is a sub-issue of the topic of compatibility with the intention of the Lawgiver or its opposition.[463] It has, however, been discussed due to its relationship with the topic of demanding an exemption in a manner that is not permitted, or demanding it when it is not due. The established rules amount to *ʿazīma* (initial general rules) that do not consist of facilities or exemptions. In this book a number of issues of this nature have been discussed, and among these are those where there are exemptions that are due. An exemption is specific to the case for which it has been specified, and it cannot be extended to other cases.[464]

Further, among circumstances associated with the servant are those that are reckoned as cases of hardship, but in the eyes of law are not so. Perhaps, an exemption can be provided in such cases without there being a basis in the *sharīʿa*. There are many benefits of such principles in issues of *fiqh*, like the rule of negation of the purpose, issues of *ḥiyal* (procedural devices), as well as others.[465]

The ninth issue: causes of exemptions not intended

It is not the intention of the Lawgiver that the causes of exemptions be attained or be removed, because these causes affect the application of the initial general rules whether prohibitive or obligatory. These causes either stand in the way of prohibition or sin or they become causes for the removal of blame or they convert something that is not permissible into the permissible. On each count they are obstacles in the absolute sense in the way of the application of the initial general rules. It has been elaborated in the discussion of obstacles that they are not intended by the Lawgiver with respect to attainment or elimination. Thus, if a person intends the occurrence of these causes for the removal of the rule of a prohibitive or obligatory cause, his act is not valid. The details mentioned with respect to conditions (*shurūṭ*) are applicable here too. The relationship of the rule with respect to the causes of exemptions is the same without any difference.

The tenth issue: ʿazīma *acquires the meaning of* wājib *with an option*

When we raise the sub-issue that an exemption is permissible in the meaning of there being a choice between it and the *ʿazīma*, the *ʿazīma* acquires the status of the *wājib mukhayyar* (unspecified obligatory act),[466] because it is said to the subject: If you like, act upon the *ʿazīma* and if you like, act upon the requirement of the exemption. Whatever he acts upon out of the two becomes the obligation for him. This is in the nature of expiation (*kaffāra*). In such a case, the *ʿazīma* for this person moves beyond the category of the *ʿazīma*.

If, however, we raise the sub-issue that the permissibility within it is in the meaning of removal of hardship, then the relationship of the *rukhṣa* with the *ʿazīma* is not of this nature, because removal of hardship does not give rise to the exercise of an option. Notice that removal of hardship is present within the obligation as well. If this is the case, it becomes obvious that the *ʿazīma* is essentially a specified obligation (*wājib muʿayyan*),[467] which is intended by the Lawgiver. If the subject acts upon the *ʿazīma* then there is no difference between him and the person who does not have an excuse, but for one who wishes to move to the exemption, giving up the initial general rule and choosing the exemption, the excuse pertains to the removal of hardship. It has been settled earlier that if the Lawgiver intends the exemption, He does so through a secondary intention. The meaning of primary intention is the occurrence of *ʿazīma*.

The issue that resembles this issue is that of the judge who is faced with two types of testimony for the rendering of judgement. One of these testimonies is based on *ʿadāla* (moral probity), while the other is not based upon such probity. Here the *ʿazīma* (initial general rule) is that he rule according to the testimony based upon *ʿadāla*, as in the words of the Exalted, "And take for witness two persons from among you, endued with moral probity, and establish the evidence for the sake of Allah",[468] and "Such as you agree should be witnesses."[469] If he decides on the testimony of those who possess *ʿadāla*, he is acting upon the *ʿazīma* and earns two rewards, but if he decides on the basis of the other testimony, there is no blame on him due to his excuse of not being aware of the true content, yet he has one reward for his *ijtihād*.[470] The award will be executed in both cases, just as the choice of the person acting upon the exemption is executed. And just as it is not said about the judge that he has a choice between ruling on the basis of *ʿadāla* and on the basis of ignoring *ʿadāla*, so also it cannot be said in the case of the exemption here that the person is in compliance through a choice between *ʿazīma* and *rukhṣa*.

Suppose it is said: How is it claimed that the Lawgiver has granted the exemption through a secondary intention, when the principle of removal of hardship stands established in the absolute sense as the primary intention? This can be seen in the words of the Exalted, "He has chosen you, and has imposed no difficulties on you in religion."[471] In the case of *rukhṣa* it has been said: "Allah intends every facility for you; He does not want to put you to difficulties."[472]

The response will be: Just as it has been said in the case of the intention about marriage that it is procreation, and this is the primary intention, while other matters besides it like making a home are intended through a secondary intention. This is seen in the words of the Exalted, "And among His Signs is this, that He created for you mates from among yourselves, that ye may dwell in tranquility with them",[473] as well as, "It is He Who created you from a single person, and made his mate of like nature, in order that he might dwell with her (in love)."[474]

Further, the removal of blame itself for the person availing the exemption, is ease and facility despite the fact that the days of fasting are numbered and not too many, which is also a facility and removal of hardship. In addition to this, the removal of hardship is intended by the Lawgiver in relation to the universals. Thus, there is no obligation creating a universal in which a complete or predominant hardship is found. This is the implication of the words of the Exalted, "He has chosen you, and has imposed no difficulties on you in religion."[475] We do find burden and hardship in some rare particulars, and no exemption has been prescribed emphasising the fact that the concern of the Lawgiver is with the universals.[476] It is for this reason that we say about the exemptions that they are not universals; they are particulars, as has been pointed in the preceding discussion under the issue of adopting the *ʿazīma* or *rukhṣa*.

Consequently, the *ʿazīma* (initial general rule), insofar as it is a universal, is the objective of the Lawgiver through the primary intention. Difficulty, insofar as it is a particular that goes against the universal, if it is intended by the Lawgiver is intended through a secondary intention. Allah knows best.

The eleventh issue: ʿazīma, rukhṣa *and practice*

When we consider the initial general rules with the exemptions, we find that the *ʿazāʾim* apply continuously to normal practices, but exemptions apply in case of disturbance in these practices.

As for the first, it is obvious. We find that the command for the performance of prayer in its complete form and at the appointed times, the observance of fasts for the fixed number of days determined for them initially, and purification with water all run their course in accordance with usual practice with respect to validity, the existence of reason, being resident in a settlement, the existence of water and so on. The same is the case with all the remaining acts of worship and practices, like the command for covering the private parts generally or for prayer, the proscription about the consumption of carrion, blood, and swine-flesh as well as other things. All these acts are performed or avoided in accordance with what is prescribed or proscribed. The existence of these is normal and general in all or the majority of the cases. There is no ambiguity about this.

As for the second, this is known too like the first. Thus, illness, journeying, absence of water or clothes or food, all lead to an exemption for omitting what has been commanded or committing what has been prohibited. The details of all these have preceded in the issues discussed earlier. From a different perspective their meaning has been established at the proper occasion in the *Book of Maqāṣid*, praise be to Allah.

The disturbance in practices is of two types: general and particular. The general is what has preceded. The particular is the disturbance of practices for saintly people when they are acting according to the requirements. All this occurs in the form of an exception, like the conversion of water into milk, sand into flour, stone into gold, the descending of food from the heavens or its derivation from the soil so that one for whom it has been obtained can consume it and utilise it. The utilisation of such a thing is by way of an exemption and not in compliance with an initial general rule (*ʿazīma*). It is stipulated for the exemption, as has preceded, that it be adopted with the condition that the person not intend it nor bring about its cause so as to avail of the facility. The matter has to be like this, because going against this condition amounts to opposing the intention of the Lawgiver. The reason is that it is not the initial intention of the Lawgiver to grant an exemption. His intention in legislating it is that if the cause of exemption occurs, permission will be directed towards its consequences, as has preceded, and here it is of greater significance. The rationale is that disturbances in practices have not been declared to be causes for removal of the rules of ritual obedience; they have been laid down for another reason. Consequently, forming an intention for facility from this perspective is an intention towards the exemption not towards the Lord. This negates the basis for determining the objectives of obedience to Allah, the Exalted.

Further, it has been mentioned in the *Book of Maqāṣid* that the rules of the *sharīʿa* are general and not particular in the meaning that they apply generally to all subjects and are not specific for some of the subjects to the exclusion of others. Praise be to Allah.

The condition is not to be objected to on the basis of the intention of the Prophet (pbuh) for manifesting a disturbance by way of miracle. The reason is that the Prophet (pbuh) intended through this a legal meaning, which is free of a requirement of personal desire. Likewise we say that it is permitted to the saintly person to intend a miracle disturbing the usual for a legal objective and not for his personal desire.[477] This category is excluded from the rule of the *rukhṣa*; rather it is in accordance with what is intended. It is in this meaning that the miracles of changing one state to another by saintly people have been manifested as is indicated by an inductive process. If this is not the case, then the condition is operative without any ambiguity. It does not apply to the general; rather it is preferable to apply it to the particular.

Suppose it is said: If the unusual is usual for the saintly person, then there is no difference in general between him and the person who lives by the usual. The reason is that a person for whom food, drink and other things are brought in a supernatural manner is at the same level with the person who has to make an effort in the natural way. Just as we cannot say about the normal person that he has been granted an exemption in consumption, likewise we cannot say this for the person following the supernatural, because there is no difference between them. The same applies to what falls under this category.

The response has two aspects.

First: The evidences adduced indicate that the relinquishment of such things is not by way of obligation, but is other than that. Thus, the Prophet (pbuh) was granted an option to be an angel or a servant, and he chose servitude.[478] He was granted an option that he be followed by Mount Tihama after turning into gold and silver, but he did not choose this.[479] The Prophet (pbuh) was one whose prayers were answered; therefore, if he had wanted he would have asked for what he wanted that would have come to pass, but he did not do so. Instead, he chose to abide by the natural course of events. He would stay hungry so that he could seek from his Lord. He would stay content another day so that he could praise and thank His Lord. He did this so that he could be like others with respect to the rules applicable to ordinary human beings. Quite often the Prophet (pbuh) would let his Companions see unusual things that would lead to curing and strengthening of faith, and sufficiency with respect to the trials of the times. When the Prophet (pbuh) spent the night in the presence of his Lord, He would provide food and drink for him. Despite this, he did not give up the seeking of livelihood for himself or for his family. Even though the normal events were made easy for him and his wants satisfied – so that ʿĀʾishah (God be pleased with her) said: I am noticing that all your desires are being met swiftly – because God made provisions for him due to his lofty status and facilitated matters for him, yet he did not rely on things other than the normal practices. This becomes a significant principle for those who possess the ability for the supernatural and miracles so that they do not indulge in what is required by the unusual. When employing the supernatural was not mandatory for the Prophets, how can it be so for the saintly people, for they are the heirs to the Prophets?

Second: The benefit of employing the unusual in their view is the strengthening of conviction, and this is accompanied by a trial that is necessary for all obligations and is applicable to all the subjects in accordance with the different grades of obedience. Consequently, it is like a strengthening factor for what they are occupied with, for it is a sign from among the signs of Allah that rises above the usual practices and has the specific characteristic of creating satisfying conviction. It is illustrated by what Abraham (pbuh) said, "My Lord! Show me how Thou givest life to the dead." He said: "Dost thou not then believe?" He said: "Yea! but to satisfy my own heart."[480] It is also visible in what our Prophet (pbuh) said when Allah mentioned the separation between Moses and Khiḍr, "May Allah bless my brother Mūsā. We wish he had shown patience so that the rest of the reports about them had been narrated to us."[481] If this is the benefit emerging from it, then it is a reward for the self, which is similar to alms given to the needy. In its consumption and utilisation it is a blessing. If he strives and demands the fulfilment of his needs in the normal manner, it becomes like the charity someone has left for him, which he utilises, but then returns to the initial general rule (*ʿazīma*). If he accepts the charity there is no harm in it, because it has been given where it was appropriate.

Further, people know that Allah has laid down causes and consequences. He has made practices by way of obligations and trials, and placed the subject in a state of compulsion to feel the need for them. Likewise he has placed obligations and trials in acts of worship too. Thus, when a supernatural event takes place conferring a benefit for which it has been intended, it contains within it the removal of hardship acquired through the obligations and a relief from them.

Acceptance by the subject of such an unusual act is the acceptance of a *rukhṣa* (exemption) insofar as it removes the hardship of the obligation and a facility from it. It is here that the rule for it becomes the rule of exemptions, but there are trials in it and something else too, which is that benefiting from what is required by it brings with it an inclination towards it: the practice of those who follow the initial general rules alone (the saintly people), that in their method they become oblivious of what is other than Allah. Likewise, the usual acquired blessings contain trials too, and it has been established (in the earlier issue) that those who adopted facility in the unqualified meaning did so by treating it as a source of exemptions. This too then belongs to the same category. Ponder over the question how the acceptance of the necessity of the supernatural becomes an exemption on both counts. It is for this reason that these people did not rely upon it, and did not have recourse to it from this perspective; rather they accepted it and derived the determined benefits from it for what they were occupied with. They relinquished anything other than this, because there are obligations and trials in it along with the fact that it is a blessing and a gift.

Al-Qushayrī has narrated something to convey this meaning: He narrates from Abū al-Khayr al-Baṣrī that a black poor man who used to live in the wilderness came in front of his house. He said, "I took something with me and started looking for him. When I came into his sight, he smiled and pointed with his hand toward the ground. I saw that the ground had all turned into shining gold. He then said, 'Give me what you have.' I gave it to him. This event put me in a state of amazement and I departed from there."[482]

He narrates a story about al-Nūrī that one night he went towards the bank of the Tigris river (to cross it) and found that both banks had come together (for him). He said: By Your Glory, I will not cross it except in a boat.[483]

From Saʿīd ibn Yaḥyā al-Baṣrī: He said, "I went up to ʿAbd al-Raḥmān ibn Zayd when he was sitting in the shade. I said to him, 'If you ask Allah to increase your sustenance, I am sure He will do it.' He replied, 'My Lord knows about the interests of His servants.' He then picked up a stone from the ground and said, 'My Lord if You wished to turn it into gold You would do it.' By Allah, there was gold in his hand at that time, which he threw at me and said, 'You go and spend it. There is no good in this world; it is only in the next.' "[484]

There were those among them who sought refuge in God from these things and from seeking them or even to be inclined towards them. This is narrated about Abū Yazīd al-Bustāmī. Among them were those who considered them at the same level as other practices for they testified that all came of His benevolence, and have come down by way of blessing. The general rule for such people is that unusual practices are themselves unusual. How then can they be inclined towards the unusual when in front of them and behind them, above them and below them, it is all the same? Nevertheless, what they possessed was the most complete in terms of worship, as has preceded. They did consider the person who inclined towards them as an ostentatious person, because these were trials, but not when they were considered signs and blessings.

Al-Qushayrī has related from Abū al-ʿAbbās al-Sharafī, who said, "We were accompanying Abū Turāb al-Nakhshabī on way to Makka, when he stepped to one side. Some of our companions said to him, 'We are very thirsty.' He struck his foot on the ground and out came a spring of sweet water. A young man said, 'I would like to drink this in a cup.' He struck with his hand on the ground and brought out a cup of glass, one of the best that I had seen. He drank from it and made us drink too. The cup stayed with us till Makka. One day Abū Turāb said to me, 'What do your companions say about such things with which Allah blesses his servants?' I said, 'I have not seen anyone who does not believe in them.' He said, 'A person who does not believe in them has denied faith. I merely asked you to make you aware of the situation.' I said, 'I do not know of anyone speaking against it.' He replied, 'In fact, your companions think that it is deception and deviation from the truth, but in reality it is not so. Deception is when you bring it to a halt. When a person does not indulge in trickery, yet does not bring them to a stop, it amounts to an attribute of divinity.'"

All this should indicate to you that what has preceded takes the rule of *rukhṣa* and not that of *ʿazīma*; therefore, penetrate this meaning, for it is a principle upon which several issues are constructed. Among these is that these are circumstances that amount to obstacles for the people, and circumstances insofar as they are circumstances cannot be sought intentionally, they are not deemed as stages, nor are they reckoned as ultimate purposes. They are also not an evidence that the person dealing in them is going through training and instruction or occupies a position of benefiting others. It is just like the spoils in the case of *jihād*, for they are not considered as the essential purpose of *jihād*, nor are they an evidence of having attained the ultimate objective. Allah knows best.

Notes

1 In this type, the Author rightly tries to point out that the same act may be a primary rule from one aspect raising an obligation or permissibility, and from another perspective it may be a cause, condition, or even an obstacle. The divine communication assigns both rules to it: an obligation creating rule and a declaratory rule. Visualising this will facilitate the understanding of the issue.

2 Editor: Thus, sale and purchase are legal rules from one aspect and declaratory rules from another. Marriage is prescribed for the legality of sexual intercourse, but it is a cause for reproduction.

3 In the Hereafter.

4 Here it falls under the declaratory rule. Theft is an act that is prohibited; it is a primary rule. Theft, however, is also a cause for the punishment awarded by the judge for whom it is obligatory to award punishment after proof. This is the relationship that the Author is concerned with here.

5 That is, marriage to another.

6 The Author elaborates here that the cause being legal is one thing and the act for which it is a cause is another thing, which will take its own independent rule. The two have to be conceptually separated to understand the relationship between causes and rules.

7 Qurʾān 20:132.

8 Qurʾān 11:6.

9 Qurʾān 51:22.

10 Qurʾān 65:2.

11 It is recorded by Ibn al-Mubārak in *al-Zuhd,* No. 559; it is also recorded by al-Tirmidhī and al-Nasāʾī.

12 Here tying of the camel is associated with the placing of trust in Allah for the protection of the camel. Had protection itself been commanded, trust in Allah and tying of the camel would not have been combined.

13 It is recorded by Ibn Ḥibbān, *al-Ṣaḥīḥ*, vol. 2, 510, Tr. No. 731.

14 Qurʾān 56:58–59. In all these verses the idea is clear that it is God Almighty who assigns the end result for He is the Creator of all things. These results are not in the control of human beings. Man brings about the cause, but it is Allah who will determine the consequences.

15 Qurʾān 56:68.

16 Qurʾān 56:63.

17 Qurʾān 56:71.

18 Qurʾān 39:62.

19 Qurʾān 37:96.

20 The Editor of the text says that if this were to be generalised, it would give rise to contradictions in the issue. According to him, it is, therefore, better to say that it is related to the effects, but not by way of obligation. The causes are numerous; some of them are within the control of the subject, while others are not.

21 The Editor of the text objects here that the distinction between commanded causes and prohibited causes is not apparent with respect to necessity. He gives the example of usurpation and theft, saying that these are prohibited causes. We feel that usurpation and theft are prohibited, but they are valid causes in the eyes of law. The distinction has to be understood, and this is not what the Author means. The Author, on the other hand, is talking about causes that are not causes in the eyes of the law. For example, *zinā* (unlawful sex) is not a cause for the legality of intercourse.

22 The Editor says that the same can be said about things commanded and things permissible. We say, again, in support of the Author, that the meaning here is, for example, that the act of *zinā* remains prohibited, whether or not the act is brought about.

23 The Editor says again that this meaning is not continuous or applicable throughout. We feel that the Author has convincingly established this point.

24 Editor: Authority has many causes. The intention to seek some of these becomes an obstacle even though assumption of authority is something that is required by law.

25 Editor: The Author means the tradition recorded by al-Bukhārī, *Ṣaḥīḥ*, vol. 13, 125, Tr. No. 7149.

26 It is recorded by al-Bukhārī, *Ṣaḥīḥ*, vol. 3, 337, Tr. No. 1473.

27 It is recorded by al-Bukhārī, *Ṣaḥīḥ*, vol. 3, 335, Tr. No. 1472.

28 Editor: Part of a lengthy tradition recorded in *al-Taysīr* from the two Shaykhs and al-Nasāʾī.

29 It is recorded by al-Bukhārī, *Ṣaḥīḥ*, vol. 3, 327, Tr. No. 1465.

30 It is recorded by al-Bukhārī, *Ṣaḥīḥ*, vol. 3, 335, Tr. No. 1472.

31 Editor: Part of a tradition related by al-Bukhārī from Abū Hurayrah, just as it is part of a tradition related by the five sound compilations other than al-Bukhārī, as stated in *al-Taysīr*.

32 It is recorded by al-Bukhārī, *Ṣaḥīḥ*, vol. 1, 114, Tr. No. 50.

33 Editor: That is, even though they are the effects, they apply to the servant without his intention.

34 The Editor asks us to ponder over the propositions used to arrive at the result. He objects to the arrangement of the propositions with respect to the result. The reality is that this is the same issue that has been objected to by him in the previous few footnotes.

35 Editor: This is not something new. The separation of the two intentions is due to the lack of convergence on a single point.

36 Editor: That is, through the evidences of the third issue. If they are not binding on him, he has the right to relinquish them.

37 Qurʾān 37:96.

38 Qurʾān 39:62.

39 Qurʾān 76:30.

40 Qurʾān 91:7–10.

41 Editor: Part of a tradition related by the two Shaykhs, al-Bukhārī and Muslim, in which a villager explains how a camel intermingled with his camels.

42 It is recorded by al-Bukhārī, *Ṣaḥīḥ*, vol. 10, 241, Tr. No. 5770.

43 It is recorded by al-Bukhārī, *Ṣaḥīḥ*, vol. 10, 179, Tr. No. 5729.

44 Editor: Part of a tradition recorded by al-Tirmidhī, who declared it sound.

45 It is recorded by al-Tabarānī, *al-Kabīr*, vol. 11, 223, Tr. No. 11560.

46 Editor: That is, from the perspective of bringing about the effect or otherwise.

47 Editor: We see on so many occasions that the cause is found, but not the effect. And, on so many occasions, we find the effect without the normal cause having been brought about. It is Allah alone who can go beyond the usual.

48 Editor: This objection is based upon the fourth issue and in this is found the excellence of craftsmanship in discussing that prior to this issue.

49 Editor: In the fourth division within the intention of the Lawgiver in the *Book of Maqāṣid*.

50 Editor: Extension of the question to the effect that the subject has an intention other than the intention of the Lawgiver when it has been assumed that the subject has no intention in this at all, either conforming or non-conforming.

51 Editor: That is, the necessity of the intention of the subject, and its evidences have preceded. It is not permissible that the meaning here should apply to the intention itself, because the evidences adduced do not apply to it.

52 Qurʾān 45:13.

53 Qurʾān 30:23.

54 Editor: It is as if he said that you should form the intention of seeking the bounty of Allah by adopting the causes leading to it, and by spreading out in the land, which is the forming of an intention for the effects through the cause. Insofar as it refers to a grant, then it continues to apply to its obvious meaning, because a grant reflects the act of the Almighty; no one else has a role to play in this. This takes place in the case of the effects and not the causes.
55 Qur'ān 62:10.
56 Editor: There is nothing in this to indicate the intention of the subject, but the verses mentioned above clearly indicate an intention with respect to matters of the Hereafter.
57 Qur'ān 65:11.
58 Editor: This supports our earlier comment on his statement that each obligation in which the intention opposes the intention of the Lawgiver is void.
59 Editor: He indicates the conformity and opposition with respect to the intention of the subject and its effect on the sixth issue in the fourth division.
60 Editor: The meaning of these two is the existence of intention with respect to the effects and its absence, irrespective of what has preceded regarding the absence of interdependence between them. The reason is that he will construct his question on the basis of necessity of intention in practices and the absence of intention in acts of worship.
61 Editor: That is, he looks at the locations of the underlying causes in order to establish in them the rule of the original case. This is a matter of reasoning, except that its adoption is through acting upon this rule that he has derived. In adopting it for practice, it is the same for the follower whether or not he considers the effects.
62 Editor: Al-Iraqī says that it is agreed upon and is the tradition of Abū Bakra. It is recorded in *al-Taysīr* as: "No one is to issue a judgement for two persons when he is angry." He said that it is recorded in the five sound compilations.
63 It is recorded by al-Bukhārī, *Ṣaḥīḥ*, vol. 13, 136, Tr. No. 7158.
64 Qur'ān 39:62.
65 Qur'ān 37:96.
66 It is recorded by al-Bukhārī, *Ṣaḥīḥ*, vol. 2, 333, Tr. No. 846. The Editor says that the remaining part of this tradition, according to *al-Taysīr*, is attributed to all six compilations except al-Tirmidhī: "Whoever says that it rained due to the bounty of Allah and His mercy believes in me and denies the stars, and whoever says that it rained due to such and such movement has denied me and believed in the stars." The words "in me" are not found after the word "denied", they are only to be found after "believes" as we verified in the main part of the book. The report will be reproduced by the Author in volume two that contains the words "in me" in both places.
67 Editor: Believing that if the cause is found the effect is found, and if it is missing the effect is missing.
68 It is recorded by al-Bukhārī, *Ṣaḥīḥ*, vol. 10, 241, Tr. No. 5770. The Editor says that this has preceded in the fifth issue.
69 Editor: That is, as a whole and in its details. The same is said in what follows. Even though the acts of each person do not relate to all the details, the particulars are ordered according to the universals.
70 Editor: It is a sound evidence for trials for the mind and the self in accordance with what he has determined.
71 Qur'ān 11:7.
72 Qur'ān 67:2.
73 Qur'ān 10:14.
74 Editor: What is prior to this verse refers to his statement: "This is to bring out their actions under the rule of *qaḍā'* and *qadr*." What comes after it, except the last verse, refers to his statement: "To bring out the requirement of preordained knowledge and binding decree that cannot be reversed."

75 Qurʾān 18:12.
76 Qurʾān 3:140–42.
77 Qurʾān 3:154.
78 Qurʾān 3:152.
79 Qurʾān 18:110.
80 Qurʾān 39:2–3.
81 The Editor says that this and what follows is an indication that it is a trial in the first meaning. He then tries to relate the different statements of the Author, but this becomes obvious after translation; therefore, the rest of the note is omitted.
82 Editor: It has preceded that a state of forgetfulness may overcome the subject, eliminating his earlier knowledge, like failing to realise the usefulness of a thing. This obstacle prevents obligation. As there is no obligation, the Author says that this is not taken into account.
83 Editor: The difference between them does not give rise to a difference in conviction about the cause giving rise to the effect. The details about the obligation of adopting the cause and the prohibition of relinquishing it will be coming up later.
84 Editor: That is, it has that status with respect to the consequences, and the rule for them is similar.
85 Qurʾān 2:195.
86 Editor: Knowledge that has become a normal state for him like natural traits.
87 Editor: That is, not for another cause.
88 Editor: In the fifth issue.
89 Editor: This too in the fifth issue.
90 It is recorded by al-Tabarānī, *al-Kabīr*, vol. 11, 223, Tr. No. 11560.
91 One can only wonder what those who are advocating hedging and other methods in Islamic finance will have to say about this.
92 Qurʾān 2:195.
93 Editor: If he is convinced about his security in taking a boat, he may do so, otherwise not.
94 It is recorded in *Tartīb al-Madārik*, vol. 2, 351, according to one editor of the book.
95 Qurʾān 20:132.
96 It is recorded by al-Tabarānī in *al-Awsat*, vol. 1, 487. The Editor provides a long list of sources for this tradition and then adds that the Prophet (pbuh) used to direct his family to do so at times of shortage of food and hardship.
97 It is recorded by Ibn Ḥibbān, *al-Ṣaḥīḥ*, vol. 2, 510, Tr. No. 731. The Editor says that these words are to be found in the version by al-Bayhaqī.
98 It is recorded by al-Bukhārī, *Ṣaḥīḥ*, vol. 11, 494, Tr. No. 6605.
99 Qurʾān 92:5–14. The Editor says that this is in one of the narrations from Muslim (vol. 8, p. 47). He adds that the tradition is recorded in *al-Taysīr* with the statement that it is found in different versions in all the sound compilations, except al-Nasāʾī.
100 Qurʾān 5:32. Editor: This is based upon the meaning that murder and saving of life are the consequences. In both places in the verse it means the departure of the soul and life. Thus, the consequences are attributed to the originator of the cause. In the second issue it has preceded that homicide is the cause and not the consequence. If that is the intended meaning then there is no evidence in it for him.
101 This has preceded.
102 Editor: Part of the tradition is mentioned in *al-Targhīb wa-al-Tarhīb* from Muslim, al-Nasāʾī, al-Tirmidhī and Ibn Māja with the words, "One who lays down a precedent in Islam …", that is, on both occasions.
103 Editor: From here up to the end of the issue it is clear that the effects are attributed to their causes, as is his purpose to show here.
104 Editor: It is found in Muslim in its complete form, except the initial sentence: "The child is a protective barrier for his parents against the Fire."

105 The Editor begins by identifying the principle the Author begins with, but then says that a distinction must be made in the case of marriage and divorce on the basis of Mālikī *fiqh*.

106 Qur'ān 5:87. The Editor says that mentioning this verse after mentioning prohibition amounts to saying that the earlier prohibition was redundant, and it amounts to saying that you should eat of the good things that you have prohibited for yourself.

107 Editor: This applies to the Mālikī and not the Shāfiʿī school where all conditional stipulations are redundant.

108 It is recorded by al-Bukhārī in his *Ṣaḥīḥ* (vol. 1, 39, Nos. 6751, 6752) and by Muslim in his *Ṣaḥīḥ* (vol. 2, 1141, No. 1504). It is related by ʿĀ'isha (God be pleased with her).

109 It is recorded by al-Bukhārī in his *Ṣaḥīḥ* (vol. 4, 376, No. 2168) and by Muslim in his *Ṣaḥīḥ* (vol. 2, 1042, No. 1504). Those who interpret traditions literally should have a close look at this tradition, because in its literal sense it appears to exclude even those conditions that are independently imposed by the *Sunna*.

110 Editor: Acts and omissions, when they are devoid of intentions, are redundant, as has been elaborated in the sixth issue of the book of *aḥkām*.

111 Editor: That is, choosing the cause so that it becomes a cause, and intending the non-occurrence of the effect.

112 Person who marries a woman in order to divorce her so she can marry her first husband.

113 Editor: He deemed the rejection of the ablution, after its completion and prior to the prayer, as nullifying prayer.

114 Editor: Just as Abū Ḥanīfa and others have given opinions about waiving the *ḥadd* penalty in certain cases, the proof of paternity, and marriage within the prohibited degree.

115 Editor: That is, combining the two factors as distinguished from the state where he looks towards the effect all the time.

116 Editor: Is this different from his elaboration in the following section?

117 Qur'ān 16:97. Editor: Applies to the good life as will be coming up. As for the rest of the verse, it applies to the Hereafter and does not serve his purpose here.

118 It is recorded by al-Quṭubī in his *Tafsīr*, vol. 10, 174.

119 That is, it is Allah who brings about all the effects from causes.

120 It is recorded by Muslim in his *Ṣaḥīḥ*, in the chapter on the proscription about cursing Time, vol. 4, 1763, Tr. No. 2246.

121 It is recorded by Ibn Māja in his *Sunan*, vol. 2, 1375, Tr. No. 4105.

122 Editor: It has been reported through three channels. The complete version is given by Aḥmad in the section on piety. Al-Bayhaqī reports it as a *mursal*. Al-Ṭabarānī provides a complete chain from Abū Hurayra.

123 Editor: This is based upon the reasoning that the effect is not in the control of the subject nor is he obliged to bring it about. His concern with the effect should be balanced and follow a mean path.

124 The Author will discuss this in volume 2.

125 Qur'ān 6:33–35.

126 Qur'ān 26:3.

127 Qur'ān 5:41.

128 Qur'ān 11:12.

129 Qur'ān 16:127.

130 Editor: He separated these verses and commented on them by saying that what is required from you is bringing about the cause.

131 Qur'ān 13:7.

132 Qur'ān 11:12.

133 Qur'ān 3:128.

134 Qur'ān 9:128.

135 Editor: It is recorded by Muslim, Aḥmad and al-Nasā'i.

136 Editor: A part of a lengthy tradition that is recorded by Muslim, al-Tirmidhī, Ibn Māja, ʿAbd al-Razzāq and al-Bayhaqī.
137 Qurʾān 41:46.
138 See volume 2 of this book.
139 See issues three and four in the second category within the *Book of Maqāṣid.*
140 Editor: As has preceded in the fourth issue.
141 Qurʾān 5:32.
142 It is recorded by Muslim in his *Ṣaḥīḥ*, vol. 2, 704–705, Tr. No. 1017.
143 It is recorded by al-Bukhārī in his *Ṣaḥīḥ*, vol. 11, 308, Tr. No. 6478.
144 Qurʾān 5:32.
145 The tradition is found in the two *Ṣaḥīḥs*.
146 It is recorded by Muslim in his *Ṣaḥīḥ*, vol. 2, 704–705, Tr. No. 1017.
147 Completion of the tradition mentioned above.
148 Editor: See above.
149 Qurʾān 36:12.
150 Qurʾān 75:13.
151 See al-Ghazālī, *Iḥyāʾ Ulūm al-Dīn*, vol. 2, 73–74.
152 Editor: The experts on traditions say they have not found this tradition anywhere.
153 It is recorded by al-Tirmidhī, al-Ṭabarānī and Ibn ʿAbd al-Barr.
154 Editor: That is with the rule of the cause.
155 Editor: Recourse is to be had, for this issue, to books on *ʿuṣūl* like *Taḥrīr* and the book by Ibn al-Ḥājib.
156 Editor: That is, repentance is not complete without actually moving out of the land, because a condition for it is undoing of the consequences and injuries.
157 Editor: As has preceded that it is not up to him to remove it nor is it within his power to do so.
158 Editor: Here the bringing about of the cause is like bringing about of the effect. He is, therefore, held accountable due to the effect.
159 Editor: The difficulty here is avoided on the basis of the upheld principle that the effects are legally acknowledged on the basis of the causes and are interpreted accordingly.
160 Editor: That is, from perspectives mentioned earlier, like the effect being in control of the subject or otherwise, and also the perspective that it is preferable not to take the effect into account.
161 He is discussing the external standards that are used to judge inner intentions in the law. Here we may mention the use of certain types of weapons as an indication of the existence of *mens rea,* as well as the objective theory of contracts. The objective theory of contracts is followed by the Ḥanafīs as well as the Shāfiʿīs.
162 Editor: This is based upon a tradition related by Mālik (God bless him).
163 Editor: That is in the previous issues and sections, because he elaborated the consideration of the effects in the light of injuries and interests.
164 Editor: That is the consideration of the effects on the basis of causes. This is mentioned within the main issue. The first principle is that the effects are not within the control of the subject nor is he an addressee with respect to them.
165 Editor: That is, that the consideration of the effect is based upon the cause dictates that there is no exemption. If the cause and effect are separated the exemption will be available in the case of the journey, because the person is a traveller.
166 Editor: In the same manner that we elaborated for the exemption above.
167 Editor: That is, it is not to be negated even if it is based upon error. It is not to be negated unless it clearly violates a text or consensus of opinion.
168 Editor: That is, these are effects that arise from prohibited causes. These in fact are interests. The meaning of interest is what the Lawgiver deems to be an interest.

169 Editor: It is, however, an injury insofar as it causes a disturbance in ownership and leads to transgression.
170 Editor: That is, they were consequential and followed them.
171 Editor: Causes in the absolute sense.
172 He is referring here to the arguments pointed out by Imam al-Rāzī in *al-Maḥṣūl* that it cannot be rationally justified that the *aḥkām* have been laid down to secure the interests of human beings. For an explanation, see Imran Ahsan Nyazee, *Theories of Islamic Law* (Islamabad: Federal Law House, 2007). The Author will discuss this briefly at the beginning of volume 2.
173 Editor: That is, the imposition of obligations is not futile.
174 Editor: That is, the error is not the object, but results from the undertaking of the act. It is an injury that does not arise from the assumption of the judicial office.
175 Editor: This will be coming up later with respect to effects after occurrence.
176 Editor: That is, with a loss. When there is an excess, there is a burden upon the buyer from this perspective.
177 Editor: This does not happen when the change is due to a rise in prices.
178 The *ʿilla* here is not hardship (*mashaqqa*), but journey (*safar*). Hardship is the underlying *ḥikma* (wisdom). The Author often treats the *ḥikma* as the *ʿilla*.
179 Editor: The preceding examples all lead to this.
180 This pertains to the rules of *ribā*. The tradition reported by ʿUbāda ibn al-Ṣāmit (God be pleased with him) prohibits the sale of gold for gold unless there is equality on both sides and both counter-values are exchanged at once through a spot sale. Thus, one gold *dīnār* cannot be exchanged for two.
181 That is, the buy-back agreement.
182 Editor: He intends elaborating the previous principle by answering objections.
183 Editor: That is with certain or probable knowledge with a counter-evidence and whatever has been stated in elaboration of this category.
184 See volume 2 of this translation.
185 Editor: Procreation is a primary objective that is based upon traditions and verses. The same applies to other primary purposes.
186 If a person has sexual intercourse with a woman under the impression that she is a stranger, but it turns out that she is his wife, he is deemed to be a *fāsiq*, and a sin is to be recorded against him for forming such an evil intention, even though his act is not treated as unlawful sexual intercourse, because such intercourse was permissible in reality.
187 Editor: That is separated from it; it does not injure it as a result of the separation.
188 Editor: Legally as is implied by the question.
189 Editor: He is the one who is bringing about the cause and his intention is not required as it is the act of another.
190 Editor: It is not one of the purposes of the *sharīʿa* due to this reason, even though it is part of the effects, like divorce and emancipation with respect to the contracts of marriage and sale.
191 Editor: Thus, they issue the ruling of validity of the effects about which it is known that the causes were not lawful.
192 Strange means not married to him.
193 The name of a book in the Mālikī school.
194 Editor: But where he does not determine the period, as will be coming up in Mālik's opinion.
195 Editor: Because no period was stipulated for divorce.
196 This contract is a matter of some controversy in the Persian Gulf states, where labour is imported for work.
197 Editor: He makes a distinction between intending a perpetual and not intending marriage for a period, and this is what Mālik stipulates.
198 Editor: It is more acute because he intends not to have intercourse with her and not to carry out the legal effects resulting from the cause, which is the contract.

199 Editor: This is the case of the *muḥallil* (person marrying for legalising another marriage).
200 Editor: The evidence requires that such causation is not lawful.
201 Editor: That is, the *mujtahid*.
202 Editor: That is, without stipulations.
203 Editor: That is, without stipulations.
204 Editor: In the tenth issue in the *Book of Maqāṣid*.
205 Editor: In actual fact.
206 Editor: In refutation of considering the validity of the subject-matter relying upon the fact that the rationale is not present in reality.
207 Editor: The comparison, as you have conceived it, is not sound as the absolute must be compared with the absolute.
208 Editor: That is, if the subject-matter is not ineligible – is eligible – and an external obstacle exists, the causation is valid. The issues formulated by al-Qarāfī are to be associated with this.
209 Editor: He said "as a whole" so as to include the issues of ownership and marriage with a woman whom he has vowed to divorce.
210 Editor: Like the marriage of the person who has vowed to divorce the woman. Assuming a rationale mentally, along with a stipulation, is not conceivable in this case.
211 Editor: Conceptually.
212 Editor: This is like marriage within the prohibited degree.
213 Editor: That is, there is a likelihood of a rationale, which is present for example in issues of ownership.
214 Editor: That is, those that are free from doubt. The differences may be due to external factors.
215 Editor: Based upon the statement that the cause is to be given effect even if the underlying rationale is not visible.
216 Editor: These issues are simpler than those of stipulations, because a stipulation does not, in reality, conform to wisdom.
217 Marriage to a man for legalising marriage to the first husband.
218 A person who facilitates marriage to the first husband.
219 Editor: Apparently, this pertains to what has been said in the Ninth Issue.
220 Tribal association that supports the offender in case of homicide that does not amount to murder.
221 Editor: That is, it leads to effects that the law acknowledges along with the rules and stipulations.
222 Slaves who are emancipated on the basis of a bequest by the owner.
223 Editor: Unqualified utilisation without compensation.
224 Editor: Even though the tradition does not identify intention. It says: "The killer will not inherit."
225 Editor: The commentators on Ibn al-Ḥājib's work convey the meaning that an obstacle is of two types: obstacle for the cause and obstacle for the *ḥukm* (rule). Likewise, a condition is a condition for the cause and condition for the rule. The unqualified condition, they say, conveys the meaning of an obstacle, but from the perspective of its absence. When the condition of the cause is absent it includes a factor that negates the wisdom underlying the rule. An example is sale as a cause of ownership where its wisdom is permissibility of benefiting from it. The condition in sale is the ability to deliver, because the inability to deliver conveys an inability to benefit from the commodity. The Editor then goes into a detailed description of the meaning of conditions. We have omitted these as they can easily be examined in any book on Islamic jurisprudence.
226 Editor: An apparent and stable attribute as distinguished from the *ʿilla* (underlying cause).
227 The Editor rightly points out that this is a very narrow meaning of the *ʿilla*, because the meaning of *ʿilla* is much wider and need not be linked to interests or injuries.

228 Editor: As internal anxiety is not an apparent attribute, but anger is an apparent cause, the rule is linked to the latter.

229 Editor: It should be based upon a factor that can be rationalised. The discussion will be coming up in what follows.

230 Editor: If the departing of life is considered a condition that completes murder, then it belongs to the first type of conditions. If, on the other hand, it is thought to complete the underlying rationale of deterrence resulting from retaliation, then it belongs to the second type of conditions.

231 Editor: The illness of the type mentioned is enough to establish their rights, but the condition is death.

232 Editor: That is, in the case of reason. As far as faith is concerned, the response will be coming up after this.

233 Editor: We say, however, that if the law has considered it a condition with respect to its relationship to the rule, it becomes a legal condition and falls within the category of legal conditions.

234 Editor: A similar view is expressed by Saᶜd in his gloss written upon Ibn al-Ḥājib's book under the issue of timely and delayed performance.

235 Editor: This is evident when the objection pertains to pardon by the injured person himself.

236 Editor: That is, whether or not it exceeds a third, because the heirs have nothing to do with it.

237 Editor: It is well known that departure of life is a condition for retaliation and claiming blood-money. The jurists agreed that if this condition is not found retaliation and blood-money for life cannot be claimed.

238 Editor: That is, marriage of the woman was not a condition for the validity of granting ownership of the right of divorce, because such ownership was completed by the statement expressing it.

239 Editor: The assumption in the issue is intercourse. The claim that ejaculation is a condition is not valid in such assumption.

240 Editor: Like marriage through which he becomes a *muḥsan*; it is permitted and is a condition for the imposition of the rule of stoning in the case of unlawful sexual intercourse.

241 Editor: That is, if he does something that realises the condition or acts in a manner that upsets it as a result of this intention, then it is void and no legal effects will be assigned.

242 It is recorded by al-Bukhārī in his *Ṣaḥīḥ*, Kitāb al-Zakāt, vol. 3, 314, Tr. No. 1450. The tradition has been related from Anas (God be pleased with him). It is also recorded by others within lengthy traditions.

243 It is recorded by al-Bukhārī in his *Ṣaḥīḥ*, Kitāb al-Buyūᶜ, vol. 4, 326, Tr. No. 2107; and Abū Dāwūd, *Sunan*, Tr. No. 3454, 3455. It is also recorded by others.

244 It is recorded by Aḥmad in his *Musnad*, vol. 3, 505; Ibn Māja, *Sunan*, vol. 2, 960, Tr. No. 2876; Abū Dāwūd, *Sunan*, vol. 3, 30, Tr. No. 2579; and by others.

245 It is recorded by al-Bukhārī in his *Ṣaḥīḥ*, Kitāb al-Buyūᶜ, vol. 4, 376, Tr. No. 2168. It is related from ᶜĀʾisha (God be pleased with her). As indicated earlier, a literal interpretation of this tradition can lead to complications as it confines the validity of all stipulations to their existence in the Book of Allah.

246 Editor: It is stated in *al-Taysīr* that this tradition is found in the three compilations of the *sunan*: "It is not permitted to combine a loan with a sale nor to impose two conditions in one sale." From Mālik: "The Messenger of Allah (pbuh) prohibited sale with a loan."

247 It is recorded by Muslim in his *Ṣaḥīḥ*, vol. 1, 122, Tr. No. 137. The rest of the words are: "... then Allah has prescribed the Fire for him."

248 It is recorded by Muslim in his *Ṣaḥīḥ*, vol. 3, 1247, Tr. No. 1353.

249 Qurʾān 3:77.

250 Qurʾān 2:229.

251 Qurʾān 2:29.

252 Qurʾān 2:29.
253 Editor: Like the passage of the year, for example, in the case of the minimum scale of wealth.
254 Editor: The principle of Islamic jurisprudence has preceded that no one is allowed to remove the legal effect of the cause for that is the prerogative of the Lawgiver.
255 Emancipation contingent upon the payment of instalments by the slave.
256 Editor: That is, they run directly counter to it. The details are in the next section.
257 Editor: In the sixth and the seventh issue he linked them to legal conditions, but here he uses the term "conditions" in the absolute sense. The discussion here is, therefore, more general.
258 Editor: These are conditions that attempt to eliminate the underlying wisdom of the cause intending thereby the removal of the legal effects of the objective.
259 Editor: That is, it is not obligatory, even though it is legally required as he will elaborate soon.
260 Editor: This is the issue of understanding the obligation creating communication. Have recourse to Ibn al-Ḥājib.
261 Editor: Like the demand for delayed performance of the fast by the menstruating woman. Is it through a renewed command, because she was not subject to the command during menses?
262 Editor: He appears to consider *jihād* among the complementary values, although in another location he has considered it a necessity or primary value. We may add here that he is calling them definitive acts of worship, and he considers them complementary only with respect to persons who fall under the effect of the obstacle.
263 Editor: Depending upon the disagreement between the Ḥanafīs and the majority as to whether the unbelievers are addressees with respect to the detailed rules.
264 Minimum amount of wealth liable to *zakāt*.
265 Qurʾān 68:17.
266 Editor: The obstacle is normal and not a legal obstacle so that the definition of obstacle cannot be applied to it.
267 Qurʾān 2:231.
268 Editor: This appears to be the case prior to the revelation of the verse that says "divorce is twice".
269 It is recorded by al-Bukhārī in his *Ṣaḥīḥ*, vol. 4, 424, Tr. No. 2236; Muslim, *Ṣaḥīḥ*, vol. 3, 1207, Tr. No. 1581.
270 It is recorded by Ibn Māja, *Sunan*, vol. 2, 1123, Tr. No. 3385.
271 It is recorded by al-Bukhārī in his *Ṣaḥīḥ*, vol. 10, 51, Tr. No. 5590.
272 Editor: It will come up in the eleventh issue under the intention of the subject that this is related from Ibn ʿAbbās (God be pleased with him) through different channels.
273 It is recorded by al-Khaṭṭābī in *Gharīb al-Ḥadīth*, vol. 1, 218.
274 Qurʾān 4:12.
275 Qurʾān 16:91.
276 Qurʾān 16:91.
277 It is recorded by al-Bukhārī in his *Ṣaḥīḥ*, vol. 5, 31, Tr. No. 2353; and Muslim, *Ṣaḥīḥ*, vol. 3, 1198, Tr. No. 1566.
278 It is recorded by al-Bukhārī in his *Ṣaḥīḥ*, vol. 10, 178–179, Tr. No. 5728.
279 The Editor says that validity and nullity are not declaratory rules, but merely rational constructs. We would like to disagree, as saying that a certain act or agreement is void definitely amounts to a legal rule.
280 Editor: Or like fasting on prohibited days.
281 Editor: Nullity and irregularity have the same meaning according to the majority of the schools other than the Ḥanafīs.
282 Editor: Like the sale of an animal along with the foetus.
283 Slave to be emancipated as part of will.
284 Slave paying instalments for freedom.
285 Giving a daughter in marriage, for example, in exchange for the daughter or sister of the other.

286 Qur'ān 2:264.
287 Qur'ān 39:65.
288 These are the words of ʿĀ'isha (God be pleased with her). They are recorded by ʿAbd al-Razzāq in *al-Muṣannaf*, vol. 8, 184–85, Tr. No. 4812, 4813.
289 Qur'ān 16:96.
290 Qur'ān 42:20.
291 Qur'ān 46:20.
292 Editor: The first part of this tradition begins with "Verily acts are dependent upon intentions." It is recorded by al-Bukhārī, Muslim, Abū Dāwūd, al-Tirmidhī and al-Nasā'ī.
293 It is recorded by al-Bukhārī, *Ṣaḥiḥ*, vol. 1, 9, Tr. No. 1; Muslim, *Ṣaḥīḥ*, vol. 3, 1515, Tr. No. 1907.
294 Editor: He says "similar to this" because it is not directly related to the issue and is an act of worship.
295 It is recorded by Muslim, *Ṣaḥīḥ*, vol. 2, 697, Tr. No. 1006.
296 According to al-Qarāfī, the entire law can be classified into two types. The first is rules that are imposed initially. These are general rules that are not specific to persons or to particular situations. The second type are provisos or exceptions to these general rules. This section is devoted to the nature of these rules.
297 Qur'ān 2:104.
298 Qur'ān 2:104.
299 Qur'ān 2:198.
300 Qur'ān 2:187.
301 Qur'ān 2:187.
302 Qur'ān 2:229.
303 Qur'ān 2:19.
304 Qur'ān 9:5.
305 A major difference between initial rules and exemptions is that a general rule can be extended to cover new cases to which the rule can apply. This is done through the process of analogy or other rational methods. The exemption or *rukhṣa*, on the other hand, cannot become the basis of extension to new cases. In other words, analogy cannot be based upon a *rukhṣa*. For example, the contract of *salam* (advance payment) has been permitted as an exemption from general rules. It cannot be used to introduce other contracts similar to it on the basis of analogy. The main reason for not allowing extension of exemptions is that if this is done, the original rule will be gradually demolished and the exemption will become the general rule.
306 This is not entirely correct, because the contract of *salam* has been termed a *rukhṣa* by the *Sunna* itself.
307 It is recorded by al-Bukhārī, *Ṣaḥiḥ*, vol. 2, 173, Tr. No. 688; Muslim, *Ṣaḥīḥ*, vol. 1, 309, Tr. No. 412.
308 Qur'ān 2:173
309 We believe that the Author is reversing the meaning of *rukhaṣ* and temporary handicaps in the performance of acts. When he says that the *rukhṣa* is one that creates a temporary excuse for the subject, he is altering the meaning usually understood by the jurists. Once this temporary condition is over, the excuse is not available. For example, take the case of a temporary fit of insanity. A person in this state is not liable for certain obligations and may have no liability for offences committed in such a state. This exception available to a person can be extended on the basis of analogy to a similar situation like an injury to the skull that temporarily causes a disturbance in the behaviour of a normal person. The *rukhṣa*, on the other hand, according to the *ʿuṣūlīs*, is a rule for a particular situation that goes against the main initial rule. This particular rule is admitted by the law as a permanent feature and continues to be in force despite the general rule. The main purpose of this division into *ʿazā'im* and *rukhaṣ* is to attain analytical consistency by noting the general rules and those

particular cases or sub-rules that go against the general rules. The classification helps in understanding the impact of principles and applying the law. If the method of the Author is accepted, this entire benefit is lost. In the following section, he appears to negate what he has said above.

310 Editor: He points towards part of a tradition that is recorded in *al-Taysīr* from the compilers of the *sunan*. It has been declared sound by al-Tirmidhī.
311 It is recorded by Aḥmad in his *Musnad*, vol. 2, 174, 178–79, 205.
312 Qurʾān 2:286.
313 Qurʾān 2:157.
314 Editor: The tradition is recorded in *al-Taysīr* from al-Bukhārī and Muslim.
315 It is recorded by al-Bukhārī, *Ṣaḥīḥ*, vol. 10, 513, Tr. No. 6101.
316 It is recorded by Aḥmad in his *Musnad*, vol. 2, 108.
317 Qurʾān 51:56.
318 Qurʾān 20:132.
319 This appears to be the reason why he felt the need to define the meaning of *rukhṣa* as he did.
320 Editor: That is, without any further detail so that it applies even to those that may be thought to be recommended or obligatory.
321 Qurʾān 2:173.
322 Qurʾān 5:3.
323 Qurʾān 4:101.
324 Qurʾān 16:106.
325 Qurʾān 2:173.
326 Qurʾān 5:3.
327 Qurʾān 2:236.
328 Qurʾān 2:198.
329 Qurʾān 2:235.
330 Qurʾān 2:185.
331 It is reported by al-Dārʾqutnī in his *Sunan*, vol. 2, 189.
332 Qurʾān 2:29.
333 Qurʾān 7:32.
334 Qurʾān 79:33.
335 Qurʾān 2:158.
336 Qurʾān 2:203.
337 It is recorded by al-Bukhārī in his *Ṣaḥīḥ*, vol. 3, 497–98, Tr. No. 1643. In this tradition the obligation of the circuit between al-Ṣafā and al-Marwa is deemed obligatory.
338 Qurʾān 2:198.
339 Qurʾān 24:61.
340 Qurʾān 24:61.
341 Qurʾān 2:235.
342 It is recorded by Aḥmad in his *Musnad*, vol. 2, 108 as a tradition that is sound according to conditions laid down by Muslim.
343 Qurʾān 2:185.
344 Qurʾān 7:32.
345 Qurʾān 2:158.
346 Qurʾān 2:158.
347 Qurʾān 2:158.
348 Qurʾān 4:29.
349 It is recorded by al-Bukhārī in his *Ṣaḥīḥ*, vol. 2, 569, Tr. No. 1090; and Muslim, in his *Ṣaḥīḥ*, vol. 1, 478, Tr. No. 685.
350 See the footnote above where the particular definition used by the Author is pointed out.
351 It is recorded by Aḥmad in his *Musnad*, vol. 2, 108.

352 Qurʾān 2:185.
353 It is recorded by Muslim in his *Ṣaḥīḥ*, vol. 1, 22, Tr. No. 89.
354 Qurʾān 2:173.
355 Qurʾān 5:3.
356 Qurʾān 2:184.
357 Qurʾān 4:101.
358 Qurʾān 16:106.
359 It is recorded by Ḥumaydī in his *Musnad*, Tr. No. 329. The implication of the tradition is that making a false promise to one's wife under some compulsion is a *rukhṣa* for the husband.
360 Qurʾān 2:223.
361 This should be understood in the meaning of lawful acts. There is no choice for an unlawful act here.
362 Qurʾān 2:35.
363 It is recorded by al-Bukhārī in his *Ṣaḥīḥ*, vol. 4, 183, Tr. No. 1946.
364 It is recorded by Muslim in his *Ṣaḥīḥ*, vol. 1, 22, Tr. No. 89.
365 It is recorded by al-Bukhārī in his *Ṣaḥīḥ*, vol. 2, 159, Tr. No. 671.
366 This is an excellent discussion of an issue that often presents some confusion for the worshipper.
367 He uses the word "definitive" here, because he has confined the meaning of *'azīma* to the necessities.
368 Qurʾān 33:10–23.
369 It is recorded by al-Bukhārī in his *Ṣaḥīḥ*, vol. 3, 262, Tr. Nos. 1399, 1400.
370 Qurʾān 16:106.
371 It is recorded by Abū Yaʿlā in his *Musnad*, vol. 1, 156, Tr. No. 167.
372 Qurʾān 39:10.
373 Qurʾān 3:186.
374 Qurʾān 46:35.
375 Qurʾān 42:41.
376 Qurʾān 42:43.
377 Qurʾān 2:284.
378 Qurʾān 2:285.
379 Qurʾān 2:173.
380 Qurʾān 2:184.
381 It is recorded by Aḥmad in his *Musnad*, vol. 2, 108.
382 Qurʾān 67:2.
383 Qurʾān 67:2.
384 Qurʾān 3:186.
385 Qurʾān 47:31.
386 Qurʾān 3:141.
387 Qurʾān 2:155–57.
388 It is part of a lengthy tradition that is recorded in al-Bukhārī, *Ṣaḥīḥ*, vol. 3, 335, Tr. No. 1469.
389 Qurʾān 8:66.
390 Al-Bukhārī, *Ṣaḥīḥ*, vol. 8, 312, Tr. No. 4653.
391 Editor: When the cause is not found, its underlying wisdom is not found either. What then is the benefit of mentioning it?
392 Editor: That is, it is not permitted to undertake the act.
393 Qurʾān 8:68.
394 Editor: This is based upon one interpretation of the verse. In *Rūh al-Maʿānī* it has been considered as an artificial interpretation; therefore, consult that book.
395 Qurʾān 42:30.

396 Editor: This is not clear. In the next section he will say that those *rukhaṣ* are preferred for which there is an established demand, and these are those in which there is an obvious hardship. This is illustrated by the saying of the Prophet (pbuh) "There is no piety in fasting during a journey." How then can it be demanded and following the general principle better?

397 To understand such statements of the Author, it has to be kept in mind that he usually considers the *ḥikma* (underlying wisdom) as the *ʿilla* (underlying cause). This meaning of the *ʿilla* differs from the meaning assigned to it by the jurists. They consider it to be something obvious and apparent like journeying. They do not consider hardship as the *ʿilla*, because hardship varies with persons and circumstances.

398 Qurʾān 9:49.

399 It is recorded by al-Tabarānī, *al-Muʿjam al-Kabīr*, vol. 2, 308. It is considered to be a weak tradition.

400 Qurʾān 9:91.

401 Qurʾān 9:91.

402 Qurʾān 9:91.

403 Qurʾān 9:41.

404 Qurʾān 9:39.

405 This is the true meaning of *rukhṣa* and *ʿazīma* as far as the legal system is concerned. His statement with respect to *qarḍ* (loan) here pertains to the issue of *ribā*. He is saying that a loan is prohibited due to an initial general rule, but an interest-free loan with its special conditions is permitted as a *rukhṣa*. This meaning has crucial significance for Islamic banking. Modern scholars permit a loan whereas it is clearly stated by the Author here that it is not permitted by an initial rule and a loan that we call *qarḍ ḥasan* is permitted as a *rukhṣa*.

406 This is the conclusion that the learned Author arrives at after an excellent discussion. The conclusion applies to the legal system, practical applications and to individuals in their personal acts of worship. We mention Islamic banking again, because it goes against the rule derived by the learned Author; it is based upon exemptions and the neglect of initial general rules that the Author is saying should be adopted.

407 The words "prescribed initially" here mean prescribed as exemptions along with the initial prohibiting rule or *ʿazīma*.

408 It is recorded by Aḥmad in his *Musnad*, vol. 2, 108.

409 It is recorded by al-Bukhārī, *Ṣaḥīḥ*, vol. 4, 183, Tr. No. 1946.

410 Qurʾān 2:185.

411 Qurʾān 4:28.

412 Qurʾān 2:184.

413 Qurʾān 4:25.

414 This is a statement that can have interesting consequences for the legal system. It is obviously based on the Qurʾānic norms that the Almighty does not desire hardship for his subjects.

415 This is crucial for those who claim that exemptions too are general rules in their own right. The Author points out that they can become general rules only by demolishing the original rule.

416 Because it is the restriction of the definitive with the definitive.

417 This passage should be treated as a lesson in legal reasoning from principles.

418 Qurʾān 22:78.

419 Qurʾān 2:185.

420 Qurʾān 4:28.

421 Qurʾān 33:38.

422 Qurʾān 7:157. These are all evidences for his statement above that initial general rules are imposed with the condition that there is no hardship.

423 Qurʾān 38:86.

424 Qurʾān 2:185.

425 It is recorded by Ibn Abī Ḥātim, *al-Tafsīr*, vol. 1, 215–16.
426 It is recorded by Muslim, *Ṣaḥīḥ*, vol. 4, 2055, Tr. No. 2670.
427 It is recorded by al-Bukhārī, *Ṣaḥīḥ*, vol. 9, 104, Tr. No. 5063.
428 Qurʾān 7:157.
429 See al-Bukhārī, *Ṣaḥīḥ*, vol. 2, 569 and vol. 1, 480, Tr. No. 690.
430 See al-Bukhārī, *Ṣaḥīḥ*, vol. 2, 173, Tr. No. 689.
431 See al-Bukhārī, *Ṣaḥīḥ*, vol. 2, 569 and vol. 1, 589, Tr. No. 1118.
432 Qurʾān 49:7.
433 Qurʾān 5:87.
434 It is recorded by al-Bukhārī, *Ṣaḥīḥ*, vol. 4, 213, Tr. No. 1969.
435 It is recorded by al-Bukhārī, *Ṣaḥīḥ*, vol. 6, 566, Tr. No. 3560.
436 It is recorded by al-Bukhārī, *Ṣaḥīḥ*, vol. 4, 205, Tr. No. 1965.
437 It is recorded by al-Bukhārī, *Ṣaḥīḥ*, vol. 13, 224, Tr. No. 7241.
438 It is recorded by al-Bukhārī, *Ṣaḥīḥ*, vol. 4, 217, Tr. No. 1975.
439 It is recorded by al-Bukhārī, *Ṣaḥīḥ*, vol. 3, 36, Tr. No. 1151.
440 It is recorded by al-Bukhārī, *Ṣaḥīḥ*, vol. 2, 192, Tr. No. 700.
441 It is recorded by al-Bukhārī, *Ṣaḥīḥ*, vol. 2, 197, Tr. No. 702.
442 It is recorded by al-Bukhārī, *Ṣaḥīḥ*, vol. 3, 36, Tr. No. 1150.
443 It is recorded by al-Bukhārī, *Ṣaḥīḥ*, vol. 4, 183, Tr. No. 1946.
444 The reader aware of the discussions of *ʿuṣūl* must note that the learned Author is treating hardship as the *ʿilla* and journey as the cause. This is different from what is stated in the authentic and established books of *ʿuṣūl*.
445 This will be discussed again in the second volume and even in later volumes.
446 This is to be noted for those cases where today people claim that the world has moved ahead and we should permit certain things on the basis of national or individual need.
447 Qurʾān 65:2, 3.
448 It is recorded by al-Ḥākam in *al-Mustadrak*, vol. 2, 492.
449 It is recorded by Ibn Abī Shayba in *al-Muṣannaf*, vol. 5, 11.
450 He has recorded it from al-Rabīʿ ibn al-Jawzī, *Zād al-Masīr*, vol. 8, 291–92.
451 Ibid.
452 Qurʾān 4:5.
453 It is recorded by al-Ḥākam in *al-Mustadrak,* vol. 2, 302.
454 Qurʾān 65:1–2.
455 It is recorded by ʿAbd al-Razzāq, *al-Muṣannaf*, vol. 6, 396, Tr. No. 11346.
456 It is recorded by Mālik in *al-Muʾaṭṭaʾ*, vol. 1, 394–95, Tr. No. 1570.
457 Qurʾān 3:54.
458 Qurʾān 2:15.
459 Qurʾān 2:9.
460 Qurʾān 65:1.
461 Qurʾān 48:10.
462 Qurʾān 41:46.
463 His major aim in his work is this: to lay out a detailed programme of intentions that conform to the intention of the Lawgiver, so that the subject leaves behind his own whims and fancies and follows the path laid down for him by the Creator.
464 This is what has been said above, that is, that exemptions cannot become a basis for analogy and extension as this will amount to demolishing the initial general rule.
465 In other words, hardship is that which is considered to be so by the *sharīʿa*. What is considered hardship by human reason or on the basis of the principle of utility may not be deemed hardship by the *sharīʿa*.
466 This type of act is required by the Lawgiver not as a specific act, but as one out of several determined acts, like the *kaffāra* (expiation) for breaking the oath: feeding ten needy persons,

or clothing them, or the freeing of a slave. If the subject is not able to perform one act, he may perform the other. Each of these three acts, however, is required by way of a choice. When one is performed, the subject is absolved of liability.

467 An obligation that has been identified.

468 Qurʾān 65:2.

469 Qurʾān 2:283.

470 This is based upon the rule that a *mujtahid* will have two rewards if his opinion is sound, and one reward if he makes an error. This in turn is related to the issue whether each *mujtahid* is right with respect to the derived opinion.

471 Qurʾān 22:78.

472 Qurʾān 2:185.

473 Qurʾān 30:21.

474 Qurʾān 7:189.

475 Qurʾān 22:78.

476 It is not clear whether this statement is similar to the assertion of some philosophers that the Creator is concerned with the universals.

477 This implies the supremacy of the *sharīʿa* over other considerations.

478 There is a lengthy tradition in *al-Targhīb wa-al-Tarhīb* about this. See also Aḥmad ibn Ḥanbal, *Musnad*, vol. 2, 231.

479 It is recorded by al-Tirmidhī in *al-Jāmiʿ*, Tr. No. 2348.

480 Qurʾān 2:260.

481 It is part of a lengthy tradition that has been recorded by al-Bukhārī, Muslim and others.

482 See *al-Risāla al-Qushayriyya*.

483 Ibid.

484 Ibid.

Glossary of Terms

ʿabd:	Slave; worshipper.
ʿadāla:	Moral probity.
adilla:	Pl. of *dalīl. See dalīl.*
adilla juzʾiyya:	The particular evidence as compared to the universal.
ʿafw:	Pardon; forgiveness.
āḥād:	*See khabar wāḥid.*
aḥkām:	Plural of *ḥukm* (rule).
ʿāmm:	General. A general word or textual evidence, as distinguished from a specific word (*khāṣṣ*).
amr:	Command.
ʿāqila:	Support group (tribal) responsible for paying blood-money on behalf of the offender.
aṣl:	Origin; root; foundation. Source of law. The established case that forms the basis of the extension of the *ḥukm* in *qiyās* (analogy). A principle of law. The principal amount in a debt.
ʿazīma:	(pl. *ʿazāʾim*) A rule initially applied as a comprehensive general principle to which exceptions or provisos are provided by the law later. The exception is called *rukhṣa.*
barāʾa aṣliyya:	Original state of no liability.
bayān:	Explanation. Technically, the explanation (*bayān*) refers to the elaboration of meanings in the texts.
bulūgh:	Puberty.
buṭlān:	Nullity; state of invalidity.
dalīl:	Evidence. In a literal sense the term means guide, but in technical terms it refers to an evidence that points to or indicates a rule (*ḥukm*).
ḍamān:	Liability; compensation; damages.
ḍarūrī:	(Pl. *ḍarūriyāt*) Necessity. The term has particular significance for the purposes of law, the preservation of which is a necessity.

dhimma:	The equivalent of legal personality in positive law. A receptacle for the capacity for acquisition.
diya:	Blood-money paid for homicide.
fāsid:	Vitiated; irregular. It is also used in the sense of voidable in the positive law. A contract, however, is voidable at the option of the parties, while the *fāsid* contract can become valid only if the offending condition is removed. It is an unenforceable contract.
fāsiq:	Disobedient. One who does not always perform the duties imposed by the *sharīʿa*.
faqīh:	(Pl. *fuqahāʾ*) Jurist.
farḍ:	Definitive obligation. An obligation proved through evidence that is definitive with respect to its transmission.
fatwā:	(Pl. *fatāwā*) Legal opinion; ruling.
fiqh:	Understanding of law; the substantive and procedural law of Islam.
furūʿ:	(Pl. of *farʿ*: branch) The detailed rules or issues of the different categories of law.
ghaḍbān:	Angry; used for the judge that he should not arrive at a decision when he is angry.
ghaṣb:	Abduction; usurpation; misappropriation.
gharar:	Hazard; uncertainty that can lead to disputes, especially in contracts.
ḥadd:	(Pl. *ḥudūd*) Limit. Fixed penalty prescribed as a right of Allah. Boundary condition laid down by the Lawgiver.
ḥadīth:	Saying. The written record of the *Sunna*. One *ḥadīth* may contain more than one *Sunna*.
ḥājāt:	Needs; necessities. Used for the secondary purposes of the law that are complementary to the five primary purposes or the *ḍarūriyāt*.
ḥalāla:	Marriage with a divorced woman with the intention of divorcing her so she can marry her first husband.
ḥawl:	One year. The prescribed period after which payment of *zakāt* becomes due.
ḥifẓ:	Preservation. The word was used by al-Ghazālī with reference to the purposes of law.
ḥikma:	Wisdom. Rationale or purpose of a law.

hīla:	(Pl. *ḥiyal*) Legal fiction; legal device.
ḥujja:	Proof; demonstrative proof. Evidence in the sources that forms the basis of persuasive legal reasoning.
ḥukm:	Rule; injunction; prescription. The word *ḥukm* has a wider meaning than that implied by most of the words of English deemed its equivalent. Technically, it means a communication from Allāh, the Exalted, related to the acts of the subjects through a demand or option, or through a declaration.
ḥukm sharʿī:	See *ḥukm*. The term *ḥukm sharʿī* is used to apply to its three elements: the Lawgiver (Ḥākim); the *maḥkūm fīh* or the act; and the subject or *maḥkūm ʿalayh*.
ḥukm taklīfī:	The obligation-creating rule. The primary rule of the legal system.
ḥukm waḍʿī:	The declaratory *ḥukm*. A secondary rule of the system that facilitates the operation of the primary rules.
ʿibāda:	(Pl. *ʿibādāt*) Worship; ritual.
ibāḥa:	Permissibility. According to some, the original rule for all things is permissibility.
iḥsān:	Good deeds; chastity; married or once married.
ijmāʿ:	Consensus of opinion. In the parlance of the jurists it is the agreement upon a *ḥukm sharʿī* by the *mujtahid*s of a determined period. This definition would exclude the employment of this principle by a political institution, unless it is composed of *mujtahids*.
ijtihād:	The effort of the jurist to derive the law on an issue by expending all the available means of interpretation at his disposal and by taking into account all the legal proofs related to the issue.
ikrāh:	Coercion.
ilhām:	Inspiration.
ʿilla:	(pl. *ʿilal*) The underlying legal cause of a *ḥukm*, its *ratio decidendi*, on the basis of which the accompanying *ḥukm* is extended to other cases.
ʿīna:	Buy-back agreement; back to back sale.
isnād:	The chain of transmission of a tradition.

istidlāl mursal: Legal reasoning that is based on a principle freed from the hold of individual texts, that is, it is let go into the realm of the purposes of the law. It is also called *maṣlaḥah mursalah.*

istiḥsān: The principle according to which the law is based upon a general principle of the law in preference to a strict analogy pertaining to the issue.

The principle is used by the Ḥanafīs as well as the Mālikīs. This method of interpretation may be employed for various reasons including hardship.

istiṣḥāb: Presumption of continuity of a rule or of its absence. A principle within the Shāfʿī system, which in general terms means: the status quo shall be maintained. In a more technical sense, it means that the original rule governing an issue shall remain operative. In such a case, the primary rule assigned to all issues is that of permissibility.

istiqrāʾ: Induction.

iʿtikāf: Seclusion in a mosque for worship, especially during Ramaḍān.

janāba: Major impurity requiring major ablution (bathing).

jihād: Striving; struggle; waging war.

kabīra: Major sin.

kaffāra: Expiation.

khabar wāḥid: It is a report from the Prophet (pbuh) that does not reach the status of *tawātur*, or of *mashhūr* according to the Ḥanafīs, that is, there are one or two narrators in its chain in the first three generations: Companions, *Tābiʿūn*, and their followers. As compared to this, the *mashhūr* report has one or two narrators among the Companions, but it reaches the status of *mutawātir* in the generation of the *Tābiʿūn.*

khamr: Wine.

khāṣṣ: Particular; specific; specific word.

khaṭaʾ: Mistake. In the case of homicide, it means manslaughter.

khiṭāb:	Communication; address; speech. The word is usually used for the communication of the Lawgiver. *Khiṭāb al-taklīf* means a communication that creates obligations or duties, while *khiṭāb al-waḍʿi* is a declaratory communication that identifies the relationship between rules.
khulʿ:	Divorce obtained by wife through monetary compensation.
kullī:	(Pl. *kulliyāt*) Universal. *Kulliyāt sharʿiyya* are the general legal principles of the *sharīʿa*.
maḍāmin:	Sale of an animal foetus along with the sale of the mother.
mafsada:	(Pl. *mafāsid*) Injury; harm.
makrūh:	Reprehensible; disapproved.
makrūh karāhat al-taḥrīm:	Disapproval that is akin to prohibition.
makrūh karāhat al-tanzīh:	Disapproval that is closer to permissibility.
māl:	Property; wealth.
manāṭ:	The support or place of suspension of another thing. The underlying cause on which the *ḥukm* is suspended.
manfaʿa:	Utility.
māniʿ:	(Pl. *mawāniʿ*) Obstacle. Obstacle in the way of operation of a rule. In criminal law: general defence.
maqāṣid al-sharīʿah:	The purposes of the *sharīʿah*, whose preservation and protection amounts to the securing of an interest (*maṣlaḥah*).
maṣāliḥ:	Interests preserved and protected by the *sharīʿah*.
mashaqqa:	Hardship. It usually leads to an exemption in the *sharīʿa*
maṣlaḥa mursala:	An interest that is not supported by an individual text, but is upheld by the texts considered collectively.
maṣlaḥa:	The principle that the *sharīʿah* has determined goals or purposes and the securing of these purposes is an acknowledged interest (*maṣlaḥah*).
mubāḥ:	Permissible.
muḍāraba:	A partnership in which the working partner has no liability for loss. It is, however, different from the *commenda* in which the working partner has unlimited liability,

	and which has given rise to the limited liability partnership.
muḥallal:	Also *muḥallal lahu*. A person (first husband) who wishes to marry a woman whom he divorced earlier for which purpose he arranges her marriage to another man, who will then divorce her so she can become lawful for the first husband. *See ḥalāla*.
muḥallil:	A person who marries a woman with the intention of divorcing her so she can become lawful for marriage to her prior husband who had divorced her. *See ḥalāla*.
muḥkam:	A meaning that is absolutely clear. A governing text.
muḥsan:	Married; chaste; free. These three meanings of the word are relevant for three different legal rules.
mujtahad fīh:	A matter that is subject to interpretation.
mujtahid:	A jurist who can derive the law independently.
naṣṣ:	Text; definitive implication of the text.
nadhr:	Vow.
nafs:	Person; self; life.
nahy:	Prohibition.
naskh:	Abrogation.
nasl:	Progeny.
niṣāb:	The minimum scale.
nikāḥ:	Marriage.
nikāḥ al-shighār:	Contract of marriage in which a daughter or sister is given away in marriage in exchange for a daughter or sister.
nisyān:	Forgetfulness.
niyya:	Intention.
qaḍāʾ:	The judicial office. Also used for delayed performance of an act.
qadhf:	False accusation of unlawful sexual intercourse.
qāḍī:	Judge.
qadr:	Predetermination.
qāʿida uṣūliya:	Principle of interpretation.
qalb:	Heart; mind.
qarḍ:	Loan without interest, also called *qarḍ ḥasan* (commendable loan).

qaṭʿī:	Definitive.
qawāʿid:	Principles.
qawānīn:	Rules.
qawānīn uṣūliyya:	Rules of interpretation.
qawānīn kulliya:	General rules.
qirāḍ:	The term used by the Mālikī school for *muḍāraba*.
qiṣāṣ:	Retaliation; *lex talionis*.
qiyās:	Analogy; syllogism. The extension of the *ḥukm* of a specific case established in the texts to a new case awaiting decision on the basis of a common underlying cause.
qubḥ:	Morally bad or evil as compared to good (*ḥasan*).
rajm:	Stoning to death.
rakʿa:	A unit of prayer.
ribā:	Interest; usury. *Ribā al-nasīʾa* is benefit derived from dealy or time-value.
rukhṣa:	(Pl. *rukhaṣ*) Exemption. See *ʿazīma*.
rukn:	Essential element; pillar.
rushd:	Discretion; maturity.
ṣāʿ:	A cubic measure.
sabab:	Cause.
ṣadaqa:	Charity
sadd al-dharīʿa:	The plugging of lawful means to an unlawful end.
safar:	Journey.
ṣaḥīḥ:	Valid.
sahw:	Error due to forgetfulness in prayer.
salam:	A contract in which advance payment is permitted.
ṣalāt:	Prayer.
sanad:	The evidence relied upon. The *sanad* of *ijmāʿ*.
sariqa:	Theft for which penalty is cutting of the hand.
ṣawm:	Fasting.
sharʿī:	Legal.
sharṭ:	(Pl. *shurūṭ*) Condition.
shubha:	(Pl. *shubhāt*) Mistake of fact or of law. *Shubhat al-milk* is mistake in ownership.
ṣiḥḥa:	Validity.
siḥḥa wa-buṭlān:	Validity and nullity.

sunna:	(Pl. *sunan*) A precedent laid down by the Prophet (pbuh) to be followed as binding law. It may be in the form of a statement, act, or silent approval.
taʿabbudāt:	Rules that require ritual obedience.
tadbīr:	Institution of emancipating a slave through bequest.
taḥqīq al-manāt:	The verification of the attributes of an established case in a new case offered for examination. This process does not need a jurist. For example, a beverage may be examined to see if it is an intoxicant. This may need a chemist or pharmacist not a jurist.
taḥsīnāt:	The third category of purposes that are complementary to the first two categories.
takhrīj:	Methodology of a *faqīh* based on reasoning from general principles.
takhrīj al-manāṭ:	Deriving the underlying cause.
takhyīr:	Picking and choosing.
taklīf:	Obligation.
ṭalāq bidʿa:	Disapproved or innovative form of divorce.
ṭalāq al-sunna:	The recommended or prescribed form of divorce.
taʿlīq:	Stipulation.
tanqīḥ al-manāṭ:	Refining the underlying cause.
taqlīd:	Following the opinion of another without questioning the *dalīl* on which reliance is placed or without lawful authority from the *sharīʿah.*
tarjīḥ:	Preference of one evidence over the other.
tawātur:	Authentic transmission of reports and texts. A text or tradition reported by so many people in the first generation that its authenticity cannot be doubted.
tayammum:	Substitute purification for ablution.
taʿzīr:	Discretionary penalty to be determined by the ruler.
thawāb:	Reward (spiritual).
umm al-walad:	Slave woman who gives birth to master's child.
wājib:	Obligatory.
wājib muʿayyan:	Specified obligation.
wājib mukhayyar:	Obligation that grants a choice among several acts.

wājib muwassaʿ:	Obligation that provides a time span in which it is to be performed.
wuḍūʾ:	Ablution.
ẓāhir:	The apparent or literal meaning.
zakāt:	Poor-due.
ẓannī:	Probable.
ẓihār:	Vow of continence. Declaring wife to be (prohibited) like mother's back.
zinā:	Unlawful sexual intercourse by person whether married or unmarried.

Index

A
action
ritual obedience, 35
spiritual reward, 84
turning away from, 83
ʿulamāʾ, 28
acts (as causes), 171
ʿadāla, 93
ʿafw, 113, 114, 119, 120
expiation, 121
ibāḥa, 131
obstacle to, 116
anger, 43
ʿazīma, 216
and *wājib*, 250
best course, 242
in practice, 252

B
bayān, 17
blessings a gift, 90
buṭlān, 212

C
causes
and consequences, 142
based on rationale, 185
bringing about, 145
effects, 159
grades of, 150
ḥikma, 185
injurious, 176
inner state, 166
intending effects, 145
intention of Lawgiver, 146
invalid, 191
legality of, 142
prohibited, 154
undoing of, 172
unexpected consequences, 171
commands (general), 13
communal obligation, 123, 125
Companions
emulation of, 47
piety, 87
status of, 49
concepts
ancillary, 33
basic, xxxi
eighth, 26
eleventh, 44
essential, 33
fifth, 10
first, 1
fourth, 8
ninth, 33
second, 3
seventh, 19
sixth, 17
tenth, 41
thirteenth, 50
twelfth, 44
conditions, 193
and purposes, 199
as attributes, 195
necessary for causes, 196
related terms, 193
types of, 194
types of rules, 205
when given up, 200
conduct, 10
and knowledge, 23
as basis, 16
consensus, 5

D
declaratory rules, 141
ʿazīma and *rukhṣa*, 216
causes, 141
conditions, 193
obstacles, 206
validity and nullity, 210
dhimma, 109–111
disagreements, 9

disapproved act when prohibited, 94
disciplines, 38
  experts, 44
  merging of, 40
  sharʿī, 19
dreams, 37

E
effects, 148
  based on interests, 175
  causing, 159
  control of subject, 160
  examining for validity, 180
  examining of, 170
  focus on, 164
  follow causes, 174
  general and particular, 175
  inner state, 166
  intention of Lawgiver, 146
  intention of subject, 147
  interests secured, 181
  turning to, 151
enjoyment of nature, 93
evidences, xxxi
  conflicting, 246
  definitive, 4
  mubāḥ, 88
  rational, 4
  separate, 6
  transmitted, 4
exegesis, 13
exemptions, 216, 217
  category of, 112
  giving up, 246
  not intended, 250

F
five categories
  ʿafw, 112
  and purposes, 103
  and exemptions, 112
  the unexpressed category, 117
forgetfulness, 114
forgiveness, 114
  obstacle to, 116

G
general defences, 206
general principles, 4
  induction, 7
gharar, 61, 122
good life, 89
good things, 89, 91
  enjoying, 92
good works, 106
grades of causes, 150
guide, xxx
  principles, 50

H
ḥalāla, 189
hardships, 51
  and facility, 246
  balancing, 129
  exemptions, 246
ḥikma, 185

I
ibāḥa, 127
  ʿafw, 131
  original rule, 130
  rukhṣa, 220, 227
ijmāʿ, 5, 8
ijtihād, xvii, xxi, xxxi, 52
  conflict of principles, 176
  error, 118
ʿilla, xix
  meaning of, 194
imām, 45
induction, 5, 10
initial rules, 216
inner state, 166
internal knowledge, 32
invalid causes, 191
istidlāl mursal, 7
istiḥsān, 7

K
knowledge, xxix, xxxii, 12
  acknowledged, 44
  and ostentation, 25
  and the ignorant, 24
  as a means, 23
  as action, 21
  as obedience, 19
  attaining, 17
  core, 39
  errors, 45
  firm in, 31
  for masses, 17
  imām, 45
  internal, 32

methods of acquisition, 47, 48
of God, 24
pleasure of, 25
preferred, 26
seekers of, 26
kulliyāt, 1

L
lawful things, 91
utilising, 92
legal reasoning, 5, 7, 37, 83

M
magic, 14
makrūh
serves prohibited, 105
manāt
taḥqīq, 60
tanqīḥ, 60
mandūb
serves *wājib*, 104
maqāṣid al-sharīʿa, xxii
mashaqqa, 238
maṣlaḥa mursala, 7
mean path, 167
meanings, xxi
general, 43
restriction of, 42
modes of address, 51
mubāḥ, 77
advantage of subject, 102
necessity, 127
niyya, 85
particular, 99
two meanings, 98
when harmless, 100
when recommended, 93
wider sense, 92
muqallid, xxx
mutʿa, 189

N
nature of things, 18
necessities, xvii
five, 6
necessity
ibāḥa, 127
nullity, 210
second meaning, 214
two meanings, 211

O
obedience
and action, 22
as a goal, 21
mubāḥ, 78
permissible, 80
obligations
communal, 123, 125
dhimma, 109
lifetime span, 107
time limit, 105
obstacles
not intended, 207
types of, 206
when given up, 208

P
particular and universal, 97
permissible
commission, 77
omission, 77
omitting, 78
philosophers, 13
philosophy, 16
piety, 54
meaning of, 87
temptation, 86
pillars, 5
pleasures, 79, 86, 90
poetry, 37
practical benefit, 15, 20, 37
preferred knowledge, 26
preventive action, 241
principles
and hardship, 51
as guide, 49
prohibited causes, 154
purposes, xviii, xxxi, 1, 6
and five categories, 103
unknown, 190

Q
qarḍ (as *rukhṣa*), 270
qawānīn, 2
questions (excessive), 11, 15

R
rational evidences, 4
reason
and anger, 43
and evil, 42

and good, 42
and morality, 42
role of, 41
reckoning, 81
commission, 82
lengthy, 79
relaxation, 93
ribā, 122
right of God
obligations, 109
ritual obedience, 35
rukhṣa, 216
and hardship, 219
and leniency, 219
and option, 230
and prohibition, 218
as additional element, 224
ibāḥa, 220, 227
in practice, 252
qarḍ, 270
two types, 228
rules
commission, 79
conditions, 205
core, xx
declaratory, 141
definitive, 3
exemptions, 216
initial, 216
interests, 146
omission, 79
particular, 95
universal, 95, 123

S
scholars
firmly established, 31
grades of, 26
lapses, 30
submission to, 46
training, 46
traits of, 46
wicked, 29
shubha, 120, 179
shurūṭ, 193
ṣiḥḥa, 210
sources
primary, 41
qiyās, 43
transmitted, 41

spiritual reward, 84
stipulations, 188
subject
ability to perform, 141
effects, 148
intention of, 148

T
tafsīr, 13
takhyīr, 100
taʿlīq, 188
taqlid, xxxi
tawḥīd, 21
temptations, 90
title of book, xxxi
traditions, xxx
authentication, 36
documentation, xxv
transmission, 36
transmitted evidences, 4
trust offered to man, xxviii

U
ʿulamāʾ and action, 28
umma (unlettered), 14, 17
universal and particular, 97
universal principles, 1, 7
unknown purposes, 190
ʿuṣūl
conduct, 10
definitive, 1, 55
disagreements, 9
disciplines, xxii
evidences, 3
grammar, 9
issues in, 8
practical benefit, 15
probable, 2
subject-matter, 8

V
validity
second meaning, 215
two meanings, 210

W
wājib
and *farḍ* distinguished, 94
mukhayyar, 9